Personal Finance For Canadians For Dummies, 4th Edition

Eric and Tony's Keys to Personal Financial Success

- Take charge of your finances. Procrastinating is detrimental to your long-term financial health. Don't wait for a crisis or major life event to spur you to get your act together. Read this book and start implementing a plan now!

- Don't buy consumer items (cars, clothing, vacations, and so on) that lose value over time on credit. Use debt only to make investments in things that gain value, such as real estate, a business, or an education.

- Use credit cards only for convenience, not for carrying debt. If you have a tendency to run up credit card debt, then get rid of your cards and use only cash, cheques, and debit cards.

- Live within your means and don't try to keep up with your co-workers, neighbours, and peers. Many who engage in conspicuous consumption are borrowing against their future; some end up bankrupt.

- Save and invest at least 5 to 10 percent of your income. Preferably, invest through a retirement savings plan to reduce your taxes and ensure your future financial independence.

- Understand and use your employee benefits. If you're self-employed, find out the best investment and insurance options available to you and use them.

- Research before you buy. Never purchase a financial product or service on the basis of an advertisement or salesperson's solicitation.

- Avoid financial products that carry high commissions and expenses. Companies that sell their products through aggressive sales techniques generally have the worst financial products and the highest commissions.

- Don't purchase any financial product that you don't understand. Ask questions and compare what you're being offered to the best sources recommended in this book.

- Invest the majority of your long-term money in ownership vehicles that have appreciation potential, such as stocks, real estate, and your own business. When you invest in bonds or bank accounts, you are simply lending your money to others and will earn a return that probably won't keep you ahead of inflation and taxes.

(continued)

For Dummies: Bestselling Book Series for Beginners

Personal Finance For Canadians For Dummies, 4th Edition

Cheat Sheet

(continued)

- Avoid making emotionally based financial decisions. For example, investors who panic and sell their stock holdings after a major market correction miss a buying opportunity. Be especially careful in making important financial decisions after a major life change, such as a divorce, job loss, or death in your family.

- Make investing decisions based upon your needs and the long-term fundamentals of what you are buying. Ignore the predictive advice offered by financial prognosticators — nobody has a working crystal ball. Don't make knee-jerk decisions based on news headlines.

- Own your home. In the long run, owning is more cost-effective than renting, unless you have a terrific rent-control deal. But don't buy until you can stay put for a number of years.

- Purchase broad insurance coverage to protect against financial catastrophes. Eliminate insurance for small potential losses.

- If you're married, make time to discuss joint goals, issues, and concerns. Be accepting of your partner's money personality; learn to compromise and manage as a team.

- Prepare for life changes. The better you are at living within your means and anticipating life changes, the better off you will be financially and emotionally.

- Read publications that have high quality standards and that aren't afraid to take a stand and recommend what's in your best interests.

- Prioritize your financial goals and start working toward them. Be patient. Focus on your accomplishments and learn from your past mistakes.

- Hire yourself first. You are the best financial person that you can hire. If you need help making a major decision, hire conflict-free advisers who charge a fee for their time. Work in partnership with advisers — don't abdicate control.

- Invest in yourself and others. Invest in your education, your health, and your relationships with family and friends. Having a lot of money isn't worth much if you don't have your health and people with whom to share your life. Give your time and money to causes that better our society and the world.

For Dummies: Bestselling Book Series for Beginners

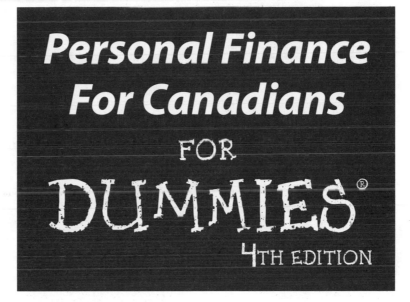

Personal Finance
For Canadians

FOR

DUMMIES®

4TH EDITION

Personal Finance For Canadians

FOR DUMMIES®

4TH EDITION

by Eric Tyson and Tony Martin

John Wiley & Sons Canada, Ltd.

Personal Finance For Canadians For Dummies, 4th Edition

Published by
John Wiley & Sons Canada, Ltd.
6045 Freemont Boulevard
Mississauga, Ontario, L5R 4J3
`www.wiley.com`

Library and Archives Canada Cataloguing in Publication

Tyson, Eric (Eric Kevin)

    Personal finance for Canadians for dummies / Eric Tyson, Tony Martin. – 4th ed.

Includes index.

First published in 1995 under title: Personal finance for dummie$ for

    Canadians.

ISBN-13: 978-0-470-83768-9

ISBN-10: 0-470-83768-3

    1. Finance, Personal–Canada. I. Martin, Tony (Tony M.) II. Title.

HG179.T97 2006   332.024'00971   C2005-906440-4

Printed in Canada

4 5 TRI 10 09 08

Distributed in Canada by John Wiley & Sons Canada, Ltd.

For general information on John Wiley & Sons Canada, Ltd, including all books published by Wiley Publishing, Inc., please call our warehouse, Tel 1-800-567-4797. For reseller information, including discounts and premium sales, please call our sales department, Tel 416-646-7992. For press review copies, author interviews, or other publicity information, please contact our marketing department, Tel 416-646-4584, Fax 416-236-4448.

For authorization to photocopy items for corporate, personal, or educational use, please contact in writing The Canadian Copyright Licensing Agency (Access Copyright). For an Access Copyright license, visit www.accesscopyright.ca or call toll free, 1-800-893-5777.

About the Authors

Eric Tyson first became interested in money matters three decades ago. After toiling as a management consultant to Fortune 500 financial-services firms, Eric took his inside knowledge of the banking, investment, and insurance industries and committed himself to making personal financial management accessible to us all.

Today, Eric is an internationally acclaimed and best-selling personal finance book author, syndicated columnist, and speaker. He has worked with and taught people from all financial situations, so he knows the financial concerns and questions of real folks just like you. Despite being handicapped by an M.B.A. from the Stanford Graduate School of Business and a B.S. in Economics and Biology from Yale University, Eric remains a master at "keeping it simple."

An accomplished personal finance writer, his "Investor's Guide" syndicated column is read by millions, and he was an award-winning columnist for the San Francisco *Examiner*. He is the author of six national best-selling financial books in the *For Dummies* series on personal finance and investing. He is also author of *Mind Over Money: Your Path to Wealth and Happiness* (CDS Books). Eric's work has been featured and quoted in hundreds of publications including *Newsweek,* the *Wall Street Journal, Forbes, Kiplinger's Personal Finance Magazine, Parenting, Money,* and *Family Money,* and on NBC's *Today Show,* ABC, CNBC, the *PBS Nightly Business Report,* CNN, CBS national radio, NPR's *Sound Money,* and Bloomberg Business Radio.

Tony Martin set off to see the world after graduating from Queen's University with a business degree. (His best buy? A two-day "cruise" from Jakarta to Singapore for $8 — which included a place on deck to roll out his sleeping bag, and fish and rice three times a day!) He then joined CBC radio, and since then has been involved in helping people understand the world of money. He excels at equipping individuals with the knowledge and tools they need to make better financial and investment choices for themselves and their family.

Tony is also the co-author with Eric of *Investing For Canadians For Dummies*. His widely read column "Me and My Money" appears in "Net Worth," *The Globe and Mail*'s weekend personal finance section. His work has been featured in many leading publications, including *ROB Magazine*, *Reader's Digest*, and *Canadian Business*. Tony is a frequent commentator and speaker on personal finance and investing. He regularly appears on television and radio, including CBC Radio, CBC Television, Report on Business Television, and TVOntario.

Tony has also been instrumental in the design and development of many online resources, including a complete online investor training program using simulated stock market transactions.

Dedication

This book is hereby and irrevocably dedicated to our families and friends, as well as our clients and customers — who ultimately have taught us everything we know about how to explain financial terms and strategies so that we all may benefit.

Authors' Acknowledgments

Being an entrepreneur involves endless challenges, and without the support and input of good friends and mentors Peter Mazonson, Jim Collins, and my best friend and wife, Judy, I couldn't have accomplished what I have. I hold many people accountable for my perverse and maniacal interest in figuring out the financial services industry and money matters, but most of the blame falls on my loving parents, Charles and Paulina, who taught me most of what I know that's been of use in the real world.

I'd also like to thank Maggie McCall, David Ish, Paul Kozak, Chris Treadway, Sally St. Lawrence, K. T. Rabin, Will Hearst III, Ray Brown, Susan Wolf, Rich Caramella, Lisa Baker, Renn Vera, Maureen Taylor, Jerry Jacob, Robert Crum, Duc Nguyen, and Maria Carmicino and all the good folks at King Features for believing in and supporting my writing and teaching.

— Eric

There is no such thing as working on one's own, as the support, good humour, and advice of many are essential to success. I owe many thanks to my wife, Jane Howard, and to my good friend Geoff Rockburn, who have both been endlessly supportive and helpful over the years. I'm grateful as always to my parents, Ruth and John, for teaching me so much about what really matters.

There are also many people in the personal finance industry who have kindly offered me their assistance in penetrating, understanding, and explaining money matters. Many thanks to everybody who has generously shared insights and expertise, including Peter Volpe, Gena Katz, Sandra McLeod, Anthony Layton, Paul Hickey, Jim Bullock, Alisa Dunbar, Alan Silverstein, and Janet Freedman. In addition, I'd like to thank Karen Benzing, David Chilton, Patricia Davies, Dorothy Engleman, Dave Pyette, Jack Fleischmann, Peggy Wente, and Richard Quinlan for their support and encouragement over the years.

Many thanks as well to all the people who provided insightful comments on this book, especially tax and financial planner *extraordinaire* Barton Francis, financial planner *par excellence* Warren Baldwin, and Mike van den Akker, Gretchen Morgensen, Craig Litman, Gerri Detweiler, Mark White, Alan Bush, Nancy Coolidge, and Chris Jensen. Special thanks to Peter Volpe for his detailed and extremely helpful technical review of this book. And a well-earned tip of the hat this time 'round to Robert Hickey for his steadying hand and ongoing guidance. Finally, thanks to the wonderful people on the front line and behind the scenes — Elizabeth McCurdy, Pamela Vokey, and Kelli Howey — for putting this 4th edition together.

— Tony

Publisher's Acknowledgments

We're proud of this book; please send us your comments at canadapt@wiley.com. Some of the people who helped bring this book to market include the following:

Acquisitions, Editorial, and Media Development

Associate Editor: Robert Hickey

Copy Editor: Kelli Howey

Cartoon: Rich Tennant, www.the5thwave.com

Composition

Publishing Services Director: Karen Bryan

Publishing Services Manager: Ian Koo

Project Manager: Elizabeth McCurdy

Project Coordinator: Pam Vokey

Layout and Graphics: Wiley Indianapolis Composition Services

Proofreader: Susan Gaines

Indexer: Colborne Communications

John Wiley & Sons Canada, Ltd

Bill Zerter, Chief Operating Officer

Jennifer Smith, Publisher, Professional and Trade Division

Publishing and Editorial for Consumer Dummies

Diane Graves Steele, Vice President and Publisher, Consumer Dummies

Joyce Pepple, Acquisitions Director, Consumer Dummies

Kristin A. Cocks, Product Development Director, Consumer Dummies

Michael Spring, Vice President and Publisher, Travel

Suzanne Jannetta, Editorial Director, Travel

Publishing for Technology Dummies

Andy Cummings, Vice President and Publisher, Dummies Technology/General User

Composition Services

Gerry Fahey, Vice President of Production Services

Debbie Stailey, Director of Composition Services

Contents at a Glance

Introduction 1

Part I: Assessing Your Financial Fitness and Setting Goals 7
Chapter 1: Improving Your Financial Fitness 9
Chapter 2: Setting and Achieving Goals 33

Part II: Saving More, Spending Less 57
Chapter 3: Determining Where Your Money Goes 59
Chapter 4: Conquering Debt and Credit Problems 73
Chapter 5: Reducing Your Spending 91
Chapter 6: Taming Taxes 121

Part III: Building Wealth through Investing 145
Chapter 7: Important Investment Concepts 147
Chapter 8: Choosing Your Investment Vehicles 175
Chapter 9: Investing in Mutual Funds 197
Chapter 10: Registered Retirement Savings Plans 217
Chapter 11: Investing in Retirement Plans 235
Chapter 12: Investing Outside Retirement Plans 249
Chapter 13: Investing for Education Expenses 261
Chapter 14: Investing in Real Estate 275

Part IV: Insurance: Protecting What You've Got 313
Chapter 15: Insurance: Getting What You Need at the Best Price.............. 315
Chapter 16: Insurance on You: Life, Disability, and Health 331
Chapter 17: Covering Your Assets... 349

Part V: Where to Go for More Help 363
Chapter 18: Working with Financial Planners 365
Chapter 19: Computer Money Management 389
Chapter 20: On Air and in Print 401

Part VI: The Part of Tens **409**

Chapter 21: Survival Guide for Ten Life Changes...411
Chapter 22: Ten Things More Important Than Money 427

Glossary...**433**

Index **447**

Table of Contents

Introduction 1
  Why This Book? 1
  What's New in This Edition 2
  Uses for This Book 3
  How This Book Is Organized 3
    Part I: Assessing Your Financial Fitness and Setting Goals 3
    Part II: Saving More, Spending Less 4
    Part III: Building Wealth through Investing 4
    Part IV: Insurance: Protecting What You've Got 4
    Part V: Where to Go for More Help 4
    Part VI: The Part of Tens 5
    Glossary 5
  Icons Used in This Book 5

Part 1: Assessing Your Financial Fitness
and Setting Goals 7

  Chapter 1: Improving Your Financial Fitness 9
    Targeting the Trouble Spots 9
      Talking money at home 11
      Teaching personal finance in schools 12
      Identifying unreliable sources of information 13
    Jumping over Real and Imaginary Hurdles 17
      Discovering the real hurdles holding you back 17
      Practising good habits 18
    Common Financial Problems: You've Got Company 20
    Defining Bad Debt and Good Debt 22
    Knowing How Much Bad Debt Is Too Much 23
    Determining Your Financial Net Worth 25
      Financial assets 25
      Financial liabilities 26
      Your net worth calculation 26
      Interpreting your net worth results 28
    Savings Analysis 28
    Measuring Your Investing Knowledge 30
    Measuring Your Insurance Savvy 32

Chapter 2: Setting and Achieving Goals 33

   Creating Your Own Definition of "Wealth" 33
      Considering what money can't buy 34
      Managing the balancing act 35
   Prioritizing Your Savings Goals 37
      Knowing what's most important to you 37
      Valuing retirement plans 38
      Dealing with competing goals 39
   Building Emergency Reserves 40
   Saving to Buy a Home or Business 41
   Funding Kids' Educational Expenses 41
   Saving for Big Purchases 42
   Preparing for Retirement 42
      Figuring what you need for retirement 44
      Understanding retirement building blocks 45
      Counting on government benefits 46
      Planning your personal savings/investment strategy 49
      Making the most of pensions 49
      Retirement planning worksheet 50
      Making up for lost time 52
      Overcoming objections to retirement plans 54

Part II: Saving More, Spending Less 57

Chapter 3: Determining Where Your Money Goes 59

   Examining the Roots of Overspending 59
      Having access to credit 60
      Using credit cards 60
      Making minimum monthly payments 61
      Taking out car loans 61
      Bending to peer pressure 62
      Spending to feel good 62
      Becoming addicted to spending 62
      Trying to keep current 63
      Ignoring your financial goals when buying 63
      Wanting the best for your children 63
   Analyzing Your Spending 64
      Tracking your spending on paper 65
      Tracking your spending on the computer .69
   Growing Rich on Your Income: The Secret 71

Chapter 4: Conquering Debt and Credit Problems 73

   Using Savings to Reduce Your Debt 74
      Understanding how you gain 74
      Discovering money to pay down consumer debts 75

Decreasing Debt When You Lack Savings 75
  Transferring balances to lower-interest-rate credit cards 76
  Cutting up your credit cards..77
  Discovering debit cards: The best of both worlds........................78
Filing Bankruptcy 79
  Understanding bankruptcy's benefits 80
  Coming to terms with bankruptcy drawbacks 81
  Seeking bankruptcy advice 83
An Alternative to Bankruptcy: The Consumer Proposal............................84
Ending the Spending-and-Debting Cycle 85
  Resisting the credit temptation...85
  Identifying and treating an addiction...86
Dealing with Credit Mistakes 87
  Obtaining a copy of your credit report 88
  Getting others to correct their mistakes 89
  Telling your side of the story...89

Chapter 5: Reducing Your Spending 91
Finding the Keys to Successful Spending...92
  Living within your means 92
  Looking for the best values..93
  Eliminating the fat from your spending...97
  Turning your back on consumer credit..98
Reducing Your Spending: Eric and Tony's Strategies 99
  Reducing food costs...100
  Saving on shelter 102
  Lowering your phone bills 105
  Cutting transportation costs 106
  Controlling clothing costs 109
  Cutting the cost of debt..110
  Indulging responsibly in fun and recreation 112
  Tending to personal care..114
  Paring down professional expenses 115
  Managing medical expenses 115
  Keeping an eye on insurance premiums 116
  Trimming your taxes...117
  Eliminating costly addictions 118

Chapter 6: Taming Taxes 121
Understanding the Taxes You Pay 121
  Recognizing the importance of your marginal tax rate.............122
  Defining taxable income 123
Getting Organized 124
Trimming Employment Income Taxes 125
  Contributing to RRSPs and retirement plans...............................125
  Shifting some income...126

Reducing Investment Income Taxes 126
    Fill up those retirement plans...127
    Select tax-friendly investments 127
    Make your profits long-term 128
Increasing Your Deductions...128
    Child care expenses 128
    Alimony and maintenance payments 129
    Child support...129
    Annual union and professional fees................................129
    Business losses...129
    Interest on investment loans 129
    Married versus common-law partners 130
    Moving expenses 130
Increasing Your Credits 131
    Basic personal tax credit...132
    Spousal credit 132
    Wholly dependent person credit......................................132
    Charitable donations credit 132
    Tuition fees credit 133
    Medical expenses credit 133
    Disability credit 134
    Pension income credit 135
    Age 65 or older..136
    Self-employment expenses..136
Getting Help from Tax Resources...138
    Assistance from the Canada Revenue Agency................138
    Preparation and advice guides 139
    Software and Web sites..139
    Professional hired help..139
Dealing with an Audit 141
    Getting your act together 142
    Surviving the day of reckoning...143

Part III: Building Wealth through Investing *145*

Chapter 7: Important Investment Concepts 147
Establishing Your Goals..147
Understanding the Major Investment Flavours 148
    Looking at lending investments.......................................148
    Exploring ownership investments 149
    Shunning gambling instruments and behaviours 150
    Provincial governments pushing gambling?...................152
Understanding Investment Returns..153

Sizing Investment Risks 154
    Comparing the risks of stocks and bonds......................154
    Focusing on the risks you can control............................155
    Discovering low-risk, high-return investments...............156
Diversifying Your Investments 157
    Spreading it around: Asset allocation.............................159
    Allocating money for the long term 160
    Sticking with your allocations: Don't trade....................161
    Investing lump sums using dollar-cost averaging...........162
Acknowledging Differences among Investment Firms 165
    Focusing on the best firms..165
    Places to consider avoiding 166
Experts Who Predict the Future...171
    Investment newsletters 171
    Investment gurus..172
Leaving You with Some Final Advice 173

Chapter 8: Choosing Your Investment Vehicles **175**
Slow and Steady Investments 175
    Transaction/chequing accounts.....................................176
    Savings and money market accounts 176
    Bonds 177
Building Wealth with Ownership Vehicles 179
    Stocks...179
    Income trusts 185
    Generating wealth with real estate 186
    Investing in small businesses 191
Off the Beaten Path: Investment Odds and Ends 193
    Precious metals 193
    Annuities...194
    Collectibles...194
    Life insurance with a cash value 195

Chapter 9: Investing in Mutual Funds **197**
Understanding the Benefits of Mutual Funds.........................197
Exploring Various Fund Types..199
    Money market funds 201
    Bond funds 202
    Stock funds...202
    Balancing bonds and stocks: Hybrid funds 204
    Canadian, U.S., international, and global funds.............204
    Index funds...205
    Specialty (sector) funds 206
Selecting the Best Mutual Funds 207
    Reading prospectuses and annual reports 207
    Keeping costs low 208

Evaluating historical performance.................................211
Assessing fund manager and fund family reputations 212
Rating tax-friendliness 212
Determining your needs and goals 213
Deciphering Your Fund's Performance.................................213
Interest and dividends 214
Capital gains...215
Share price changes 215
Following and Selling Your Funds 216

Chapter 10: Registered Retirement Savings Plans 217

How RRSPs Work...217
The benefit of tax-deferred contributions.................................218
Tax-deferred compound growth 219
Maximizing Your RRSP Savings 220
Starting an RRSP early in life...220
Increasing your returns 221
Understanding the Contribution Rules 222
Checking out the contribution limits.................................222
Calculating your allowable contribution 224
Withdrawing money from your RRSP 226
Getting support from spousal RRSPs.................................226
Getting to Know the Different Types of RRSPs.................................227
Guaranteed RRSPs...227
Mutual fund RRSPs 228
Self-directed and brokerage-house RRSPs 228
Closing Down Your RRSP...228
Wrapping up your RRSP: Your three options.................................229

Chapter 11: Investing in Retirement Plans 235

Allocating Your Money in Retirement Plans 235
Understanding the difference between an RRSP
and the investments inside your RRSP 236
Prioritizing retirement contributions 236
Allocating money when your employer selects
the investment options 236
Allocating money in RRSPs 239
Franklin Templeton Investments.................................241
Phillips, Hager & North...242
Self-directed or discount brokerage portfolios 242
Index funds and exchange-traded funds 243
Discount brokers 244
Inappropriate Retirement Plan Investments 244
Annuities...244
Limited partnerships 245
Transferring Retirement Plans 246
Transferring accounts you control 246
Moving money from an employer's plan.................................248

Chapter 12: Investing Outside Retirement Plans 249

Getting Started 249
Paying off high-interest debt...............................250
Taking advantage of tax breaks 250
Understanding Taxes on Your Investments 251
Fortifying Your Emergency Reserves 251
Bank and credit union accounts...........................252
High-interest savings accounts.............................252
Money market mutual funds 254
Investing Money for the Longer Term 256
Defining your time horizons 256
Allocating assets for the long haul.......................257

Chapter 13: Investing for Education Expenses 261

Neglecting RRSPs: A Big Mistake............................261
How Will You Pay for Education Expenses?................262
Estimating the cost of university or college 263
Setting realistic savings goals 263
How to Save for Education Expenses 264
Registered Education Savings Plans (RESPs) 265
In-trust accounts 267
Loans, Grants, and Scholarships.............................269
Government student loans program.......................269
Canada Access Grants 271
Tips for getting loans, grants,and scholarships 272
Investing Education Funds.....................................272
Good investments: No-load mutual funds
and exchange-traded funds 273
Bad investments 273
Overlooked investments 274

Chapter 14: Investing in Real Estate 275

Deciding Whether to Buy or Continue Renting...............275
Assessing your timeline.......................................276
Determining what you can afford to buy.................276
Calculating how much lenders will allow you to borrow..............277
Comparing the cost of owning versus renting............279
Considering the long-term costs of renting 281
Financing Your Home..282
Understanding the different types of mortgages 283
Understanding amortization — How long
you'll take to pay off your home loan 283
Understanding your mortgage term 284
Open and closed mortgages 286
Understanding fixed- and variable-rate mortgages.........287
Shopping for mortgages 288
Avoiding the down-payment blues.........................289

The RRSP Home Buyers' Plan 291
Cut your costs at renewal time...294
Finding the best lender..294
Increasing your approval chances 296
Finding the Right Property and Location..297
Condo, town house, co-op, or detached home?............................298
Casting a broad net 298
Finding out actual sale prices 299
Researching the neighbourhood and area 299
Working with Real Estate Agents 300
Recognizing real estate agents' conflicts of interest 300
Looking for the right qualities in real estate agents 301
Putting Your Deal Together...303
Negotiating 101 303
Inspecting before you buy..304
After You Buy..305
Refinancing your mortgage 306
Mortgage life insurance..307
Is getting a reverse mortgage a good idea?...................................308
Selling your house 309

Part IV: Insurance: Protecting What You've Got 313

Chapter 15: Insurance: Getting What You Need at the Best Price 315

Discovering Our Three Laws of Buying Insurance.................................315
Law I: Insure for the big stuff, not the small stuff........................316
Law II: Buy broad coverage 320
Law III: Shop around and consider buying direct 322
Dealing with Insurance Problems 325
Knowing what to do if you're denied coverage 325
Getting your due on claims 326

Chapter 16: Insurance on You: Life, Disability, and Health 331

Providing for Your Loved Ones: Life Insurance....................................332
Determining how much life insurance to buy.................................332
Looking at the Canada Pension Plan's survivor benefits 333
Comparing term life insurance to cash value life insurance 334
Making your decision...337
Buying term insurance..338
Getting rid of cash value life insurance 340
Considering the purchase of cash value life insurance.................340
Preparing for the Unpredictable: Disability Insurance.......................341
Determining how much disability insurance you need.................342
Identifying other features you need in disability insurance........343
Deciding where to buy disability insurance 344

Getting Care for the Road: Travel Medical Insurance 345
    Buying travel medical insurance 346
Looking at Long-Term Care Insurance 346
Discovering the Most Overlooked Form of Insurance 347

Chapter 17: Covering Your Assets 349

Protecting Where You Live 349
    Dwelling coverage: The cost to rebuild 350
    Personal property coverage: For your things 350
    Liability insurance: Coverage for hurting others 351
    Flood and earthquake insurance: Protection from
        Mother Nature 352
    Deductibles: Your cost with a claim 353
    Special discounts 353
    Buying homeowner's or renter's insurance 353
Auto Insurance 101 354
    Bodily injury/property damage liability 354
    Uninsured or underinsured motorist liability 355
    Deductibles 356
    Special discounts 356
    Little-stuff coverage to skip 357
    Buying auto insurance 358
Protecting Against Mega-Liability: Umbrella Insurance 358
You Can't Take It with You: Planning Your Estate 359
    Wills, living wills, and medical powers of attorney 359
    Avoiding probate through living trusts 360
    Planning your estate to minimize taxes
        triggered by your death 361

Part V: Where to Go for More Help 363

Chapter 18: Working with Financial Planners 365

Alice in Financial Planner–Land 365
    Alice's (mis)adventures 366
    Learning from Alice's journey 368
Surveying Your Financial-Management Options 369
    Doing nothing 370
    Doing it yourself 370
    Hiring financial help 371
Deciding Whether to Hire a Financial Planner 374
    How a good financial planner can help 374
    Why financial planners aren't for everyone 376
The Frustrations of Finding Good Financial Planners 376
    Regulatory problems 377
    Recognizing financial planners' conflicts of interest 377

Finding a Good Financial Planner 382
    Soliciting personal referrals 382
    Seeking advisers through associations 382
Interviewing Financial Advisers: Asking the Right Questions...............383
    What percentage of your income comes from clients' fees vs.
      commissions from the products that you sell? 383
    What percentage of fees paid by your clients is for ongoing
      money management vs. hourly financial planning? 384
    What is your hourly fee? 384
    What work and educational experience qualifies you
      to be a financial planner?..385
    Have you ever sold limited partnerships?
      Options? Futures? Commodities? 385
    Do you carry liability (errors and omissions) insurance? 385
    Can you provide references from clients
      with needs similar to mine?..386
    Will you provide specific strategies and product
      recommendations that I can implement
      on my own if I choose?...386
    How is implementation handled?..387

Chapter 19: Computer Money Management 389
Surveying Software and Web Sites...389
    Adding up financial software benefits 390
    Treading carefully on the Web..391
    Shun short-term thinking 392
Accomplishing Money Tasks Using Your Computer................................393
    Doing your banking online 393
    Using chequebook software..393
    Using online bill payment services 394
    Planning for retirement...395
    Preparing your taxes...395
    Researching investments 397
    Trading online..397
    Reading and searching periodicals 398
    Buying life insurance...399
    Preparing legal documents 399

Chapter 20: On Air and in Print 401
Observing the Mass Media 401
    Alarming or informing us?..402
    Teaching what kind of values?...402
    Perpetuating prognosticating pundits? 403
Rating Radio and Television Financial Programs.....................................403
Surveying the Internet..404
Navigating Newspapers and Magazines..404
Betting on Books 405

Part VI: The Part of Tens *409*

Chapter 21: Survival Guide for Ten Life Changes .... .411
Starting Out: Your First Job 412
Changing Jobs or Careers 413
Getting Married 414
Buying a Home...416
Having Children..416
Starting a Small Business 419
Caring for Aging Parents 420
Divorcing 421
Receiving a Windfall..423
Retiring 424

Chapter 22: Ten Things More Important Than Money 427
Putting Your Family First..427
Making and Keeping Friends..428
Investing in Your Health 428
Caring for Kids...428
Knowing Your Neighbours 429
Appreciating What You Do Have..429
Minding Your Reputation 430
Continuing Your Education..430
Having Fun 430
Solving Social Problems 431

Glossary *433*

Index *447*

Introduction

· ·

*W*elcome to *Personal Finance For Canadians for Dummies,* 4th Edition. The publication of this edition marks the eleventh anniversary of the 1st edition. As you can see from the quotes in the front of this edition, readers and reviewers alike were pleased with the previous editions.

However, we don't rest on our laurels. So the book you hold in your hands reflects more hard work and brings you the freshest material for addressing your personal financial quandaries.

Why This Book?

Many Canadians are financially illiterate. If your knowledge is limited when it comes to your finances, it's probably not your fault. Personal Finance 101 is not offered in most schools — not in high school, and not even in the best universities and graduate schools. It should be. (Of course, if it were, we wouldn't be able to write fun and useful books such as this — or maybe they would use this book in the course!)

People keep making the same common financial mistakes over and over — procrastinating and not planning, wasteful spending, falling prey to financial salespeople and pitches, failing to do sufficient research before making important financial decisions, and so on. This book, like a good friend, can whop you upside the head and keep you from falling into the same traps.

As unfair as it may seem, many of these traps await you when you seek help for your financial problems. The world is filled with biased and bad financial advice. We regularly see and hear about the consequences of poor advice. Of course, every profession has bad apples, but too many of the people calling themselves "financial planners" have conflicts of interest and an inadequate level of competence.

All too often, financial advice ignores the big picture and focuses narrowly on investing. Because money is not an end in itself but a part of your whole life, this book helps connect your financial goals and problems to the rest of your life. You need a broad understanding of personal finance that includes all areas of your financial life: spending, taxes, saving and investing, insurance, and planning for major goals like education, buying a home, and retirement.

Even if you understand the financial basics, thinking about your finances in a holistic way can be difficult. Sometimes you're too close to the situation to be objective. Like the organization of your desk or files (or disorganization, as the case may be), your finances may reflect the history of your life more than they reflect a comprehensive plan for your future.

You're likely a busy person who doesn't have enough hours in the day to get things done. Thus, you want to know how to diagnose your financial situation quickly (and painlessly) and determine what you should do next. Unfortunately, after figuring out which financial strategies make sense for you, choosing specific financial products in the marketplace can be a nightmare. You have literally thousands of investment, insurance, and loan options to choose from. Talk about information overload!

To complicate matters even more, you probably hear about most products through advertising that can be misleading, if not downright false. Of course, some ethical and useful firms advertise, but so do those that are more inter-ested in converting your hard-earned income and savings into their profits. And they may not be here tomorrow when you need them.

You want to know the best places to go for your circumstances, so we fill this book with specific, tried-and-proven product recommendations. We also sug-gest where to turn next if you need more information and help.

What's New in This Edition

To make solid financial decisions, you need up-to-date information and advice, and that's what this book provides. Every page in this book has been updated and freshened.

Here are some of the major updates you may notice as you peruse the pages of this book:

- ✔ Tax law changes were enacted since the last edition was published. In addition to the coverage provided in Chapter 6, you can also find a discussion of how tax law changes affect Registered Retirement Savings Plans in Chapter 10.

- ✔ Updated investment recommendations, especially in the area of mutual funds, throughout Part III.

- ✔ Added coverage of new options that can help you save and invest for university and other educational expenses.

- ✔ Revised recommendations for where to get the best insurance deals in Part IV.

- ✔ Expanded and updated coverage of money resources (especially online resources).

Uses for This Book

You can use this book in one of three ways:

- ✔ If you want to find out about a specific topic, such as getting out of high-interest consumer debt, planning for major goals, or investing, you can flip to that section and get answers quickly.

- ✔ If you want a crash course in personal finance, read this book cover-to-cover. Reading the whole book helps solidify major financial concepts and gets you thinking about your finances in a more comprehensive way.

- ✔ If you're tired of picking up scattered piles of bills, receipts, and junk mail every time the kids chase the cat around the den, you can use this book as a paperweight!

Seriously though, this book is basic enough to help a novice get his or her arms around thorny financial issues. But advanced readers will be challenged, as well, to think about their finances in a new way and identify areas for improvement. Check out the table of contents for a chapter-by-chapter rundown of what this book offers. You can also look up a specific topic in the index. Or you can turn the page and start at the beginning: Chapter 1.

How This Book Is Organized

This book is organized into six parts, with each covering a major area of your personal finances. The chapters within each part cover specific topics in detail. You can read each chapter (and part) without having to read what comes before, which is useful if you have better things to do with your free time. This book also makes for great reading anywhere you may be sitting for a length of time (perhaps the bathroom?). You may be referred occasionally to somewhere else in the book for more details on a particular subject. Here is a summary of what you'll find in each part.

Part 1: Assessing Your Financial Fitness and Setting Goals

This part explains how to diagnose your current financial health and explores common reasons for any missing links in your personal finance knowledge. We all have dreams and goals, so in this part, we also encourage you to think about your financial aspirations and figure out how much you should be saving if you want to retire someday or accomplish other important goals.

Part II: Saving More, Spending Less

Most people don't have gobs of extra cash. Therefore, this part shows you how to figure out where all your dollars are going and tells you how to reduce your spending. Chapter 4 is devoted to helping you get out from under the burden of high-interest consumer debt (such as credit card debt). We also provide specifics for reducing your tax burden.

Part III: Building Wealth through Investing

Earning and saving money is hard work, so you should be careful when it comes to investing what you have worked so hard to save (or waited so long to inherit!). In this part, we assist you with picking investments wisely and help you understand investment risks, returns, and a whole lot more. We explain all the major, and best, investment options. We recommend specific strategies and investments to use both inside and outside of tax-sheltered retirement plans such as RRSPs. We also discuss buying, selling, and investing in real estate, as well as other wealth-building investments.

Part IV: Insurance: Protecting What You've Got

Insurance is an important part of your financial life. Unfortunately, for most people, insurance is a thoroughly overwhelming and dreadfully boring topic. But perhaps we can pique your interest in this esoteric topic by telling you that you're probably paying more than you should for insurance, and you probably don't have the right coverage for your situation. This part tells you all you ever wanted to know (okay, fine — all you *never* wanted to know but probably should know anyway) about how to buy the right insurance at the best price.

Part V: Where to Go for More Help

As you build your financial knowledge, more questions and issues may arise. In this part, we discuss where to go and what to avoid when you seek financial information and advice. We also discuss hiring a financial planner as well as investigating resources in print, on the air, and online.

Part VI: The Part of Tens

The chapters in this part can help you manage major life changes, survive tough financial times, and keep money in the proper perspective with the rest of your life.

Glossary

The world of money is filled with jargon, so you'll be happy to know that this book includes a comprehensive glossary of financial terms that are often tossed around but seldom explained.

Icons Used in This Book

 This nerdy looking guy appears beside discussions that aren't critical if you just want to understand basic concepts and get answers to your financial questions. You can safely ignore these sections, but reading them can help deepen and enhance your personal financial knowledge. This stuff can also come in handy if you're ever on a game show, or if you find yourself stuck on an elevator with a financial geek.

 This target flags strategy recommendations for making the most of your money (for example, paying off your credit card debt with your lottery winnings).

 This icon highlights the best financial products in the areas of investments, insurance, and so on. These products can help you implement our strategy recommendations.

 This icon points out information that's discussed elsewhere in the book or stuff you'll definitely want to remember.

This icon marks things to avoid and common mistakes people make when managing their finances.

 This icon alerts you to scams and scoundrels that prey on the unsuspecting.

 This icon tells you when you should consider doing some additional research. Don't worry — we explain what to look for and what to look out for.

Lobby your schools! Make sure that financial basics are taught in schools at all levels. If you think that you're powerless to change the situation, you're mistaken. Many changes to our education system have started as grassroots movements.

Identifying unreliable sources of information

Some people are smart enough to realize that they're not financial geniuses. So they set out to take control of their finances by reading or consulting a financial adviser. Because the pitfalls are so numerous and the challenges so mighty when choosing an adviser, we devote Chapter 18 to the financial planning business and tell you what you need to know to avoid being fooled.

Reading is good. Reading is fundamental. But reading to find out how to manage your money can be dangerous if you're a novice. Misinformation can come from popular and seemingly reliable information sources, as we explain in the following sections.

Won't investment gurus make me rich?

One formerly best-selling personal finance book (*Wealth Without Risk,* by Charles Givens) advises you to "Buy disability insurance only if you are in poor health or accident prone." Putting aside the minor detail that no insurance company (at least, not one interested in making a profit) is going to issue you a disability policy *after* you fall into poor health, how do you know when you're going to be accident-prone? Because health problems and auto accidents cause many disabilities, you can't see most disabilities coming!

Consider the investment seminars by Wade Cook. These seminars lured people in by promising outrageous and unrealistic returns. The stock market has generated average annual returns of about 10 percent over the long term. Cook, a former taxicab driver, promoted his seminars as follows: "A live, hands-on, do the deals, two-day intense course in making huge returns in the stock market. If you aren't getting 20 percent per month, or 300 percent annualized returns on your investments, you need to be there."

Cook's get-rich-quick seminars — which cost more than $6,000 — were so successful at attracting people that his company went public in the late 1990s and generated annual revenues of more than $100 million U.S.

Cook's "techniques" included trading in and out of stocks and options on stocks after short holding periods of weeks, days, or even hours. His trading strategies can best be described as techniques based upon technical analysis — that is, charting a stock's price movements and volume history and then making predictions based on those charts.

The perils of following an approach that advocates short-term trading with the allure of high profits are numerous:

- You're going to rack up enormous brokerage commissions.

- You're not going to make big profits — quite the reverse. You're going to underperform the market averages if you stick with this approach.

- You're going to make yourself a nervous wreck. This type of trading is gambling, not investing. Get sucked up in it and you'll lose more than money — you may also lose the love and respect of your family and friends.

"The past history of stock prices cannot be used to predict the future in any meaningful way. Technical strategies are usually amusing, often comforting, but of no real value," says Burton Malkiel, a Princeton University business professor and author of the investment classic, *A Random Walk Down Wall Street*.

If Cook's followers were indeed earning the 300-percent annual returns his seminars claim to help you achieve, any investor starting with just $10,000 would vault to the top of the list of the world's wealthiest people (ahead of Bill Gates and Warren Buffett) in just 11 years!

Understanding how undeserving investment gurus get popular

You may be wondering how Charles Givens and Wade Cook became so popular despite the obvious flaws in their advice. Givens made the most of his talent for working the media and his great self-promotion through seminars. One of the problems with the mass media is that hucksters like Givens can get good coverage and publicity. Many members of the media are themselves financially illiterate. And they love a good story. So Givens got all sorts of free publicity, getting quoted in the press and invited to appear on a number of popular programs such as *The Today Show*, *Oprah*, and *Larry King Live*.

Thousands of people went to seminars conducted by Givens, partly because of the credibility Givens built through media appearances. As has now been well documented by some of those same members of the media, many unsuspecting investors were sold commission-laden products, including risky limited partnerships, through his organization.

Consider the case of Helen Giszczak, a 69-year-old retired secretary. She invested nearly two-thirds of her modest life savings in limited partnerships, which she said were described to her by Givens as "probably the most conservative investments we know of." But some of her limited partnerships ended up in bankruptcy, while the others lost much of their value.

Helen Giszczak appeared on the *Donahue* talk show with John Allen, an investment broker turned securities lawyer who helped her sue Givens's organization to get her money back. After a lengthy dialogue with Giszczak and Allen, Phil Donahue asked Helen how a smart person like her could get sucked in like that. She replied, "He was on your show and Oprah's. You gave him credibility. You gave him free advertising."

Wade Cook promoted his seminars through infomercials and other advertising, including radio ads on respected news stations. The high stock market returns of the 1990s brought greed back into fashion. Our experience has been that you see more of this greed when the market is hitting new highs than when it's in the basement.

The attorneys general of numerous U.S. states sued Cook's company and sought millions of dollars in consumer refunds. The suits alleged that the company lied about its investment track record (not a big surprise — this is the company that claimed you'd make 300 percent per year in stocks!).

Cook's company settled the blizzard of state and U.S. Federal Trade Commission (FTC) lawsuits against his firm by agreeing to accurately disclose its trading record in future promotions and give refunds to customers who were misled by past inflated return claims.

According to a news report by Bloomberg News, Cook's firm disclosed that it lost a whopping 89 percent of its own money trading during the last reporting year. As Deb Bortner, director of the Washington State Securities Division and president of the North American Securities Administrators Association, observed, "Either Wade is unable to follow his own system, which he claims is simple to follow, or the system doesn't work."

Don't assume that someone with something to sell, who is getting good press and running lots of ads, is going to take care of you. That "guru" may just be good at press relations and self-promotion. Certainly, talk shows and the media at large can and do provide useful information on a variety of topics, but you need to be aware that bad eggs sometimes turn up. These bad eggs may not always smell bad upfront. In fact, they may hoodwink people for many years before finally being exposed.

Pandering to advertisers

Thousands of publications and media outlets — newspapers, magazines, Web sites, radio, television, and so on — dole out personal financial advice and perspectives. Although many of these "service providers" collect revenue from subscribers, virtually all are dependent — in some cases, fully dependent (especially those on the Internet, radio, and television) — on advertising dollars. Although advertising is a necessary part of capitalism, advertisers can taint and, in some cases, dictate the content of what you read, listen to, and view.

Consider this case from a non-financial publication — _Modern Bride_ magazine. _Harper's_ magazine got hold of an apologetic letter (which it humorously entitled "To Love, Honor and Obey Our Advertisers") that _Bride's_ fashion advertising director sent to the magazine's advertisers. Here's an excerpt:

> _Bride's_ recommends that its readers (your customers) negotiate price, borrow a slip or petticoat, and compare catalogue shoe prices, and tells its readers that the groom's tuxedo may be free. It is difficult to understand why _Bride's_ was compelled to publish this information. With 57 years of publishing experience and support to the bridal industry, _Bride's_ could and should have been more sensitive to the retailers that it purports to serve. All of us in the bridal business must concentrate on projecting full-service bridal retailing in a positive light.

We don't find it difficult to understand why the writer of the criticized _Bride's_ article revealed cost-saving strategies to its readers — she was trying to give them useful information and advice! Now, revealing letters like this one are hard to come by, so how can you, a consumer of financial information, separate the good publications from the advertiser-biased publications? After writing and working for a number of publications, and observing the workings of even more, we've developed some ideas on the subject.

First, consider how dependent a publication or media outlet is on advertising. We find that "free" publications, radio, and television are the ones that most often create conflicts of interest by pandering to advertisers. (All three derive all of their revenue from advertising.) Much of what is on the Internet is advertiser-driven, as well. Many investing sites cater to offering advice about individual stocks. Interestingly, such sites derive much of their revenue from online brokerage firms seeking to recruit customers. (See Part III for more information about your investment options.)

Next, as you read various publications, watch TV, or listen to the radio, note how consumer-oriented these media are. Do you get the feeling that they're looking out for your interests? Or are they primarily creating an advertiser-friendly broadcast or publication? For example, if lots of auto manufacturers advertise, does the media outlet ever tell you how to save money when shopping for a car, or the importance of buying a car within your means?

Jumping over Real and Imaginary Hurdles

Perhaps you know that you should be living within your means, buying and holding sound investments for the long term, and securing proper insurance coverage. However, you can't bring yourself to do these things. We all know how difficult it is to break the detrimental habits we've practised for many years. The temptation to spend money lurks everywhere we turn. Ads show attractive and popular people enjoying the fruits of their labours — a new car, an exotic vacation, and a lavish home.

Maybe you felt deprived by your tightwad parents as a youngster, or maybe you're bored with life and you like the adventure of buying new things. If only you could hit it big on one or two investments, you think, you could get rich quick and do what you really want with your life. As for disasters and catastrophes, well, those things happen to other people, not to you. Besides, you'll probably have advance warning of pending problems, so you can prepare accordingly.

Your emotions and temptations can get the better of you. Certainly, part of successfully managing your finances involves coming to terms with your shortcomings and the consequences of your behaviours. If you don't, you may end up enslaved to a dead-end job so that you can keep feeding your spending addiction. Or you can spend more time with your investments than you do with your family and friends. Disasters and catastrophes can happen to anyone at any time.

Discovering the real hurdles holding you back

A variety of personal and emotional hurdles can get in the way of making the best financial moves. As we discuss earlier in this chapter, a lack of financial knowledge (which stems from a lack of personal financial education) can stand in the way of making good decisions.

However, we've seen some people get caught in the psychological trap of blaming something else for their financial problems. For example, some people believe that all our adult problems can be traced back to our childhood and how we were raised. Our roots supposedly cause behaviors ranging from substance abuse and credit card addiction to sexual infidelity.

We don't want to diminish the negative impact particular backgrounds can have on some people's tendency to make the wrong choices during their lives. Exploring your personal history can certainly yield clues to what makes you tick. That said, we are adults making choices and engaging in behaviours that affect ourselves as well as others. We shouldn't blame our parents for our own inability to plan for our financial futures, live within our means, and make sound investments. At the very least, if they are indeed partly to blame, it's still up to you — and certainly to your benefit — to change your ways.

Some people also have a common tendency to blame their financial shortcomings on not earning more income. Such people believe that if they only earned more income, their financial (and personal) problems would melt away.

Our experience with people from diverse economic backgrounds has taught us that achieving financial success — and, more importantly, personal happiness — has virtually nothing to do with how much income a person makes but rather with what she makes of what she does have. We know financially wealthy people who are emotionally poor even though they have all the material goods they want. Likewise, we know people who are quite happy, contented, and emotionally wealthy even though they're struggling financially.

Canadians — even those who have not had an "easy" life — should be able to come up with numerous things to be happy about and grateful for: a family who loves them; friends who laugh at their stupid jokes; the freedom to catch a movie or play, or read a good book; a great singing voice, sense of humour, or a full head of hair; or the fact that they live in a country not at war with any other country.

Financially speaking, Canadians are pretty spoiled. The majority of the people in the world have a standard of living that is a fraction of the Canadian average.

Practising good habits

After you understand the basic concepts and know where to buy the best financial products when you need them, you'll soon see that managing your personal finances well is not much more difficult than other things you do regularly, like tying your shoelaces and getting yourself to and from work each day.

Regardless of your income, you can make your dollars stretch farther if you practise good financial habits and avoid mistakes. In fact, the lower your income, the more important it is that you make the most of your income and savings (because you don't have the luxury of falling back on your next fat paycheque to bail you out).

More and more industries are subject to global competition, and you need to be on your financial toes now more than ever. Job security is on the wane. Layoffs and retraining for new jobs are on the increase. Putting in 20 or 30 years for one company and retiring with the gold watch and lifetime pension are becoming as rare as never having problems with your computer.

Speaking of company pensions, odds are increasing that you work for an employer that has you save toward your own retirement rather than provide a pension for you. Not only do you need to save the money, you must also decide how to invest it.

Managing your personal finances involves much more than just managing and investing money. It also includes making all the pieces of your financial life fit together. It means lifting yourself out of financial illiteracy. Like planning a vacation, managing your personal finances means formulating a plan for making the best use of your limited time and dollars. (We discuss common financial problems in the next section.)

Intelligent personal financial strategies have little to do with your gender, ethnicity, or marital status. We all need to manage our finances wisely. Some aspects of financial management become more or less important at different points in your life, but for the most part, the principles remain the same for all of us.

Knowing the right answers isn't enough. You have to practise good financial habits just as you practise other good habits, such as brushing your teeth. Don't be overwhelmed. As you read this book, make a short list of your financial marching orders and then start working away. Throughout this book, we highlight ways you can overcome temptations and keep control of your money rather than let your emotions and money rule you.

You probably don't like being made to feel stupid or told that you're doing something wrong. And what you do with your money is a quite personal and confidential matter. We endeavour not to be paternalistic in this book, but to provide guidance and advice that is in your best interest. You don't have to take it all — pick what works best for you and understand the pros and cons of your options. But from this day forward, please don't make the easily avoidable mistakes or overlook the sound strategies that we discuss throughout this book.

If you're young, congratulations for being so forward-thinking as to realize the immense value of investing in your personal financial education. You'll reap the rewards for decades to come. But even if you're not so young, you surely have many years to make the most of the money you currently have, the money you're going to earn, and even the money you may inherit!

Throughout our journey together, we hope to challenge and even change the way you think about money and about making important personal financial decisions — and sometimes even about the meaning of life. No, we're not philosophers, but we do know that money — for better but more often for worse — is connected to many other parts of our lives.

Common Financial Problems: You've Got Company

How financially healthy are you? You may already know the bad news. Or perhaps things aren't quite as bad as they seem.

When was the last time you sat down surrounded by all your personal and financial documents and took stock of your overall financial situation, including reviewing your spending, savings, future goals, and insurance? If you're like most people, you've either never done this exercise, or you did so a long time ago.

Financial problems, like many medical problems, are best detected early (clean living doesn't hurt, either). Here are some common personal financial problems we've seen:

- **Not planning.** Human beings were born to procrastinate. That's why we have deadlines — and deadline extensions. Unfortunately, you may have no explicit deadlines with your overall finances. You can allow your credit card debt to accumulate, or you can leave your savings sitting in lousy investments for years. You can pay higher taxes, leave gaps in your retirement and insurance coverage, and overpay for financial products. Of course, planning your finances isn't as much fun as planning a vacation, but doing the former can help you take more of the latter.

- **Overspending.** The average Canadian saves less than 5 percent of his or her after-tax income (in contrast to those in other industrialized countries, where the savings rate is two to three times that rate). Simple arithmetic helps you determine that savings is the difference between what you earn and what you spend (assuming that you're not spending more than you're earning!). To increase your savings, you either have to work more (yuck!), know a wealthy family who wants to leave its fortune to you, or spend less. For most of us, the thrifty approach is the key to building savings and wealth.

- **Buying with consumer credit.** Even with the benefit of today's lower interest rates, carrying a balance month-to-month on your credit card or buying a car on credit means that even more of your future earnings are going to be earmarked for debt repayment. Buying on credit encourages you to spend more than you can really afford.

In this part . . .

We discuss the concepts that underlie sensible personal financial management. You also find out why you didn't know all these concepts before now (and whom to blame). Here, you undergo a (gentle) financial physical exam to diagnose your current economic health. We also cover how to plan for and accomplish your financial goals.

Part I
Assessing Your Financial Fitness and Setting Goals

The 5th Wave   By Rich Tennant

"I find it easier to say 'No', if I imagine them saying, 'Mommy, can I have the latest over-hyped, over-priced, commercial exploitation of an obnoxiously adorable cartoon character'."

Chapter 1

Improving Your Financial Fitness

· ·

In This Chapter

▶ Understanding and conquering obstacles to personal financial success

▶ Overcoming real and imagined financial hurdles

▶ Comprehending common money problems

▶ Understanding bad debt, good debt, and too much debt

▶ Determining assets, liabilities, and your (financial) net worth

▶ Calculating your rate of savings

▶ Assessing your investments and insurance

· ·

*W*e're barely acquainted, but we do know that you're not dumb. Real dummies don't read and educate themselves. And real dummies don't understand the value of investing in their education. Real dummies also can't deflate their egos enough to admit that they need help and guidance.

Here's what dumb is: Dumb is the crook who walked into a convenience store, put a $20 bill on the counter, and asked for change. When the cashier opened the register, the man pulled a gun and demanded all the cash. The thief took the loot — $15 — and fled, leaving his $20 bill on the counter. Or how about the criminal who robbed a person who lacked cash? The victim offered the assailant a cheque, which the assailant later attempted to cash at the bank, where — surprise, surprise — he was arrested. Both of these stories are true!

So you're most definitely not dumb! But you may not be literate when it comes to personal finances.

Targeting the Trouble Spots

Unfortunately, most Canadians don't know how to manage their personal finances because they were never taught how to do so. Nearly all our high schools and universities lack even one course that teaches this vital skill we all need throughout our lives.

In the handful of schools that do offer a course remotely related to a personal finance class, the class is typically an economics course (and an elective at that). "Archaic theory is being taught and it doesn't do anything for the students as far as preparing them for the real world," says one high school principal we know. Having taken more than our fair share of economics courses, we understand the principal's concerns.

Some people are fortunate enough to learn the financial keys to success at home, from knowledgeable friends, and through good books like this one. Others either never learn the keys to financial success, or they learn them the hard way — by making lots of costly mistakes. The lack of proficiency in personal financial management causes not only tremendous anxiety but also serious problems. Consider the following sobering statistics:

- About 75,000 personal bankruptcies are filed in Canada annually. That's about one in every 100 households. So in the next ten years, nearly one in every ten households in Canada — one of the most affluent countries in the world — will file bankruptcy.

- Studies show that many people aren't saving adequately for retirement. Most years only about half of Canadians even intend to make an RRSP contribution, and only around 10 percent contribute the maximum they are allowed in their plan.

- One out of every two marriages ends in divorce. Studies show that financial disagreement is one of the leading causes of marital discord. In a survey conducted by *Worth* magazine and the market research firm of Roper/Starch, couples admitted to fighting about money more than anything else (more than three times more often than they fight about their sex lives). And a staggering 57 percent of those surveyed agreed with the statement, "In every marriage, money eventually becomes the most important concern."

- Almost half of all Canadians think one can deduct the interest on a home mortgage (they can't!), and that they reduce their risk by only putting their money into Canadian investments (they don't!). Further, one survey found that almost 80 percent of people feel that the lowest-risk investments make the most sense when saving for retirement (they don't because most people need to make their money grow in order to be able to retire).

- In a Princeton Survey Research Associates investing basics test, approximately one-third of the people who took the quiz answered fewer than 50 percent of the questions correctly. These results are all the more stunning when you consider that the questions offered only two or three multiple-choice answers as options!

> ✓ Nearly 80 percent of consumers do not know how the grace period on a credit card works. An even greater percentage doesn't understand that interest starts accumulating immediately for new purchases on credit cards with outstanding balances.
>
> ✓ Fifty-three percent of people who took a multiple-choice investing quiz did not know that total return was the best measure of a mutual fund's performance.

The overall costs of personal financial illiteracy to our society are huge. The high rate of spending and low rate of saving in Canada leads to lower long-term economic growth and higher interest rates. Annually, billions of dollars are wasted in North America through the purchase of inferior and inefficient financial products.

Talking money at home

We were both fortunate that our parents taught and instilled in us the importance of personal financial management. Our moms and dads taught us a lot of useful things that have been invaluable throughout our lives — among them were sound principles for earning, spending, and saving money. Our parents *had* to know how to do these things, because they were raising large families on (usually) one income. They knew the importance of making the most of what you have and of passing that vital skill on to your kids.

In many families, however, money is a taboo subject — parents don't level with their kids about the limitations, realities, and details of their budgets. Some parents we talk with believe that dealing with money is an adult issue, and that kids should be insulated from it so that they can enjoy being kids. In many families, kids may hear about money only when disagreements and financial crises bubble to the surface. Thus begins the harmful cycle of children having negative associations with money and financial management.

In other cases, parents with the best of intentions pass on their money-management habits. Unfortunately, some of those habits are bad habits. Now, we're not saying that you shouldn't listen to your parents. But in the area of personal finance, as in any other area, poor family advice can be problematic. Think about where your parents learned about money management, and then consider whether they had the time, energy, or inclination to research choices before making their decisions. For example, your parents may mistakenly think that banks are the best places for investing money. (You can find the best places for investing your money in Part III of this book.)

In still other cases, the parents have the right approach, but the kids go to the other extreme out of rebellion. For example, if your parents spent money carefully and thoughtfully, you may tend to do the opposite, such as buying yourself gifts the moment any extra money comes your way.

Although we can't change what the educational system and your parents did or didn't teach you about personal finances, you now have the ability to find out what you need to know to manage your finances. And if you have children of your own, we're sure you'll agree that kids really are amazing. Don't underestimate their potential or send them out into the world without the skills they need to be productive and happy adults. Teach them about personal finance as they are growing up, just as you do manners, personal hygiene, and staying safe — and do it *before* they head off to university or begin their first job.

Teaching personal finance in schools

Nancy Donovan teaches personal finance to her grade five math class as a way to illustrate how math can be used in the real world. "Students choose a career, find jobs, and figure out what their taxes and take-home paycheques will be. They also have to rent apartments and figure out a monthly budget," says Donovan, adding, "Students like it and parents have commented to me how surprised they are with how much financial knowledge their kids can handle." Donovan also has her students invest $10,000 (play money) and then track the performance of their investments.

Urging our schools to teach the basics of personal finance is just common sense. We should be teaching our children about how to manage a household budget, about the importance of saving money for future goals, and about the consequences and dangers of overspending. Unfortunately, few schools offer classes like Nancy Donovan's. In most cases, the financial basics aren't taught at all.

Some people argue that teaching children financial basics is the job of parents. However, this well-meaning sentiment is what we're relying on now, and for all too many it isn't working. In some families, financial illiteracy is passed on from generation to generation.

We must recognize that education takes place in the home, on the streets, *and* in the schools. Therefore, schools must bear some responsibility for teaching this very important life skill. And with more and more teenage students holding down after-school jobs, teaching money management know-how through the schools makes even more sense.

✔ **Delaying saving for retirement.** Most people say that they want to retire by their mid-60s or sooner. But in order to accomplish this goal, most people need to save a reasonable chunk (around 10 percent) of their income, starting sooner rather than later. The longer you wait to start saving for retirement, the harder it will be to reach your goal. And you'll pay much more in taxes to boot if you don't take advantage of the tax benefits of investing through particular retirement plans.

✔ **Falling prey to financial sales pitches.** Great deals that can't wait for a little reflection or a second opinion are often disasters waiting to happen. A sucker may be born every minute, but a slick salesperson is born every second! Steer clear of those who pressure you to make decisions, promise you high investment returns, and lack the proper training and experience to help you.

✔ **Not doing your homework.** To get the best deal, you need to shop around, read reviews, and get advice from disinterested, objective third parties. You need to check references and track records so that you don't hire incompetent, self-serving, or fraudulent financial advisers. But with all the different financial products available, making informed financial decisions has become an overwhelming task. We do a lot of the homework for you with the recommendations in this book. We also explain what additional research you need to do and how to go about doing it.

✔ **Making decisions based on emotion.** You're most vulnerable to making the wrong financial moves after a major life change (a job loss or divorce, for example), or when you feel under pressure. Maybe your investments plunged in value. Or perhaps a recent divorce has you fearing that you won't be able to afford to retire when you planned, so you pour thousands of dollars into some newfangled financial product. Take your time and keep your emotions out of the picture. In Chapter 21, we discuss how to approach major life changes with an eye to determining what changes you may need to make to your financial picture.

✔ **Not separating the wheat from the chaff.** In any field in which you're not an expert, you run the danger of following the advice of someone who you think is an expert but really isn't. This book shows you how to separate the financial fluff from the financial facts. Look in any mirror to see the person who is best able to manage your personal finances. Educate and trust yourself!

✔ **Exposing yourself to catastrophic risk.** You're vulnerable if you and your family don't have insurance to pay for financially devastating losses. People without a savings reserve and support network can end up homeless. Many people lack sufficient insurance coverage to replace their income. Don't wait for a tragedy to strike to find out whether you have the right insurance coverages.

✔ **Focusing too much on money.** Placing too much emphasis on making and saving money can warp your perspective on what's important in life. Money is not the first or even the second priority in happy people's lives. Your health, relationships with family and friends, career satisfaction, and fulfilling interests should be more important.

Most financial problems can be fixed over time with changes in your behaviour. (That's what the rest of the book is all about.)

The rest of this chapter guides you through a *financial physical* to help you detect problems with your current financial health. But don't get depressed and dwell on your "problems." View them for what they are — opportunities for improving your financial situation. In fact, the more areas for improvement that you can identify, the greater the potential you have to build real wealth and accomplish your financial and personal goals.

Defining Bad Debt and Good Debt

Why do you borrow money? Usually, you borrow money because you don't have enough of it to buy something you want or need — like a university education. If you want to buy a four-year post-secondary education, you can easily spend $30,000 or more. Not too many people have that kind of spare cash. So borrowing money to finance part of that cost enables you to buy the education.

How about a new car? A trip to your friendly local car dealer shows you that a new set of wheels will set you back at least $15,000 ... and usually much more. Although more people may have the money to pay for that than, say, the university education, what if you don't? Should you finance the car the way you finance the education?

The auto dealers and bankers who are eager to make you an auto loan say that you deserve and can afford to drive a nice, new car, and they tell you to borrow away.

We say, "*NO! NO! NO!*"

Why do we disagree with the auto dealers and lenders? For starters, we're not trying to sell you a car or loan from which we derive a profit! More importantly, there's a *big* difference between borrowing for something that represents a long-term investment and borrowing for short-term consumption.

If you spend, say, $1,500 on a vacation, the money is gone. Poof! You may have fond memories and even some Kodak moments, but you have no financial value to show for it. "But," you say, "vacations replenish my soul and make me more productive when I return. In fact, the vacation more than pays for itself!"

Great. We're not saying that you shouldn't take a vacation. By all means, take one, two, three, or as many as you can afford yearly. But that's the point — *take what you can afford.* If you have to borrow money in the form of an outstanding balance on your credit card for many months in order to take the vacation, you *can't* afford it.

We refer to debt incurred for consumption as *bad debt,* because such debt is harmful to your long-term financial health.

You'll be able to take many more vacations during your lifetime if you save the cash in advance. If you get into the habit of borrowing and paying all that interest for vacations, cars, clothing, and other consumer items, you'll spend more of your future income paying back the debt and interest, leaving you with *less* money for vacations and all your other goals.

The relatively high interest rates banks and other lenders charge for bad debt is one of the reasons why you have less money when using such debt. Money borrowed through credit cards, auto loans, and other types of consumer loans not only carry a relatively high interest rate but also is not tax-deductible.

We're not saying that you should never borrow money and that all debt is bad. Good debt, such as that used to buy real estate or a small business, is generally available at lower interest rates than bad debt and is usually tax-deductible. If well managed, these investments may also increase in value. Borrowing to pay for educational expenses can also make sense. Education is generally a good long-term investment, because it can increase your earning potential.

Knowing How Much Bad Debt Is Too Much

Calculating how much debt you have relative to your annual income is a useful way to size up your debt load. Ignore, for now, good debt — the loans you may owe on real estate, a business, an education, and so on. We're focusing on bad debt, the higher-interest debt used to buy items that depreciate in value.

For example, suppose that you earn $30,000 per year. Between your credit cards and an auto loan, you have $15,000 of debt. In this case, your bad debt represents 50 percent of your annual income.

$$\frac{\text{bad debt}}{\text{annual income}} = \text{bad debt danger ratio}$$

The financially healthy amount of bad debt is zero. (Not everyone agrees with us. One major U.S. credit card company says — in its "educational" materials, which it gives to schools to teach students about supposedly sound financial management — that carrying consumer debt amounting to 10 to 20 percent of your annual income is just fine.)

Playing the credit card float

Given what we have to say about the vagaries of consumer debt, you may think that we're always against using credit cards. But if you pay your balance in full each month, there's a benefit in addition to the convenience credit cards offer in not having to carry around extra cash. You get free use of the bank's money extended to you through your credit card charges. (Some cards offer other benefits, such as frequent flyer miles. Also, purchases made on credit cards may be contested if the seller of the product or service doesn't stand behind what it sells.)

When you charge on a credit card that does not have an outstanding balance carried over from the prior month, you typically have several weeks (known as the *grace period*) from the date of the charge to the time when you must pay your bill. Financial types call this *playing the float*. Had you paid for this purchase by cash or cheque, you would have had to shell out the money sooner.

If you have difficulty saving money, and plastic tends to burn holes through your budget, forget the float game. You're better off not using credit cards. The same applies to those who pay their bills in full but spend more because it's so easy to do so with a piece of plastic.

When your *bad debt danger ratio* starts to push beyond 25 percent, it can spell real trouble. Such high levels of high-interest consumer debt on credit cards and auto loans are like cancer. As with cancer, the growth of the debt can snowball and get out of control unless something significant intervenes. If you have consumer debt beyond 25 percent of your annual income, see Chapter 4 to find out how to get out of debt.

How much good debt is acceptable? The answer varies. The key question is: Are you able to save sufficiently to accomplish your goals? In the "Savings Analysis" section later in this chapter we help you figure out how much you're actually saving, and in Chapter 2 we help you determine what you should be saving to accomplish your goals. Take a look at Chapter 13 to find out how much mortgage debt is appropriate to take on when buying a home.

Avoid borrowing money for consumption (bad debt) — for spending on things that decrease in value and eventually become financially worthless, such as cars, clothing, vacations, and so on. Borrow money only for investments (good debt) — for purchasing things that retain and hopefully increase in value over the long term, such as an education, real estate, or your own business.

Determining Your Financial Net Worth

Your financial net worth is an important barometer of your monetary health. Your net worth indicates your capacity to accomplish major financial goals, such as buying a home, retiring, and withstanding unexpected expenses or loss of income.

Your financial net worth has absolutely, positively *no* relationship to your worth as a human being. This is not a test. You don't have to compare your number with your neighbour's. Financial net worth is not the scorecard of life.

Your *net worth* is your financial assets minus your financial liabilities.

```
Financial Assets - Financial Liabilities = Net Worth
```

Financial assets

A *financial asset* is worth real money or is something you can convert to hard dollars that you can use to buy things now or in the future.

Financial assets generally include the money you have in bank accounts, stocks, bonds, and mutual fund accounts (see Part III, which deals with investments). Money that you have in retirement plans (including those with your employer) and the value of any businesses or real estate that you own are also included.

We generally recommend that you exclude your personal residence when figuring your financial assets. Include your home only if you expect to someday sell it or otherwise live off the money you now have tied up in it (perhaps by taking out a reverse mortgage, which we discuss in Chapter 14). If you plan on someday tapping into the *equity* (the difference between the market value and any debt owed on the property) in your home, add that portion of the equity that you expect to use to your list of assets.

Assets also include your future expected Canada Pension Plan (Or Quebec Pension Plan) benefits and company pension payments (if your employer has such a plan). These assets are usually quoted in dollars per month rather than as a lump sum. We explain in a moment how to account for these monthly benefits when tallying your financial assets.

Personal property such as your car, clothing, stereo, and wine collection does *not* count as a financial asset. We know that adding these things to your assets makes your assets *look* larger (and some financial software packages and publications encourage you to list these items as assets), but you can't live off them unless you sell them.

Financial liabilities

To arrive at your financial net worth, you must subtract your *financial liabilities* from your assets.

Liabilities include loans and debts outstanding, such as credit card and auto loan debts. When figuring your liabilities, include money you borrowed from family and friends (unless you're not gonna pay it back — we won't tell). Include mortgage debt on your home as a liability *only* if you include the value of your home in your asset list. Be sure to also include debt owed on other real estate — no matter what.

Your net worth calculation

Table 1-1 provides a place for you to figure your financial assets. Go ahead and write in the spaces provided, unless you plan to lend this book to someone and you don't want to put your money situation on display.

Important note: See Table 2-1 in Chapter 2 to estimate your Canada Pension Plan benefits.

Table 1-1	Your Financial Assets
Account	*Value*
Savings and investment accounts (including retirement plans):	
Example: Bank savings account	$5,000
_____	$_____
_____	$_____
_____	$_____
_____	$_____
_____	$_____
_____	$_____
Total =	$_____

Account	Value
Benefits earned that pay a monthly retirement income:	
Employer's pensions	$_____ / month
Canada Pension Plan (or QPP)	$_____ / month
	× 240*
Total =	$_____
Total Financial Assets (add the two totals) =	$_____

* To convert benefits that will be paid to you monthly into a total dollar amount, and for purposes of simplification, assume that you will spend 20 years in retirement. (Ah, think of two decades of lolly-gagging around — vacationing, harassing the kids, spoiling the grandkids, starting another career, or maybe just living off the fat of the land.) As a shortcut, multiply the benefits that you'll collect monthly in retirement by 240 (12 months per year times 20 years). Inflation may reduce the value of your employer's pension if it doesn't contain a cost-of-living increase each year in the same way that Canada Pension Plan does. Don't sweat this now — you can take care of it in the section on planning for retirement in Chapter 2.

Now comes the potentially depressing part — figuring out your debts and loans in Table 1-2.

Table 1-2	Your Financial Liabilities
Loan	**Balance**
Example: Gouge 'Em Bank Credit Card	$4,000
_____	$_____
_____	$_____
_____	$_____
_____	$_____
_____	$_____
_____	$_____
Total Financial Liabilities =	$_____

Now you can subtract your liabilities from your assets to figure your net worth in Table 1-3.

Table 1-3	Your Net Worth	
Find		*Write It Here*
Total Financial Assets (from Table 1-1)		$_____
Total Financial Liabilities (from Table 1-2)		– $_____
	Net Worth =	$_____

Interpreting your net worth results

Your net worth is important and useful only to you and your unique situation and goals. What seems like a lot of money to a person with a simple lifestyle may seem like a pittance to a person with high expectations and a desire for an opulent lifestyle.

In Chapter 2, you can crunch some more numbers to determine your financial status more precisely for such goals as retirement planning. We also discuss saving toward other important goals in that chapter. In the meantime, if your net worth (excluding expected monthly retirement benefits such as those from the Canada Pension Plan or Quebec Pension Plan and company pensions) is negative or less than half your annual income, take notice. You have lots of company — in fact, you're with the majority of Canadians. If you're in your 20s, and you're just starting to work, a low net worth is less concerning. Getting rid of your debts — the highest-interest ones first — is the most important thing. Then you need to build a safety reserve equal to three to six months of living expenses. You should definitely find out more about getting out of debt, reducing your spending, and developing tax-wise ways to save and invest your future earnings.

Savings Analysis

How much money have you actually saved in the past year? By savings, we mean the amount of new money you added to your nest egg, stash, or whatever you like to call it.

Most people don't know or have only a vague idea of the rate at which they're saving money. The answer may sober, terrify, or pleasantly surprise you. In order to calculate your savings over the past year, you need to calculate your net worth as of today *and* as of one year ago.

The amount you actually saved over the past year is equal to the change in your net worth over the past year — in other words, your net worth today minus your net worth from one year ago. We know it may be a pain to find statements showing what your investments were worth a year ago, but bear with us; it's a useful exercise.

If you own your home, ignore this in the calculations. (You can consider the extra payments you make to pay off your mortgage principal faster as new savings.) And don't include personal property, such as your car, computer, clothing, and so on, with your assets.

When you have your two figures, plug them into Step 1 of Table 1-4. If you're anticipating the exercise and are already subtracting your net worth of a year ago from what it is today in order to determine your rate of savings, your instincts are correct, but the exercise is not quite that simple. You need to do a few more calculations in Step 2 of Table 1-4. Why? Well, counting the appreciation of the investments you've owned over the past year as savings wouldn't be fair. Suppose that you bought 100 shares of a stock a year ago at $17 per share, and now the value is at $34 per share. Your investment increased in value by $1,700 during the past year. Although you'd be the envy of your friends at the next party if you casually mentioned your investments, the $1,700 of increased value is not really savings. Instead, it represents appreciation on your investments, so you must remove this appreciation from the calculations.

Note: Just so you know, we're not unfairly penalizing you for your shrewd investments — you also get to add back the decline in value of your less-successful investments.

Table 1-4	Your Savings Rate over the Past Year		
Step 1: Figuring your savings.			
Today		*One Year Ago*	
Savings & investments	$_____	Savings & investments	$_____
– Loans & debts	$_____	– Loans & debts	$_____
= Net worth today	$_____	= Net worth 1 year ago	$_____
Step 2: Correcting for changes in value of investments you owned during the year.			
Net worth today		$_____	
– Net worth 1 year ago		$_____	
– Appreciation of investments (over past year)		$_____	
+ Depreciation of investments (over past year)		$_____	
= Savings rate		$_____	

If all this calculating gives you a headache, you get stuck, or you just hate crunching numbers, try the intuitive, seat-of-the-pants approach: Save a regular portion of your monthly income. You can save it in a separate savings or retirement plan.

How much do you save in a typical month? Get out the statements for accounts you contribute to or save money in monthly. It doesn't matter if you're saving money in a retirement plan that you can't access — money is money.

Note: If you save, say, $200 per month for a few months, and then you spend it all on auto repairs, you're not really saving. If you contributed $3,000 to a Registered Retirement Savings Plan (RRSP), for example, but you depleted money that you had from long ago (in other words, it wasn't saved during the past year), you should not count the $3,000 RRSP contribution as new savings.

You should be saving at least 5 to 10 percent of your annual income for longer-term financial goals such as retirement. If you're not, be sure to read Chapter 5 to find out how to reduce your spending so that you can increase your savings.

Measuring Your Investing Knowledge

Congratulations! If you stuck with us from the beginning of this chapter, you completed the hardest part of your financial physical. The physical is a whole lot easier from here on in!

Regardless of how much or how little money you have invested in banks, mutual funds, or other types of accounts, you want to invest your money in the wisest way possible. Knowing the rights and wrongs of investing is vital to your long-term financial well-being. Few people have so much extra money that they can afford major or frequent investing mistakes.

Answering yes or no to the following questions can help you determine how much time you need to spend with our "Investing Crash Course" in Part III, which focuses on investing. *Note:* The more "no" answers you reluctantly scribble, the more you need to find out about investing, and the faster you should turn to Part III.

_____ Do you understand the investments you currently hold?

_____ Is the money that you'd need to tap in the event of a short-term emergency in an investment where the principal does not fluctuate in value?

_____ Do you know what marginal income-tax bracket (combined federal and provincial) you're in, and do you factor that in when choosing investments?

_____ For money outside of retirement plans, do you understand how these investments produce income and gains, and whether these types of investments make the most sense from the standpoint of taxes?

_____ Do you have your money in different, diversified investments that aren't dependent on one or a few securities or one type of investment (that is, bonds, Canadian and foreign stocks, real estate, and so on)?

_____ Is the money that you're going to need for a major expenditure in the next few years invested in conservative investments rather than in riskier investments such as stocks?

_____ Is the money that you have earmarked for longer-term purposes (more than five years) invested to produce returns that are well ahead of inflation?

_____ If you currently invest in or plan to invest in individual stocks, do you understand how to evaluate a stock, including reviewing the company's balance sheet, income statement, business strategy, competitive position, price–earnings ratio versus its peer group, and so on?

_____ If you work with a financial adviser, is that person compensated in a way that minimizes potential conflicts of interest in the strategies and investments he or she recommends?

Making and saving money is not a guarantee of financial success but rather a prerequisite. If you don't know how to choose sound investments that meet your needs, you'll more than likely end up throwing money away, which leads to the same end result as never having earned and saved it in the first place. Worse still, you won't be able to derive any enjoyment from spending the lost money on things that you perhaps need or want. Turn to Part III to discover the best ways to invest; otherwise, you may wind up spinning your wheels working and saving.

Measuring Your Insurance Savvy

In this section, you must deal with the prickly subject of protecting your assets and yourself with *insurance*. (The following questions help you get started.) If you're like most people, reviewing your insurance policies and coverages is about as much fun as a root canal. Open wide!

_____ Do you understand the individual coverages, protection types, and amounts of each insurance policy you have?

_____ Does your current insurance protection make sense given your current financial situation (as opposed to your situation when you bought the policies)?

_____ If you wouldn't be able to make it financially without your income, do you have adequate long-term disability insurance coverage?

_____ If you have family members who are dependent on your continued income, do you have adequate life insurance coverage to replace your income should you die?

_____ Do you buy insurance through discount brokers, fee-for-service advisers, and companies that sell directly to the public (bypassing agents)?

_____ Do you carry enough liability insurance on your home, car (including umbrella/excess liability), and business to protect all your assets?

_____ Have you recently (in the last year or two) shopped around for the best price on insurance policies?

_____ Do you know whether your insurance companies have good track records when it comes to paying claims and keeping customers satisfied?

That wasn't so bad, was it? If you answered "no" more than once or twice, don't feel dumb — more than nine out of ten people make major mistakes when buying insurance. Find your insurance salvation in Part IV. If you answered "yes" to all the preceding questions, you can spare yourself from reading Part IV, but bear in mind that many people need as much help in this area as they do in other aspects of personal finance.

Chapter 2

Setting and Achieving Goals

In This Chapter

▶ Defining your own happiness

▶ Establishing and prioritizing your financial goals

▶ Saving for a rainy day, a real estate purchase, a small business, or educational needs

▶ What you need to get through retirement, and ways to make up for lost time

*I*n our work, we regularly ask people what their short- and long-term personal and financial goals are. Quite a large portion of people report that reflecting on this question is incredibly valuable, because they hadn't considered it for a long time — if ever.

In this chapter, we help you dream about what you want to get out of life. Although our expertise is in personal finance, we wouldn't be doing our job if we didn't get you to consider your non-financial plans and how money fits into the rest of your life goals. So before we jump into how to establish and save toward common financial goals, we want to take a moment to discuss how you think about making and saving money, and how to best fit your financial goals into the rest of your life.

Creating Your Own Definition of "Wealth"

Pick up just about any major financial magazine or newspaper, or scan stories on the Internet, and you'll quickly see our culture's obsession with financial wealth. The more money financial executives, movie stars, or professional athletes make and have, the more publicity and attention they seem to get. In fact, many publications go as far as ranking those people who earn the most or have amassed the greatest wealth!

We're frankly perplexed at why many of the most affluent and highest-income earners maintain workaholic schedules despite being married and having kids. From what we observe, our society seems to define "wealth" as the following:

- Fat pay cheques

- Huge investment account balances

- The ability to hire full-time employees to raise your children

- Being too busy at your career to maintain friendships or take an interest in your neighbours, community, or important social problems

- The freedom to be unfaithful and dump your spouse when you're no longer pleased with him or her

Considering what money can't buy

Recall the handful of moments in your life that you wouldn't trade for anything. Odds are, those moments don't include the time you bought a car or found a designer sweater that you liked. The old saying is true: The most enjoyable and precious things of value in your life can't be bought.

The following statement should go without saying, but we must say it, because too many people act as if it weren't so: Money can't buy happiness. It's tempting to think that if you could only make 10 or 20 percent more money, you'd be happier. You'd have more money to travel, eat out, and buy that new car you've been eyeing, right? Not so. A great deal of thoughtful research suggests that little relationship exists between money and happiness.

"Wealth is like health: Although its absence can breed misery, having it is no guarantee of happiness," summarizes Dr. David Myers, professor of psychology at Michigan's Hope College, in his book *The Pursuit of Happiness: Discovering the Pathway to Fulfillment, Well-Being, and Enduring Personal Joy* (Avon Books). (This guy has it good! Imagine studying happiness for a living.)

Despite cheap air travel, DVD players, cell phones, microwaves, computers, voice mail, and all the other stuff that's supposed to make our lives easier and more enjoyable, people aren't any happier than they were four decades ago. According to research conducted in the U.S. by the National Opinion Research Center, 35 percent of Americans in 1957 said that they were "very happy" — and now, two generations later, fewer say the same. These unexpected results occur even though incomes, after adjusting for inflation, have more than doubled during that time.

As Dr. Myers observes in *The Pursuit of Happiness*, "if anything, to judge by soaring rates of depression, the quintupling of the violent crime rate since 1960, the doubling of the divorce rate, and the tripling of the teen suicide rate, we're richer and less happy."

What is your relationship to money?

Over the years in our work, we've come to find that how a person relates to and feels about money has a great impact on how good he is at managing his money and making important financial decisions. For example, knowing that you have a net worth of –$13,200 because of credit card debt is useful, but it's probably not enough information for you to do something constructive about your problem. A logical next step would be to examine your current spending and take steps to reduce your debt load.

Although we cover practical solutions to common financial quandaries later in this book, we also discuss the more touchy-feely side of money. For example, some people who continually rack up consumer debt have a spending addiction. Other people who jump in and out of investments and follow them like a hawk have psychological obstacles that prevent them from holding investments.

And then you have those somewhat philosophical and psychological issues relating to money and the meaning of life. Saving more money and increasing your net worth isn't always the best approach. In our work, we've come across numerous people who attach too much significance to personal wealth accumulation and neglect important human relationships in their pursuit of more money. Some retirees have a hard time loosening the purse springs and actually spending some of the money they worked so hard to save for their golden years.

Balancing your financial goals with other important life goals is key to your happiness. What's the point, for example, of staying in a well-paying, admired profession if you don't care for the work and you're mainly doing it for the financial rewards? Life is too short and precious for you to squander away your days.

So, as you read through the various chapters and sections of this book, please consider your higher life goals and purposes. What are your non-financial priorities (family, friends, causes), and how can you best accomplish your goals with the financial resources you do have?

Managing the balancing act

Believe it or not, some people save too much. If making and saving money is a good thing, then the more the better, right?

Well, take the admittedly extreme case of Anne Scheiber, who, on a modest income, started saving at a young age, allowing her money to compound in wealth-building investments such as stocks over many years. As a result, she was able to amass $20 million before she passed away at the age of 101.

Scheiber lived in a cramped studio apartment and never used her investments. She didn't even use the interest or dividends — an American, she lived solely on her Social Security benefits and the small pension from her employer. Scheiber was extreme in her frugality and obsessed with her savings. As reported by James Glassman in the *Washington Post*, "She had few friends . . . she was an unhappy person, totally consumed by her securities accounts and her money."

Most people, ourselves included, wouldn't choose to live and save the way that Scheiber did. She saved for the sake of saving: no goal, no plan, no reward for herself. Saving should be a means to an end, not something that makes you mean to the end.

Even those who are saving for an ultimate goal can become consumed by their saving habits. We see some people pursuing higher-paying jobs and pinching pennies in order to retire early. But sometimes they make too many personal sacrifices today while chasing after some vision of their lives tomorrow. Others get consumed by work and then don't notice or understand why their family and friends feel neglected.

Another problem with seeking to amass wealth is that tomorrow may not come. Even if all goes according to plan, will you know how to be happy when you're not working if you spend your entire life making money? More importantly, who will be around to share your leisure time? One of the costs of an intense career is time spent away from friends and family. You may indeed realize your goal of retiring early, but you may be putting off too much living today in expectation of living tomorrow.

As Charles D'Orleans said in 1465, "It's very well to be thrifty, but don't amass a hoard of regrets."

Of course, at the other extreme are spendthrifts who live only for today. A friend once said, "We're not into delayed gratification." Shop 'til you drop seems to be the motto of this personality type. "Why bother saving when we might not be here tomorrow?" reasons this type of person.

The danger of this approach is that tomorrow may come after all, and most people don't want to spend all their tomorrows working for a living. The earlier neglect of saving, however, may make it necessary for you to work when you're older. And if for some reason you can't work, and you have little money to live on, much less live enjoyably, the situation can be tragic. The only difference between a person without any savings or access to credit and some homeless people is a few months of unemployment.

Making and saving money is like eating food. If you don't eat enough, you may suffer. If you eat too much, the overage may go to waste or make you overweight. The right amount, perhaps with some extra to spare, affords you a healthy, balanced, peaceful existence. Money should be treated with respect and acknowledged for what it is — a means to an end, and a precious resource that shouldn't be thoughtlessly squandered and wasted.

As Dr. David Myers, whom we introduce earlier in this chapter, says: "Satisfaction isn't so much getting what you want as wanting what you have. There are two ways to be rich: one is to have great wealth, the other is to have few wants." Find ways to make the most of the money that does pass through your hands, and never lose sight of all that is far more important than money.

Prioritizing Your Savings Goals

Most people we know have financial goals. The rest of this chapter discusses the most common financial goals and how to work toward accomplishing them.

- ✔ **Becoming part of the landed gentry.** Renting and dealing with landlords can be a financial and emotional drag, so most folks want to buy into the Canadian dream and own some real estate — the most basic of which is to own your own home.

- ✔ **Retiring.** No, retiring does not imply sitting on a rocking chair watching the world go by while hoping that some long lost friend, your son's or daughter's family, or the neighbourhood dog comes by to visit. *Retiring* is a catch-all term for discontinuing full-time work or perhaps not even working for pay at all.

- ✔ **Educating the kids.** No, all those diaper changes, late-night feedings, and trips to the zoo aren't enough to get junior out of your house and into the real world as a productive, self-sufficient adult. You may want to help your children get a university or college education — unfortunately, that can cost a truckload of dough.

- ✔ **Owning your own business.** Many employees want to face the challenges and rewards that come with being the boss. The primary reason that most people continue to dream without actually plunging into their own small businesses is that they lack the money to do so. Although many businesses don't require gobs of start-up cash, almost all require that you withstand a substantial reduction in your income during the early years.

Because each of us is different, we can have goals (other than those in the previous list) that are unique to our own situation. Accomplishing such goals almost always requires saving money. As one of our favourite Chinese proverbs says, "Do not wait until you are thirsty to dig a well." In other words, don't wait to save money until you're ready to accomplish a personal or financial goal!

Knowing what's most important to you

Unless you earn really big bucks or have a large family inheritance to fall back on, your personal and financial desires will probably outstrip your resources. Thus, you must prioritize your goals if you want to accomplish them.

One of the biggest mistakes we see people make is rushing into financial decisions without considering what's really important to them. Because many of us get caught up in the responsibilities of our daily lives, we often never find time for reflection.

From the experience we've had working in the world of personal finance, we can tell you that the people who accomplish their goals aren't necessarily smarter or higher-income earners than those who don't. People who identify their goals and then work toward them are the ones who accomplish their goals.

Valuing retirement plans

Where possible, you should try to save and invest in plans that offer a tax advantage. Registered accounts — known by such enlightening acronyms and names as RRSP (Registered Retirement Savings Plan), RPP (Registered Pension Plan), and so on — offer tax breaks to people of all economic means. (You can find the details of the different types of retirement plans in Chapter 11.) Consider the following advantages to investing in retirement plans:

✔ Contributions are usually tax-deductible. Retirement plans should really be called *tax-reduction plans*. If they were, people might be more excited about contributing to them. For many Canadians, avoiding higher taxes is the motivating force to open the plan and start the contributions.

By putting money in a retirement plan, you not only plan wisely for your future but also get an immediate financial reward: lower taxes — and lower taxes means more money available for saving and investing. Retirement plan contributions are generally not taxed at either the federal or provincial level until withdrawal. If you're paying, say, 35 percent between federal and provincial taxes (refer to Chapter 6 to determine your tax bracket), a $5,000 contribution to a retirement account will lower your taxes by $1,750.

✔ Returns on your investments compound over time without taxation. After you put money into a retirement plan, you aren't taxed on any interest, dividends, or appreciation that money earns. Of course, there's no such thing as a free lunch — these plans don't allow for complete tax avoidance. Yet you can get a really great lunch at a discount — you get to defer taxes on all of the accumulating gains and profits until you withdraw the money down the road. Thus, more money is working for you over a longer period of time.

✔ In some retirement plans, companies will match a portion of your own contribution. Thus, in addition to tax breaks, you get free extra money courtesy of your employer!

Dealing with competing goals

Unless you enjoy paying higher taxes, why would you save money outside of retirement plans? The reason is that some financial goals are not easily achieved by saving in retirement plans. Also, retirement plans have limits on the amount you can contribute annually, and the type of investments you can choose.

If you're accumulating money to purchase a vehicle or to start or buy a business, for example, you'll probably need to save that money outside of a retirement plan. Why? Because if you withdraw funds from retirement plans, you have to include that money in your income and pay tax on it. (See the sidebar "Avoiding RRSP early withdrawal penalties," where we discuss exceptions to this rule.)

Because you're constrained by your financial resources, you must prioritize your goals. Before funding your retirement plans and racking up those tax breaks, read on to consider your other goals.

Avoiding RRSP early-withdrawal penalties

There are times and ways to avoid the early-withdrawal penalties that the tax gods normally apply. You can now make penalty-free withdrawals from an RRSP for either a first-time home purchase (limit of $20,000 per person) or expenses for higher education for you or your spouse (up to $10,000 a year with a total maximum of $20,000), your children, or your grandchildren. Note, though, that in both cases you have to repay the money over time to your plan.

If you lose your job and withdraw RRSP money simply because you need it to live on, that money has to be included in your annual income and is taxed accordingly. However, if you're not working and earning so little income that you need to raid your retirement plan, you are surely in a low tax bracket. The lower income taxes you pay as compared to the taxes you would have paid on that money had you not sheltered it in a retirement plan in the first place should make up for most or all of the penalty.

When you do make a withdrawal from your RRSP, the plan administrators are required by the government to hold back some of the money as a sort of tax down payment. The withholding tax rates (unless you live in Quebec) are 10 percent on the first $5,000, 20 percent on the next $10,000, and 30 percent on any amount beyond $15,000. In Quebec, the rates are 21 percent on the first $5,000, 30 percent on the next $10,000, and 35 percent on any amount over $15,000. These tax rates are calculated on each individual transaction. If you need to withdraw a large amount, consider breaking the amount you need into separate withdrawals of no more than $5,000 each. This will minimize the amount of tax held back, and maximize the amount of money you can get your hands on. However, don't forget that the withholding tax may not be sufficient to cover all the tax you'll owe, given that the withdrawals will be included in that year's annual income come tax time. Plan ahead.

Building Emergency Reserves

No one can predict the future. You simply have no reliable way to tell what may happen with your job, health, or family. Because you don't know what the future holds, preparing for the unexpected is financially wise. Even if you're the lucky sort who sometimes finds $5 bills on street corners, you can't control the sometimes chaotic world in which we live.

Conventional wisdom says that you should have approximately six months of living expenses put away for an emergency. This particular amount may or may not be right for you, because it depends, of course, on how expensive the emergency is. Why six months, anyway? And where should you put it? Unfortunately, no hard and fast rules exist. How much of an emergency stash you need depends on your situation.

We recommend saving the following emergency amounts under differing circumstances (in Chapter 12, we recommend good places to invest this money):

- **Three months' living expenses** if you have other accounts, such as an RRSP, or family members and close friends that you can tap for a short-term loan. This minimalist approach makes sense when you're trying to maximize investments elsewhere (for example, in retirement plans), or you have stable sources of income (employment or otherwise).

- **Six months' living expenses** if you don't have other places to turn for a loan, or you have some instability in your employment situation or source of income.

- **Up to one year's living expenses** if your income fluctuates wildly from year to year, or if your profession involves a high risk of job loss and it could take you a long time to find another job, and you don't have other places to turn for a loan.

Don't buy cash-value life insurance plans

Life insurance salespeople are often eager to sell you *cash-value life insurance policies*, which combine life insurance protection with a type of savings account. A salesperson may very well try to sucker you into buying a cash-value life insurance policy as a savings vehicle for accomplishing goals such as retiring or paying for a child's educational costs. Don't fall for this sales trap.

Cash-value life insurance policies give you no immediate tax deduction. By contrast, a retirement savings plan such as an RRSP allows you to deduct your contributions from your taxable income.

Most people should buy term life insurance. (See Chapter 15 for more details.) Because agents earn far larger commissions selling cash-value policies, they usually push those policies.

In the event that your only current source of emergency funds is a high-interest credit card, you should first save at least three months' worth of living expenses in an accessible account before funding a retirement plan or saving for other goals.

Saving to Buy a Home or Business

When you're starting out financially, deciding whether to save money to buy a home or to put money into a retirement plan presents a dilemma. In the long run, owning your own home is a wise financial move. On the other hand, saving sooner for retirement makes achieving your goal easier.

Presuming both goals are important to you, you should be saving toward both buying a home *and* for retirement. If you're eager to own a home, you can throw all your savings toward achieving that goal and temporarily put your retirement savings on hold. Save for both purposes simultaneously if you're not in a rush.

When saving money for starting or buying a business, most people encounter the same dilemma they face when deciding to save to buy a house: If you fund your retirement plans to the exclusion of earmarking money for your small-business dreams, your entrepreneurial aspirations may never become a reality. Generally, we advocate hedging your bets by saving some money in your tax-sheltered retirement plans as well as some toward your business venture. As we discuss in Part III, an investment in your own small business can produce great rewards, so you may feel comfortable focusing your savings on your own business.

Funding Kids' Educational Expenses

 Wanting to provide for your children's future is perfectly natural. But doing so before you've saved adequately toward your own goals can be a major financial mistake.

It may sound selfish, but you need to take care of *your* future first. You should first take advantage of saving through your tax-sheltered retirement plans before you set aside money in custodial savings accounts or registered education savings plans for your kids. This practice isn't selfish — do you really want to have to leech off your kids when you're old and frail, because you didn't save any money for yourself?

See Chapter 13 for a complete explanation of how to save for educational expenses.

Saving for Big Purchases

If you want to buy a car, a canoe, or a plane ticket to France, do not, we repeat, *do not* buy such things with *consumer credit* (that is, carrying debt month-to-month to finance the purchase on a credit card or auto loan). As we explain in Chapter 4, cars, boats, vacations, and the like are consumer items, not investments that build wealth, such as real estate or small businesses. A car begins to depreciate the moment you drive it off the sales lot. A plane ticket to France is worthless the moment you arrive back home. (We know your memories will be priceless, but they won't pay the bills.)

Paying for high-interest consumer debt can cripple your ability not only to save for long-term goals like retirement or a home but also to make major purchases in the future. Interest on consumer debt is exorbitantly expensive — up to 18 percent or higher for most credit cards. When contemplating the purchase of a consumer item on credit, add up the total interest you end up paying on your debt and call it the price of instant gratification.

Don't deny yourself gratification; just learn how to delay it. Get into the habit of saving for your larger consumer purchases to avoid paying for them over time with high-interest consumer credit. When saving up for a consumer purchase such as a car, a money market account or short-term bond fund (see Chapter 11) is a good place to store your short-term savings.

Preparing for Retirement

Many people toil away at work, dreaming about a future in which they can stop the daily commute and grind; get out from under that daily deluge of faxes, voice mails, and e-mails; and do what they want, when they want. People often assume that this magical day will arrive either on their next true day off or when they retire or win the lottery — whichever comes first.

We've never cared much for the term *"retire."* This word seems to imply idleness or the end of usefulness to society. But if retirement means not having to work at a job (especially one you don't enjoy) and having financial flexibility and independence, then we're all for it.

Being able to retire sooner rather than later is part of the Canadian dream. But this idea has some obvious problems. First, you set yourself up for disappointment. If you want to retire by your mid-60s (when the Canada Pension Plan kicks in), you'll need to save enough money to support yourself for 20 years, maybe longer. Two decades is a long time to live off your savings. You're going to need a good-sized chunk of money — more than most people realize. The earlier you hope to retire, the more money you need to set aside, and the sooner you have to start saving — unless you plan to work part-time in retirement to earn more income!

Many of the people we speak to say that they do want to retire, and most say "the sooner, the better." Yet only about half of Canadians even plan to put money into their RRSP each year, and just 10 percent put in the maximum they're allowed to contribute. One sardonic middle-aged person we know who had saved little for retirement, when asked when he would like to retire, deadpanned, "Sometime before I die." If you're in this group (and even if you're not), determine where you stand financially regarding retirement. If you're like most working people, you need to increase your savings rate for retirement.

Don't neglect non-financial preparations for retirement

Investing your money is just one (and not even the most important) aspect of preparing for your retirement. In order to enjoy the lifestyle that your retirement savings will provide you, you need to invest energy into other areas of your life, as well.

- Few things are more important than your health. Without your health, enjoying the good things in life can be hard. Unfortunately, many people are not motivated to care about their health until after they discover problems. By then, it may be too late.

  Although exercising regularly, eating a balanced and nutritious diet, and avoiding substance abuse can't guarantee you a healthful future, these good habits go a long way toward preventing many of the most common causes of death and debilitating disease. Regular medical exams also are important in detecting problems early.

- In addition to your physical health, be sure to invest in your psychological health. People live longer and have happier and healthier lives when they have a circle of family and friends around them for support.

Unfortunately, many people become more isolated and lose regular contact with business associates, friends, and family members as they grow older.

Happy retirees tend to stay active, getting involved in volunteer organizations and new social circles. They may travel to see old friends or younger relatives who may be too busy to visit them.

Treat retirement life like a bubbly, inviting hot tub. You want to ease yourself in, nice and slow; jumping in hastily can take most of the pleasantness out of the experience. Abruptly leaving your job without some sort of plan for spending all that free time is an invitation to boredom and depression. Everyone needs a sense of purpose and a sense of routine. Establishing hobbies, volunteer work, or a sideline business while gradually cutting back your regular work schedule can be a terrific way to ease into retirement.

Lower yourself into the tub slowly. Take some time to get used to the temperature change. Ahhh . . . nice, isn't it?

Figuring what you need for retirement

If you hope to someday reduce the time you spend working, or cease working completely, you'll need sufficient savings to support yourself. Many people — particularly young people and those who don't work well with numbers — underestimate the amount of money needed to retire. To figure out how much you should be saving per month to achieve your retirement goals, you need to crunch a few numbers. (Don't worry — this number-crunching should be easier than doing your taxes.)

Luckily for you, you don't have to start cold. Studies show how people typically spend money before and during retirement. Most people need about 70 to 80 percent of their pre-retirement income throughout retirement to maintain their standard of living. For example, if your household earns $40,000 per year before retirement, you're likely to need $28,000 to $32,000 (70 to 80 percent of $40,000) per year during retirement to live the way you're accustomed to living. The 70 to 80 percent is an average. Some people may need more simply because they have more time on their hands to spend their money. Others adjust their standard of living and live on less.

You, of course, are not average in any way — you're unique! So how do you figure out what you're going to need? The simplest method for estimating what you need is for us to tell you what percentage you need. (We know we've only known each other a short time, but we're going to offer some friendly counselling.) The following three profiles provide a rough estimate of the percentage of your pre-retirement income you're going to need during retirement. Pick the one that most accurately describes your situation. If you fall between two descriptions, pick a percentage that fits in between the two.

To maintain your standard of living in retirement:

✔ You need **65 percent of your pre-retirement income** if you

  • save a large amount (15 percent or more) of your annual earnings

  • are a high-income earner

  • will own your home free of debt by the time you retire

  • do not anticipate leading a lifestyle in retirement that reflects your current high income

If you're an especially high-income earner who lives well beneath your means, you may be able to do just fine with even less than 65 percent. Try picking an annual dollar amount or percentage of your current income that will allow the kind of retirement lifestyle you desire.

> ✔ You need **75 percent of your pre-retirement income** if you
>
>   • save a reasonable amount (5 to 14 percent) of your annual earnings
>
>   • will still have some mortgage debt or a modest rent to pay by the time you retire
>
>   • anticipate having a standard of living in retirement that is comparable to what you have today
>
> ✔ You need **85 percent of your pre-retirement income** if you
>
>   • save little or none of your annual earnings (less than 5 percent)
>
>   • will have a significant mortgage payment or sizeable rent to pay in retirement
>
>   • anticipate wanting or needing to maintain your current lifestyle throughout retirement

Of course, you can use a more precise approach to figure out how much you need per year in retirement. Be forewarned, though, that this more personalized method is far more time-consuming, and because you're making projections into an uncertain future, it may not be any more accurate than the simple method we explain earlier in this section. If you're data-oriented, you may feel comfortable tackling this method: You need to figure out where you're spending your money today (worksheets are available in Chapter 3) and then work up some projections for your expected spending needs in retirement (the information in Chapter 19 may help you, as well).

Understanding retirement building blocks

Did you play with Lego blocks or Tinker Toys when you were a child? You start by building a foundation on the ground, and then you build up. Before you know it, you're creating bridges, castles, and panda bears. Although preparing financially for retirement isn't exactly like playing with blocks, the concept is the same: You need a basic foundation so that your necessary retirement reserves can grow.

If you've been working steadily, you may already have a good foundation, even if you haven't been actively saving toward retirement. In the pages ahead, we walk you through the probable components of your future retirement income and show you how to figure how much you should be saving to reach particular retirement goals.

Counting on government benefits

It's old news that no one should depend on the Canada Pension Plan (CPP) or Quebec Pension Plan (QPP) and other programs such as Old Age Security (OAS) if they want anything but a bare bones existence when they retire. One poll found that around two-thirds of Canadians believe that government programs won't provide them with a secure income in their retirement years.

Contrary to widespread cynicism, some form of various government programs should be around to provide you with some income when you retire, no matter how old you are today. In fact, the Canada Pension Plan is one of the sacred cow political programs. Imagine what would happen to the group of politicians that voted not to pay any more benefits!

If you think that you can never retire because you don't have any money saved, we're happy to inform you that you're probably wrong. You likely have some CPP/QPP and Old Age Security benefits coming to you. But they generally won't be enough to live on comfortably.

The CPP/QPP, for example, is only intended to provide you with a subsistence level of retirement income for the basic necessities: food, shelter, and clothing. It's not intended to be your sole source of income. The Canada Pension Plan (or QPP) is designed to replace about a quarter of your pre-retirement income — but only up to a certain limit. Few people could maintain their current lifestyles without supplementing their CPP/QPP with personal savings and company retirement plans.

How much will I get from CPP/QPP?

The retirement pension you'll receive from the Canada Pension Plan (or QPP) is determined by two factors. The first is the number of years you contribute to the plan. The second is how much you contribute to the plan. When you're working, you pay a percentage of your earnings above $3,500 — in 2005, the maximum payment was $41,100; this ceiling is regularly adjusted for inflation. The amount you have to put in is determined by the *contribution rate,* which also is often adjusted — in 2005, it was 9.9 percent. If you earn a salary, you pay half of your required CPP/QPP contributions and your employer pays half (so, using the 2005 rate, you each would pay 4.95 percent). If you're self-employed, you pay the full amount. However, you don't make CPP/QPP contributions if you are receiving disability or retirement payments from the CPP/QPP. Also, even if you are still working and haven't yet started receiving your CPP/QPP retirement benefits, you stop paying into the plan when you turn 70.

In 2005, the average monthly benefit (assuming you retired at age 65) was just over $450, and the maximum possible monthly payment was about $828. The payments are set for life, and are fully indexed to inflation. An adjustment is made to reflect the change in the cost of living once a year, in January.

If you qualify for CPP/QPP and are no longer able to work due to a disability, you may be eligible for a *disability pension.* The maximum is slightly higher than regular CPP/QPP benefits. In 2005, the average disability benefit was $750, while the maximum was $1,010.

If you make CPP/QPP contributions, you should receive a statement summarizing your contributions every few years. If you want to get an estimate of the size of Canada Pension Plan benefits you can expect, contact Health and Welfare Canada. (If you live in Quebec, contact the Quebec Pension Plan.)

You can start collecting as early as age 60 or as late as age 70. The amount of your monthly benefits will be permanently reduced by half a percent for every month before age 65 that you start drawing your pension. This works out to 6 percent a year; the reduction continues for the rest of your life. On the other hand, if you choose to delay receiving your CPP/QPP, your benefits will be increased by the same 0.5 percent a month for each month beyond your 65th birthday.

If you are a member of the CPP/QPP and die, there are three different types of survivor benefits your family may be eligible to receive, depending on how long you have been making contributions.

The first is a one-time lump-sum death benefit. Like most CPP/QPP payments, how much you get will depend on how long — and how much — you've paid into the system. This payment is six times what your CPP/QPP retirement pension was — or would have been — at age 65, but can't be higher than a set maximum, which in 2005 was $2,500.

The second death benefit is called the *survivor's pension,* and is paid to your surviving spouse or common-law partner. The amount of the payment is a percentage of the deceased's benefits. This is calculated using the survivor's age and other factors. For survivors under the age of 65, the average monthly survivor's benefit in 2005 was about $340, and the maximum was $462. For those 65 or over, the average survivor's benefit in 2005 was just over $275, with the maximum set at just under $500. However, if the surviving spouse is also eligible to receive retirement benefits from his or her own CPP/QPP contributions, the total will usually be less than the sum of the two benefits.

The third death-related CPP/QPP benefit is a children's benefit. This is paid to your natural or adopted children, or children in your care and control, at the time you die and continues until the child turns 18. The benefits may continue up to age 25 as long as your child is going to school full-time at a recognized institution. If the benefits are stopped and then your child goes back to school and is still between the ages of 18 and 25, the benefits can be reinstated. This benefit is a flat rate that is adjusted annually. The maximum in 2005 was around $195.

How much will I get from Old Age Security?

Old Age Security is paid out to all Canadians who are 65 and older. The only problem is that, depending on your other income, you may have to give some or even all of it back!

The rules as to who is eligible and how much you receive are somewhat complicated. In general, to receive the maximum (which in 2005 was $473 a month, with the average being around $450 a month) you must have lived in Canada for at least 40 years since you turned 18.

In addition, you may also qualify for the maximum amount if you meet the following three conditions: You were born on or before July 1, 1952, you lived in Canada "for a period" between the time you turned 18 and July 1, 1977, and you lived in Canada for the ten years immediately before your application is approved. (Even if you haven't lived in Canada for the full ten years leading up to your application being approved, you may also qualify for the full amount if, prior to these last ten years, you lived in Canada after age 18 for at least three times as long as the total amount of time you lived outside Canada during those last ten years.) To earn at least the minimum OAS monthly benefit you must have lived in Canada for at least 10 years.

There are further and different eligibility rules. For the specifics, contact the Income Securities Program Branch of Social Development Canada at 800-277-9914, or visit the government Web site at www.sdc.gc.ca.

OAS payments are adjusted four times a year for inflation. Your payments don't start automatically when you hit the big 65 — you have to fill out a formal application. Be sure to send it in well ahead of time.

The big question for many people, though, isn't how much they'll receive from OAS, but how much of it they'll be able to hang on to. The government will recoup or claw back some or all of your OAS payments if your net income is over a certain level. In 2005, for instance, the threshold was $59,790 of net income. If your net income was higher than that, you had to repay a portion of your OAS benefits. The repayment rate is 15 percent of the amount that your net income exceeds the threshold amount. Because of this formula, if your net income exceeds a certain level you end up repaying every single cent of OAS benefits. In 2005, if your net income exceeded $96,483, for example, then you would end up losing all of your OAS payments.

Extra support for low-income retirees

If you have a very low retirement income, you may be eligible to receive a form of top-up to Old Age Security known as the Guaranteed Income Supplement, or *GIS*. To receive the GIS, you must be getting OAS pension benefits and also must meet the income requirements. There are different maximums depending on whether you are single, married, or if your spouse is a pensioner. In 2005, for instance, the average monthly GIS payment for a single person was about $389, and the maximum was around $562. To qualify, your income had to be no greater than $13,512. The figure includes all income — including CPP/QPP payments — except Old Age Security. For households where both spouses are receiving OAS benefits, the average monthly GIS benefit in 2005 was around $237 and the maximum $366, with the maximum income allowable to receive GIS benefits set at $17,616.

Planning your personal savings/ investment strategy

Money you're saving toward retirement can include money under the mattress as well as money in a Registered Retirement Savings Plan (RRSP). You may have also earmarked investments in non-retirement plans for your retirement.

Equity (the difference between the market value less any mortgage balances owed) in rental real estate can be counted toward your retirement, as well. Deciding whether to include the equity in your primary residence (your home) is trickier. If you don't want to count on using this money in retirement, don't include it when you tally your stash. You may want to count a portion of your home equity in your total assets for retirement. Many people sell their homes when they retire and move to a cheaper region of the country, move closer to family, or downsize to a more manageable household. And increasing numbers of older retirees are tapping their homes' equity through reverse mortgages.

Making the most of pensions

Pension plans are a benefit offered by some employers — mostly larger organizations and government agencies. Even if your current employer doesn't offer a pension, you may have earned pension benefits through a previous job.

The plans we're referring to are known as *defined benefit plans*. With these plans, you qualify for a monthly benefit amount to be paid to you in retirement based on your years of service for a specific employer.

Although each company's plan differs, all plans calculate and pay benefits based on a formula. A typical formula might credit you with 1.5 percent of your salary for each year of service (full-time employment). For example, if you work for ten years, you earn a monthly retirement benefit worth 15 percent of your monthly salary.

Pension benefits can be quite valuable. In the better plans, employers put away the equivalent of 5 to 10 percent of your salary to pay your future pension. This money is not quoted as part of your salary — it's in addition to your salary. You never see it in your paycheque, and it isn't taxed. The employer puts this money away in an account for your retirement.

To qualify for pension benefits, you don't have to stay with an employer long enough to receive the 25-year gold watch. Depending on your province, an employee must generally be fully *vested* (entitled to receive full benefits based on years of service upon reaching retirement age) after either two or five years of full-time service.

Defined-benefit pension plans are becoming rare for two major reasons:

- ✔ First, they are costly for employers to maintain. Many employees don't understand how these plans work and why they're so valuable, so companies don't get mileage out of their pension expenditures — employees don't see the money, so they don't appreciate how generous the company is being.

- ✔ Second, most of the new jobs being generated in today's economy are with small companies that typically don't offer these types of plans.

More employers are offering plans in which employees elect to save money out of their own paycheques. Known as *defined contribution plans*, these plans allow you to save toward your retirement at your own expense rather than at your employer's expense. (To encourage participation in defined contribution plans, some employers "match" a portion of their employees' contributions.) More of the burden and responsibility of investing for retirement falls on your shoulders with these plans, so it's important to understand how these plans work. Most people are ill-equipped to know how much to save and how to invest the money. The retirement planning worksheet in the next section should help get you started with figuring out the amount you need to save. (Part III shows you how to invest.)

Retirement planning worksheet

Now that you've toured the components of your future retirement income, we want you to take a shot at tallying where you stand in terms of retirement preparations. Don't be afraid to do this exercise — it's not difficult, and you may find that you're not in such bad shape. We even explain how to catch up if you find that you're behind in saving for retirement.

Note: The following worksheet (Table 2-1) and the growth multiplier (Table 2-2) assume that you're going to retire at age 66 and that your investments will produce an annual rate of return that is 4 percent higher than the rate of inflation. (For example, if inflation averages 3 percent, this table assumes that you will earn 7 percent per year on your investments.)

Table 2-1	Retirement Planning Worksheet	
1. Annual retirement income needed in today's dollars (see earlier in this chapter).	$ _____ / year	
2. Government benefits.	– $ _____ / year	
3. Annual pension benefits (ask your benefits department). (Multiply by 60 percent if your pension won't increase with inflation during retirement.)	– $ _____ / year	
4. Annual retirement income needed from personal savings (subtract lines 2 and 3 from line 1).	= $ _____ / year	
5. Savings needed to retire at age 66 (multiply line 4 by 15).	$ _____	
6. Value of current retirement savings.	$ _____	
7. Value of current retirement savings at retirement (multiply line 6 by Growth Multiplier in Table 2-3).	$ _____	
8. Amount you still need to save (line 5 minus line 7).	$ _____	
9. Amount you need to save per month (multiply line 8 by Savings Factor in Table 2-3).	$ _____ / month	

Table 2-2	Growth Multiplier	
Your Current Age	**Growth Multiplier**	**Savings Factor**
26	4.8	.001
28	4.4	.001
30	4.1	.001
32	3.8	.001
34	3.5	.001
36	3.2	.001
38	3.0	.002
40	2.8	.002
42	2.6	.002
44	2.4	.002

(continued)

Table 2-2 *(continued)*

Your Current Age	Growth Multiplier	Savings Factor
46	2.2	.003
48	2.0	.003
50	1.9	.004
52	1.7	.005
54	1.6	.006
56	1.5	.007
58	1.4	.009
60	1.3	.013
62	1.2	.020
64	1.1	.041

Making up for lost time

If the amount you need to save per month to reach your retirement goals seems daunting, don't despair. All is not lost. Here are our top recommendations for making up for lost time.

- ✔ **Question your spending.** You have two ways to boost your savings: Earn more money or cut your spending (or do both). Most people don't spend their money nearly as thoughtfully as they earn it. Refer to Chapter 5 for suggestions and strategies for reducing your spending.

- ✔ **Be more realistic about your retirement age.** If you extend the age at which you plan to retire, you get a double financial benefit: You're earning and saving money for more years, and you're spending your nest egg over fewer years. Of course, if your job is making you crazy, this option may not be too appealing. Try to find work that makes you happy, and consider working, at least part-time, during the early years typically considered the retirement years.

- ✔ **Use your home equity.** The prospect of tapping the cash in your home can be troubling. After getting together the down payment, you probably worked for many years to pay off that sucker. You're delighted not to have to mail a mortgage payment to the bank anymore. But what's the use of owning a house free of mortgage debt when you lack sufficient retirement reserves? All the money that's tied up in the house can be used to help increase your standard of living in retirement.

You have a number of ways to tap your home's equity. You can sell your home and either move to a lower-cost property or rent an apartment. Another option is a *reverse mortgage*, where you get a monthly income cheque as you build a loan balance against the value of your home. The loan is paid when your home is finally sold. (See Chapter 14 for more information about reverse mortgages.)

✔ **Get your investments growing.** The faster the rate at which your money grows and compounds, the less you need to save each year to reach your goals. Earning just a few extra percentage points per year on your investments can dramatically slash the amount you need to save. The younger you are, the more powerful the effect of compounding interest. For example, if you're in your mid-30s, and your investments appreciate 6 percent per year (rather than 4 percent) faster than the rate of inflation, the amount you need to save each month to reach your retirement goals drops by about 40 percent!

✔ **Turn a hobby into supplemental retirement income.** Even if you've earned a living in the same career over many decades, you have skills that are portable and can be put to profitable use. Pick something you enjoy and are good at, develop a business plan, and get smart about how to market your services and wares. Remember, as people get busier, more specialized services are created to support their hectic lives. A demand for quality, homemade goods of all varieties also exists. Be creative! You never know — you may wind up profiled in a business publication!

✔ **Invest in a tax-wise way.** By investing in a tax-wise fashion, you can boost the effective rate of return on your investments without taking on additional risk. Many people don't save and invest money in a way that minimizes their taxes.

Direct your savings into a tax-favoured retirement plan like an RRSP. You get an immediate tax deduction for your contribution. For a typical person, one-third or more of your contribution represents money you would have had to pay in federal and provincial income taxes. This money gets to work for you, rather than for the government, in the years ahead. Plus, the money compounds over the years without taxation.

As for money outside of tax-sheltered retirement plans, if you're in a relatively high tax bracket you may earn more by investing in investments and other vehicles that do not make a great amount of taxable distributions. (We discuss tax-friendly investments and retirement plans in detail in Chapters 10 and 11.)

✔ **Take a look at jobs that offer retirement plans.** When you're evaluating employers, cash is usually king. As long as the position includes extended health benefits, most people are concerned only about the salary. But having access to a retirement savings plan is a valuable benefit. Even more beneficial is a pension plan, which pays you a monthly retirement benefit based on your years of service (a completely pain-free way to build wealth for retirement). If you're lucky enough to have choices, check out these plans when considering a job offer.

✔ **Think about inheritances.** Although you should never count on an inheritance to support your retirement, you may inherit money someday. If you want to see what impact an inheritance has on your retirement calculations, simply add a conservative estimate of the amount you expect to inherit to your current total savings in Table 2-1.

Overcoming objections to retirement plans

Despite all the great tax benefits of investing through RRSPs and other retirement plans, many people aren't jumping at the opportunity to take advantage of them. Each of us has unique priorities. Maybe you're saving for a home purchase or paying off student loans. Some reasons for not taking advantage of retirement plans, however, stem from a lack of knowledge and understanding. The following sections cover the objections to contributing to tax-favoured plans that we hear most frequently. Some of these objections can be overcome, whereas others are legitimate reasons for not funding retirement plans.

Retirement's a long way away

When you're in your 20s or 30s, age 65 seems like the distant future. For many people, warning bells don't stimulate thoughts about one's golden years until middle age.

Delaying the age at which you start to sock away money is usually a financial mistake. The sooner you start to save, the less painful it is to save each year, because your contributions have more years to compound. For each decade you procrastinate, the percentage of your earnings that you should save to meet your goals approximately doubles. For example, if saving 5 percent per year in your early 20s would get you to your retirement goal, waiting until your 30s may mean that you have to sock away 10 percent, waiting until your 40s may mean that you have to save 20 percent, and so on.

When should you start saving for retirement? Ideally, you should start saving a small portion of your employment earnings with your very first pay cheque — another reason why we recommend you start your kids' saving habits while they're young!

Only losers who don't know how to have fun save for retirement

Some people really believe this statement. But we also know "losers" who don't save for retirement and still don't know how to have a good time (none of our colleagues and friends, of course).

This attitude is just a rationalization. The reality is that if you manage your finances efficiently and start working toward your goals sooner, you can spend more and have more fun in the long run. Besides, who says spending all your money is the only way to have fun?

There are greener investment pastures elsewhere

Some people find investing in RRSPs boring and believe that they can get a better return in the real estate market. Rental real estate can appreciate in value and produce increasing rental income over the years. Investing in real estate is a legitimate reason for not maximizing retirement plan contributions.

Although real estate provides some tax breaks, you need to also consider its drawbacks:

- ✔ While you accumulate the down payment, you may pay higher income taxes if you're sacrificing contributions to retirement plans that are tax-deductible.
- ✔ Rental real estate produces income that is taxable and is added to all your other income during the year, which may push you into a higher tax bracket. Even if the extra real estate income doesn't push you into a higher tax bracket, this income is taxable immediately at the ordinary income tax rates rather than deferred for many years.

In an RRSP, the earnings continue to compound without taxation, and you decide when you want to start drawing on the money.

You may be able to invest in what you want and gain tax relief, too. Many types of investments — stocks, bonds, mutual funds, precious metals, and even real estate — can be held in retirement plans. (See Chapter 10 for more details.)

I have no money left over to save

The more you spend, the less you're able to fund retirement plans. Thus, the extra taxes that you pay because you can't afford retirement plan contributions are an additional cost of overspending today. So if you can reduce your expenditures (refer to Chapter 5), you can more easily meet your retirement goals. You'll have more money to contribute to retirement plans, and you'll save on your taxes, too!

In some cases, people have a pile of money invested outside of tax-sheltered RRSPs that's not earmarked for specific future needs. They may use all of their monthly employment income to meet their ongoing living expenses. As a result, they believe that they can't afford to save in a retirement plan.

If you believe that you can't afford to save in an RRSP or other retirement savings plan because you spend all of your income on living expenses, you're compartmentalizing your finances. Look at the big picture. For example, what if you save $300 per month through your tax-deductible retirement plan? Suppose that doing so reduces your taxes by $100 and therefore really costs you only $200 a month. You then can take $200 from your savings outside the retirement plan and put it toward living expenses.

What you're effectively doing is transferring your savings from outside retirement plans to inside an RRSP or other retirement plan. You're not really saving new money, but you're getting terrific tax savings by playing this perfectly legal investing shell game. Just be careful not to drain your emergency savings reserve down too far.

I love my job and will work forever

Are you one of those people who loves his or her work? Do you feel that because you don't plan to retire, you don't need to amass a pile of money to live on for 20-plus years? If so, you can get away with saving a lot less than your eager-to-retire friends.

You may not, however, be *able* to work at your current job forever. What if you lose your job? What if something happens to your health? You can't assume that you will always be able to work — plan ahead for these what-ifs.

I've saved enough already

Congratulations! This is the single best excuse for not saving more for retirement. If you have a lot of money outside of tax-sheltered retirement plans, you may still want to contribute to retirement accounts for the tax benefits.

Part II
Saving More, Spending Less

The 5th Wave   By Rich Tennant

"I bought a software program that should help us monitor and control our spending habits, and while I was there, I picked up a few new games, a couple of screen savers, 4 new mousepads, this nifty pullout keyboard cradle..."

In this part . . .

We show you how to identify where your hard-earned dollars are going. We detail numerous ways to make them go toward helping you build up your savings rather than wasteful spending. What? You're buried in debt with little to show for it? Well, it's never too late to start digging out. Here you find out how to reduce your debt burden. We also devote an entire chapter to discussing taxes and how to legally minimize them, because too much of your money may be going to pay taxes.

Chapter 3

Determining Where Your Money Goes

In This Chapter

▶ Understanding the roots of overspending

▶ Assessing your spending

▶ Finding the road to salvation

*I*f you're like most people, you must live within your means in order to accomplish your financial goals. This requires spending less than you earn and then taking your "savings" and hopefully investing it intelligently.

Many folks earn just enough to make ends meet. And some can't even do that; they simply spend more than they make. The result of such spending habits is, of course, an accumulation of debt — witness the Canadian government and its debt of some $500 million.

No matter what your financial dreams are, you need to save and invest (unless you plan on winning the lottery or gaining a large inheritance). To put yourself in a position that allows you to start saving, you need to take a close look at your spending habits.

Examining the Roots of Overspending

Most influences in society encourage you to spend; credit is so widely and easily available. Think about it. More often than not, you're referred to as a *consumer* in the media and even in the hallowed halls of our government. You're not referred to as a person, a citizen, or a human being.

Here are some of the adversaries you're up against as you attempt to control your spending.

Having access to credit

As you probably already know, spending your money is easy. Thanks to innovations like bank machines and credit cards, your money is available for spending 24 hours a day, 365 days a year (except during leap years, when your money is available 366 days a year!). Every outlet imaginable is pitching its own credit card, including the gas station on the corner and the convenience store across the road. It certainly won't surprise us when kids down the block start taking credit cards at their lemonade stand. We can hear it now: "We take Visa, but we don't take American Express."

Sometimes it may seem as though lenders are trying to give away money by making credit so easily available. But this free money is a dangerous illusion. When it comes to consumer debt (credit cards, auto loans, and the like), lenders aren't giving away anything except the opportunity for you to get in over your head, rack up high interest charges, and delay your progress toward your financial and personal goals.

Credit is most dangerous when you make consumption purchases you can't afford in the first place.

Using credit cards

The modern–day bank credit card was invented by Bank of America near the end of the baby boom. The credit industry has been booming along with the boomers ever since.

If you pay your bill in full every month, credit cards offer a convenient way to buy things with an interest-free, short-term loan. But if you carry your debt over from month to month at high interest rates, credit cards encourage you to live beyond your means. Credit cards make it easy and tempting to spend money that you don't have.

 If you have a knack for charging up a storm and spending more than you should with those little pieces of plastic, only one solution exists: Get rid of your credit cards. Put scissors to the plastic. Go cold turkey. You can function without them. (See Chapter 4 for details on how to live without credit cards.)

Making minimum monthly payments

You'll never get your credit card debt paid off if you keep charging on your card and making only the minimum monthly payment. Interest continues to pile up on your outstanding debt. Paying only the minimum monthly payment is like using a paper cup to bail water from a sinking boat with a basketball-sized hole in its bottom.

Taking out car loans

Walking onto a car lot and going home with a new car that you could never afford if you had to pay cash is easy. The dealer gets you thinking in terms of monthly payments that sound small when compared to what that four-wheeler is *really* gonna cost you. Auto loans are easy for just about anyone to get (except maybe a recently paroled felon).

Suppose that you're tired of driving around in your old clunker. The car is battle-scarred and boring, and you don't like to be seen in it. Plus, the car is likely to need more repairs in the months ahead. So off you go to your friendly local car dealer.

You start looking around at all the shiny, new cars and then — like the feeling you experience when spotting a water fountain on a scorching hot day — there it is: the replacement for your old clunker. This new car is sleek and clean, and it has A/C, stereo, and power everything.

Before you have an opportunity to read the fine print on the sticker page on the side window, the salesperson moseys on up next to you. He gets you talking about how nice the car is, the weather, the hockey game. In short, anything *but* the sticker price of that car.

"How," you begin to think to yourself, "can this guy afford to spend time with me without knowing if I can afford this thing?" After a test drive and more talk about the car, the weather, and your love life (or lack thereof) comes your moment of truth.

The salesperson, it seems, doesn't care about how much money you have. Whether you have lots of money or very little money, it doesn't matter. Either way, it's no problem!

The car is only $299 a month.

"That price isn't bad," you think. Heck, you were expecting to hear that the car costs at least 20 grand. Before you know it, the dealer runs a credit report on you and has you sign a few papers, and minutes later you're driving home — the proud owner of a new car.

The dealer wants you to think in terms of monthly payments because the cost *sounds* so cheap: $299 for a car. But, of course, that's $299 per month, every month, for many, many months. You're gonna be payin' forever — after all, you just bought a car that cost a huge chunk (perhaps 100, 200, 300 percent or more) of your yearly take-home income!

But it gets worse. What does the total sticker price come to when interest charges are added in? (Even if interest charges are low, you may still be buying a car with a sticker price you can't afford.) And what about insurance, registration, and maintenance over the seven or so years that you'll own the car? Now you're probably up to more than a year's worth of your income. Ouch! (See Chapter 5 for info on how to spend what you can afford on a car.)

Bending to peer pressure

You go out with some friends to dinner, a ballgame, or a show. Try to remember the last time one of you said, "Let's go someplace (or do something) cheaper. I can't afford to spend this much."

On the one hand, you don't want to be a stick in the mud. But on the other hand, some of your friends have more money than you do — and the ones who don't may be running up debt fast.

Spending to feel good

Life is full of stress, obligations, and demands. "I work hard," you say, "And darn it, I deserve to indulge!" Especially after your boss took the credit for your last great idea or blamed you for his last major screw-up. So you buy something expensive or go to a fancy restaurant. Feel better? You won't when the bill arrives. And the more you spend, the less you save — and the longer you'll be stuck working for jerks like your boss!

Becoming addicted to spending

Just as people can become addicted to alcohol, tobacco, television, and the Internet, some people also become addicted to the high they get from spending. A number of psychological causes for spending addiction can be identified, with some relating to how your parents handled money and spending. (And you thought you had already identified all the problems you can blame on mom and dad!)

If your spending and debt problems are chronic, Debtors Anonymous — a 12-step support group program patterned after Alcoholics Anonymous — can help. See Chapter 4 for more information.

Trying to keep current

You just have to see the latest hit movie, wear the latest designer clothes, or get the new, super-improved, oversized tennis racquet with shock absorbers, double-wishbone suspension, and polyxylitol handgrips. All your friends are getting one, so you'd better get one, too. Right?

Wrong. Besides, many new technologies or products don't live up to their billing. Be smart. Wait until a product is proven and you can afford it.

Ignoring your financial goals when buying

When was the last time you heard someone say that he decided to forgo a purchase because he was saving for retirement or a home purchase? It doesn't happen often, does it? Just dealing with the here-and-now and forgetting your long-term needs and goals is tempting. This mindset leads people to toil away for too many years in jobs they dislike.

Living for today has its virtues: Tomorrow may *not* come. But the odds are good that it will. Will you still feel the same way about today's spending decisions tomorrow? Or will you feel guilty that you again failed to stick to your goals?

If you haven't set any goals yet, you may not know how much you should be saving. Chapter 2 helps you kick-start the planning and saving process.

Wanting the best for your children

For children, many of the best things in life are free, just as they are for you. Junior can live without the latest $100 sneakers. Later on in life, your children will thank you for teaching them that they don't need everything they see in ads: Better to pass on sound judgment and wise thriftiness than the worship of material goods.

Education can cost good money. However, education experts are the first to dissuade you of the assumption that you're doing the best for your children when you spend lots of money to live in an area with a supposedly top-of-the-line school or fund the tuition of a costly private school education. If you aren't home enough to take care of your children's other wants and needs, even the best education won't help your children succeed in life.

Education begins in (and is best done in) the home. We see some parents spend so much time running around and working to afford all the supposedly best things for their kids, that they neglect to spend *time* and get involved with them — the most important ingredient to their children's long-term happiness and success.

Analyzing Your Spending

Washing your face, brushing your teeth, and exercising regularly are good habits. Spending less than you earn and saving enough to meet your future financial objectives are the financial equivalents of these habits.

Despite relatively high incomes compared with the rest of the world, most Canadians have a hard time saving a good percentage of their incomes. Why? Because we spend too much — often far more than is necessary.

The first step to saving more of the income that you work so hard for is to figure out where that income typically gets spent. The spending analysis in the next section helps you determine where your income is going.

You should do the spending analysis if any of the following apply to you:

- ✔ You aren't saving enough money to meet your financial goals. (If you're not sure whether this is the case, please see Chapter 2.)

- ✔ You feel as though your spending is out of control, or you don't really know where all your income goes.

- ✔ You're anticipating a significant life change (for example, marriage, leaving your job to start a business, having children, retiring, and so on).

If you're already a good saver, you may not need to complete the spending analysis. If you're saving enough to accomplish your goals, we don't see much value in continually tracking your spending. You've already established the good habit — saving. Tracking exactly where you spend your money month after month is *not* the good habit. As long as you're saving enough, we say who cares where the leftover money is being spent! (You may still benefit from perusing our smarter spending recommendations in Chapter 5.)

The immediate goal of a spending analysis is to figure out where you're typically spending your money. The long-range goal is to establish a good habit: Maintaining a regular, automatic savings routine.

Notice the first four letters in the word *analysis*. (You may never have noticed, but we feel the need to bring it to your attention.) Knowing where your money is going each month is useful. Making changes in your spending behaviour and cutting out the fat so that you can save more money and meet your financial goals is terrific. But you may make yourself and those around you miserable if you try to be anal-retentive about documenting precisely where you're spending every single dollar and cent.

Remember: Saving what you need to achieve your goals is what matters most.

Tracking your spending on paper

Doing a spending analysis is a little bit like being a detective. Your goal is to reconstruct the crime of spending. You probably have some major clues at your fingertips or piled somewhere on the desk or table where you plop yourself down to pay bills.

Unless you keep meticulous records that detail every dollar you spend, you won't have perfect information. Don't sweat it! A number of available sources should allow you to reconstruct where you've been spending the bulk of your money. To get started, get out your:

- ✔ Recent pay stubs
- ✔ Tax returns
- ✔ Chequebook register or cancelled cheques
- ✔ Credit and charge card bills.

Ideally, you want to assemble the documents needed to track one year (12 months) of spending. But if your spending patterns don't fluctuate greatly from month to month (or if your dog ate some of the old bills), you can reduce your data gathering to one six-month period, or to every second or third month for the past year. If you take a major vacation or spend a large amount on gifts during certain months of the year, make sure that you include these months in your analysis.

Purchases made with cash are the hardest to track, because they don't leave a paper trail. Over the course of a week or perhaps even a month, you *could* keep a record of everything you buy with cash. Tracking cash can be an enlightening exercise, but it can also be a hassle. If you're lazy like we sometimes are or you lack the time and patience, try *estimating*. Think about a typical week or month — how often do you buy things with cash? For example, if you eat lunch out four days a week, paying around $6 a shot, that's about $100 a month. You may also want to try adding up all the cash withdrawals from your bank account statement and then working backward to try to remember where you spent the cash. If you regularly use a debit card, your bank statements will detail where you spent your money. You only need to recall what specific items you purchased. If you don't have your bank statements mailed out to you, you may be able to access them over the internet.

Try to separate your expenditures into as many useful and detailed categories as possible. Table 3-1 gives you a suggested format — you can tailor it to fit your needs. Remember, if you lump too much of your spending into broad, meaningless categories like "Other," you'll end up right back where you started: wondering where all the money went. (*Note:* When completing the tax section in Table 3-1, you should report the total tax you paid for the year as tabulated on your annual income tax return — and take the total Canada Pension Plan (or Quebec Pension Plan) and Employment Insurance deductions paid from your end-of-year pay stub — rather than the tax withheld or paid during the year.)

Table 3-1	Detailing Your Spending	
Category	*Monthly Average ($)*	*Percentage of Total Gross Income (%)*
Taxes, taxes, taxes (income)	_____	_____
Federal	_____	
Provincial	_____	
CPP (or QPP)	_____	
Employment Insurance premiums	_____	
The roof over your head		_____
Rent	_____	
Mortgage	_____	
Property taxes	_____	

The roof over your head _____

Gas/electric/oil _____

Water/garbage _____

Phone _____

Cable TV & Internet _____

Gardener/housekeeper _____

Furniture/appliances _____

Maintenance/repairs _____

Food, glorious food _____

Supermarket _____

Restaurants and take-out _____

Getting around _____

Gasoline _____

Maintenance/repairs _____

Provincial registration fees _____

Tolls and parking _____

Bus or subway fares _____

Style _____

Clothing _____

Shoes _____

Jewellery _____

Dry cleaning _____

Debt repayments (excluding mortgage) _____

Credit/charge cards _____

Auto loans _____

Student loans _____

Other _____

(continued)

Table 3-1 *(continued)*

Category	Monthly Average ($)	Percentage of Total Gross Income (%)
Fun stuff		_____
Entertainment (movies, concerts)	_____	
Vacation and travel	_____	
Gifts	_____	
Hobbies	_____	
Subscriptions/memberships	_____	
Pets	_____	
Other	_____	
Personal care		_____
Haircuts	_____	
Health club or gym	_____	
Makeup	_____	
Other	_____	
Personal business		_____
Accountant/lawyer/financial adviser	_____	
Other	_____	
Health care		_____
Physicians and hospitals	_____	
Drugs	_____	
Dental and vision	_____	
Therapy	_____	
Insurance		_____
Homeowner's/renter's	_____	
Auto	_____	
Health	_____	
Life	_____	

Insurance _____

Disability _____

Umbrella liability _____

Educational expenses _____

Tuition _____

Books _____

Supplies _____

Children _____

Day care _____

Toys _____

Child support _____

Charitable donations _____

Other _____

_____ _____

_____ _____

_____ _____

_____ _____

_____ _____

Tracking your spending on the computer

Numerous software programs can assist you with paying bills and tracking your spending. The main advantage of using software is that you can continually track your spending as long as you keep entering the information. These software packages can even help speed up the cheque-writing process (after you figure out how to use them, which is not always an easy thing to do).

But you don't need a computer and fancy software to pay your bills and figure out where you're spending money. Many people we know give up entering data into the software after a few months. If tracking your spending is what you're after, you need to enter information from the bills you pay by cheque and the expenses you pay by credit card and cash.

Don't waste time on financial administration

Tom is the model of financial organization. His financial documents are neatly organized into colour-coded folders. Every month, he enters all his spending information into his computer. He even carries a notebook to detail his cash spending so that every penny is accounted for.

Tom also balances his chequebook, "To make sure that everything is in order." He can't remember the last time his bank made a mistake, but he knows someone who once found a $50 error.

If you spend seven hours per month balancing your chequebook and detailing all your spending (as Tom does), you may be wasting nearly two weeks' worth of time per year — the equivalent of two-thirds of your vacation time if you take three weeks annually.

Suppose that, every other year, you're "lucky" enough to find a $100 error the bank made in its favour. If you spend just three hours per month tracking your spending and balancing your chequebook to discover this glitch, you'll be spending 72 hours over two years to find a $100 mistake. Your hourly pay: a wafer-thin $1.39 per hour. You can make more flipping burgers at a burger joint. (*Note:* If you make significant-sized deposits or withdrawals, however, make sure that you capture them on your statement.)

To add insult to injury, you may not have the desire and energy to do the more important stuff after working a full week and doing all your financial and other chores. Your big personal financial picture — establishing goals, choosing wise investments, securing proper insurance coverage — may continue to be shoved to the back burner. As a result, you may lose thousands of dollars annually. Over the course of your adult life, this amount could translate into tens or even hundreds of thousands of lost dollars.

Tom, for example, didn't know how much he should be saving to meet his retirement goals. He didn't review his employer's benefit materials, so he didn't understand his insurance and retirement plan options. He knew that he paid a lot in taxes, but he wasn't sure how to reduce his taxes.

You want to make the most of your money. Unless you truly enjoy dealing with money, you need to prioritize the money activities you work on. Time is limited and life is short. Working harder on financial administration doesn't earn you bonus points. The more time you spend dealing with your personal finances, the less time you have available to gab with friends, watch a good movie, read a good novel, and do other things you really enjoy.

Don't get us wrong — nothing is inherently wrong with balancing your chequebook. In fact, if you regularly bounce cheques because you don't know how low your balance is, the exercise may save you a lot in returned cheque fees. However, if you keep enough money in your chequing account so that you don't have to worry about the balance reaching $0.00, or if you have overdraft protection, balancing your chequebook is probably a waste of your valuable time, even if your hourly wages aren't lofty.

If you're busy, consider ways to reduce the amount of time you spend on mundane financial tasks like bill paying. Many companies, for example, allow you to pay your monthly bills electronically via your bank chequing account or your credit card. (Don't use this option unless you pay your credit card bill in full each month.) The fewer bills you have to pay, the fewer separate cheques and envelopes you must process each month. That translates into more free time *and* fewer paper cuts!

Like home exercise equipment and exotic kitchen appliances, such software often ends up in the consumer graveyard. Paper, pencil, and a calculator work just fine for tracking your spending.

If you want to try computerizing your bill payments and expense tracking, we recommend the best software packages in Chapter 18.

Growing Rich on Your Income: The Secret

We've dealt with people who bring in tiny incomes, people who have incomes of hundreds of thousands of dollars or more, and everyone in between. At every income level, people fall into one of the following three categories:

- ✔ People who spend more than they earn (accumulating debt)
- ✔ People who spend all that they earn (saving nothing)
- ✔ People who save 2, 5, 10, or even 20 percent (or more!)

We've seen $30,000 earners who save 20 percent of their income ($6,000), $60,000 earners who save just 5 percent ($3,000), and people earning well into six figures annually who save nothing or accumulate debt.

Suppose that you currently earn $40,000 per year and spend all of it. You may wonder, "How can I save money?"

Good question!

Rather than knock yourself out at a second job or hustle for that next promotion, you may want to try living below your income — in other words, spend less than you earn. (We know spending less than you earn is hard to imagine, but you can do it.) Consider that for every discontented person earning and spending $40,000 per year, someone else is out there making do on $35,000.

A great many people live on less than you make. If you spend as they do, you can save and invest the difference.

Chapter 4

Conquering Debt and Credit Problems

· ·

In This Chapter

▶ Using your savings to lower your debt

▶ Getting out of debt when you don't have savings

▶ Understanding the pros and cons of filing bankruptcy

▶ Halting your spending

▶ Handling credit problems

· ·

*W*hen debt is used for investing in your future, we call it *good debt* (see Chapter 1). Borrowing money to pay for an education, buy real estate, or invest in a small business is like eating foods rich in calcium to build strong bones, or eating fruits and vegetables for their vitamins.

But accumulating *bad debt* (consumer debt) by buying things like new living room furniture or a new car that you really can't afford is like living on a diet of sugar and caffeine: a quick fix with little nutritional value. Borrowing on your credit card to afford that vacation to Mexico is costly and detrimental to your long-term financial health.

In this chapter, we help you battle the increasingly common problem of consumer debt. Getting rid of your bad debts may be even more difficult than giving up the junk foods you love. But in the long run, you'll be glad you did; you'll be financially healthier and emotionally happier. And after you get rid of your high-cost consumer debts, make sure that you practise the best way to avoid future credit problems: *Don't borrow with bad debt.*

Before you decide which debt-reduction strategies make sense for you, you first must consider your overall financial situation and assess your alternatives. (Strategies for reducing your current spending — which help you free up more cash to pay down your debts — are discussed in the next chapter.)

Using Savings to Reduce Your Debt

Many people build a psychological brick wall between their savings and investment accounts and their debt accounts. By failing to view their finances holistically, they simply fall into the habit of looking at these accounts individually. The thought of putting a door in that big brick wall doesn't occur to them.

Understanding how you gain

When you use savings to pay down debts, it may seem like you're losing money, but you're actually gaining money. Although your savings and investments may be earning decent returns, odds are that the interest you're paying on your consumer debts is higher.

Paying off consumer loans on a credit card at, say, 12 percent is like finding an investment with a guaranteed return of 12 percent — *tax-free*. You would actually need to find an investment that yielded even more — anywhere from 16 to 24 percent, depending on your marginal tax rate — to net 12 percent after paying taxes in order to justify not paying off your 12-percent loans. The higher your tax bracket (see Chapter 6), the higher the return you need on your investments to justify keeping high-interest consumer debt.

If you have the savings to pay off high-interest credit card and auto loans, do so. Sure, you diminish your savings, but you also reduce your debts. You benefit financially because the interest on your savings is far less than the interest accruing on your consumer debt. Make sure you pay off the loans with the highest interest rates first.

Even if you think that you're an investment genius and you can earn more on your investments, swallow your ego and pay down your consumer debts anyway. In order to chase that higher potential return from investments, you need to take substantial risk. You *may* earn more investing in that hot stock tip or that bargain real estate located on a toxic waste site, but more than likely you won't.

If you use your accessible savings to pay down consumer debts, be careful to leave yourself a sufficient emergency cushion. (In Chapter 2, we tell you how to determine how large of an emergency reserve you should have.) You want to be in a position to withstand an unexpected large expense or temporary loss of income. On the other hand, if you use savings to pay down credit card debt, you can run your credit card balances back up in a financial pinch (unless your card gets cancelled), or you can turn to a family member or wealthy friend for a low-interest loan.

Discovering money to pay down consumer debts

Have you ever reached into the pocket of an old winter parka and found a rolled-up $20 bill you forgot you had? Stumbling across some forgotten funds is always a pleasant experience. But before you root through all your closets in search of stray cash to help you pay down that nagging credit card debt, check out some of these financial jacket pockets you may have overlooked:

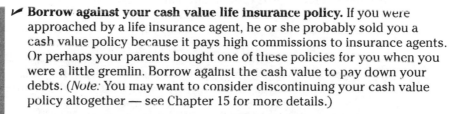

- ✔ **Borrow against your cash value life insurance policy.** If you were approached by a life insurance agent, he or she probably sold you a cash value policy because it pays high commissions to insurance agents. Or perhaps your parents bought one of these policies for you when you were a little gremlin. Borrow against the cash value to pay down your debts. (*Note:* You may want to consider discontinuing your cash value policy altogether — see Chapter 15 for more details.)

- ✔ **Sell investments held outside of RRSPs or RRIFs.** Maybe you have some shares of stock or a Canada Savings Bond gathering dust in your safety deposit box. Consider cashing in these investments to pay down your loan balances. Just be sure to consider the tax consequences of selling these investments. If possible, sell only those investments that won't generate a big tax bill.

- ✔ **Borrow against the equity in your home.** If you're a homeowner, you may be able to tap into your home's *equity,* which is the difference between the property's market value and your outstanding loan balance (that is, what's left to pay off on your mortgage). You can generally borrow against real estate at a lower interest rate.

- ✔ **Borrow from friends and family.** They know you, love you, realize your shortcomings, and — heck — probably won't be as cold-hearted as some bankers we know. Money borrowed from family members can have strings attached, of course. Treating the obligation seriously is important. To avoid misunderstandings, write up a simple agreement listing the terms and conditions of the loan. Unless your family members are like the worst bankers we know, you'll probably get a fair interest rate, and your family will have the satisfaction of helping you out — just don't forget to pay them back.

Decreasing Debt When You Lack Savings

If you lack savings to throw at your consumer debts, not surprisingly, you have some work to do. If you're currently spending all your income (and more!), you need to figure out how you can decrease your spending (see Chapter 5 for lots of great ideas) and/or increase your income. In the meantime, you need to slow the growth of your debt.

Transferring balances to lower-interest-rate credit cards

Different credit cards charge different interest rates. Why in the world should you pay 14, 16, or 18 percent (or more) when you can pay less? The credit card business has become quite competitive. Gone are the days when all banks charged 18 percent or more for Visa and MasterCard.

Until you get your debt paid off, make it more difficult for your debt to grow. You may be able to slow the growth of your debt by reducing the interest rate you're paying. Here are sound ways to do that:

✔ **Apply for a lower-rate credit card.** If you're earning a decent income, you're not too burdened with debt, and you have a clean credit record, qualifying for lower-rate cards is relatively painless. Some persistence (and cleanup work) may be required if you have income and debt problems or nicks in your credit report. After you're approved for a new, lower-interest-rate credit card, you can simply transfer your outstanding balance from your higher-rate card.

Often, the lowest-rate cards are available from smaller financial institutions. Worth looking at are the low-rate cards offered by Desjardins and Laurentian Bank, National Bank, and Meridian Credit Union. As for the big banks, CIBC, Bank of Montreal, and HSBC also have low-rate cards available. (As we point out in the "Credit cards with a 1.9-percent interest rate" sidebar, when assessing low-rate cards make sure you consider the regular interest rate, not just the rate offered during the "introductory" period.)

The Financial Consumer Agency of Canada tracks credit card interest rates. You can find the recent rates on low-rate cards at the agency's Web site: www.fcac-acfc.gc.ca.

✔ **Call the bank(s) that issued your current high-interest-rate credit card(s) and say that you want to cancel your card(s) because you found a competitor that offers no annual fee and a lower interest rate.** Your bank may choose to match the terms of the competitor rather than lose you as a customer.

✔ **While you're paying down your credit card balance(s), stop putting new charges on cards that have outstanding balances.** Many people don't realize that interest starts to accumulate immediately when they carry a balance. You have no grace period — the 20-odd days you normally have to pay your balance in full without incurring interest charges — if you carry a credit card balance month to month.

Credit cards with a 1.9-percent interest rate!

Avoid getting lured into applying for a credit card that hypes an extremely low interest rate. One such card advertises a 1.9-percent rate, but you have to dig into the fine print for the rest of the story.

First, any card that offers such a low interest rate will honour that rate for only a short period of time — in this case, six months. After six months, the interest rate skyrockets to nearly 15 percent.

But wait, there's more. Make just one late payment or exceed your credit limit, and the company raises your interest rate to 19.8 percent and slaps you with a $29 fee for each such infraction. If you want a cash advance on your card, you get socked with a fee equal to 3 percent of the amount advanced. (During the economic slowdown in the early 2000s, some banks were even advertising 0-percent interest

rates — although that rate generally applied only to balances transferred from another card, and such cards were subject to all of the other vagaries discussed in this sidebar.)

Now, we're not saying that everyone should avoid this type of card. Such a card may make sense for you if you want to transfer an outstanding balance and then pay off that balance within a matter of months, cancel the card, and avoid getting socked with the high fees on the card.

If you hunt around for a low-interest-rate credit card, be sure to check out all the terms and conditions. Start by reviewing the rates and terms disclosure, which details the myriad fees and conditions. Also, be sure that you understand how the future interest rate is determined on cards that charge variable interest rates.

Cutting up your credit cards

If you have a pattern of living beyond your means by buying on credit, get rid of the culprit — the credit card, that is. To kick the habit, a smoker needs to toss *all* the cigarettes, and an alcoholic needs to get rid of *all* the booze. Cut up *all* of your credit cards and call the issuers of the cards to cancel your accounts. And when you buy consumer items such as cars and furniture, do not apply for E-Z credit.

The world worked fine back in the years B.C. (Before Credit). Think about it: Just a couple of generations ago, credit cards didn't even exist. People paid with cash and cheques — imagine that! You *can* function without buying anything on a credit card. In certain cases, you may need a card as collateral — like when you rent a car. When you bring back the rental car, however, you can pay with cash or cheque. Leave the card at home in the back of your sock drawer or freezer, and pull (or thaw) it out only for the occasional car rental.

If you can trust yourself, keep a separate credit card *only* for new purchases that you know you can absolutely pay in full each month. No one needs three, five, or ten credit cards! You can live with one (and actually none), given the wide acceptance of most cards. Count 'em up, including retail store and gas cards, and get rid of 'em. Retailers such as department stores and gas stations just love to give you their cards. These cards not only charge outrageously high interest rates, but also duplicate Visa and MasterCard. Virtually all retailers accept Visa and MasterCard. More credit lines mean more temptation to spend what you can't afford.

If you decide to keep one widely accepted credit card instead of getting rid of them all, be careful. You may be tempted to let debt accumulate and roll over for a month or two, starting up the whole horrible process of running up your consumer debt again.

Discovering debit cards: The best of both worlds

Credit cards are one of the main reasons why today's consumers are consuming more than they can afford. So logic would say that one way you can keep your spending in check is to not use your credit cards. But in a society used to flashing the widely accepted Visa and MasterCard plastic for purchases, changing habits is hard. And you may be legitimately concerned that carrying your chequebook or cash can mean hassles if it is lost or stolen.

Well, *debit cards* truly offer the best of both worlds. The beauty of the debit card is that it offers you the convenience of making purchases with a piece of plastic without the temptation and ability to run up credit card debt. Since purchase amounts are deducted electronically from your account the moment the transaction is approved, a debit card keeps you from spending money you don't have and helps you live within your means.

If you keep your chequing account balance low and don't ordinarily balance your chequebook, you may need to start balancing your chequebook if you switch to a debit card. Otherwise, you could be facing unnecessary bounced cheque charges. Of course, if you use a debit card for many items that you might have purchased with cheques in the past, balancing your chequebook will become easier.

Here are some other differences between debit and credit cards:

- If you pay your credit card bill in full and on time each month, your credit card gives you free use of the money you owe until it's time to pay the bill; debit cards take the money out of your chequing account almost immediately. (Note that some credit cards charge a fee even if you pay your balance in full each month.)

> ✓ Credit cards make it easier for you to dispute charges for problematic merchandise through the issuing bank. Most banks allow you to dispute charges for up to 60 days after purchase and will credit the disputed amount to your account pending resolution. Most debit cards offer a much shorter window, typically less than one week, for making disputes.

Be sure to protect your PIN number — the four digit secret code you enter that tells the bank machine or the store where you're making a purchase that you have the right to use the card. Don't keep it written down on the card or in the wallet or purse in which you carry your debit card. Also, ensure that no one can see which numbers you are entering when you punch in your PIN.

Filing Bankruptcy

For consumers in over their heads, the realization that their monthly income is increasingly exceeded by their bill payments is usually traumatic. In many cases, years can pass before drastic measures like filing bankruptcy are considered. Both financial and emotional issues come into play in one of the most difficult and painful, yet potentially beneficial, decisions of a lifetime.

When Helen, a mother of two and a sales representative, contacted lawyer Harry Orr, her total credit card debt equalled her annual gross income. As a result of her crushing debt load, she could not meet her minimum monthly credit card payments. Rent and food gobbled up most of her earnings. What little was left over went to the squeakiest wheel.

Creditors were breathing down Helen's back. "I started getting calls from collection departments at home and work — it was embarrassing," relates Helen. Helen's case is typical in that credit card debt was the prime cause of her bankruptcy. Of course, credit cards often aren't the cause of bankruptcy, but simply a tool that helps people overspend faster. If you're addicted to spending, for instance, plastic lets you spend money you don't actually have. Other factors, from gambling to costly divorces, are also major causes of bankruptcy.

Helen's case is typical in other regards. Her debt accumulated over a number of years. Helen, a former homeowner with a master's degree from a prestigious university, had good credit until a couple of years before. After getting a divorce, Helen rented an apartment with her two children while holding down a job. Unfortunately, she was laid off when her employer encountered tough times.

At first, bills to her dentist and doctor went unpaid. When Helen went into business for herself, she used her credit cards for office furniture and other start-up expenses. "I would have done more corner cutting, but the credit cards were easily available cash and allowed me to think in terms of monthly payments," says Helen.

As the debt load grew (partly exacerbated by the high interest rates on the cards), more and more purchases got charged — from the kids' clothing to repairs for the car. Finally, after running out of cash, she had to take a large cash advance on her credit cards to pay for rent and food.

Despite trying to work out lower monthly payments to keep everyone happy, most of the banks to which Helen owed money were inflexible. "When I asked one bank's Visa department if it preferred that I declare bankruptcy because it was unwilling to lower my monthly payment, the representative said yes," Helen says. After running out of options, Helen filed personal bankruptcy.

Understanding bankruptcy's benefits

Every year, more than 50,000 Canadian households (that's about 1 in every 200) file for personal bankruptcy. With bankruptcy, certain types of debts can be completely eliminated, or *discharged*. Debts that typically can be discharged include credit card, medical, auto, utilities, and rent.

Debts that may *not* be cancelled generally include child support, alimony, student loans, taxes, and court-ordered settlements. Also, debt that's rung up by fraud isn't covered. And if a creditor isn't included in the bankruptcy, they still have the right to demand repayment, even after other debts have been discharged.

You'll need to consider some other wrinkles, too. Student loans are generally not cancelled if bankruptcy is filed within ten years of completing your studies. And if you have an outstanding car loan the lender can simply repossess your automobile, as the car usually secures the debt. Typically the person going bankrupt claims a provincial exemption and keeps the vehicle, but this means continuing to repay the loan to the lender.

The roof over your head may also not be as secure as it first seems. Utilities are prevented from shutting your service off typically only during the winter months, and you may be required to pay a security deposit before they turn things back on. If you are a renter, bankruptcy can eliminate owed rent, but it doesn't prevent your landlord from proceeding to evict you.

(At the time we were writing this edition of the book, changes to the bankruptcy law were being proposed through Bill C-55. In particular, new rules were being considered that would give income tax debts a different status in order to prevent high-income earners from using bankruptcy to eliminate substantial income tax debt.)

What you can keep if you file for bankruptcy

You can retain certain property and assets even though you're filing for bankruptcy. In most provinces, you're allowed to keep only a few thousand dollars' worth of clothing and personal effects. You likely will also be able to keep a few thousand dollars' worth of the tools of your trade if such items are necessary for you to earn a living. Depending on the province that you live in, you may also be able to hang on to a vehicle worth no more than $3,000 to $5,000, and possibly a small amount of equity in your home. One major exception is Alberta, which allows you to keep $40,000 worth of equity in your home.

Eliminating your debt also allows you to start working toward your financial goals. Depending on the amount of debt you have outstanding relative to your income, you may need a decade or more to pay it all off. In Helen's case, at the age of 48 she had no money saved for retirement, and she was increasingly unable to spend money on her children.

Filing bankruptcy offers not only financial benefits but also emotional benefits. Says Helen, "I was horrified at filing, but it is good to be rid of the debts and collection calls — I should have filed six months earlier. I was constantly worried. When I saw homeless families come to the soup kitchen where I sometimes volunteer, I thought that someday that could be me and my kids."

Coming to terms with bankruptcy drawbacks

Filing bankruptcy, needless to say, has a number of drawbacks. When you file bankruptcy, the trustee takes control of your assets. They can then be sold, and the proceeds distributed to your creditors. In practice, though, the trustee will often make arrangements with you so that you can buy your assets back from your estate.

Going bankrupt also means giving up a good deal of control over your financial life. You can't simply sell or dispose of your own property, for example. In addition, a portion of your income goes to your creditors, month in and month out. And if you happen to come into a lot of money before your bankruptcy is discharged, that too goes to the trustee to pay off your creditors.

After the paperwork is filed, you're officially "bankrupt" for nine months. However, bankruptcy appears on your credit report for many years, as dictated by the consumer reporting act legislation in your province. In Ontario, for example, it is seven years from the date of discharge. This means you will have difficulty obtaining credit, especially in the years immediately following your filing.

However, if you already have problems on your credit report (because of late payments or a failure to pay previous debts), the damage usually has largely been done. And, without savings, you're probably not going to be making major purchases (such as a home) in the next several years anyway.

If you do file bankruptcy, getting credit in the future is still possible. If you go bankrupt for reasons other than high credit card debt — loss of a job, a costly divorce, or dental or veterinary bills, for example — you likely will be able to obtain a credit card if you can make a case that you will be able to meet your monthly payments. You can usually obtain a *secured credit card*, which requires

Getting help from the Credit Counselling Service (CCS)

If you having trouble with debt, one source you can turn to for information and advice is Credit Counselling Canada (www.credit counsellingcanada.ca), an association that represents non-profit credit counselling agencies, along with provincially legislated Orderly Payment of Debt programs.

Some of these agencies are run by the government, some are attached to Family Services departments, and some are independent. Funding for CCS offices comes from a variety of different sources, including provincial governments, the United Way, local government, and creditors. Different offices have different funding arrangements.

The goal of the members of Credit Counselling Canada is to offer no-cost (or low-cost) credit counselling. Depending on your situation, you may simply be given some ideas for free about how to manage your savings better, and assistance in budgeting. The agencies also put a strong emphasis on education to assist people in not continuing with debt-happy habits. A member organization can also contact creditors for you, set you up with a third-party mediator, or assist you in obtaining a consolidation loan.

Another way in which a Credit Counselling Canada member can help out is by working out a debt management program. This would typically be recommended only if you were so deeply in debt you were unable to meet your minimum monthly payments and the interest was ballooning your outstanding debt. In such cases, the counselling agency would work out your monthly living costs, which would include your mortgage, and determine what was left over. The agency would then negotiate with creditors to see if it can get them to stop any further interest charges or perhaps even reduce your debt. You then make one monthly payment to the agency, which distributes the money to your various creditors. Depending on your situation, you may also be asked to pay a fee (which can range up to 10 percent of your payments) to the agency for its services in this case.

The usual maximum length of time you can take to repay your debts under such an arrangement is four years. If that isn't possible, bankruptcy may be a better choice. While enrolling in a debt-management program will affect your credit rating, your history is wiped clean two years after it is completed. By contrast, bankruptcy remains on your credit rating for seven years.

you to deposit money in a bank account equal to the credit limit on your credit card. Of course, as we advocate earlier in this chapter, you'll be better off without the temptation of any credit cards and better served with a debit card. Also know that if you can hold down a stable job, most creditors will be willing to give you loans within a few years of your filing bankruptcy. Almost all lenders ignore bankruptcy after five to seven years.

Another drawback of bankruptcy is that it costs money. We know this seems terribly unfair. You're already in financial trouble — that's why you're filing bankruptcy! Nevertheless, filing bankruptcy may set you back anywhere from several hundred dollars to $1,000 in court filing and legal fees.

And, finally, most people find that filing bankruptcy causes emotional stress. Admitting that your personal income can't keep pace with your debt obligations is a painful thing to do. Although filing bankruptcy clears the decks of debt and gives you a fresh financial start, feeling a profound sense of failure (and sometimes shame) is common. Despite the increasing incidence of bankruptcy, bankruptcy filers are reluctant to talk about it with others, including family and friends.

Some people also feel that they're shirking responsibility by filing for bankruptcy. One client Eric worked with should have filed, but she couldn't bring herself to do it. She said, "I spent that money, and it's my responsibility to pay it back." (Incidentally, this is just the sort of person that should consider a consumer proposal, which we talk about a little later.)

Most banks make gobs and gobs of money from their credit card businesses. We can tell you that credit cards are one of the most profitable lines of business for banks. If you don't believe us, consider that, at a banking conference sponsored by the investment bank Salomon Brothers, CEO John Reed referred to the credit card business for banks as a "high-return, low-risk" business. Now you know why your mailbox is always filled with solicitations for more cards.

Seeking bankruptcy advice

Be careful where you get advice about whether to file for bankruptcy. Trustees in bankruptcy who earn a fee from doing bankruptcy filings, for example, have a conflict of interest. All things being equal, their bias is to — you guessed it — *recommend bankruptcy*, which generates their fees.

If you want to learn more about the pros, cons, and details of filing for bankruptcy, pick up a copy of the *Bankruptcy Guide* by Earl Sands, published by Self Counsel Press.

If history has shown that you're likely to fall back into old habits, the best and only solution is to go cold turkey. Eliminate your access to credit and pay for everything with cash, cheques, and debit cards.

An Alternative to Bankruptcy: The Consumer Proposal

If your debts total $75,000 or less, a *consumer proposal* can be a good alternative to filing bankruptcy. A consumer proposal is similar to a debt repayment plan that a credit counselling agency might work out for you. It's an option if you have money coming in that will allow you to pay off a good portion of your debts but need more time to do so.

With a consumer proposal, you can negotiate to repay only a portion of the money you owe. At the time you file your proposal, the debts covered by the proposal are frozen, and no more interest can be charged on them from that point on. In addition, your creditors are restricted from taking further legal action against you, and any garnishing of your wages is stopped (except for support and alimony payments).

Typically, a trustee assists you in assessing your assets and income, organizes a budget for you, and provides a few counselling sessions. Your trustee will present a detailed plan to your creditors detailing how much and when you'll pay them, to which the creditors have 45 days to respond. If a majority of your creditors accept the proposal, it is deemed to have been accepted by all of them. *The agreement is legally binding.*

A consumer proposal covers common unsecured debts, such as credit cards, lines of credit, and personal loans, as well as income taxes. In general, secured debt isn't covered under a consumer proposal. (*Secured debt* is money borrowed with an agreement that the lender can take possession of some of your property and sell it to recover their money if you fail to repay the loan.) In addition, alimony, child support, and legal fines aren't covered by the proposal. They remain payable in full.

 A consumer proposal is often a sensible route to take, especially if you have a lot of assets and a regular income. In a regular bankruptcy, almost all your assets are sold. Under a consumer proposal, that may not be necessary if your creditors are willing to settle for a piece of your paycheque.

A consumer proposal is likely to be accepted only if your unsecured lenders foresee getting paid more than they would if you file bankruptcy. Also, some lenders may prefer you to file bankruptcy as it is a much more short-term, finite process for them. In contrast, under a consumer proposal you can arrange to spread your payments out over as much as five years. Once you have completed your payments under the proposal, a record of the agreement remains in your credit history for two years.

(Note that new legislation being considered at the time of writing proposed raising the maximum dollar amount of debt that can be dealt with by a consumer proposal to $250,000. The idea is to make it an option for those with larger debts who also have a higher income that can support larger repayments.)

Ending the Spending-and-Debting Cycle

Regardless of how you deal with paying off your debt, you're in real danger of falling back into old habits. Backsliding happens not only to people who file bankruptcy, but also to those who use savings or home equity to eliminate their debt. This section speaks to that risk and tells you what to do about it.

Resisting the credit temptation

Getting out of debt can be challenging, but we have confidence that you can do it with this book by your side and us as your guides. In addition to the ideas we discuss earlier in this chapter (such as eliminating all your credit cards and making better use of your debit card), the following list provides some additional tactics you can use to limit the influence credit cards hold over your life:

- **Reduce your credit limit.** If you're not going to take the advice we give you earlier in this chapter and get rid of all of your credit cards, be sure to keep a lid on your credit card's limit (the maximum balance allowed on your card). Just because your bank keeps raising your credit limit to reward you for being such a profitable customer, you don't have to accept the increase. Call your credit card provider's toll-free phone number and lower your credit limit to a level you're comfortable with.

- **Replace your credit card with a charge card.** A *charge card* (such as the American Express card) requires you to pay your balance in full each billing period. You have no credit line or interest charges. Of course, spending more than you can afford to pay when the bill comes due is possible. But you'll be much less likely to overspend if you know you have to pay in full monthly.

- **Never buy on credit anything that depreciates in value.** Meals out, cars, clothing, and shoes all depreciate in value. Never buy these things on credit. Borrow money only for sound investments — education, real estate, or your own business, for example.

- **Think in terms of total cost.** Everything sounds cheaper in terms of monthly payments — that's how salespeople entice you into buying things you can't afford. Take a calculator along, if necessary, to tally up the sticker price, interest charges, and upkeep. The total cost will scare you. It should.

✔ **Stop the junk mail avalanche.** Look at your daily mail — we bet half of it is solicitations and mail-order catalogues. You can save some trees and time sorting junk mail by removing yourself from most mailing lists. To remove your name from mailing lists, contact the Canadian Marketing Association and register with their Do Not Contact service. You can write them at 1 Concord Gate, Suite 607, Don Mills, Ontario, M3C 3N6. You can also register through the association's Web site at www.the-cma.org. To remove your name from the major credit reporting agency lists that are used by credit card solicitation companies, call 888-567-8688. Also, be sure to tell any credit card companies you keep cards with that you want your account marked to indicate you do not wish to have any of your personal information shared with telemarketing firms.

✔ **Limit what you can spend.** Go shopping with a small amount of cash and no plastic or cheques. That way, you can only spend what little cash you have with you!

Identifying and treating an addiction

No matter how hard they try to break the habit, some people become addicted to spending and accumulating debt. It becomes a chronic problem that starts to interfere with other aspects of their lives. Financial problems can lead to problems at work and with family and friends.

Debtors Anonymous (DA), which was officially started in 1976, is a non-profit organization that provides support (primarily through group meetings) to people trying to break their debt accumulation and spending habits. DA is modelled after the 12-step Alcoholics Anonymous (AA) program.

Like AA, Debtors Anonymous works with people from all walks of life and socioeconomic backgrounds. At DA meetings you can find people who are financially on the edge, $100,000-plus income earners, and everybody in between. Even former millionaires join the program.

DA has a simple questionnaire that helps determine whether you're a problem debtor. If you answer yes to at least 8 of the following 15 questions, you may be developing or already have a compulsive spending and debt accumulation habit:

1. Are your debts making your home life unhappy?

2. Does the pressure of your debts distract you from your daily work?

3. Are your debts affecting your reputation?

4. Do your debts cause you to think less of yourself?

5. Have you ever given false information in order to obtain credit?

6. Have you ever made unrealistic promises to your creditors?

7. Does the pressure of your debts make you careless when it comes to the welfare of your family?

8. Do you ever fear that your employer, family, or friends will learn the extent of your total indebtedness?

9. When faced with a difficult financial situation, does the prospect of borrowing give you an inordinate feeling of relief?

10. Does the pressure of your debts cause you to have difficulty sleeping?

11. Has the pressure of your debts ever caused you to consider getting drunk?

12. Have you ever borrowed money without giving adequate consideration to the rate of interest you're required to pay?

13. Do you usually expect a negative response when you're subject to a credit investigation?

14. Have you ever developed a strict regimen for paying off your debts, only to break it under pressure?

15. Do you justify your debts by telling yourself that you are superior to the "other" people, and when you get your "break," you'll be out of debt?

Debtors Anonymous is headquartered in the U.S., but the organization holds meetings in several Canadian cities. To find a Debtors Anonymous (DA) support group in your area, check your local phone directory (in the "Business" section) or visit the DA website at www.debtorsanonymous.org. You can write to DA's headquarters for meeting locations in your area and a literature order form at the following address: Debtors Anonymous General Service Office, P.O. Box 920888, Needham, MA 02492-0009. You can also contact DA's Toronto Self-Help Clearinghouse by phone at 416-487-4355. If you live in Ontario or Manitoba, you can find details for meetings in Ottawa, Toronto, Kingston, and Winnipeg at mywebpage.netscape.com/torontoda/Meetings.html. If you live outside an area that has meetings, you can still benefit from the group by participating in telephone meetings and online chats. Details are provided on the DA Web site.

Dealing with Credit Mistakes

You may not know it, but you probably have a personal credit report. Creditors generally examine your credit report before granting you a loan or credit line.

Many people don't realize that they have a blemish on their credit report until they are turned down for a loan or questioned by a creditor about the glitch. Although dealing with credit report problems takes up some of your time, it isn't difficult if you know what to do — and what not to do.

Obtaining a copy of your credit report

If you're turned down for rental housing, employment, or a loan because of derogatory information on your credit report, ask the credit reporting bureaus to give you a copy of the report.

If you're applying for a mortgage or other major loan, most lenders will give you a copy of your credit report if you simply ask. And why shouldn't they, if you're paying them to obtain the copy!

Reading a credit report is a challenge given all the abbreviations and jargon, so we recommend that, in addition to getting the report, you ask the lender what specific information on the report led to the denial of credit.

To get a copy of your credit rating, contact the following credit bureaus. You'll need to send them signed photocopies of two pieces of identification along with your name, address, and social insurance number.

- ✔ Equifax Canada Inc.
  Consumer Relations Dept.
  Box 190, Jean-Talon Station
  Montreal, QC, HIS 2Z2
  1-800-465-7166
  www.equifax.com/EFX_Canada/

  (You can also email them at consumer.relations@equifax.com. Equifax will fax you an application to obtain your report.)

- ✔ Trans Union Consumer Relations Centre
  P.O. Box 338, LCD 1
  Hamilton, ON, L8L 7W2
  1-866-525-0262
  1-905-525-0262
  www.tuc.ca

Getting others to correct their mistakes

If you obtain your credit report and find a boo-boo on it that you don't recognize as being your mistake or fault, do *not* assume that the information is correct. Credit reporting bureaus and the creditors who report credit information to these bureaus often make mistakes.

You hope and expect that, if a credit bureau has negative and incorrect information in your credit report and you bring the error to their attention, they will graciously and expeditiously fix the mistake. If you believe that, you're the world's greatest optimist; perhaps you also believe that you won't have to wait in line at the vehicle licensing office, the post office, or your local bank at noon on payday.

Odds are you're going to have to make some phone calls or write a letter or two to fix the problems on your credit report. Here's how most errors that aren't your fault are corrected:

- ✔ **The credit problem is someone else's.** A surprising number of personal credit report glitches are the result of someone else's negative information getting on your credit report. If the bad information on your report is completely foreign-looking to you, tell the credit bureau and explain that you need more information because you don't recognize the creditor.

- ✔ **The creditor made a mistake.** Creditors make mistakes, too. You need to write or call the creditor to get them to correct the erroneous information that they sent to the credit bureau. Phoning first usually works best. (The credit bureau should be able to tell you how to reach the creditor if you don't know how.) If necessary, follow up with a letter.

Whether you speak with a credit bureau or an actual lender, make notes of your conversations. If representatives say that they can fix the problem, get their names and extensions and follow up with them if they don't deliver as promised. If you're ensnared in bureaucratic red tape, escalate the situation by speaking with a department manager.

Telling your side of the story

With a minor credit infraction, some lenders may simply ask for an explanation. Eric once had a credit report glitch that was the result of being away for several weeks and missing the payment due date for a couple of small bills. When his proposed mortgage lender saw the late payments, all he had to do was provide a written explanation.

Chapter 5

Reducing Your Spending

• •

In This Chapter

▶ Discovering the keys to successful spending

▶ Reducing your spending through proven techniques

• •

A highly paid, professional gentleman (whom we'll call Bart) lived in one of the most prestigious communities in North America. He owned his own business, drove top-of-the-line cars outfitted with all the latest toys and gadgets, and belonged to the most expensive country club in the area. The problem was, however, that he was a workaholic. In fact, he seemed to be a workaholic in order to support his spending habits. Over time, his wife tired of the life they were leading and filed for divorce. Bart called Eric for a consultation soon after his divorce was finalized. He looked beaten and depressed. He said that he needed help making some financial decisions, but what he appeared to need more than anything else was a good, long vacation — and some personal counselling.

At the other end of the spending extreme was Justin, a young man in his mid-20s who, like Bart, was well-educated and intelligent. Justin lived a Spartan lifestyle even though he lived in the same costly metropolitan area as Bart. Justin took a leave from his work to sail partway around the world with some friends. He was passionate about music; he played in a band outside of work and found time to produce a CD. Justin spent little money, yet he was happy.

Too often, movies and the media portray people who make more money and have more toys as being happier and more powerful than people who don't have these things, but in our experience we have come across far more Barts than Justins. In part because of his high income, Bart took no interest in learning how to spend smarter — as a result, he had little savings to show for all his earnings. Justin, by contrast, viewed spending well beneath his means as a welcome challenge and a means to an end. The better use he made of his money, the more freedom he felt he had.

No matter where you are or where you go today, you're bombarded with advertising and spending temptations. Therefore, we're not surprised to find that so many people could spend their money more wisely than they currently do.

Telling people how and where to spend their money is a risky undertaking, because most people like to spend money and hate to be told what to do. You'll be glad to hear that we're *not* going to tell you exactly where you must cut your spending. We're simply going to give you numerous strategies that have worked for other people. The final decision for what to cut rests solely with you. Only you can decide what's important to you and what's dispensable — should you cut out your weekly poker games, or cut back on your shoe collection?

We assume throughout these recommendations that you value your time. Therefore, we're not going to tell you to scrimp and save by doing things like cutting open a tube of toothpaste so that you can use every last bit of it. And we won't tell you to have your spouse do your ironing to reduce your dry-cleaning bills — no point in having extra money in the bank if your significant other walks out on you!

The fact that you're busy all the time may be part of the reason why you spend money the way you do. Therefore, the recommendations in this chapter focus on methods that produce significant savings but don't involve a lot of time. In other words, these strategies provide bang for the buck.

Finding the Keys to Successful Spending

For most people, spending money is a whole lot easier and more fun than earning it. We're certainly not going to tell you to stop having fun and turn into a penny-pinching, stay-at-home miser. Of course you can spend money. But there's a world of difference between spending money *carelessly* and spending money *wisely*.

If you spend too much and spend unwisely, you put pressure on your income and your future need to continue working. Savings dwindle, debts may accumulate, and you can't achieve your financial goals.

If you dive into details too quickly, you may miss the big picture. So before we jump into the specific areas where you can trim your budget, we give you our four overall keys to successful spending. These four principles run through most of the recommendations we provide in this chapter.

Living within your means

Spending too much is a *relative* problem. Two people can each spend $40,000 per year yet still have drastically different financial circumstances. How? Suppose that one of them earns $50,000 annually, while the other makes $35,000. The $50,000 income earner saves $10,000 each year. The $35,000 wage earner, on the other hand, accumulates $5,000 of new debt (or spends that amount from prior savings). Spend within your means.

Don't let the spending habits of others dictate your spending habits. Certain people — and you know who they are — bring out the big spender in you. Do something else with them besides shopping and spending. If you can't find any other activity to share with them, try shopping with limited cash and no credit cards. That way, you can't overspend on impulse.

How much you can safely spend while still working toward your financial goals depends on what your goals are and where you are financially. Chapter 2 assists you with figuring how much you should be saving and what you can afford to spend to accomplish your financial goals.

Looking for the best values

You can find high quality and low cost in the same product. Conversely, paying a high price is no guarantee that you're getting high quality. Cars are a good example. Whether you're buying a subcompact, a sports car, or a luxury four-door sedan, some cars are more fuel-efficient and cheaper to maintain — not to mention better for the environment — than rivals that carry the same sticker price.

When you evaluate the cost of a product or service, you need to think in terms of total, long-term costs. Suppose that you're comparing the purchase of two used cars: the Solid Sedan, which costs $16,995, and the Clunker Convertible, which weighs in at $14,995. On the surface, the convertible appears to be cheaper. However, the price that you pay for a car is but a small portion of what that car ultimately costs you. If the convertible is costly to operate, maintain, and insure over the years, it could end up costing you much more than the sedan would have. Sometimes, paying more upfront for a higher-quality product or service ends up saving you money in the long run.

People who sell particular products and services may initially appear to have your best interests at heart when they steer you toward buying something that isn't costly. However, you may be in for a rude awakening when you discover the ongoing service, maintenance, and other fees you face in the years ahead. Salespeople are generally trained to pitch you a lower-cost product if you indicate that's what you're after.

We urge you to be especially careful when you shop on the Internet for the supposed purpose of saving money. You won't have much difficulty finding relatively low advertised prices on the Internet. However, many people overlook shipping costs, the cost of their computer equipment, and monthly Internet service fees when weighing how great a deal they're really getting online. Also, what about the possibility that you're not going to be happy with the product after it's delivered? You'll probably be stuck with paying the shipping costs back to the online retailer, which you hope is still in business, not to mention the hassle and inconvenience of returning the product.

Don't waste money on brand names

You don't want to compromise on quality, especially in the areas where quality is important to you. But you also don't want to be duped into believing that brand-name products are better or worth a substantially higher price. Be suspicious of companies that spend gobs on image-oriented advertising. Why? Because heavy advertising costs many dollars, and, as a consumer of those companies' products and services, you pay for all that advertising.

All successful companies advertise their products. Advertising is cost-effective and good business if it brings in enough new business. But you need to consider the products and services and the claims that companies make.

Does a cola beverage really taste better if "It's the real thing" or "The choice of a new generation"? Consider all the silly labels and fluffy marketing of colas. Blind taste testing demonstrates little if any difference between the expensive brand-name products and the cheaper, less heavily advertised ones.

Now, if you can't live without your Coca-Cola or Pepsi, and you think that these products are head and shoulders above the rest, drink them to your heart's content. But question the importance of the name and image of the products you buy. Companies spend a lot of money creating and cultivating an image, which has zero impact on how their products taste or perform.

Branding is used in many fields to sell overpriced, mediocre products and services to consumers. Take the lowly can of paint. Tests show some differences among different brands of paint. However, when you can buy high-quality paints for about $20 to $30 a gallon, do you really think that a $50 or $100 can of paint blessed with the name of Ralph Lauren or Martha Stewart is that much better?

D/L Laboratories, a testing firm, compared these expensive snooty paints to low-cost, high-quality alternatives and found little difference — or at least no difference that was worth paying for. In fact, one of the "gourmet" paints splattered more, had a less uniform sheen, didn't cover the surface as well, was more prone to run when applied, and emitted a high level of volatile organic compounds! Some other snooty brands didn't fare much better. As people in the trade will tell you, if you find a particular colour of paint you like in a highbrow line, thanks to computer-based matching you can probably match it and buy it from a high-quality but far less costly line.

Consumer Reports is a reputable publication that evaluates products and services based on quality and performance, not brand image. Consult it on major consumer purchases.

Getting your money back

Take a look around your home for items you never use. Odds are you have some (maybe even many). Returning such items to their retail origin can be cathartic; it also reduces your home's clutter and puts more money in your pocket.

Also, think about the last several times you bought a product or service and didn't get what was promised. What did you do about it? Most people do nothing and let the derelict company off the hook. Why? Here are some common explanations for this type of behaviour:

- ✔ **Low standards:** We've come to expect shoddy service and merchandise because of the common lousy experiences we've had.

- ✔ **Conflict avoidance:** Most people shun confrontation. It makes us tense and anxious, and it churns our stomachs. Sometimes it seems like avoiding confrontation is part of what makes us Canadian.

- ✔ **Hassle aversion:** Most companies don't make it easy for complainers to get their money back or obtain satisfaction. To get restitution from some companies, you need the tenacity and determination of a pit bull.

You can increase your odds of getting what you expect for your money by doing business with companies that:

- ✔ **Have fair return policies.** Don't purchase any product or service until you understand the company's return policy. Be especially wary of buying from companies that either charge hefty "restocking" fees for returned merchandise or that simply don't allow returns at all. Reputable companies offer full refunds and don't make you take store credit (although taking credit is fine if you're sure that you'll use it soon, and you're sure that the company will still be around).

- ✔ **Can provide good references.** Suppose that you're going to install a fence on your property, and therefore you're going to be speaking with fencing contractors for the first time. You can weed out many inferior firms by asking each contractor that you interview for at least three references from people in your local area who have had a fence installed in the past year or two.

- ✔ **Are committed to the type of product or service they provide.** Suppose that your chosen fencing contractor does a great job, and now that you're in the market for new gutters on your home, the contractor says that he does gutters, too. Although the path of least resistance would be for you to simply hire the same contractor for your gutters, you should inquire about how many gutters the contractor has installed and also interview some other firms that specialize in such work. Because your fencing contractor may have done only a handful of gutter jobs, he may not know as much about such work.

Following these guidelines can greatly diminish your chances of having unhappy outcomes with products or services you buy. And here's another important tip: Pay with plastic whenever possible (if you pay off your credit card in full every month, that is!). Doing so enables you to dispute a charge within 60 days and gives you more leverage for getting your money back.

Recognizing the Better Business Bureau's conflicts of interest

The Better Business Bureau (BBB) states that its mission is "to promote and foster the highest ethical relationship between businesses and the public." The reality of the typical consumer's experience of dealing with the BBB doesn't live up to the BBB's marketing.

"They don't go after local established businesses — they are funded by these same businesses. The BBB certainly has a good public relations image, better than what is warranted. They don't do all that much for consumers," says consumer advocate Ralph Nader.

"It's a business trade organization and each local BBB is basically independent like a franchise. By and large, when somebody has a problem with a company and they fill out a complaint form with the BBB, if the company is a member of the BBB, there's ample evidence that consumers often end up not being satisfied. The BBB protects their members," says John Bear, an author of consumer advocacy books, including *Send This Jerk the Bedbug Letter: How Companies, Politicians, and the Mass Media Deal with Complaints & How to Be a More Effective Complainer* (Ten Speed Press).

Particularly problematic among the BBB's pro-business practices are the company reports the BBB keeps on file. The BBB will consider a legitimate complaint satisfactorily resolved even though you're quite unhappy and the company is clearly not working to satisfy the problems for which it is responsible.

Bear also cites examples of some truly troubling BBB episodes. In one case, he says that a diploma mill company called Columbia State University was being run in Louisiana, and the business was a member of the local BBB. "When complaints started coming in, the BBB's response was always that the company met their standards and that the complaints were resolved. The reality was that the complaints weren't satisfactorily resolved and it took about two years until complaints reached into the hundreds for the BBB to finally cancel the diploma mill's membership and give out a bland statement about complaints. Two months later, the FBI raided the company. Millions of consumers' dollars were lost because the BBB didn't do its job," says Bear.

The Toronto office of the BBB also had its share of troubles. In the late nineties, the branch was engulfed in a spending scandal, including the finding of a forensic audit that the then-president had been given a $1-million "termination" package, and then immediately rehired. And in 2000, a former director and chair of the Toronto BBB was found guilty of securities violations. The office had its license revoked by the governing body in 2001.

The President of a South Florida BBB (the fifth largest in the country, according to Bear) was ultimately imprisoned for taking bribes from companies in exchange for maintaining favourable reports on file.

The truth about the BBB is unfortunate, because as consumer protection agencies are being cut back and dissatisfied consumers are being shunted to the BBB, more people are in for unsatisfactory experiences with an organization that does not go to bat for them.

If you find that you're not able to make progress when trying to get compensation for a lousy product or service, here's what we recommend that you do:

✔ **Document:** Taking notes whenever you talk to someone at a company can help you validate your case down the road should problems develop. However, how realistic is it for any of us to take notes every time we buy a product or service? Obviously, the bigger the purchase and the more you have at stake, the more carefully you should document what you've been promised. In many cases, though, you probably won't start carefully noting each conversation until a conflict develops. Keep copies of companies' marketing literature, because such documents often make promises or claims that companies fail to live up to in practice.

✔ **Escalate:** Some front-line employees either aren't capable of resolving disputes or lack the authority to do so. No matter what the cause, speak with a department supervisor and continue escalating from there. If you're still not making progress, lodge a complaint to whatever regulatory agency (if any) oversees such companies. Also, be sure to tell your friends and colleagues not to do business with the company (and let the company know that you're doing this until your complaint is resolved to your satisfaction). Also consider contacting a consumer help group — these groups are typically sponsored by broadcast or print media in metropolitan areas. They can be helpful in resolving disputes or shining adverse publicity on disreputable companies or products.

✔ **Litigate:** If all else fails, consider taking the matter to small claims court if the company continues to be unresponsive. (Depending on the amount of money at stake, this tactic may be worth your time.) The maximum dollar limit that you may recover varies by province, but you're usually limited to several thousand dollars. For larger amounts than those allowed in small claims court in your province, you can, of course, hire a lawyer and pursue the traditional legal channels — although you may end up throwing away more of your time and money. Mediation and arbitration are generally a better option than following through on a lawsuit.

Eliminating the fat from your spending

If you want to reduce your overall spending by, say, 10 percent, you can just cut all of your current expenditures by 10 percent. Or you can reach your 10-percent goal by cutting some categories a lot and others not at all. You need to set priorities and make choices about where you want and don't want to spend your money.

What you spend your money on is sometimes a matter of habit rather than a matter of what you really want or value. For example, some people shop at whatever stores are close to them; they never bother to look elsewhere.

Eliminating fat doesn't necessarily mean cutting back on your purchases. You save money by buying in bulk. Some stores specialize in selling larger packages or quantities of a product at a lower price, because they save money on the packaging and handling. And even though that 10-kg bag of rice means more cash upfront than the little box of Uncle Ben's, every meal that you make from the 10-kg bag will be a great deal cheaper than a meal out of the little box. (If you're single, shop with a friend and split the bulk purchases.)

Turning your back on consumer credit

As we discuss in Chapters 3 and 4, buying items that depreciate — such as cars, clothing, and vacations — on credit is hazardous to your long-term financial health. Buy only what you can afford today. If you're going to be forced to carry a debt for months or years on end, you can't really afford what you're buying on credit today.

Without a doubt, *renting to own* is the most expensive way to buy. Here's how it works. You see a huge ad blaring "$12.95 for a DVD player!"

Well, the ad has a big hitch: That's $12.95 per week, for many weeks. When all is said and done (and paid), buying a $200 DVD player through a rent-to-own store costs a typical buyer more than $750!

Welcome to the world of rent-to-own stores, which offer cash-poor consumers the ability to lease consumer items and, at the end of the lease, an option to buy.

If you think that paying an 18-percent interest rate on a credit card is expensive, consider this: The effective interest rate charged on many rent-to-own purchases exceeds 100 percent; in some cases, it may be 200 percent or more! Renting to own makes buying on a credit card look like a great deal.

We're not sharing this information with you to encourage you to buy on credit cards, but to point out what a rip-off renting to own is. Such stores prey on cashless consumers who either can't get credit cards or don't understand how expensive renting to own really is.

Consumer credit is expensive, and it reinforces a bad financial habit: spending more than you can afford.

Budgeting to save more money

Kind of like the word *dieting,* when most people hear the word *budgeting* they usually think unpleasant thoughts — and rightfully so. But budgeting can help you move from knowing how much you spend on various things to successfully reducing your spending.

The first step in the process of budgeting, or planning your future spending, is to analyze where your current spending is going (refer to Chapter 3). After you do that, calculate how much more you'd like to save each month. Then comes the hard part: deciding where to make cuts in your spending.

Suppose that you're currently not saving any of your monthly income, and you want to save 10 percent. If you can save and invest money through a Registered Retirement Savings Plan, you don't actually need to cut your spending by 10 percent to reach a savings goal of 10 percent (of your gross income).

When you contribute money to a tax-deductible retirement plan, you reduce your federal and provincial taxes. If you're a moderate income earner and pay, say, 35 percent in federal and provincial taxes on your marginal income, you actually need to reduce your spending by only 6.5 percent to save 10 percent, if you contribute the money you don't spend to your RRSP. (The "other" 3.5 percent of the savings comes from the lowering of your taxes.) The higher your tax bracket, the less you need to cut your spending to reach a particular savings goal.

So, in this example, to boost your savings rate to 10 percent, go through your current spending category by category until you come up with enough proposed cuts to reduce your spending by 6.5 percent. Make your cuts in the areas that will be the least painful and where you're getting the least value from your current level of spending.

Another method of budgeting involves starting completely from scratch rather than examining your current expenses and making cuts from that starting point. Ask yourself how much you'd like to spend on different categories. The advantage of this approach is that it doesn't allow your current spending levels to constrain your thinking. You'll likely be amazed at the discrepancies between what you think you should be spending and what you actually are spending in certain categories.

Reducing Your Spending: Eric and Tony's Strategies

As you read through the following strategies for reducing your spending, please keep in mind that some of these strategies will make sense for you and some of them won't. Start your spending-reduction plan with the strategies that come easily. Work your way through them. Keep a list of the options that are more challenging for you — ones that may require more of a sacrifice but that you can make work if necessary to achieve your spending and savings goals.

No matter which of the ideas in this chapter that you choose for yourself, rest assured that keeping your budget lean and mean pays enormous dividends. After you implement a spending-reduction strategy, you'll reap the benefits for years to come. Take a look at Figure 5-1: For every $1,000 that you shave from your annual spending (that's just $83 per month), check out how much more money you'll have down the road. (This chart assumes that you invest your new-found savings in a tax-favoured retirement plan, you average a 10 percent per year return on your investments, and you're in a moderate combined federal and provincial tax bracket of 35 percent — see Chapter 6 for information on tax brackets.)

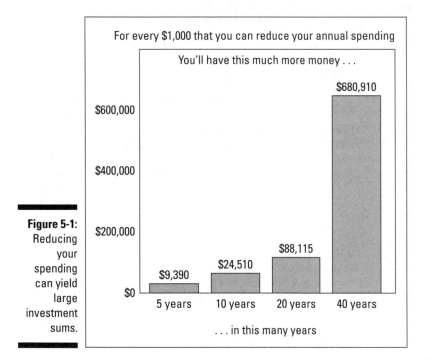

Figure 5-1:
Reducing
your
spending
can yield
large
investment
sums.

Reducing food costs

Stopping eating is one way to reduce your food expenditures. However, this method tends to make you weak and dizzy, so it's probably not a viable long-term strategy. The following culinary strategies will help you save money — and maybe even improve your health.

Joining a wholesale superstore

Superstores such as Costco and Sam's Club enable you to buy groceries in bulk at wholesale prices. And, contrary to popular perception, you *don't* have to buy 1,000 rolls of toilet paper at once — just 24.

We performed price comparisons between wholesale superstores and retail grocery stores, and found that wholesalers often charge about 30 to 40 percent less for the exact same stuff — all without the hassle of clipping coupons or hunting for which store has the best price on crackers this month! (At these discount prices, you need to spend only about $100 to $200 per year to recoup Costco and Sam's Club's membership fees, which start at around $40 to $45 per year.)

In addition to saving you lots of money, buying in bulk requires fewer shopping trips. You'll have more supplies around your humble abode — so you'll have less need to eat out (which is costly) or make more trips (wasted time and gasoline).

Mom was right about eating those vegetables

Not only is meat expensive, but it's also coming under increasing scrutiny as being bad for your health. In a landmark report entitled "The Surgeon General's Report on Nutrition and Health" (produced under former U.S. Surgeon General C. Everett Koop, M.D.), reliance on a meat- and dairy-based diet — with its fat and cholesterol — was found to be the cause of the majority of premature deaths in the United States. In fact, five out of the top ten causes of death in North America — heart disease, certain types of cancer, stroke, diabetes, and arteriosclerosis — are caused largely by poor diets. A World Health Organization report estimated Canada experiences about 217,000 preventable deaths annually. Of those, it attributed some 10,000 to physical inactivity, 12,000 to inadequate consumption of fruits and vegetables, and 17,000 to being overweight. Further, it estimated high cholesterol was responsible for another 20,000 deaths, and high blood pressure, 32,000.

In developing countries that are poorer economically, people eat mainly grains, beans, and vegetables, and have significantly lower rates of heart disease and diet-related cancers, such as cancer of the prostate and colon.

Meat is expensive, so the less meat you eat, the more money you save. Even if you choose to merely reduce your meat consumption rather than eliminate it, you can still save significant dough. If you decide to eliminate meat from your diet, make changes in your diet gradually.

Besides saving you money and bolstering your health, vegetarian diets are also friendlier to the environment. Raising cattle requires a great deal more land and water than does growing vegetables. Here's a tidbit sure to liven up a dull cocktail party conversation: Livestock also produce a great deal of flatulence, which adds more methane to the atmosphere. One hundred million tons of the world's annual methane emissions — 20 percent of the total — are from cattle!

Unfortunately, most of these outlets are designed for car-owners, and aren't easy to get to by public transit.

Perishables run the risk of living up to their name, so don't buy what you can't use. Repackage bulk packs into smaller quantities and store them in the freezer if possible. If you're single, shop with a friend or two and split the order.

Be careful when you shop at the warehouse clubs — you may be tempted to buy things you don't really need. These stores carry all sorts of items, including wide-screen TVs, computers, furniture, clothing, complete sets of baseball cards, and giant canisters of M&Ms and biscotti — so beware! Try not to make impulse purchases, and be especially careful when you have kids in tow.

To find a superstore near you, check your local phone directory. You can also find a Costco store near you by visiting the Costco Web site at `www.costco.ca` or calling 888-426-7826 or 800-774-2678. Sam's Club is on the Internet at `www.samsclubcanada.ca`.

Eating out frugally

Eating meals out and getting takeout can be timesavers, but they rack up big bills if done too often and too lavishly. Eating out is a luxury — think of it as hiring someone to shop, cook, and clean up for you. Of course, some people either hate to cook or don't have the time, space, or energy to do much in the kitchen. If this sounds like you, choose restaurants carefully and order from the menu selectively. Here are a couple of tips for eating out:

- **Avoid beverages, especially alcohol.** Most restaurants make big profits on beverages. Drink water instead. (Water is healthy for you, and it reduces the likelihood that you'll want a nap after a big meal.)

- **Order vegetarian.** Vegetarian dishes generally cost less than meat-based entrées (and they're generally healthier for you).

We don't want to be killjoys. We're not saying that you should live on bread and water. You can have dessert — heck, have some wine, too! Just try not to eat dessert with every meal. Try eating appetizers and dessert at home, where they're a lot less expensive (especially if you follow our advice on shopping for food).

Saving on shelter

Housing and all the costs associated with it (utilities, furniture, appliances, and, if you're a homeowner, maintenance and repairs) can gobble a large chunk of your monthly income. We're not suggesting that you live in an igloo or teepee (even though they're probably less costly), but rather just to be aware of some commonly overlooked opportunities to save money in this category.

Reducing rental costs

Rent can take up a sizable chunk of your monthly take-home pay. Many people consider rent to be a fixed and inflexible part of their expenses, but it's not. Here are some things you can do to cut down your rental costs:

- ✔ **Move to a lower-cost rental.** Of course, a lower-cost rental may not be as nice — it may be smaller, lack a private parking spot, or be located in a less popular area. Remember that the less you spend renting, the more you can save toward buying your own place. Just be sure to factor in all the costs of a new location, including the possible higher commuting costs.

- ✔ **Share a rental.** Living alone has some benefits, but financially speaking, it's a luxury. If you rent a larger place with roommates, your rental costs will go way down, and you'll get more home for your rental dollars. You have to be in a sharing mood, though. Roommates can be a hassle at times, but they can also be a plus — you get to meet all sorts of new people, and you have someone else to blame when the kitchen's a mess.

- ✔ **Negotiate your rental increases.** Every year, like clockwork, your landlord bumps up your rent by a certain percentage. If your local rental market is soft or your living quarters are deteriorating, stand up for yourself! You have more leverage and power than you probably realize. A smart landlord doesn't want to lose good tenants who pay rent on time. Filling vacancies takes time and money. State your case: You've been a responsible tenant, and your research shows comparable rentals going for less. Crying "poor" may help, too. At the very least, if you can't stave off the rent increase, maybe you can wrangle some improvements to the place.

- ✔ **Buy rather than rent.** Purchasing your own place can be costly, yes, but in the long run owning should be cheaper than renting, and you'll have something to show for it in the end. If you purchase real estate with a mortgage spread — *amortized* — over 25 years, your mortgage payment (which is your biggest ownership expense) will bounce around a certain amount, depending on interest rates each time you renew. Only your property taxes, maintenance, and insurance costs are exposed to the vagaries of inflation.

  As a renter, your entire monthly housing cost can rise with increases in the cost of living (unless you're the beneficiary of a rent-controlled apartment). See Chapter 14 to find out how to buy real estate, even if you're short on cash.

Reducing homeowner expenses

As every homeowner knows, houses suck up money. You should be especially careful to watch your money in this area of your budget.

- ✔ **Know what you can afford.** Don't make the mistake of overspending when buying a home. Whether you're on the verge of buying your first home or trading up to a more costly property, crunch some realistic numbers before you jump. When too little money is left over for your other needs and wants — such as taking trips, eating out, enjoying hobbies, or saving for retirement — your new dream house may become a financial prison.

Calculate how much you can afford to spend monthly on a home by figuring your other needs first. (Doing the exercises in Chapter 3, about where you're spending your money, and Chapter 2, about saving for retirement, will help you calculate the amount you can afford.)

Although real estate can be a good long-term investment, you can end up pouring a large portion of your discretionary dollars into your home. In addition to decorating and remodelling, some people feel the need to trade up to a bigger home every few years. Of course, after they're in their new home, the remodelling and renovation cycle simply begins again, which costs even more money. Appreciate what you have, and remember that homes are for living in, not museums for display. If you have children, why waste a lot of money on expensive furnishings that take up valuable space and require you to constantly nag your kids to tread carefully? And don't covet — the world will always have people with bigger houses and more toys than you.

✔ **Rent out a room.** Because selling your home to buy a less expensive place can be a big hassle, consider taking in a tenant to reduce your housing expenses. Check out the renter thoroughly: Get references, run a credit report, and talk about ground rules and expectations before sharing your space. Don't forget to check with your insurance company to see whether your homeowner's policy needs adjustments to cover potential liability from renting.

✔ **Appeal your property-tax assessment.** If you bought your property during a period when housing prices were higher in your area than they are now, you may be able to save money by appealing your assessment. Also, if you live in a region of the country where your assessment is based upon how the local assessor valued the property (rather than what you paid for your home), your home may be over-assessed. Check with your local assessor's office for the appeals procedure you need to follow. You generally have to prove that your property is worth less today than it was when you bought it, or that the assessor incorrectly valued your property. In the first case, an appraiser's recent evaluation of your property will— do. In the latter case, review how the assessor valued your property compared with similar ones nearby — mistakes happen.

✔ **Reduce utility costs.** Sometimes you have to spend money to save money. Old refrigerators, for example, can waste a lot of electricity. Insulate to save on heating and air-conditioning bills. Install water flow regulators in showerheads and toilet bowls. When planting your yard, don't select water-guzzling plants, and keep your lawn area reasonable. Even if you don't live in an area susceptible to droughts, why waste water (which isn't free)? And be sure to recycle — recycling means less garbage, which not only translates into lower trash bills but also benefits the environment by reducing landfill.

Lowering your phone bills

Thanks to increased competition and technology, telephone costs are falling. If you haven't looked for lower rates recently, you're probably paying more than you need to for quality phone service. Unfortunately, shopping among the many service providers is difficult. Plans come with different restrictions, minimums, and bells and whistles. Here are our recommendations for saving on your phone bills:

✔ **Look at your phone company's other calling plans.** You may have to switch companies to reduce your bill, but we find that many people can save significantly with their current phone company simply by getting onto a better calling plan. So, before you spend hours shopping around, contact your current local and long distance providers and ask them which of their calling plans offer the lowest cost for you based on the patterns of your calls.

✔ **Get help when shopping for other providers.** One good useful source is Consumer Reports (800-234-1645; www.consumerreports.org). At www.telecomparisons.com you can input information about when, how often, and to where you call long distance and get reports on what you'll pay with different phone companies. Similarly, you can compare different cell company plans at www.cellphones.ca.

The cell phone business is booming. And while being able to make calls from wherever you are can be enormously convenient, you can spend a lot of money for service given the myriad extra charges. On the other hand, if you're able to take advantage of the free minutes many plans offer (on weekends, for example), a good cell phone service can save you money. Here's how to get your money's worth from cell phone service:

✔ **Question the need for a cell phone.** Okay, we realize that this is a risky point to be raising for those cell phone addicts among us. If you enjoy having a cell phone to use during downtime when commuting or for emergency purposes, we won't try to talk you out of it. However, many people really don't have a need for a cell phone.

✔ **Shop around.** Make sure that you sign up with the best calling plan and carrier given your typical usage. Reputable carriers allow you to test out their service. They also offer full refunds if you're not satisfied after a week or two of service.

✔ **Assess VOIP.** VOIP — *voice over internet protocol* — is a newer service that lets you make phone calls over a high-speed Internet connection. Depending on the features, and how much long-distance calling you do, using VOIP may mean lower phone costs.

Finally, keep in mind that sending a thoughtful letter is usually cheaper, more appreciated, and longer lasting than placing a phone call. Just block out an hour, grab a pen and paper, and rediscover the lost art form of letter writing.

Formulating your thoughts on paper can be clarifying and therapeutic, as well. Computer users may find that they can also save money by sending e-mail.

Cutting transportation costs

Canada is a car-driven society. In most other countries, cars are a luxury. More than 90 percent of the people in the rest of the world can't afford a new car. If more people in Canada thought of cars as a luxury, Canadians might have far fewer financial problems (and accidents). Cars not only pollute the air and clog the highways, but they also cost you a bundle. Purchasing a quality car and using it wisely can save you money. So can using other transportation alternatives.

Contrary to advertising slogans, cars are not built to last — car manufacturers don't want you to stick with the same car year after year. New models are constantly introduced, with new features and styling changes. Getting a new set of wheels every few years is an expensive luxury.

Don't try to keep up with the Joneses as they show off their new cars every year — for all you know, they're running themselves into financial ruin just trying to impress you. Let your neighbours admire you for your thriftiness and wisdom instead.

Are satellite television and unlimited Internet access making our lives better?

Things — at least in the world of home entertainment technology — were much simpler when we were growing up. We remember being able to choose among a handful of local channels. Now, many cable and satellite services offer hundreds of channels. And, of course, you can surf millions of Web sites for one monthly fee.

While we enjoy choices and convenience as much as the next person, we also see the detrimental impact these technologies are having on our families' lives. As it is, most families struggle to find quality time together given their work obligations, long school days, and various other activities. At home, all of these technology choices and options compete for attention and often pull families apart. The cost for all these services and gadgets adds up, leading to a continued enslavement to our careers.

Err on the side of keeping your life simple. Doing so costs less, reduces stress, and allows for more time for the things that really do matter in life.

Research before you buy a car

When you buy a car, you don't just pay the initial sticker price: You also have to pay for gas, insurance, registration fees, maintenance, and repairs. Don't compare simple sticker prices; think about the total, long-term costs of car ownership.

Speaking of total costs, remember that you're also trusting your life to the car. With about 3,500 Canadians killed in auto accidents annually, safety should be an important consideration. The U.S. National Highway Traffic Safety Administration Web site (www.nhtsa.gov) has lots of crash test data, as well as information on other car safety issues. You can also find information on related topics from the Web sites of the Insurance Institute for Highway Safety (www.iihs.org) and the Traffic Injury Research Foundation (www.trafficinjuryresearch.com).

Consumer Reports publishes a number of useful buying guides for new and used cars. You find *Consumer Reports* on the Internet at www.consumerreports.org. For a detailed assessment of defects, repair costs, and safety ratings, check out the annual *Lemon-Aid* books put out by Phil Edmonston. He has separate books dealing with new cars, used cars, new trucks and vans, and used trucks and vans (including minivans). The books also detail average resale prices by model and year. For you data jocks, *The Complete Car Cost Guide*, which is published by Intellichoice (800-227-2665; www.intellichoice.com), is packed with information about all categories of ownership costs, warranties, and dealer costs. The guide rates new cars based on total ownership costs (note that they are stated in U.S. dollars). But can you *really* afford a new car?

Buy your car with cash

The main reason why people end up spending more than they can afford on a car is that they finance the purchase. As we discuss in Part I, you should avoid borrowing money for consumption purchases, especially for items that depreciate in value (like cars). A car is most definitely *not* an investment.

When buying a car, leasing is generally more expensive than borrowing money. Leasing is like a long-term car rental. We all know how well rental cars get treated — well, leased cars are treated just as well, which is one of the reasons why leasing is so costly.

Unfortunately, the practice of leasing cars or buying them on credit is increasingly becoming the norm in our society. This approach is certainly attributable to a lot of the misinformation that's spread by car dealers and, in some cases, the media. Consider a magazine article entitled "Rewards of Car Leasing." The article claims that leasing is a great deal when compared to buying. Ads for auto dealers advertising leasing were placed next to the article. The magazine, by the way, is free to subscribers — which means that 100 percent of its revenue comes from advertisers such as auto dealers. Also be aware that, because of the influence of advertising (and ignorance), leasing is widely endorsed on Web sites that purport to provide information on cars.

Replace high-cost cars

Maybe you've realized by now that your car is too expensive to operate because of insurance, gas, and maintenance costs. Or maybe you bought too much car — people who lease or borrow money to buy a car frequently buy a far more expensive car than they can realistically afford.

Dump your expensive car and get something more financially manageable. The sooner you switch, the more money you'll save. Getting rid of a car on a lease is a challenge, but it can be done. We know of one person who, when he lost his job and needed to slash expenses, convinced the dealer (by writing a letter to the owner) to take the leased car back.

Keep cars to a minimum

We've seen households that have one car per person — four people, four cars! Some people have a "weekend" car that they use only on days off! For

---

But I can't buy a new car with cash!

"Come on, guys," you may be thinking, "how can I and most wage earners today afford to buy a new car with cash — who has that kind of dough sitting around?"

Some people feel that it's unreasonable to expect them to use cash to buy a new car. After all, many publications effectively endorse and encourage loaning and leasing to buy a car. Of course, these same publications also derive great advertising revenue from auto dealers and lenders. (Coincidence? We think not.)

We're reasonable guys. So believe us when we say that we're trying to look out for your best long-term financial interests. Please consider the following:

✔ If you lack sufficient cash to buy a new car, we say "DON'T BUY A NEW CAR!" Most of the world's population can't even afford a car, let alone a new one! Buy a car that you can afford — which for most people is a used one.

✔ Don't fall for the rationalization that says buying a used car means lots of maintenance, repair expenses, and problems. Do your homework and buy a good-quality used car. That way, you can have the best of both worlds. A good used car costs less to buy and, thanks to lower insurance costs, less to operate.

✔ A fancy car is not needed to impress people for business purposes. Some people we know say that they absolutely must drive a nice, brand-spanking-new car to set the right impression for business purposes. We're not going to tell you how to manage your career, but we will ask you to consider this: If your clients — and potential clients — see you driving an expensive new car, they may think that you spend money wastefully or you're getting rich off of them!

most households, maintaining two or more cars is an expensive extravagance. Try to find ways to make do with fewer cars.

You can move beyond the confines of owning a car by either carpooling or riding buses or trains to work. Some employers give incentives for taking public transit to work, and some cities and regions offer assistance for setting up vanpools or carpools along popular routes. By leaving the driving to someone else, you can catch up on reading or just relax on the way to and from work. You also help reduce pollution.

When you're considering the cost of living in different areas, don't forget to factor in commuting costs. One advantage of living close to work, or at least close to public transit systems, is that you may be able to make do with fewer cars (or no car at all) in your household.

Buy commuter passes

In many areas, you can purchase train, bus, or subway passes to help reduce the cost of commuting. Many toll bridges also have booklets of tickets that you can buy at a discount. Some booths don't advertise that they offer these plans — maybe as a strategy to help keep revenues up.

Buy regular unleaded gas

A number of studies have shown that "super-duper-ultrapremium" gasoline is not worth the extra expense. But make sure that you buy gasoline that has an octane rating recommended for your vehicle. Paying more for the higher-octane "premium" gasoline just wastes money. Your car won't run better; you just pay more for gas. Also, don't use credit cards to buy your gas if you have to pay a higher price to do so.

Service your car regularly

Sure, servicing your car (for example, changing the oil every 5,000 or 10,000 kilometres) costs money, but it saves you dough in the long run by extending the operating life of your car. Servicing your car also reduces the chance that your car will crap out in the middle of nowhere, which may require a humongous towing charge to a service station. Stalling on the highway during peak rush hour and having hundreds of angry commuters stuck behind you is even worse.

Controlling clothing costs

Given the amount of money that some people spend on clothing and related accessories, we've come to believe that people in nudist colonies must be great savers! But you probably live among the clothed mainstream of society, so here's a short list of economical ideas:

- ✔ **Avoid clothing that requires dry cleaning.** When you buy clothing, try to stick with cottons and machine-washable synthetics rather than wools or silks that require dry cleaning. Check labels before you buy clothing.

- ✔ **Don't chase the latest fashions.** Fashion designers and retailers are constantly working to tempt you to buy more. Don't do it. Ignore publications that pronounce this season's look. In most cases, you simply don't need to buy racks of new clothes or an entire new wardrobe every year. If your clothes are not lasting at least ten years, you're probably tossing them before their time or buying clothing that isn't very durable.

   Fashion, as defined by what people wear, changes quite slowly. In fact, the classics don't ever go out of style. If you want the effect of a new wardrobe every year, store last year's purchases away next year and then bring them out the year after! Or rotate your clothing inventory every third year. Set your own fashion standards. Buy basic, and buy classic — if you let fashion gurus be your guide, you'll end up with the biggest wardrobe in the poorhouse.

- ✔ **Minimize accessories.** Shoes, jewellery, handbags, and the like can gobble large amounts of money. Again, how many of these accessory items do you really need? The answer is probably very few, because each one should last many years.

Go to your closet or jewellery box and tally up the loot. What else could you have done with all that cash? Do you see things you regret buying or forgot you even had? Don't make the same mistake again. Have a garage sale if you have a lot of stuff that you don't want.

Cutting the cost of debt

In Chapter 4, we discuss strategies for reducing the cost of carrying consumer debt. The *best* way to reduce the costs of such debt is to avoid it in the first place when you're making consumption purchases. You can avoid consumer debt by eliminating your access to credit or by limiting your purchase of consumer items to what you can pay off each month. Remember, borrow only for long-term investments (see Chapter 1 for more information).

Don't keep a credit card that charges you an annual fee, especially if you pay your balance in full each month. Many no-fee credit cards exist — and some even offer you a benefit for using them:

- ✔ **Bank of Montreal Mosaik MasterCard** (1-800-263-2263; `www.bmo.com/mastercard`) is a somewhat customizable rewards card. You can choose either a higher interest rate, no-fee combination, or a low rate

coupled with an annual fee. On the rewards front, you can choose
between ringing up Air Miles or getting 0.5 percent back on purchases.

✔ **CIBC** (1-800-465-4653; www.cibc.com/ca/visa) offers a few Visa
options. The CIBC Dividend Card gives you a credit of 0.25 percent on
the first $1,500 you spend annually, 0.5 percent on the next $1,500, and
1.0 percent on any amount beyond $3,000. CIBC also has a Shoppers
Optimum/Pharmaprix card, with which you can earn Shoppers Optimum
points. You get points on all your purchases, but earn more when you
use the card at a Shoppers outlet. The points earn you a discount on
purchases from Shoppers, and you can also donate the points to charity.

✔ **Citibank** (1-800-387-1616; www.citibank.com/canada) offers several
rewards cards. Their Driver's Edge cards give you a 2-percent rebate on
transactions to put toward the purchase of a vehicle. Unlike some other
programs, you aren't restricted to buying from any specific car maker, and
can also purchase a used car. The card offers three different levels — the
higher levels let you earn more and come with a higher credit limit. The
Enrich card earns a straight 1-percent cash back, while the KidsFutures
card lets you earn anywhere from 0.5 to 2 percent toward your child's
postsecondary education. There is also a Petro-Points card, which saves 2
cents a litre on Petro-Canada gas while earning 10 Petro-Points.

✔ **National Bank** (1-800-465-4653; www.nbc.ca) offers several different
MasterCard options that earn a discount on purchases made at selected
gas retailers, as well as a small refund on other purchases put on the
card. Cards available include those for Sunoco and Husky/Mohawk.

✔ **President's Choice Financial MasterCard** (1-866-246-7262; www.pc
financial.ca) lets you earn PC points, which can be used to buy groceries, tools, and a variety of other items from different merchants. The
points work out to a 1-percent rebate. This card is also an excellent
choice if you are currently carrying a large balance on another card. The
interest rate on balance transfers is very low — less than 4 percent at
the time of writing — and instead of rising to a much higher level after 6
months, as is the case with many other cards, the rate stays low on the
transferred amount until it is all paid off.

✔ **RBC Rewards Visa Classic** (1-800-769-2512; www.rbcroyalbank.com) lets
you earn rewards points that can be redeemed for gift certificates accepted
at a range of retailers, including The Bay, Zellers, Home Outfitters, and
Future Shop. The program gives about a 0.4-percent rebate.

✔ **Scotiabank Moneyback Visa** (1-888-882-8958; www.scotiabank.com) is
a few-frills card that gives you up to 1 percent back on purchases. You're
also eligible for a discount on car rentals with Avis.

✔ **TD Visa** (1-800-983-8472; www.tdcanadatrust.com) offers a GM Visa,
on which you earn 3 percent of your charges toward the purchase of a
GM-manufactured vehicle, to a maximum of $3,500. The TD Green Visa is
a basic, no-fee card.

Consider the cards in the previous list only if you pay your balance in full each month, because no-fee cards typically levy high interest rates for balances carried month-to-month. The small rewards that you earn really won't do you much good if they're negated by interest charges.

If you have a credit card that charges an annual fee, try calling the company and saying that you want to cancel the card because you can get a competitor's card without a fee. Some banks will agree to waive the fee on the spot. Some require you to call back yearly to cancel the fee — a hassle that can be avoided by getting a true no-fee card.

Some cards that charge an annual fee and offer credits toward the purchase of a specific item, such as a car or airline ticket, may be worth your while if you pay your bill in full each month and charge $10,000 or more annually. *Note:* Be careful — you may be tempted to charge more on a card that rewards you for more purchases. Spending more than you would otherwise in order to rack up bonuses defeats the purpose of the credits.

Indulging responsibly in fun and recreation

Having fun and taking time out for R&R can be money well spent. But when it comes to fun and recreation, financial extravagance can wreck an otherwise good budget.

Entertainment

If you adjust your expectations, entertainment doesn't have to cost a great deal of money. Many movies, theatres, museums, and restaurants offer discount prices on certain days and times.

Cultivate some interests and hobbies that are free or low-cost. Visiting with friends, hiking, reading, and playing sports can be good for your finances as well as your health.

Vacations

For many people, vacations are a luxury. For others, regular vacations are essential parts of their routine. Regardless of how you recharge your batteries, remember that vacations are not investments, so you shouldn't borrow through credit cards to finance your travels. After all, how relaxed will you feel when you have to pay all those bills?

Try taking shorter vacations that are closer to home. Have you been to a national or provincial park recently? Take a vacation at home, visiting the

Using thrift with gifts

Think about how you approach buying gifts throughout the year — especially during the holidays. We know people who spend so much on their credit cards during the December holidays that it takes them until late spring or summer to pay their debts off!

Although we don't want to deny your loved ones gifts from the heart — or you the pleasure of giving them — spend wisely. Homemade gifts are less costly to the giver and may be dearer to recipients. Many children actually love durable, classic, basic toys. If the TV commercials dictate your kids' desires, it may be time to toss the TV (or set better rules for what the kids are allowed to watch).

Some people forget their thrifty shopping habits when gift buying, perhaps because they don't like to feel cheap when buying a gift. As with other purchases you make, paying careful attention to where and what you buy can save you significant dollars. Don't make the mistake of equating the value of a gift with its dollar cost.

And here's a good suggestion for getting rid of those old, unwanted gifts. One of the most entertaining and memorable holiday parties you can throw is a "white elephant" gift exchange: Everyone brings a wrapped, unwanted gift from the past and exchanges it with someone else. After the gifts are opened, trading is allowed. (Just be sure not to bring a gift that was given to you by any of the exchange participants!)

sights in your local area. Great places that you've always wanted to see but haven't visited for one reason or another are probably located within 300 kilometres of you. Or you may want to just block out some time and do what cats do: Take lots of naps and relax around your home.

If you do travel a long way to a popular destination, travel during the off-season for the best deals on airfares and hotels. Keep an eye out for discounts and "bought-but-unable-to-use" tickets advertised in your local paper. The *Consumer Reports Travel* newsletter and Web site (www.consumerwebwatch.org/travel.cfm), as well as numerous other Web sites such as

- ✓ www.itravel2000.com,
- ✓ www.redtag.ca
- ✓ www.escapes.ca
- ✓ www.selloffvacations.com
- ✓ www.travelocity.ca
- ✓ www.jetvacations.ca

can help you find low-cost travel options as well. Senior citizens generally qualify for special fares at most airlines — ask the airline what programs it offers.

Also, be sure to shop around, even when working with a travel agent. Travel agents are on commission, so they may not work hard to find you the best deals. Tour packages, when they meet your interests and needs, can also save you money. If you have flexible travel plans, offering to make deliveries for courier services can cut your travel costs significantly (but make sure that the company is reputable).

Tending to personal care

You have to take care of yourself, but as with anything else, you can find ways to do it that are expensive, and you can find ways that save you money.

- ✔ **Hair care:** If you have hair to be trimmed, a number of no-frills, low-cost hair-cutting joints can do the job: Supercuts is one of the larger chains. You may insist that your stylist is the only one who can manage your hair the way you like it. At the prices charged by some trendy hair places, you have to *really* adore what they do to justify the cost. Consider going periodically to a no-frills stylist for maintenance after getting a fabulous cut at a more expensive place. If you're daring, you can try getting your hair cut at a local training school. For parents of young children, buying a simple-to-use home haircutting electric shaver can be a great time and money saver — no more agonizing trips with little ones to have their hair cut by a "stranger." The kit pays for itself after just two to three haircuts!

- ✔ **Other personal-care services:** As long as we're on the subject of outward beauty, we have to say that, in our personal opinion, the billions spent annually on cosmetics are largely a waste of money (not to mention all that time spent applying and removing them). And having regular facials, pedicures, and manicures can add up quickly.

- ✔ **Health club expenses:** Money spent on exercise is almost always money well spent. But you don't have to belong to a trendy club to receive the benefits of exercise. If you belong to a gym or club for the social scene (whether for dating or business purposes), you have to judge whether it's worth the cost.

  Low-cost exercise facilities are everywhere — look for them anywhere you see children and young adults. Local schools, colleges, and universities often have tennis courts, running tracks, swimming pools, basketball courts, and exercise rooms, and they may even provide instruction. Community centres offer fitness programs and classes, too. Metropolitan areas that have lots of health clubs undoubtedly have the widest range of options and prices. Note: When figuring the cost of membership, be sure to factor in the cost of travel to and from the club and any parking costs (and the realistic likelihood of actually going there regularly to work out).

  Don't forget that healthy exercise can be done indoors or out, free of charge. Isn't biking in the park at sunset more fun than pedalling away on a stationary bike, anyway? You may want to buy some basic gym equipment for use at home. Be careful though: Lots of rowing machines and free weights languish in a closet after their first week at home.

Look for value in the publications to which you subscribe

Everyone has a favourite and not-so-favourite publication. Some people don't realize how much they spend on publications, partly because they never tally up the cost.

Free publications are often driven by advertisers, so we don't encourage you to load up on them. But take a close look at the total amount you spend on publications and how much each one costs. Keep the ones that you're getting sufficient value from and cancel the rest. You can always read them at your local library.

If you took the money that you're spending on one of your regular papers — say, $23 a month, or $276 a year — and invested it in your RRSP and earned 10 percent a year, in 25 years you'd have more than $27,000. And this example assumes that the subscription prices won't increase every year, which they always do. After seeing these figures, you'd really have to believe that you're getting good value from the paper to keep subscribing!

Paring down professional expenses

Accountants, lawyers, and financial advisers can be worth their expense if they're good. But be wary of professionals who create or perpetuate work and have conflicts of interest with their recommendations.

Make sure you get organized before meeting with a professional for tax, legal, or financial advice. Do some background research to evaluate his or her strengths and biases. Set goals and estimate fees in advance so that you know what you're getting yourself into.

Computer and printed resources (see Chapters 18 and 19) can be useful, low-cost alternatives to hiring professionals.

Managing medical expenses

Health care is a big topic nowadays. The cost of health care is going up fast, and some services that once were covered by universal heath insurance you now have to personally pay for. Canada's system probably covers most of your basic health care needs, but you may also need to pay for certain expenses, like dental, vision, and chiropractic care, out of your own pocket. (Chapter 16 explains how to shop for additional health insurance.)

Medical and health care and supplies are like any other services and products — prices and quality vary. And medicine in Canada, like any other profession, is a business. A conflict of interest exists whenever the person recommending treatment benefits financially from providing that treatment. Health care professionals generally get paid piece-meal or by the hour for much of their work, so there is a substantial financial incentive to do their work in the way that pays the most. Many studies have documented some of the unnecessary surgeries and medical procedures that have resulted from this conflict of interest. This is a concern for all Canadians. Even if a particular health care service is covered by your provincial health care plan, you are still paying for it through your taxes.

Therapy, for instance, can be useful and even lifesaving. However, visits to some types of therapists typically aren't fully covered — or covered at all — by provincial health care plans. If you are consdering — or have already begun — seeing a therapist, have a frank talk with them about how much total time and money you can expect to spend and what kind of results you can expect to receive. As with any professional service, a competent therapist will give you a straight answer if he or she is looking out for your psychological *and* financial well-being.

Alternative medicine (holistic, for example) is gaining attention because of its focus on preventive care and the treatment of the whole body or person. Although alternative medicine can be dangerous if you're in critical condition, alternative treatment for many forms of chronic pain or disease may be worth investigating.

If you have to take certain drugs on an ongoing basis and pay for them out-of-pocket, ordering through a mail-order company can bring down your costs and help make refilling your prescriptions more convenient. Your health plan should be able to provide more information about this option.

The following mail-order companies also offer generic drugs, which are medically equivalent to brand-name drugs but cost a lot less:

- ✔ MediTrust (1-888-792-3667 or www.meditrust.com)
- ✔ Pharmacy.ca (Central Medical Pharmacy) (800-727-5048 or www.pharmacy.ca)
- ✔ Pharmex Direct (800-663-8637 or www.pharmexdirect.com)

Keeping an eye on insurance premiums

Insurance is a vast minefield. In Part IV, we explain the different types of coverage, suggest what to buy and avoid, and detail how to save on policies.

The following list explains the most common ways people waste money on insurance.

✔ **Keeping low deductibles:** The *deductible* is the amount of a loss that must come out of your pocket. For example, if you have an auto insurance policy with a $100 collision deductible, and you get into an accident, you pay for the first $100 of damage and your insurance company picks up the rest. Low deductibles, however, translate into much higher premiums for you. In the long run, you save money with a higher deductible, even when factoring in the potential for greater out-of-pocket costs to you when you do have a claim. Insurance should protect you from economic disaster. Don't get carried away with a really high deductible, which can cause financial hardship if you have a claim and lack savings.

If you have a lot of claims, you won't come out ahead with lower deductibles, because your insurance premiums will escalate. Plus, low deductibles mean more claim forms to file for small losses (creating more hassle). Filing an insurance claim is usually not an enjoyable or quick experience.

✔ **Covering small potential losses or unnecessary needs:** You shouldn't buy insurance for anything that won't be a financial catastrophe if you have to pay for it out of your own pocket. Although the postal service isn't perfect, insuring inexpensive gifts sent in the mail is not worth the price. Buying extended warranties on electronic goods and appliances also doesn't make financial sense for the same reason. And, if no one is dependent on your income, you don't need to buy life insurance either. (Who will be around to collect when you're gone?)

✔ **Failing to shop around:** Rates vary tremendously from insurer to insurer. In Part IV, we recommend the best companies to call for quotes and other cost-saving strategies.

Trimming your taxes

Taxes are probably one of your largest expenditures — if not *the* largest—. (So why is it discussed last here? Read on to find out.)

Retirement savings plans are one of the best and simplest ways to reduce your tax burden. (We explain more about retirement savings plans in Chapter 10.) Unfortunately, most people can't take full advantage of these plans because they spend everything they make. So they not only have less savings, but also pay higher income taxes — a double whammy.

We've attended presentations where a fast-talking investment guy in an expensive suit lectures about the importance of saving for retirement and explains how to invest your savings. Yet details and tips about finding the money to save (the hard part for most people) are left to the imagination.

In order to take advantage of the tax savings that come through retirement savings plans, you must first spend less than you earn. Only then can you afford to contribute to these plans. That's why the first part of this chapter is all about strategies to reduce your spending.

Reduced sales taxes are another benefit of spending less and saving more. When you buy most consumer products, you pay sales tax. Therefore, when you spend less money and save more in retirement plans, you reduce both the income *and* sales tax you pay. (See Chapter 6 for detailed tax-reduction strategies.)

Eliminating costly addictions

Human beings are creatures of habit. We all have habits we wish we didn't have, and breaking those habits can be very difficult. Costly habits are the worst. The following tidbits may nudge you in the right direction toward breaking your own financially-draining habits.

- ✔ **Kick the smoking habit.** Canadians spend about $6 billion annually on tobacco products. If you smoke just a pack a day, you're spending around $3,000 a year to damage your health. The increased medical costs and the costs of lost work time are even greater, as they're estimated at anywhere from $3 billion to $7 billion every year. Of course, if you continue to smoke, you may eliminate the need to save for retirement.

  Check with local hospitals for smoking-cessation programs. If you want to quit, the Canadian Cancer Society (1-888-939-3333; www.cancer.ca) offers a self-help program, along with a hotline. The Society can also refer you to local programs. The Canadian Lung Association (1-888-566-5864; www.lung.ca) produces a Quit Smoking guide, and can refer you to provincial associations, many of which offer programs to help you stop smoking.

- ✔ **Stop abusing alcohol and other drugs.** Thousands of Canadians seek treatment annually for alcoholism or drug abuse. These addictive behaviours, like spending, transcend all educational and socioeconomic lines in our society. Even so, studies have demonstrated that only one in seven alcohol or drug abusers seek help. Three of the ten leading causes of death — cirrhosis of the liver, accidents, and suicides — are associated with excessive alcohol consumption.

To find a local Alcoholics Anonymous chapter, look in the telephone book or visit www.alcoholics-anonymous.org. For drug addiction, start by contacting your provincial ministry of health. You can also dig up lists of sources for help online. One good example is Ontario's Drug and Alcohol Registry of Treatment (www.dart.on.ca). Another starting point is the Centre for Addiction and Mental Health (www.camh.net).

✔ **Don't gamble.** The house always comes out ahead in the long run. Why do you think so many governments run lotteries? Because governments make money on people who gamble, that's why.

Video lottery terminals and lotteries, as well as casinos, horse and dog racetracks, and other gambling establishments are sure long-term losers for you. So, too, is the short-term trading of stocks, which isn't investing but gambling. Getting hooked on the dream of winning is easy and tempting. And sure, occasionally you win a little bit (just enough to keep you coming back). Every now and then, a few folks win a lot. But your hard-earned capital mostly winds up in the pockets of the casino owners.

If you gamble just for the entertainment, take only what you can afford to lose. Gamblers Anonymous (213-386-8789; www.gamblersanonymous.org) helps those for whom gambling has become an addiction. Also, contact your provincial ministry of health and inquire about the availability of treatment programs.

Chapter 6

Taming Taxes

In This Chapter

▶ Understanding the baffling tax system

▶ Reducing employment income taxes

▶ Lowering investment income taxes

▶ Discovering ways to increase your deductions

▶ Preparing your return with help from tax resources

▶ Handling an audit notice

*Y*ou pay a lot of money in taxes — probably more than you realize. Believe it or not, few people know just how much they pay in taxes each year. Most people remember only whether they received a refund or owed money on their return. But when you file your tax return, all you're doing is settling up with tax authorities over the amount of taxes you paid during the year versus the total tax that you owe based on your income and deductions.

Understanding the Taxes You Pay

Some people feel lucky when they get a refund, but all a refund really indicates is that you overpaid in taxes during the year. You should have had this money in your own account all along. If you're consistently getting big refunds, you need to pay less tax throughout the year.

Instead of focusing on whether you're going to get a refund when you complete your annual tax return, you should be focusing on the *total* taxes you pay. To find out the total taxes you pay, you need to get out your tax return. On the federal T1 General form, there will be a line called "Total payable." On recent returns, this was line 435. Next, subtract any credits — including your provincial tax credits — deducted from your total tax payable, except for tax that you've already had deducted (line 437) or tax you paid in instalments (line 476). The resulting number you'll see is probably one of your largest expenses.

The goal of this chapter is to help you legally and permanently reduce the total taxes you pay. Understanding the tax system is the key to reducing your tax burden — if you don't, you'll surely pay more taxes than necessary. Your tax ignorance can lead to mistakes, which can be costly if the Canada Revenue Agency (which until recently was called the Canada Customs and Revenue Agency, and for a long period before that, Revenue Canada) catches your underpayment errors. With the proliferation of computerized information and data tracking, discovering mistakes has never been easier.

The tax system, like other public policy, is built around incentives to encourage *desirable* behaviour and activity. Home ownership, for example, is considered desirable because it encourages people to take more responsibility for maintaining buildings and neighborhoods. Clean, orderly neighbourhoods are often the result of home ownership. Therefore, the government offers all sorts of tax perks, which we discuss later in this chapter, to encourage people to buy homes.

Not all people follow the path the government encourages — after all, it's a free country. However, the fewer desirable activities you engage in, the more you pay in taxes. If you understand the options, you can choose the ones that meet your needs as you approach different stages of your financial life.

Recognizing the importance of your marginal tax rate

When it comes to taxes, not all income is treated equally. This fact is far from self-evident. If you work for an employer and earn a constant salary during the course of a year, a steady and equal amount of federal and provincial taxes is deducted from each paycheque. Thus, it appears as though all that earned income is being taxed equally.

In reality, however, you pay less tax on your first dollars of earnings and more tax on your last dollars of earnings. For example, if you're single and your taxable income (a term we define in the next section) totals $40,000 during 2005, you would not pay any tax on the first $8,148 because of a tax credit that offsets the tax on that income. Your combined federal and provincial tax rate would be approximately 24 percent on income from $8,148 to $35,595. Your tax rate would be 34 percent on income between $35,595 and $71,190, 41 percent on income from $71,190 to $115,739, and 45 percent on income above $115,739. Table 6-1 gives approximate combined federal and provincial tax rates. Your actual marginal bracket may be somewhat higher or lower, depending on the tax rate in your province.

Table 6-1	Approximate 2005 Combined Federal and Provincial Income Tax Brackets and Rates	
Taxable Income	**Tax Rate (Bracket)**
$0–$8,000	0% (Due to tax credit)
$8,000–$35,500	24%
$35,500–$71,000	34%
$71,000–$116,000	41%
over $116,000	45%

Your marginal tax rate is the rate of tax you pay on your last, or so-called highest, dollars of income. In the example of a single person with taxable income of $40,000, that person's combined federal and provincial marginal tax rate is approximately 34 percent. In other words, she effectively pays 34 percent tax on her last dollars of income — those dollars in excess of $35,000.

Marginal tax rates are a powerful concept. Your marginal tax rate allows you to quickly calculate the additional taxes you'd have to pay on additional income. Conversely, you can delight in quantifying the amount of taxes you save by reducing your taxable income, either by decreasing your income or by increasing your deductions.

Defining taxable income

Taxable income is the amount of income on which you actually pay income taxes. (In the sections that follow, we explain strategies for reducing your taxable income.) The following reasons explain why you don't pay taxes on your total income:

- ✔ **Not all income is taxable.** For example, any profit you make when you sell the home you live in — your principal residence — generally isn't taxable.

- ✔ **You get to subtract deductions from your income.** Some deductions are available just for being a living, breathing human being. In 2005, every taxpayer resident in Canada got a federal exemption — known as the basic personal amount — on their first $8,149 of income (this amount is scheduled to increase gradually over the next several years). When you contribute to qualified retirement plans such as an RRSP, you also effectively get a deduction.

Alternative minimum tax (Say what?)

You may find this hard to believe, but a *second* tax system actually exists (as if the first tax system weren't already complicated enough). This second system may raise your taxes even higher than they would normally be. We'll explain while you reach for some Aspirin.

Over the years, as the government grew hungry for more revenue, taxpayers who slashed their taxes by claiming lots of deductions or exclusions from taxable income came under greater scrutiny. So the government created a second method of assessing taxes — the alternative minimum tax (AMT) — to ensure that those with high deductions or exclusions pay at least a certain percentage of taxes on their incomes.

If you have a lot of deductions or exclusions from income taxes, you may fall prey to AMT. Even if you're not claiming a lot of deductions or using tax-sheltered investments such as limited partnerships, you may also get tripped up by AMT. For instance, someone who receives a substantial capital gain — say, a farmer who

sells off a large plot of land — may find that the AMT kicks in.

AMT restricts you from claiming certain deductions and requires you to add back in some capital gains that are normally not taxed. You then take a $40,000 exemption, and calculate your federal tax at 16 percent. You can use most personal tax credits, except for the dividend tax and the investment tax credits, just as you would when calculating your regular tax. You also need to carry about a similar calculation for your provincial taxes. The minimum tax rate will range from around 35 percent to 62 percent of the federal minimum tax (with adjustments for provincial credits), depending on the province in which you live. (If you live in Quebec there are different rules. Contact the provincial tax authorities for more information.) You have to figure your tax under the AMT system and under the other system, and then pay whichever amount is higher. We hope that Aspirin is starting to kick in.

Getting Organized

Locating your tax slips and all the other scraps of paper you need when you're completing your tax return can be a hassle. Setting up a filing system can be a big timesaver:

> ✔ **One receptacle:** If you have limited patience for setting up neat file folders, and you lead an uncomplicated financial life (that is, you haven't saved receipts throughout the year), you can confine your filing to January and February. During those months, you should receive tax summary statements on wages paid by your employer (T4), taxable dividend income from Canadian corporations (T5), income from profit-sharing plans (T4PS), and interest income (T5 for bank account and regular interest Canada Savings Bond "R" bonds, T5008 for T-bills). If you're older, you may also get a slip for Old Age Security income (T4AOAS) and

the Canada Pension Plan or Québec Pension Plan (T4A(P)). Set up a folder that's labelled with something easy to remember ("2005 Taxes" is a brilliant choice) and dump these papers as well as your tax booklet into it. When you're ready to crunch numbers, you should have everything you need to complete the form.

✔ **Many receptacles:** Organizing the bills you pay into individual folders during the entire year is a more thorough approach. This method is essential if you own your own business and need to tabulate your expenditures for office supplies each year. No one is going to send you a form totalling your office expenditures — you're on your own.

✔ **Software as a receptacle:** Software programs can help organize your tax information during the year and save you time and accounting fees come tax-preparation time. See Chapter 18 for more information about tax and financial software.

Trimming Employment Income Taxes

You're supposed to pay taxes on income you earn from work. Countless illegal ways are available to reduce your employment income — for example, not reporting it — but if you use them you can very well end up paying a heap of penalties and extra interest charges on top of the taxes you owe. And you may even get tossed in jail. Because we don't want you to serve jail time or lose even more money by paying unnecessary penalties, this section focuses on the *legal* ways to reduce your taxes.

Contributing to RRSPs and retirement plans

An RRSP or your employer's retirement plan is one of the few painless and completely legal ways to reduce your taxable employment income. Besides reducing your taxes, retirement plans help you build up a nest egg so that you don't have to work for the rest of your life.

You can deduct money from your taxable income by tucking it away in an RRSP or employer-based retirement plan. If your marginal tax rate is 34 percent, and you contribute $1,000 to one of these plans, you reduce your taxes by $340. Do you like the sound of that? How about this: Contribute another $1,000, and your taxes drop another $340 (as long as you're still in the same marginal tax rate). And when your money is inside a retirement plan, it can compound and grow without taxation.

Cutting back on expenses to fund retirement plans

Many people miss this great opportunity for reducing their taxes because they spend all (or too much) of their current employment income and, therefore, have nothing (or little) left to put into an RRSP or other retirement plan. If you're in this predicament, you need to reduce your spending before you can contribute money to a retirement plan. (Chapter 5 explains how to decrease your spending.)

If your employer doesn't offer the option of saving money through a retirement plan, an RRSP is your next best bet. In many cases, you may be able to contribute to an RRSP after putting the maximum you can into your employer's pension plan and have it matched by a company contribution in your name. Chapter 10 can help you determine whether you should contribute to an RRSP and how to make the most out of registered retirement plans.

Shifting some income

Income shifting is a more esoteric tax-reduction technique that's an option only to those who can control when they receive their income.

For example, suppose that your employer tells you in late December that you're eligible for a bonus. You're offered the option to receive your bonus in either December or January. If you're pretty certain that you'll be in a higher tax bracket next year, you should choose to receive your bonus in December.

Or suppose that you run your own business, and you think that you'll be in a lower tax bracket next year. Perhaps you plan to take time off to be with a newborn or take an extended trip. You may be able to push a big contract off until January so the income is earned and taxed in the next tax year.

Reducing Investment Income Taxes

You don't need to worry about taxes for investments that you hold in tax-sheltered retirement plans — RRSPs and RRIFS, for example. This money is generally not taxed until you actually withdraw funds from the retirement plan.

The distributions and profits on investments that you hold outside of tax-sheltered retirement plans are exposed to taxation when you receive them. Interest, dividends, and profits from the sale of an investment at a price that is higher than the purchase price (called *capital gains*) are all taxed.

Although this section explains some of the best methods for reducing the taxes on investments exposed to taxation, Chapter 11 discusses how and where to invest money held outside of tax-sheltered retirement plans.

Fill up those retirement plans

Taking advantage of opportunities to direct money into retirement plans gives you two possible tax benefits. First, your contributions to the retirement plan are generally immediately tax-deductible (see Chapter 10 for details). Second, the distributions and growth of the investments in the retirement plans aren't generally taxed until withdrawal.

Select tax-friendly investments

Too often, when selecting investments people mistakenly focus on past rates of return. We all know that the past is no guarantee of the future. But choosing an investment with a reportedly high rate of return without considering tax consequences is an even worse mistake. What you get to keep — after taxes — is what matters in the long run.

For example, when comparing two similar funds, most people prefer a fund that averages returns of 14 percent per year to one that earns 12 percent per year. But what if the 14-percent-per-year fund forces you to pay a lot more in taxes? What if, after factoring in taxes, the 14-percent-per-year fund nets just 9 percent, while the 12-percent-per-year fund nets an effective 10-percent return? In such a case, you'd be unwise to choose a fund solely on the basis of the higher (pre-tax) reported rate of return.

We call investments that appreciate in value and don't distribute much in the way of taxable income *tax-friendly*. (Some in the investment business use the term *tax efficient*.) See Chapter 9 for more information on tax-friendly stocks and stock mutual funds.

If you are investing outside of a retirement plan and want to regularly receive income, stocks that pay dividends are generally a good choice. Typically, the after-tax yield of these investments is better than that on interest-paying GICs or bonds. The yield is not guaranteed, but especially for preferred shares, major companies try to maintain their dividends. If you are in the 34-percent tax bracket, that's the rate you'll pay on interest income. Compare that to the tax rate on dividend income of about 19 percent.

(In late 2005, the liberal government promised changes that would significantly alter the way dividends are taxed, and in many cases, make them even more tax friendly. Whether they are in fact now law will depend on the outcome of the 2006 federal election. Under the amendments, dividend income is "grossed up" by 45%. At the same time, the federal dividend tax credit increases by about 50 percent to 19%. Assuming the provinces boost their dividend tax credits by a similar percentage, the tax rate those in the top marginal tax bracket pay on dividend income falls from around 32% to around 21% by 2010. The tax rate on dividends also falls for those in lower tax brackets, but the changes are no where near as pronounced, since rates were already quite low. Those in the 24% marginal tax bracket, for example only paid tax at a rate of about 7% on dividend income under the old rules. Still, if you only received dividend income, the amount you could receive before you began being taxed would increase from about $32,000 to $65,000 under the proposed new rules.

Make your profits long-term

As we discuss in Part III, when you buy growth investments such as stocks and real estate, you should do so for the long term — ideally 10 or more years. The tax system rewards your patience since you don't have to pay taxes on your profits until you sell the shares. Similarly, if you invest in real estate, the value can rise substantially and for many years. That profit is taxable only if and when you sell the property.

Increasing Your Deductions

Deductions are just what their name implies: You subtract them from your income after totalling your income and before calculating the tax you owe. To determine just what a deduction is worth, multiply it by your marginal tax rate.

In the sections that follow, we detail some of the more common deductions you may be able to take advantage of. The dollar figures we use are for 2005 — many will likely have been revised for subsequent years.

Child care expenses

The joy parents get from children is usually endless. It may also seem like there is no end to the expenses that come with them. The good news is that many of the costs of having others take care of your children can be deducted from your income. Babysitters, day nurseries, daycare, day camps, and boarding school expenses all qualify. However, the expenses must be incurred to enable you either to work or to take an occupational training course.

You can deduct $7,000 for each child who is under age 7 at the end of the year, and $4,000 for each child age 7 to 16. Your total deduction can't be greater than two-thirds of your salary or net business income (technically your earned income). Note that for Quebec residents, child care expenses give you a refundable credit, not a deduction, and different limits apply.

Alimony and maintenance payments

Alimony or maintenance payments you make to an ex-spouse can be deducted, as long as they are made following a decree, order, judgment, or written agreement. To be deductible, they must be an allowance that is paid out in regular, predetermined payments. You can't deduct any transfers of property or one-time payments you make as part of a settlement.

Child support

Child support payments that are made according to an agreement that was reached before May 1, 1997, and that are established in advance as an allowance that involves recurring payments, are generally deductible. Like alimony payments, the amounts must be predetermined, paid under a written agreement or under a decree, order, or judgment of a competent tribunal, and paid on a periodic basis. You also must be living apart from your spouse or ex-spouse because of a marriage breakdown at the time the payment is made.

Annual union and professional fees

Regular annual dues are deductible, but you can't claim initial fees or special assessments. (These dues are generally deducted from your paycheque.) Fees paid to professional organizations are deductible only if they must be paid to maintain a professional standing recognizable by law. If you are self-employed, however, you can generally deduct dues you pay to voluntarily belong to work-related organizations.

Business losses

If you work and run your own unincorporated business or professional practice, you can use business losses from the other businesses you're involved in to reduce your employment or professional income. Say that you have a salaried job in a car plant, and you start up a contracting business. If your business expenses are greater than the income it brings in, you can subtract your losses from your other income.

Interest on investment loans

Any interest you pay on money you borrow to buy investments or to earn income from a business may be deducted. (Note: This rule doesn't apply to money borrowed to make an RRSP contribution.) You'll need to keep a record of any money you borrow and use to invest and the interest you pay during the year.

Married versus common-law partners

Your mother likely won't agree, but you're as good as married in the eyes of the tax authorities if you have been living in a common-law relationship for more than a year. If so, you are subject to the same tax rules that apply to legally married couples. For instance, if you are living common-law, you can't claim the "equivalent-to-married" credit for a child. On the other hand, you can take advantage of planning opportunities including setting up a spousal RRSP and pooling some expenses to take the most advantage of various credits.

You are considered to be common-law spouses if you and your partner "cohabit in a conjugal relationship," and either have had a child together or have been living together continuously for at least 12 months. You are deemed to have "separated" — or lost your common-law status — only if you are separated for more than 90 days due to the relationship breaking down.

Beginning in 2001, same-sex couples who have lived together for at least one year have been treated by the tax authorities in the same way as opposite-sex common-law couples.

Moving expenses

Eligible moving expenses are often overlooked, but they can be a very valuable deduction. The rules are straightforward. If you start a business or start working at a new location and move to a home that is at least 40 kilometres closer by road to your new business or job location than your old home, you can generally deduct most of the associated costs. However, moving to Canada from another country — or moving from Canada *to* another country — doesn't qualify.

Expenses that are eligible include the travelling costs to move you and your family (including food and lodging along the way) and your household belongings, as well as any related storage costs. In addition, you can deduct the cost of selling your old home, including the real estate commissions, and the legal bills on purchasing your new home. Expenses can be deducted only against income that is earned in the new location. If you are unable to deduct all the expenses in the year of the move, the remainder can be deducted in future years. So don't forget to carry that deduction forward.

Students who move so they can attend university or another post-secondary institution full time can also deduct moving expenses. The expenses must be deducted against taxable scholarships, bursaries, research grants, or fellowships. Students can also claim moving expenses if the move is in order to take a job — including a summer job — or to start a business.

Increasing Your Credits

Tax credits are credited to you as if you've already paid that amount in taxes. Once your tax bill has been calculated from your taxable income, any tax credits reduce your taxes by the full amount of the credit. A $500 credit is worth the same amount to everybody — it reduces the tax you have to pay by $500. Most credits are *non-refundable*, which means that they can't be used to make your tax liability less than zero. If you have $1,500 in credits left over after wiping out your federal tax payable, that's as good as it gets. The government won't send you a cheque for $1,500.

Tax credits are worth the same to you regardless of your tax bracket. This is not the case with deductions. Deductions are subtracted from your income before your tax is calculated, so a deduction is worth what you would otherwise have paid on that amount of income, which is determined by your marginal tax bracket.

All the provinces (except Quebec) calculate their piece of your tax bill by applying their marginal rates directly to your taxable income. This is known as a *tax-on-income,* or *TONI* method. Previously, provincial taxes were calculated as a percentage of your basic federal tax bill; this was known as the *tax-on-tax* method.

With the old tax-on-tax method, credits were usually deducted from your federal tax bill before your provincial taxes and surtaxes were calculated. With the TONI method, both the federal and provincial governments calculate your tax by multiplying your income by their respective tax rate. You then separately deduct your federal and provincial tax credits from the corresponding gross tax payable to arrive at what's called your basic federal and basic provincial tax.

Under the old tax-on-tax system, a tax credit was worth anywhere from around 50 to 70 percent more than the straight federal credit, because by cutting your federal taxes you also reduced your provincial taxes and surtaxes. When they moved to the TONI method, the provinces were required to maintain the basic credits that are offered at the federal level. The value of a federal credit will be about 40 to 70 percent more once the provincial tax credit is factored in.

In the following sections are some common credits that may be available to you and your family, and some tips on how to maximize them. *Note:* Most of the dollar figures are from the 2005 tax year. Check your tax guide for the specific amounts for the year you're filing for.

Basic personal tax credit

Everyone gets a basic federal credit of $1,304. (When you're going through the form, you claim a "basic personal amount" of $8,148, which is then multiplied by 16 percent to work out to $1,304.)

Spousal credit

You can claim a federal spousal credit of $1,107 if your spouse (including a common-law spouse) earned less than $692 during the year, and a smaller credit if he or she made between $692 and $7,611. If the spouse makes more than the cut-off amount of $7,611, the lower-earning partner may be able to get under the threshold by making an RRSP contribution.

Wholly dependent person credit

You can claim this credit if you're single, separated, divorced, or widowed and you support a relative who lives with you. (This used to be known as the *equivalent-to-married* credit.) The most common example of this is a single mother. However, whether you're a man or a woman, you can claim this credit if you're financially responsible for supporting a child, parent, or other relative. The only conditions are that the dependant must be related to you, completely financially dependent on you, living in Canada, and, except in the case of a parent or grandparent, under 18 years old at some point in the tax year. (The age limit doesn't apply if the person is dependent on you because of a mental or physical disability.) You can't claim this credit if you have a common-law or same-sex spouse. The amounts are the same as the spousal credit.

Charitable donations credit

As long as you get an official tax receipt, you can earn credits from most contributions made to charities. In addition to cash contributions, you can often gain tax credits if you donate items of significant value, such as a used computer. The amount of the receipt must reflect the item's fair market value. However, you can't get a receipt for your time or the expenses you ring up while doing charitable work.

The first $200 you donate earns you a 16 percent federal tax credit, which works out to about 23 to 27 percent once your savings on provincial taxes are accounted for. Once you're past the $200 level, though, your donations give you a 29-percent federal tax credit, worth about 45 percent once the savings on provincial taxes are counted. This makes your donations above $200 worth about as much as a deduction if you're in the top tax bracket.

If you donate only small amounts each year, pool several years' contributions to put you over the $200 donation level. You can also combine your spouses' and your own contributions on one return. This avoids both of you having to get the lower credit on the first $200. You don't have to claim a charitable deduction in the year that it's made. Unclaimed contributions can be carried forward and claimed on your return in any of the five years after the year in which you make the charitable contribution.

Tuition fees credit

You receive a credit worth 16 percent of tuition fees (as long as they total more than $100 per institution) paid to a Canadian university, college, or other post-secondary institution during the year. Fees paid to an institution certified by Employment and Immigration Canada are also eligible. Tuition paid to universities outside Canada may be eligible as well, but fees paid to private elementary schools or high schools don't earn you a tax credit.

If you study full-time, you also get to claim a federal educational status credit that in 2005 was $64. Students with qualifying disabilities can generally claim this amount even if they are studying only part-time.

If you are studying part-time, for every month in which you attended an eligible program for at least three consecutive weeks, and which involved at least 12 hours of course work per month, the education amount is about $20 a month.

Beginning in 2004 you are able to claim the education tax credit for post-secondary education that's related to your job, as long as your employer doesn't reimburse you for any of the costs.

Tuition fees cover much more than just the standard admission charges. You can also claim library and lab costs, exam fees, and mandatory computer service fees. As well, you can include mandatory associated fees such as those for health services and athletics.

Sometimes the student in the family doesn't need to use all — or any — of the tuition fee tax credit or the education credit to bring her federal tax bill to zero. In this case, the credits don't go to waste. Up to $800 of the unused portion of either — or both — credits generally can be transferred to a parent, grandparent, or spouse. Unused tuition and education amounts can also be carried forward and claimed against your income in future years.

Medical expenses credit

Despite provincial health care coverage, you'll likely find that you are responsible for the cost of an increasing number of medical expenses. It pays to hang on to your receipts. A surprisingly wide range of medical costs and health-related expenditures are eligible for a credit, but you have to generally submit all your receipts.

After totalling your expenses, you can claim only the amount that exceeds 3 percent of your net income. The federal credit for 2005 is 16 percent of that allowable amount. If your net income is $60,464 or more, you can claim 16 percent of any expenses exceeding $1,813.

To maximize the benefit of this credit, one spouse can and should claim the entire family's medical expenses. The spouse with the lowest income generally should make the claim, to get over the 3 percent floor as quickly as possible. Further, in any tax year you can claim your expenses for any 12 months ending in that particular year. If you have a lot of bills in the fall and spring, for example, it may pay to make your claim run from August 1 to July 31.

You can include a broad range of medical costs in calculating this credit. Add up any payments to doctors, nurses, dentists, and public or licensed private hospitals for medical or dental care. In addition, you can include payments for any prescription drugs and medications, eyeglasses, and therapy for speech or hearing problems. You can also include any premiums for private health insurance plans. (That includes the cost of travel insurance for your vacations out of the country; see Chapter 17 for more information.) You can't claim any expenses that you are reimbursed for from, say, a company dental plan, but any deductibles you pay do qualify.

Low-income earners who have high medical bills may also be able to take advantage of the medical expense supplement. The supplement is 25 percent of the medical expenses that are used to calculate your medical expenses credit — those beyond 3 percent of your income. The maximum this is worth is $562, and it gets reduced by 5 percent of your family's net income over $21,301.

Disability credit

You are eligible for a federal credit if you have a severe and prolonged mental or physical impairment. The credit was $1,038 for the 2005 tax year. Depending on the type of disability, it must be certified by the relevant professional (medical doctor, optometrist, audiologist, occupational therapist, or psychologist).

Families that care for children with severe disabilities can also receive a supplementary credit of up to $605. This will be reduced by childcare expenses and attendant care expenses in excess of $2,216 claimed with respect to that child.

Shifting or bunching expenses

Because you can control when you make some expenditures that earn you a credit, you can shift or bunch more of them into selected years to boost your tax savings. Take medical expenses: You're allowed to claim a deduction for medical bills for any 12-month period, as long as it ends within the tax year. If you anticipate a large medical bill, perhaps for some major dental work, and your 12-month period runs October to September, try to pay for the work in September rather than October. By having the expense included in the earlier 12-month period, you're able to get a credit for the expense a full year earlier.

Charitable donations are another expense category where grouping and timing your claims makes sense. You and your spouse are allowed to pool your contributions on one return. You can also group donations from up to six years together.

You're also allowed to pool charitable contributions from up to five consecutive years. If you regularly make donations that are smaller than $200, hold on to your receipts and claim them every few years. Again, this puts more of your donations over the $200 level, earning you a credit at a higher percentage.

If a dependent relative doesn't earn enough income to use all of his or her disability credit, a supporting relative can use any unused amount. The eligible dependant can be a spouse, child, grandchild, parent, grandparent, sibling, aunt, uncle, niece, or nephew. In addition, lower-income families caring for a child eligible for the disability tax credit may also qualify for Child Disability Benefit payments.

If a parent supports a disabled child who is over 18 years old, the parent is allowed an additional federal credit. This credit was $605 for the 2005 tax year. However, the credit is reduced by 16 percent of the income the dependant earns beyond $5,368. The credit gets eliminated if the dependant's income exceeds $9,152.

A *caregiver's credit* is also available to caregivers who provide in-home care for elderly or infirm relatives living in the same house. In 2005, the maximum credit was $605. This credit is reduced if the infirm relative has an income of between $12,921 and $16,705, and eliminated if their income exceeds $16,705. Also, you cannot claim this credit if you claim the eligible dependant or other dependent tax credits in connection with the relative.

Pension income credit

If you earn pension income, you can claim a credit of 16 percent on the first $1,000 of this income, which generally means money paid out by a life annuity as private pension income. Income from Old Age Security or the Canada Pension Plan isn't eligible. If you're unable to use the credit, it may be transferred to your spouse.

If you're 65 or older or are receiving benefits due to your spouse's death, the pension income definition expands to include annuities from an RRSP or deferred profit-sharing plan, the income portion of a regular annuity, or an RRIF payment.

Age 65 or older

Another credit is for those over 65: If this means you, you can claim a federal tax credit — the so-called *age credit* — of up to $625 for 2005. However, this credit is reduced if your net income is more than $29,124, and is completely eliminated if your income is more than $55,240.

Self-employment expenses

When you're self-employed, you can deduct a multitude of expenses from your income before calculating the tax you owe. If you buy a computer or office furniture, you can deduct those expenses. (Sometimes they need to be gradually deducted or depreciated over time.) Salaries for your employees, office supplies, rent or mortgage interest for your office space, and phone expenses are also generally deductible.

Many self-employed folks don't take all the deductions they're eligible for. In some cases, people simply aren't aware of the wonderful world of deductions. Others are worried that large deductions will increase the risk of an audit. Spend some time finding out more about tax deductions; you'll be convinced that taking full advantage of your eligible deductions makes sense and saves you money.

The following are common mistakes made by people who are their own bosses:

- ✔ **Being an island unto yourself:** When you're self-employed, going it alone is usually a mistake when it comes to taxes. You must educate yourself to make the tax laws work for rather than against you. Hiring tax help is well worth your while. (See "Professional hired help," later in this chapter, for info on hiring tax advisers.)

- ✔ **Making administrative tax screw-ups:** As a self-employed individual, you're responsible for the correct and timely filing of all taxes owed on your income and employment taxes on your employees. You need to make estimated tax payments on a quarterly basis. And if you have employees, you also need to withhold taxes from each paycheque they receive, and make timely payments to Canada Revenue Agency. In addition to federal and provincial taxes, you also need to withhold and send in Canada Pension Plan (or QPP) contributions and Employment Insurance premiums.

✔ **Failing to document expenses:** When you pay with cash, following the paper trail for all the money you spent can be hard for you to do (and for the Canada Revenue Agency, in the event you're ever audited). At the end of the year, how are you going to remember how much you spent for parking or client meals if you fail to keep a record? How will you survive a tax audit without proper documentation? You need a system for recording your daily petty cash purchases. Most pocket calendars or daily organizers include ledgers that allow you to track these small purchases. If you aren't that organized, at least get a receipt for cash transactions and stash them in a file folder in your desk. Or keep receipts in envelopes labelled with the month and year.

✔ **Choosing the wrong business entity:** When you set up your own business, you can structure its legal and tax organization in a variety of ways. A corporation is a separate legal entity from you, the individual. For example, if you're incorporated, and a customer slips on a stray banana peel at your office, the customer can sue your company but he can't go after your personal assets. Incorporating makes more sense if you have employees or customers visit your office, or if you do business with many vendors.

Incorporating is not always the right answer. For professional service providers such as self-employed lawyers, physicians, or tax advisers, incorporating isn't necessarily useful as protection against professional negligence suits related to their work. *Professional liability insurance* is the answer for these folks. Check with the professional associations in your field for information on insurers who offer such policies.

✔ **Failing to fund a retirement plan:** You should be saving money toward retirement anyway, and you can't beat the tax break. People who are self-employed are allowed to contribute up to 18 percent of their net income to an RRSP. If they also belong to a registered pension plan, the maximum amount they are allowed to contribute is decreased by a *pension adjustment.* To find out more about RRSPs, see Chapter 10.

✔ **Failing to use numbers to help manage business:** If you're a small-business owner who doesn't track her income, expenses, staff performance, and customer data on a regular basis, your tax return may be the one and only time during the year when you take a financial snapshot of your business. After you go to all the time, trouble, and expense to file your tax return, make sure that you reap the rewards of all your work: Use those numbers to help analyze and manage your business.

Some bookkeepers and tax preparers can provide you with management information reports on your business from the tax data they compile for you. Just ask! Software packages can also help. See "Software and Web sites," later in this chapter, for our recommendations.

✔ **Failing to pay family help:** If your children, spouse, or other relatives help with some aspect of your business, consider paying them for the work. Besides showing them that you value their work, this practice may reduce your family's tax liability. For example, children are usually in a lower tax bracket than you are. So by shifting some of your income to your child, you cut your tax bill.

Getting Help from Tax Resources

All sorts of ways to prepare your tax return exist. Which approach makes sense for you depends on the complexity of your situation and your knowledge of taxes.

Regardless of which approach you use, you should be making financial moves during the year to reduce your taxes. By the time you actually file your return in the following year, it's often too late for you to take advantage of many tax-reduction strategies.

Assistance from the Canada Revenue Agency

If you have a simple, straightforward tax return, filing it on your own using only the Canada Revenue Agency (CRA) instructions is fine. This approach is as cheap as you can get. The main costs are time, patience, photocopying expenses (you should always keep a copy for your files), and postage for mailing the completed tax return.

CRA publications don't have Tip or Warning icons. And the CRA has been known to give wrong information from time to time. When you call the CRA with a question, be sure to take notes about your conversation to protect yourself in the event of an audit. Date your notes and include the name and identification number of the tax employee you talked to, the questions you asked, and the employee's responses. File your notes in a folder with a copy of your completed return.

In addition to the standard instructions that come with your tax return, Canada Revenue Agency offers a number of free and helpful tax guides that you can pick up at your nearest taxation centre, or you can call to request them. These guides serve as useful references and provide more detail and insight than the basic Canada Revenue Agency publications. For the self-employed, many booklets are available depending on your occupation, including *Business and Professional Income*, *Farming Income*, *Fishing Income*, and *Rental Income*. Other guides deal with specific circumstances. To inquire about and request these documents, call 1-800-959-2221, or 905-712-5813 in the Toronto area. You can also visit the Canada Revenue Agency Web site at www.cra-arc.gc.ca.

Preparation and advice guides

Books about tax preparation and tax planning that highlight common problem areas and are written in clear, simple English are invaluable. They supplement the official instructions not only by helping you complete your return correctly but also by showing you how to save as much money as possible. Quite a few preparation guides are on the market. Our favourites are

- ✔ *Tax Planning For You and Your Family* (prepared by KPMG and published by Thomson Carswell)
- ✔ *Tax Tips For Canadians For Dummies* (please excuse our shameless self-promotion, but this book has everything you need to prepare and save on your tax return)
- ✔ *Winning the Tax Game* (written by Tim Cestnick and published by John Wiley & Sons Canada Ltd.)

Software and Web sites

If you have access to a computer, good tax-preparation software can be helpful. QuickTax and UFile are two programs that are well put together, as is TaxTron, which also has the added benefit of working with Mac computers. (Mac users can also prepare their returns online using ufile (www.ufile.ca) and QuickTax (www.intuit.ca).) If you go the software route, we highly recommend having a good tax advice book by your side.

For you Websurfers, the Canada Revenue Agency Web site (www.cra-arc.gc.ca) is among the better Internet tax sites, believe it or not. The Tax Organizations and Other Tax Sites section at www.taxes.ca is another good site with many useful links. The Certified General Accountants of Ontario Web site (www.cga-ontario.org), as well as www.taxtips.ca, are also worth visiting.

Professional hired help

Competent tax preparers and advisers can save you money — sometimes more than enough to pay their fees — by identifying tax-reduction strategies you may overlook. They can also help reduce the likelihood of an audit, which can be triggered by blunders. Mediocre and lousy tax preparers, on the other hand, may make mistakes and not be aware of sound ways to reduce your tax bill.

Tax practitioners come with varying backgrounds, training, and credentials. One credential is not necessarily better than another. The four main types are preparers, certified general accountants (CGAs), chartered accountants (CAs), and tax lawyers (tricked ya — no acronym!). The more training and specialization a tax practitioner has (and the more affluent his or her clients), the higher the hourly fee usually is. Fees and competence at all levels of the profession vary significantly. If you do hire a tax adviser and you're not sure of the quality of work performed and the soundness of the advice, try getting a second opinion.

Preparers

Preparers generally have the least amount of training of all the tax practitioners, and a greater proportion of them work part time. As with financial planners, no national regulations apply to preparers, and no licensing is required.

Preparers are appealing because they're relatively inexpensive — they can do most basic returns for around $100 or so. The drawback of using a preparer is that you may hire someone who doesn't know much more than you do.

Preparers make the most sense for folks who have relatively simple financial lives, who are budget minded, and who hate doing their own taxes. If you're not good about hanging onto receipts, or you don't want to keep your own files with background details about your taxes, you should definitely shop around for a tax preparer who's committed to the business. You may need all that stuff someday for an audit, and many tax preparers keep and organize their clients' documentation rather than return everything each year. Also, going with a firm that is open year-round may be a safer option (some small shops are open only during tax season) in case tax questions or problems arise.

Certified general accountants

CGAs are often a sound, economical choice for tax advice. Many certified general accountants have large personal income tax practices.

CGAs are best for people with moderately complex returns who don't necessarily need complicated tax-planning advice throughout the year. Many CGAs also have expertise in preparing returns for small businesses. A professional who is familiar with the peculiarities of your industry may be able to give you more complete advice on opportunities for saving and how to organize your business to minimize your tax bill. What's more, he or she will likely be able to do your return more quickly, meaning a lower bill.

CGAs don't close down when the tax season ends. That means you can go to them for advice and help on your schedule, and you'll be able to get help if you have problems after filing your return. Fees for a straightforward return should be about $100, while more complex situations (for example, a part-time business or investment income) might mean a bill for several hundred dollars.

Chartered accountants (CAs)

CAs are the folks who audit public companies. They tend to have specialties in specific industries or types of businesses. Many CAs work for large firms that have international operations in both accounting and consulting, so they have the expertise to prepare complicated returns involving investments and earnings in different countries.

CA fees vary tremendously. Most charge around $100 per hour, but CAs at large companies and in high-cost of living areas tend to charge somewhat more. The cost of having a CA prepare your return can range anywhere from $150 to several thousand dollars.

CAs are of greatest value to people completing some of the more unusual and less user-friendly schedules, or who have to file in several countries. A typical CA user might be a Canadian who, because she works a portion of the year in the United States, has to file in both countries and who has numerous tax shelters and real estate investments.

If your return is uncomplicated and your financial situation is stable, hiring a high-priced CA year after year to fill in the blanks is a waste of money. Sometimes you'll be granted an initial interview with a partner, who then has a less qualified — and lower-paid — associate carry out the work. However, the bill you receive for the associate's advice often will reflect the CA's rate.

Paying for the additional cost of a CGA or CA on an ongoing basis makes sense if you can afford it and if your situation is reasonably complex or dynamic. If you're self-employed and/or file lots of other schedules, it may be worth hiring a CGA or CA. But you needn't do so year after year. If your situation grows complex one year and then stabilizes, consider getting help for the perplexing year and then using preparation guides, software, or a lower-cost preparer in the future.

Tax lawyers

Tax lawyers deal with complicated tax problems and issues that usually have some legal angle. Unless you're a super-high-income earner with a complex financial life, hiring a tax lawyer to prepare your annual return is prohibitively expensive. In fact, many tax lawyers don't prepare returns as a normal practice.

Because of their level of specialization and training, tax lawyers tend to have the highest hourly billing rates — $200 to $300+ per hour is not unusual.

Dealing with an Audit

On a list of real-life nightmares, most people would rank tax audits right up there with root canals, rectal exams, and court appearances. Many people are traumatized by audits because they feel like they're on trial and being accused of a crime. Take a deep breath and don't panic.

You may be getting audited simply because a business that reports tax information on you, or someone at the Canada Revenue Agency, made an error regarding the data on your return. You may also work in an industry or run a type of business that the CRA has targeted in a particular year. CRA regularly focuses on certain types of employees and professions. In the vast majority of cases, the CRA conducts its audit by corresponding with you through the mail.

Audits that require you to schlep to the local CRA office are the most feared type of audit. Unfortunately, you'll most likely be one of the majority of audit survivors who end up owing more tax money. The amount of additional tax that you owe in interest and penalties hinges on how your audit goes.

Getting your act together

Preparing for an audit is sort of like preparing for a test at school. The CRA will let you know which sections of your tax return it wants to examine.

The first decision you face when you get an audit notice is whether to handle it yourself or to hire a tax adviser to represent you. Hiring representation may help you save time, stress, and money.

If you normally prepare your own return, and you're comfortable with your understanding of the areas being audited, handle the audit yourself. When the amount of tax money in question is small when compared to the fee you'd pay the tax adviser to represent you, self-representation is probably your best option. However, if you're likely to turn into a babbling, intimidated fool, and you're unsure of how to present your situation, hire a tax adviser to represent you. (See "Professional hired help," earlier in this chapter, for information about whom to hire.)

If you decide to handle the audit yourself, get your act together sooner rather than later. Don't wait until the night before to start gathering receipts and other documentation. You may need to contact others to get copies of documents you can't find.

You need to document and be ready to speak only about the areas the audit notice says are being investigated. Organize the various documents and receipts into folders. You want to make it as easy as possible for the auditor to review your materials. Don't show up, dump shopping bags full of receipts and paperwork on the auditor's desk, and say, "Here it is — you figure it out."

Whatever you do, don't ignore your audit request letter. The CRA is the ultimate bill-collection agency. And if you end up owing more money (the unhappy result of most audits), the sooner you pay, the less interest and penalties you'll owe.

Surviving the day of reckoning

Two people with identical situations can walk into an audit and come out with very different results. The loser can end up owing much more in taxes and have the audit expanded to include other parts of the return. The winner can end up owing less tax money.

Here's how to be a winner in your tax audit:

- **Treat the auditor as a human being.** This advice may be obvious, but it isn't practised by taxpayers very often. You may be resentful or angry about being audited. You may be tempted to gnash your teeth and tell the auditor how unfair it is that an honest taxpayer like you had to spend hours getting ready for this. You may feel like ranting and raving about how the government wastes too much of your tax money, or that the party in power is out to get you. Bite your tongue.

  Believe it or not, most auditors are decent people just trying to do their job. They are well aware that taxpayers don't like seeing them. Don't suck up, either — just relax and be yourself. Behave as you would around a boss you like — with respect and congeniality.

- **Stick to the knitting.** Your audit is for discussing only the sections of your tax return that are in question. The more you talk about other areas or things that you're doing, the more likely the auditor will probe into other items. Don't bring documentation for parts of your return that aren't being audited. Besides creating more work for yourself, you may be opening up a can of worms that doesn't need to be opened. Should the auditor inquire about areas that aren't covered by the audit notice, politely say that you're not prepared to discuss those other issues and that another meeting should be scheduled.

- **Don't argue when you disagree.** State your case. When the auditor wants to disallow a deduction or otherwise increase the taxes you owe, and you disagree with him, state once why you don't agree with his assessment. If the auditor won't budge, don't get into a knock-down, drag-out confrontation. He or she may not want to lose face and is inclined to find additional tax money — that's the auditor's job. Remember: When necessary, you can plead your case with several people who work above your auditor. If this method fails, and you still feel wronged, you can take your case to tax court.

- **Don't be intimidated.** Most auditors are not tax geniuses. The work is stressful — being in a job where people dislike seeing you is not easy. Turnover is quite high. They may know less about tax and financial matters than you do. The basic CRA tax boot camp that auditors go through doesn't — no, *can't* — come close to covering all the technical details and nuances in the tax code. So you may not be at such a disadvantage in your tax knowledge after all, especially if you work with a tax adviser.

Part III
Building Wealth through Investing

The 5th Wave   By Rich Tennant

Being Dracula's slave didn't pay much, but Renfield always found extra money to invest.

In this part . . .

We lay out the basics of investing and show you how to choose your investments wisely. Earning and saving are hard work, so you need to be careful where you invest the fruits of your labour. This part is where you find out the real story on such things as stocks, bonds, mutual funds, investing in RRSPs and other retirement plans, investing in non-retirement accounts, and how to invest for university or college. Canadians are big on investing in real estate, and we look at how to decide between renting and buying, purchasing a home, and navigating the mortgage maze.

Chapter 7

Important Investment Concepts

In This Chapter

▶ Determining your investment goals

▶ Major types of investments

▶ Expected investment returns and risks

▶ Understanding diversification and asset allocation

▶ The different types of investment firms

▶ Investment gurus and their prognostications

*M*aking wise investments doesn't have to be complicated. However, many investors get bogged down in the morass of the thousands of investment choices out there. This chapter helps you grasp the important "bigger picture" issues that will help you ensure that your investment plan meshes with your needs and the realities of the investment marketplace.

Establishing Your Goals

Before you select a specific investment, you should first determine your investment needs and goals. Why are you saving this pile of money? What are you going to use it for? You don't need to earmark every dollar, but you should set some major objectives. Setting objectives is important because the expected use of the money helps you determine how long it's going to be invested. And that, in turn, helps you determine which investments to choose.

The risk level of your investments should factor in your time frame *and your comfort level.* Investing in high-risk vehicles doesn't make sense if you're going to spend all your profits on stress-induced medical bills. For example, suppose you've been accumulating money for a down payment on a home you want to buy in a few years. You can't afford much investment risk with that money — you're going to need it sooner rather than later. Putting that money in the stock market, then, is probably not a wise move. As we discuss later in this chapter, the stock market can drop a lot in a year or over several consecutive years. So stocks are probably too risky a place to invest money you plan to use soon.

Perhaps you're saving toward a longer-term goal, such as retirement, that is 20 or 30 years away. In this case, you're in a position to make riskier investments, because your holdings have more time to bounce back from temporary losses or setbacks. You may want to consider investing in growth investments, such as stocks, in an RRSP that you leave alone for 20 years or longer. You can tolerate year-to-year volatility in the market — you have time on your side. If you haven't yet done so, take a tour through Chapter 2, which helps you contemplate and establish your financial goals.

Understanding the Major Investment Flavours

For most people, jumping right into picking a particular investment is the fun and exciting part of investing. Perhaps you're tired of thinking about where to invest and watching others make profits while you sit on the sidelines. You may have an idea about where you want to invest after doing some reading or watching some entertaining investment type tout investments on television or online. Or maybe Uncle Louie is whispering in your ear that he's gonna get you in on the ground floor of a great new opportunity — a real sure thing.

Looking at lending investments

For a moment, forget all the buzzwords, jargon, and product names you've heard tossed around in the investment world — in many cases, they're meant only to obscure what an investment really is and to hide the hefty fees and commissions. Imagine a world with only two investment flavours — chocolate and vanilla ice cream (or low-fat, non-dairy frozen dessert for you health-minded folks).

The investment world is really just as simple. You have only two major investment choices: You can be a lender or an owner.

You're a *lender* when you invest your money in a bank guaranteed investment certificate (GIC), a Treasury bill, or a bond issued by a company like Bombardier, for example. In each case, you lend your money to an organization — a bank, the federal government, or Bombardier. You're paid an agreed-upon rate of interest for lending your money. The organization also promises to have your original investment (the *principal*) returned to you on a specific date.

Getting paid all of the interest in addition to your original investment (as promised) is the best that can happen with a lending investment. Given that the investment landscape is littered with carcasses of failed investments, this is not a result to take for granted.

The worst that can happen with a lending investment is that you don't get everything you're promised. Promises can be broken under extenuating circumstances. When a company goes bankrupt, for example, you can lose all or part of your original investment.

Another risk associated with lending investments is that, even though you get what you were promised, the ravages of inflation may make your money worth less — it has less purchasing power than you thought it would. Back in the 1960s, for example, high-quality companies issued long-term bonds that paid approximately 4-percent interest. At the time, buying a long-term bond seemed like a good deal, because the cost of living was increasing by only 2 percent per year.

When inflation rocketed to 6 percent and higher, those 4-percent bonds didn't seem so attractive. The interest and principal didn't buy nearly the amount they did years earlier when inflation was lower. Table 7-1 shows the reduction in the purchasing power of your money at varying rates of inflation after just ten years.

Table 7-1	Reduction in Purchasing Power Due to Inflation
Inflation Rate	*Reduction in Purchasing Power after 10 Years*
6 percent	–44 percent
8 percent	–54 percent
10 porcent	–61 percent

Some conservative-minded investors make the common mistake of thinking that they are diversifying their long-term investment money by buying several bonds, some GICs, and a Treasury bill. The problem, however, is that all these investments pay a relatively low fixed rate of return that is exposed to the vagaries of inflation.

A final drawback to lending investments is that you don't share in the success of the organization to which you lend your money. If the company doubles or triples in size and profits, your principal and interest rate don't double or triple in size along with it; they stay the same. Of course, such success should ensure that you get your promised interest and principal.

Exploring ownership investments

You're an *owner* when you invest your money in an asset, such as a company or real estate, that has the ability to generate earnings or profits. Suppose you own 100 shares of Bombardier stock. With many hundreds of millions of shares of stock outstanding, Bombardier is a mighty big company — your 100 shares represent a tiny piece of it.

What do you get for your small slice of Bombardier? As a shareholder, you share in the profits of a company in the form of annual dividends and an increase (you hope) in the share price if the company grows and becomes more profitable. Of course, you receive these benefits if things are going well. If Bombardier's business declines, your shares may be worth less (or even worthless!).

Real estate is another one of our favourite financially rewarding and time-honoured ownership investments. Real estate can produce profits when it is rented out for more than the expense of owning the property or sold at a higher price than what you paid for it. We know numerous successful real estate investors who have earned excellent long-term profits.

The value of real estate depends not only on the particulars of the individual property but also on the health and performance of the local economy. When companies in the community are growing and more jobs are being produced at higher wages, real estate often does well. When local employers are laying people off and excess housing is sitting vacant because of previous over-building, rent and property values are likely to fall.

Many Canadians have also built substantial wealth through small businesses. According to *Forbes* magazine, more of the world's wealthiest individuals have built their wealth through their stake in small businesses than through any other vehicle. Small business is the engine that drives much of North America's economic growth. Although firms with fewer than 20 employees account for about one-quarter of all employees, such small firms were responsible for nearly half of all new jobs created in the past two decades.

You can participate in small business in a variety of ways. You can start your own business, buy and operate an existing business, or simply invest in promising small businesses. In the chapters ahead, we explain each of these major investment types in detail.

Shunning gambling instruments and behaviours

Although investing is often risky, it's not gambling — at least not the way we advocate investing. *Gambling* is putting your money into schemes that are sure to lose you money over time. That's not to say that everyone loses or that you lose every time you gamble. However, the deck is stacked against you. The house wins most of the time.

Horse racing tracks, gambling casinos, and lotteries are set up to pay out 50 to 60 cents on the dollar. The rest goes to profits and the administration of the system — don't forget that these are businesses. Sure, your chosen horse may win a race or two, but in the long run, you're almost guaranteed to lose about 40 to 50 percent of what you bet. Would you put your money in an "invest-ment" where your expected return was –40 percent?

Forsake futures, options, and other derivatives

Futures, options, and commodities are *derivatives,* or financial investments whose value is derived from the performance of another security such as a stock or bond.

You may have heard the radio ad for the firm Fleecem, Cheatem, and Leavem, advocating that you buy heating oil futures because the cold weather months lead to the use of more heating oil. You call the firm and are impressed by the smooth-talking vice president who spends so much time with little ol' you. His logic makes sense, and he spent a lot of time with you, so you send him a cheque for $10,000.

Buying futures isn't much different from blowing $10,000 at the craps tables in Las Vegas. Futures prices depend on short-term, highly volatile price movements. As with gambling, you occasionally win when the market moves the right way at the right time. But in the long run, you're gonna lose. In fact, you can lose it all.

Options are as risky as futures. With options, you're betting on the short-term movements of a specific security. If you have inside information (such as knowing in advance when a major corporate development is going to occur), you can get rich. But don't forget one minor detail — insider trading is illegal. You may end up in the slammer.

Honest brokers who help their clients invest in stocks, bonds, and mutual funds will tell you the truth about commodities, futures, and options. Consider the comments of a former broker who worked for Merrill Lynch and Salomon Smith Barney for 12 years: "I had one client who made money in options, futures, or commodities, but the only reason he came out ahead was because he was forced to pull money out to close on a home purchase just when he happened to be ahead. The commissions were great for me, but there's no way a customer will make money in them." Remember these words if you're tempted to gamble with futures, options, and the like.

Futures and options are not always used for speculation and gambling. Some sophisticated professional investors use them to hedge, or actually reduce the risk of, their broad investment holdings. Even the supposed professionals fail to get good results when using them in this fashion. You, the individual investor, should steer clear of futures and options.

Provincial governments pushing gambling?

The provinces have got hooked on the gambling business in a big way as a way to bring in tax revenue. Lotteries have now become a mainstream source of cash for governments. This is wrong for many reasons. It's been well documented that lotteries and casinos obtain most of their business from those least able to afford them — primarily middle and low-income earners. They end up creating an additional tax on the less economically well off and operate on the basis of false hopes.

Even worse is government support for video lottery terminals, or *VLTs*. A few premiers even tried to defend their support of VLTs by using the twisted logic that it would curtail criminal involvement in electronic gambling. In fact, experts say government-backed VLTs mean new opportunities for organized crime. In part, this is because one thing VLTs are good at is creating new gambling addicts, and add to the perception that gambling is a socially acceptable and even positive pastime.

Unfortunately, a disproportionate amount of revenues comes from the quickly emptied pockets of problem gamblers with an addiction. Broken families, depression, and even suicides have all been pointed to as direct outcomes of VLTs. Some studies suggest that they are much more efficient at minting new problem gamblers, saying that with most forms of gambling, it takes about four years to become addicted, but VLTs supercharge the downslide, and get gamblers addicted in just one year.

Government endorsement of gambling also promotes the get-rich-quick mentality. Why get an education and work hard over the years when you can solve all your financial concerns with the next ticket you buy or slot you pull? Gambling also contributes to our nationally low personal savings rate.

Finally, gambling, like alcohol and tobacco, can be addictive and destructive. In the worst cases, gambling and gambling debts can split up families and lead to divorce or even suicides and murders. Governments should not be involved in this destruction of the lives of Canadians.

It's bad enough that legalized gambling exists. It's even worse that, in the pursuit of short-term profits and a quick fix, local governments are piling into this business. Government is fostering an irresponsible attitude toward money. Ditch daytrading

Daytrading — which is the rapid buying and selling of securities online — is an equally foolish vehicle for individual investors to pursue. Placing trades via the Internet is far cheaper than the older methods of trading (such as telephoning a broker), but the more you trade, the more trading costs eat into your investment capital.

You can certainly make some profits when daytrading. However, over an extended period of time, you'll inevitably underperform the broad market averages. In those rare instances where you may do a little better than the market averages, it's rarely worth the time and personal sacrifices that you and your family and friends endure.

Understanding Investment Returns

The previous sections describe the difference between ownership and lending investments, and help you distinguish gambling and speculation from true investments. "That's all well and good," you say, "but how do I choose which type of investments to put my money into? How much can I make, and what are the risks?"

Good questions. We'll start with the returns you *might* make. We say "might" because we're looking at history, and history is a record of the past. Using history to predict the future — especially the near future — is dangerous. History may repeat itself, but not always in exactly the same fashion, and not necessarily when you expect it to.

During this past century, ownership investments such as stocks and real estate returned around 10 percent per year, handily beating lending investments such as bonds (around 5 to 7 percent) and savings accounts (roughly 3 to 4 percent) in the investment performance race. Inflation has averaged 3 percent per year.

If you already know that the stock market can be risky, you may be wondering why investing in stocks is worth the anxiety and potential losses. Why bother for a few extra percentage points per year? Well, over many years, a few extra percent per year can really magnify the growth of your money (see Table 7-2). The more years you have to invest, the greater the difference a few percent makes in your returns.

Table 7-2	The Difference a Few Percent Makes	
At This Rate of Investment Return on $10,000	*You'll Have This Much in 25 Years*	*You'll Have This Much in 40 Years*
4% (savings account)	$26,658	$48,010
5% (bond)	$33,863	$70,400
10% (stocks and real estate)	$108,347	$452,592

Investing is not a spectator sport. You can't earn good returns on stocks and real estate if you keep your money in cash on the sidelines. If you invest in growth investments such as stocks and real estate, don't chase one new investment after another trying to beat the market average returns. *The biggest value is to be in the market, not to beat it.*

Sizing Investment Risks

Many investors have a simplistic understanding of what risk means and how to apply it to their investment decisions. For example, when compared to the yo-yo motions of the stock market, a bank savings account may seem like a less risky place to put your money. Over the long term, however, the stock market usually beats the rate of inflation, while the interest rate on a savings account does not. Thus, if you're saving your money for a long-term goal like retirement, a savings account can be a "riskier" place to put your money.

Before you invest, ask yourself these three questions:

- ✔ "What am I saving and investing this money for? In other words, what's my goal?"
- ✔ "What is my timeline for this investment — when will I use this money?"
- ✔ "What is the historical volatility of the investment I'm considering, and does that suit my comfort level and timeline for this investment?"

After you answer these questions, you'll have a better understanding of *risk,* and you'll be able to match your savings goals to their most appropriate investment vehicles. In Chapter 2, we help you consider your savings goals and timeline. We address investment risk and returns in the sections that follow.

Comparing the risks of stocks and bonds

Given the relatively higher historical returns we mention for ownership investments in the previous section, some people think that they should put all of their money in stocks and real estate. So what's the catch?

Investments with a potential for higher returns carry greater risks. Risk and return go hand in hand. If you're not willing to accept more risk, you're not going to be able to achieve higher rates of return.

The risk with ownership investments is the short-term fluctuations in their value. During the last century, stocks declined, on average, by more than 10 percent (in one particular year) every five years. Drops in stock prices of more than 20 percent occurred, on average, once every ten years. Real estate prices suffer similar periodic setbacks.

As a result, in order to earn those generous long-term returns from owner-ship investments like stocks and real estate, you must be willing to tolerate volatility. You absolutely should not put all your money in the stock or real estate market. You should not invest your emergency money or money you expect to use within the next five years in such volatile investments.

The shorter the time period that you have for holding your money in an invest-ment, the less likely that growth-oriented investments like stocks will beat out lending-type investments like bonds. Table 7-3 illustrates the historical relation-ship between U.S. stock and bond returns based on number of years held.

Table 7-3	Stocks versus Bonds
Number of Years Investment Held	*Historical Likelihood of Stocks Beating Bonds*
1	60%
5	70%
10	80%
20	91%
30	99%

Some types of bonds have higher yields than others, but the risk–reward rela-tionship remains intact. A bond generally pays you a higher rate of interest when it has a

- Lower credit rating — to compensate for the higher risk of default and the higher likelihood of losing your investment

- Longer-term maturity — to compensate for the risk that you'll be unhappy with the bond's set interest rate if the market level of interest rates moves up

Focusing on the risks you can control

When asked what they want to learn about personal finance, it's not unusual for people to reply like this student of Eric's did: "I want to learn what to invest my money in now as the stock market is overvalued and interest rates are about to go up, so bonds are dicey and banks give lousy interest — HELP!"

This student recognizes the risk of price fluctuations in her investments, but she also seems to believe, like too many people, that you can predict what's going to happen. How does *she* know that the stock market is overvalued, and why hasn't the rest of the world figured it out? How does *she* know that interest rates are about to go up, and why hasn't the rest of the world figured that out, either?

When you invest in stocks and other growth-oriented investments, you must accept the volatility of these investments. Invest the money that you have earmarked for the longer term in these vehicles. Minimize the risk of these investments through diversification. Don't buy just one or two stocks; buy a number of stocks. Later in this chapter, we discuss what you need to know about diversification.

Discovering low-risk, high-return investments

Despite what professors teach in leading business and finance graduate school programs, low-risk investments that almost certainly will lead to high returns are available. We can think of at least four such investments:

- **Paying off consumer debt.** If you're paying 10-, 14-, or 18-percent interest on an outstanding credit card or other consumer loan, pay it off before investing. To get a comparable return through other investment vehicles (after the government takes its share of your profits), you'd have to start a new career as a loan shark. If, between federal and provincial taxes, you're in a 34-percent tax bracket, and you're paying 12-percent interest on consumer debt, you'd need to annually earn a whopping 18 percent on interest-earning investments pre-tax to justify not paying off the debt. Good luck!

  When your only source of funds for paying off debt is a small emergency reserve equal to a few months' living expenses, paying off your debt may involve some risk. Tap into your emergency reserves only if you have a backup source — for example, the ability to borrow from a willing family member.

- **Investing in your health.** Eat healthy, exercise, and relax.

- **Investing in friends and family.** Invest time and effort in improving your relationships with loved ones.

- **Investing in personal and career development.** Pick up a new hobby, improve your communication skills, or read widely. Take an adult education course or go back to school for a degree. Your investment should lead to greater happiness and perhaps even higher paycheques.

Diversifying Your Investments

Diversification is one of the most powerful investment concepts. It refers to saving your eggs (or investments) in different baskets.

Diversification requires you to place your money in different investments with returns that are not completely correlated. This is a fancy way of saying that when some of your investments are down in value, odds are that others are up in value.

To decrease the chances of all your investments getting clobbered at the same time, you must put your money in different types of investments, such as bonds, stocks, real estate, and small business. (We cover all these investments and more in Chapter 9.) You can further diversify your investments by investing in domestic as well as international markets.

Within a given class of investments — say, stocks — investing in different types of stocks that perform well under various economic conditions is important. For this reason, *mutual funds,* which are diversified portfolios of securities such as stocks or bonds, are a highly useful investment vehicle. When you buy into a mutual fund, your money is pooled with the money of many others and invested in a vast array of stocks or bonds.

You can look at the benefits of diversification in two ways:

- ✔ Diversification reduces the volatility in the value of your whole portfolio. In other words, your portfolio can achieve the same rate of return that a single investment can provide, with less fluctuation in value.

- ✔ Diversification allows you to obtain a higher rate of return for a given level of risk.

Keep in mind that no one, no matter whom he works for or what credentials he has, can *guarantee* returns on an investment (except for specifically guaranteed investments such as GICs). You can do good research and get lucky, but no one is free from the risk of losing money. Diversification allows you to hedge the risk of your investments. See Figures 7-1, 7-2, and 7-3 to get an idea of how diversifying can reduce your risk. (The figures in these charts use the longer historical data available in the U.S. and are adjusted for inflation.) Notice that different investments did better during different time periods. Because the future can't be predicted, diversifying your money into different investments is safer. (In the 1990s, stocks appreciated greatly, and bonds did pretty well, too, while gold and silver did poorly. In the early 2000s, stocks did poorly while bonds and precious metals did well.)

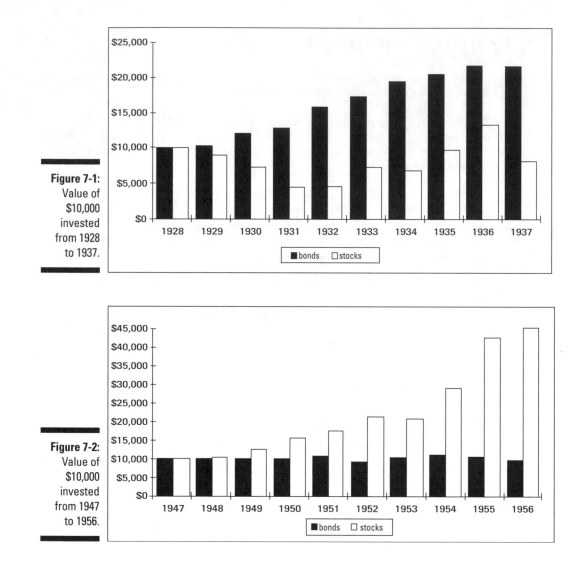

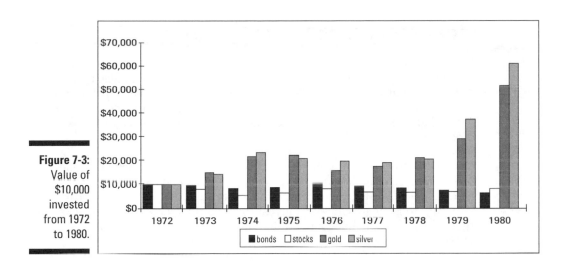

Figure 7-3:
Value of
$10,000
invested
from 1972
to 1980.

Spreading it around: Asset allocation

Asset allocation refers to how you spread your investing dollars among different investment options (stocks, bonds, high-interest savings accounts, and so on). Before you can intelligently decide how to allocate your assets, you need to ponder a number of issues, including your present financial situation, your goals and priorities, and the pros and cons of various investment options.

Although stocks and real estate offer attractive long-term returns, they can sometimes suffer significant declines. Thus, these investments are not suitable for money that you think you may want or need to use within, say, the next five years.

Money market and bond investments are good places to keep money that you expect to use soon. Everyone should have a reserve of cash — about three to six months' worth of living expenses — in a money market fund or high-interest savings account that they can access in an emergency. Shorter-term bonds or bond mutual funds can serve as a higher-yielding, secondary emergency cushion. (Refer to Chapter 2 for more on emergency reserves.)

Bonds can also be useful for some longer-term investing for diversification purposes. For example, when investing for retirement, placing a portion of your money in bonds helps buffer stock market declines. The remaining chapters in this part of the book detail your various investments options and tell you how to select those that best meet your needs.

Allocating money for the long term

Investing money for retirement is a classic long-term goal for most of us. Your current age and the number of years until you retire are the biggest factors to consider when allocating money for long-term purposes. The younger you are and the more years you have before retirement, the more comfortable you should be with growth-oriented (and more volatile) investments, such as stocks and investment real estate.

One useful guideline for dividing or allocating your money between longer-term–oriented growth investments such as stocks and more-conservative lending investments such as bonds is to subtract your age from 100 (or 120 if you want to be aggressive) and invest the resulting percentage in stocks. You then invest the remaining amount in bonds.

For example, if you're 30 years old, you invest from 70 (100 – 30) to 90 (120 – 30) percent in stocks. The portion left over — 10 to 30 percent — is invested in bonds.

Table 7-4 lists some guidelines for allocating long-term money. All you need to figure out is how old you are and the level of risk you're comfortable with.

Table 7-4	Allocating Long-Term Money	
Your Investment Attitude	*Bond Allocation (%)*	*Stock Allocation (%)*
"Play it safe"	= Age	= 100 – age
"Middle-of-the-road"	= Age – 10	= 110 – age
"Aggressive"	= Age – 20	= 120 – age

For example, if you're the conservative sort who doesn't like a lot of risk but recognizes the value of striving for some growth and making your money work harder, you're a *middle-of-the-road* type. Using Table 7-4, if you're 40 years old, you may consider putting 30 percent (40 – 10) in bonds and 70 percent (110 – 40) in stocks.

In most employer retirement plans, mutual funds are the typical investment vehicle. If your employer's retirement plan includes more than one stock mutual fund as an option, you may want to try discerning which options are best by using the criteria we outline in Chapter 10. In the event that all your retirement plan's stock fund options are good, you can simply divide your stock allocation equally among the choices.

When one or more of the choices is an international stock fund, consider allocating a percentage of your stock fund money to overseas investments: At least 20 percent for *play-it-safe* investors, 25 to 35 percent for *middle-of-the-road* investors, and as much as 35 to 50 percent for *aggressive* investors.

If the 40-year-old middle-of-the-roader from the previous example is investing 70 percent in stocks, about 25 to 35 percent of the stock fund investments (which works out to be about 18 to 24 percent of the total) can be invested in international stock funds.

Historically, most employees haven't had to make their own investing decisions with retirement money. Pension plans, in which the company directs the investments, were more common in previous years. It's interesting to note that in a typical pension plan, companies choose to allocate the majority of money to stocks (about 60 percent), with a bit less placed in bonds (about 35 percent) and other investments. For more information on investing in retirement plans, see Chapter 11.

Sticking with your allocations: Don't trade

The allocation of your investment dollars should be driven by your goals and desire to take risk. As you get older, gradually scaling back on the riskiness (and therefore growth potential) of your portfolio generally makes sense.

Don't tinker with your portfolio daily, weekly, monthly, or even annually. (Consider reviewing your portfolio annually in case major price changes in an investment or two have thrown your allocation out of whack. Otherwise, every three to five years or so, you may want to rebalance your holdings to get your mix to a desired asset allocation, as discussed in the previous section.) You should not engage in trading with the hopes of buying into a hot investment and selling your losers. Jumping onto a "winner" and dumping a "loser" may provide some short-term psychological comfort, but in the long term such an investment strategy can produce below-average returns.

When an investment gets front-page coverage and everyone is talking about its stunning rise, it's definitely time to take a reality check. The higher the value of an investment rises, the greater the danger that it's overpriced. Its next move may be downward. Don't follow the herd.

During the late 1990s, many technology stocks (especially Internet-related companies) had spectacular rises, thus attracting a lot of attention. Just because the economy was increasingly becoming technology-based, it didn't mean that any price you pay for a technology stock is fine. Some investors who neglected to do basic research and bought into the attention-grabbing, high-flying technology stocks lost 80 percent or more of their investments in early 2000 and 2001 — ouch!

Conversely, when things look bleak, giving up hope is easy — who wants to be associated with a loser? However, investors who panic and sell after major declines miss out on tremendous buying opportunities.

Many people like buying everything from clothing to cars to ketchup on sale — yet whenever the stock market has a clearance sale, most investors stampede for the exits instead of snatching up great buys. Demonstrate your courage; don't follow the herd. After all, lemmings die because they follow the herd. (By the way, how is it that lemmings aren't extinct?)

Investing lump sums using dollar-cost averaging

When you have a large chunk of cash to invest — whether you received it from an accumulation of funds over the years, an inheritance, or a recent windfall from work you've done — you may have a problem deciding what to do with it. Many people, of course, would like to have your problem. (You're not complaining, right?) You want to invest your money, but you're a bit skittish, if not outright terrified, at the prospect of investing the lump of money all at once.

If the money is residing in a savings or money market account, you may feel like it's wasting away. You want to put it to work! Our first words of advice are "Don't rush." Nothing is wrong with earning a small return in a safe investment. (See Chapter 12 for our recommendations of the best money market funds and high-interest savings accounts.) Remember that a money market fund or high-interest savings account beats the heck out of rushing into an investment in which you may lose 20 percent or more. We know people who suddenly whip themselves into a state of near panic. Typically, these folks have GICs coming due, and they feel that they must decide exactly where they want to invest the money in the 48 hours before the GIC matures.

 Take a deeeep breath. You have absolutely no reason to rush into an important decision. Tell your friendly banker that, when the GIC matures, you want to put the proceeds into the bank's highest-yielding savings or money market account. That way, your money continues to earn interest while you buy yourself some breathing room.

One approach to investing is called dollar-cost averaging (DCA). With DCA, you invest your money in equal chunks on a regular basis — such as once a month — into a diversified group of investments.

For example, if you have $60,000 to invest, you can invest $2,500 per month until it's all invested, which takes a couple of years. The money that's awaiting future investment isn't lying fallow. You keep it in a money market account so that it can earn a bit of interest while waiting its turn.

The attraction of DCA is that it allows you to ease into riskier investments instead of jumping in all at once. If the price of the investment drops after some of your initial purchases, your plan means you'll buy some later at lower prices. If you dump all your money into the "sure win" investment all at once, and then it drops like a stone, you'll be kicking yourself for not waiting. (The flip side of DCA is that, when your investment of choice appreciates in value, you may wish that you had invested your money faster.)

One appealing benefit of DCA is that if you commit to invest a set sum at regular intervals, you end up buying more units of a fund (or shares in a company) when prices are lower. Say you invest $1,000 each month and a fund's units are selling for $100; at that price you'll get 10 units. If the next month the price has fallen to $90.90, your $1,000 will buy you 11 units. Conversely, if the price has risen, you'll get fewer units for your $1,000. Over time, this means your average price will be less than the simple average price of the units over the same period.

One potentially big drawback of DCA is that you may get cold feet as you continue to pour money into an investment that's dropping in value. Many people who are attracted to DCA because they fear that they may buy before a price drop end up jumping out what feels like a sinking ship. A bigger criticism of DCA is that it goes against the basic premise of investing in the stock market — that over the long term, the market tends to rise. Dollar-cast averaging means that it will be some time before you have all your money invested and working for you, and if the market is moving up, that means lower returns than if you had simply invested a lump sum in the first place. One study that compared making a lump-sum investment to spreading your purchases out using dollar-cost averaging found that for almost all different historical periods, the lump-sum approach offered better returns.

Remember, the stock market is for your long-term money, and if the long-term trend of the market is up, then there's an argument to be made that you should invest with that in mind. Don't DCA, as that is simply a strategy for mitigating some of the market's short-term volatility.

DCA can also cause headaches with your taxes when the time comes to sell investments held outside retirement plans. When you buy an investment at many different times and prices, the accounting becomes muddied as you sell blocks of the investment.

DCA is most valuable when the money you want to invest represents a large portion of your total assets and you can stick to a schedule. Make DCA automatic so that you're less likely to chicken out should the investment fall after your initial purchases.

Keeping your investing wits during uncertain times

During times like the early 2000s, some investors abandon the stock market for good. That's why the rebound from a severe bear market — and the down-cycle that began in 2000 was the worst in magnitude and duration in decades — takes time to develop. While some people who have been burned badly learn that they're not cut out for stock investing, the rest of us should reassess our investing approaches and adjust our practices and expectations.

In the early 2000s, the stock market began falling — with some growth stocks, especially technology stocks, plunging like stocks do in a depression. Layoffs mounted, and the events of September 11, 2001 undermined consumer confidence. Then the general public learned that some major companies — Enron, WorldCom, and Global Crossing — pulled the wool over investors' eyes with shady accounting techniques that artificially inflated earnings. Here at home, we had our own share of sketchy stock market promoters, including over-hyped dot.coms like Book4Golf and bid.com. And many conservative investors who felt safe owning the all-but universally approved-of Nortel saw their portfolios get sideswiped as it became clear the company had offered a far more rosy picture of its finances then reality would have suggested, and the stock price fell from well over $100 to less than $1.00. Concern about further terrorist attacks, the fallout from SARS, the war with Iraq, and scandals within the Liberal party hung like dark storm clouds on the horizon, and often overhead.

We see many similarities between the early 2000s and the early 1970s, when a multitude of problems (that could not have been predicted) unfolded. The early seventies saw record trade and budget deficits, inflation was rearing its ugly head, and we had the invasion of Cambodia, the Arab oil embargo, gas lines, and the FLQ crisis.

Then news of Watergate broke, and then–U.S. president Richard Nixon's impeachment hearings began. After flirting with the 1,000 level since 1966, the Dow Jones Industrial Average plunged below 600 after Nixon resigned in 1974 — a 45-percent drop. Here at home the TSE also plummeted, falling 38 percent. Many investors soured on stocks and swore off the market forever. That reaction was unfortunate, because even with the recent, severe stock market decline, stocks are still some 15-fold higher today than they were back in 1974.

Don't let a string of negative events sour you on stock investing. History has repeatedly proven that continuing to buy stocks during down markets increases your long-term returns. Throwing in the towel is the worst thing you can do in a slumping market. And don't waste your time trying to find a way to beat the system. Buy and hold a diversified portfolio of stocks. Remember that the financial markets reward investors for accepting risk and uncertainty.

Acknowledging Differences among Investment Firms

Thousands of firms sell investments and manage money. Banks, mutual fund companies, securities brokerage firms, and even insurance companies all vie for your hard-earned dough.

Just to make matters more complicated, each industry plays in the others' backyards. You can find mutual fund companies that offer securities brokerage, insurance firms that are in the mutual fund business, and mutual fund companies that offer bank-like accounts and services. You benefit somewhat from all this competition and one-stop-shopping convenience. On the other hand, some firms are novices at particular businesses, and they count on the fact that many people shop by brand-name recognition.

Focusing on the best firms

Make sure that you do business with a firm that

- ✔ **Offers the best value investments in comparison to their competitors.** Value is the combination of performance and cost. Given the level of risk that you're comfortable with, you want investments that offer higher rates of return, but you don't want to have to pay a small fortune for them. Commissions, management fees, maintenance fees, and other charges can turn a high-performance investment into a mediocre or poor one.

- ✔ **Employs representatives who do not have an inherent self-interest in steering you into a particular type of investment.** This criterion has nothing to do with whether an investment firm hires polite, well-educated, or well-dressed people. The most important factor is the way the company compensates its employees. If the investment firm's personnel are paid on commission, it can be a challenge for employees not to focus on their compensation. Give preference to investing firms that don't tempt their employees to push one investment over another in order to generate more fees.

No-load (commission-free) mutual fund companies

Mutual funds are an ideal investment vehicle for most investors. *No-load mutual fund companies* are firms through which you can invest in mutual funds without paying sales commissions. In other words, every dollar you invest goes to work in the mutual funds you choose — nothing is siphoned off to pay sales commissions. See Chapter 10 for details on investing in mutual funds.

Discount brokers

In one of the most beneficial changes for investors in this century, the Securities and Exchange Commission (SEC) deregulated the U.S. retail brokerage industry on May 1, 1975. In 1983, the Toronto and Montreal stock exchanges followed suit. Prior to this date, investors were charged fixed commissions when they bought or sold stocks, bonds, and other securities. In other words, no matter which brokerage firm an investor did business with, the cost of the firm's services was set (and the level of commissions was high). After the deregulation, brokerage firms could then charge people whatever their little hearts desired.

Competition inevitably resulted in more and better choices. Many new brokerage firms (that did not do business the old way) opened. They were dubbed *discount brokers* because the fees they charged customers were substantially lower than what brokers charged under the old fixed-fee system.

Even more important than saving customers money, discount brokers established a vastly improved compensation system that greatly reduced conflicts of interest. Discount brokers generally pay the salaries of their brokers. The term *discount broker* is actually not an enlightening one. It's certainly true that this new breed of brokerage firm saves you lots of money when you invest. You can easily save 50 to 80 percent through the major discount brokers. But these firms' investments are not "on sale" or "second-rate." Discount brokers are simply brokers without major conflicts of interest. Of course, like any other for-profit enterprise, they're in business to make money, but they're much less likely to steer you wrong for their own benefit.

Be careful of discount brokers selling load mutual funds. (We discuss the reasons why you should shun these brokers in Chapter 10.)

Places to consider avoiding

The worst places to invest are those that charge you a lot, have mediocre- or poor-performing investments, and have major conflicts of interest. The prime conflict of interest arises when investment firms pay their brokers commissions on the basis of what and how much they sell. The result: The investment firms sell lots of stuff that pays fat commissions, and they *churn,* or cause a rapid turnover of, your account. (Because each transaction has a fee, the more you buy and sell, the more money they make.)

Some folks who call themselves *financial planners* or *financial consultants* work on commission. In addition to working at the bigger brokerage firms, many of them belong to so-called *broker–dealer networks,* which provide back-office support and investment products to sell. When a person claiming to be a financial planner or adviser is part of a broker–dealer network, odds are quite high that you're dealing with an investment salesperson. See Chapter 18 for more background on the financial planning industry and questions to ask an adviser you're thinking about hiring.

Commissions and their impact on human behaviour

Investment products bring in widely varying commissions. The products that bring in the highest commissions tend to be the ones that money-hungry brokers push the hardest.

Table 7-5 lists the commissions that you pay and that come out of your investment dollars when you work with brokers, financial consultants, and financial planners who work on commission.

Table 7-5	Investment Sales Commissions	
Investment Type	**Average Commission on $20,000 Investment**	**Average Commission on $100,000 Investment**
Annuities	$1,400	$7,000
Initial public offerings (new stock issue)	$1,000	$5,000
Limited partnerships	$1,800	$9,000
Load mutual funds	$1,000	$5,000
Options and futures	$2,000+	$10,000+

Besides the fact that you can never be sure you're getting an unbiased recommendation from a salesperson working on commission, you may be wasting money unnecessarily. All good investments can be bought on a *no-load* (commission-free) basis. No-load mutual funds are a good example of an investment that can be purchased without paying a commission. Many discount brokers will also sell you load funds without a commission, charging only a relatively small transaction fee.

When you're unsure about an investment product that's being pitched to you (and even when you *are* sure), ask for a copy of the prospectus. In the first few pages, check out whether the investment includes a commission (also known as a *load*). While salespeople can hide behind obscure titles such as vice president or financial consultant, a prospectus must detail whether the investment carries a commission.

Investment salespeople's conflicts of interest

Financial consultants (sometimes known as stockbrokers), financial planners, and others who sell investment products can have enormous conflicts of interest when recommending strategies and specific investment products. Commissions and other financial incentives can't help but skew the advice of even the most earnest and otherwise well-intentioned salespeople.

What to do when you're fleeced by a broker

You can't sue a broker just because you lose money on that person's investment recommendations. However, if you have been the victim of one of the following cardinal financial sins, you may have some legal recourse:

- **Misrepresentation and omission.** If you were told, for example, that a particular investment guarantees returns of 15 percent per year, and then the investment ends up plunging in value by 50 percent, you were misled. Misrepresentation can also be charged if you're sold an investment with hefty commissions after you were originally told that it was commission-free.

- **Unsuitable investments.** Retirees who need access to their capital are often advised to invest in limited partnerships (or LPs, discussed in Chapter 9) for safe, high yields. The yields on most LPs end up being anything but safe. LP investors have also discovered how *illiquid* (or not readily converted into cash) their investments are — some can't be liquidated for up to ten years or more.

- **Churning.** If your broker or financial planner is constantly trading your investments, odds are that his or her weekly commission cheque is benefiting at your expense.

- **Rogue-elephant salespeople.** When your planner or broker buys or sells without your approval or ignores your request to make a change, you may be able to collect for losses caused by these actions.

Two major types of practitioners — securities lawyers and arbitration consultants — stand ready to help you recover your lost money. You can find securities lawyers by looking "in the Yellow Pages or calling your local bar association for referrals. If your claim is for $100,000 or less, the Investment Dealers Association offers an arbitration service. You can find out more by calling their complaints line (1-877-442-4322) or by visiting their Web site at www.ida.ca and looking under "Investor" information.

Most lawyers and consultants will ask for a fee to be paid upfront — called a retainer — of anywhere from a few hundred to several thousand dollars as an advance to cover their time and expenses. You generally don't end up in a John Grisham—style courtroom scene. You'll probably go to *arbitration* — an agreement you made (probably without realizing it) when you set up an account to work with the broker or planner. Arbitration is usually much quicker, cheaper, and easier than going to court. You can even choose to represent yourself. Both sides present their case to a panel of three arbitrators. The arbitrators then make a decision that neither side can squabble over or appeal.

If you decide to prepare for arbitration by yourself, the non-profit American Arbitration Association can send you a package of background materials. Contact the association's headquarters (335 Madison Avenue, 10th Floor, New York, NY 10017-4605; phone 800-778-7879; Web site www.adr.org). While there are similar Canadian organizations, they are largely professional development bodies.

Numerous conflicts of interest can damage your investment portfolio. The following are the most common conflicts to watch out for:

- **Pushing higher-commission products.** As we discuss earlier in this chapter, commissions on investment products vary tremendously. Products like limited partnerships, commodities, options, and futures are at the worst end of the spectrum for you (and the best end of the spectrum for a salesperson). Investments such as no-load mutual funds and Treasury bills that are 100-percent commission-free are at the best end of the spectrum for you (and, therefore, the worst end of the spectrum for a salesperson).

- **Recommending active trading.** Investment salespeople often advise you to trade frequently into and out of different securities. They usually base their advice on current news events or an analyst's comments on the security. Sometimes these moves are valid, but more often they're not. In extreme cases, brokers trade on a monthly basis. By the end of the year, they've churned through your entire portfolio. Needless to say, all these transactions cost you big money in trading fees.

  Diversified mutual funds (discussed in Chapter 10) make more sense for most people. You can invest in mutual funds free of sales commissions. Besides saving money on commissions, you earn better long-term returns by having an expert money manager work for you.

- **Failing to recommend investing through a company retirement plan.** An investment salesperson is not likely to recommend that you contribute to your employer's retirement plan. Such contributions cut into the money you have available to invest with your friendly salesperson.

- **Pushing high-fee products.** Many of the brokerage firms that used to sell investment products only on commission moved into fee-based investment management. This change is an improvement for investors because it reduces some of the conflicts of interest caused by commissions.

  On the other hand, these brokers often charge extraordinarily high fees (which are usually quoted as a percentage of assets under management) on their managed investment (or wrap) accounts. For more on wrap accounts, see the "Wrap (or managed) accounts" sidebar.

Valuing brokerage research

Brokerage firms and the brokers who work for them frequently argue that their research is better. With their insights and recommendations, they say, you'll do better and "beat the market averages."

Brokerage firm analysts are often overly optimistic when it comes to predicting corporate profits. If analysts were simply inaccurate or bad estimators,

Wrap (or managed) accounts

Wrap accounts (which are also referred to as managed accounts) are all the rage among commission-based brokerage firms. These accounts go by a variety of names, but they are all similar in that they charge a fixed percentage of the assets under management to invest your money through money managers.

Wrap accounts can be poor investments because their management expenses may be extraordinarily high — up to 3 percent per year (some even higher) of assets under management. Remember that, in the long haul, stocks can return about 10 percent per year before taxes. So if you're paying 3 percent per year to have your money managed in stocks, 30 percent of your return (before taxes) is siphoned off. But don't forget — because the government sure won't — that you pay a good chunk of money in taxes on your 10-percent return as well. So the 3-percent wrap actually ends up depleting 40 to 50 percent of your after-tax profits!

The best no-load (commission-free) mutual funds offer investors access to the nation's best investment managers for a fraction of the cost of wrap accounts. You can invest in dozens of top-performing funds for an annual expense of 2 percent per year or less. Some of the best fund companies offer excellent funds for a cost as low as 0.5 to 1.5 percent (see Chapter 10).

You may be told, in the marketing of wrap accounts, that you're getting access to investment managers who don't normally take money from small-fry investors like you. Not a single study shows that the performance of money managers has anything to do with the minimum account they handle. Besides, no-load mutual funds hire many of the same managers who work at other money management firms.

You also may be told that you'll earn a higher rate of return, so the extra cost is worth it. "You could have earned 18 to 25 percent per year," they say, "had you invested with the 'Star of Yesterday' investment management company." The key word here is "had." History is history. Many of yesterday's winners become tomorrow's losers or mediocre performers.

You also need to remember that wrap account performance records may include marketing hype. Showing only the performance of selected accounts — those that performed the best — is the most common ploy.

you'd expect that they'd sometimes underestimate and, at other times, overestimate companies' earnings. The discrepancy identifies yet another conflict of interest among many of the brokerage firms.

Brokerage firm analysts are reluctant to write a negative report about a company, because the firms these analysts work for also solicit companies to issue new shares to the public. What better way to display your potential for selling shares at a high price to the public than by showing how much you believe in certain companies and writing glowing reports about their future prospects?

Brokerage analysts have great difficulty being objective. *Investment banking* (the business of helping companies sell new securities) can't objectively be done by companies supposedly evaluating and rating the same securities for the investing public.

Experts Who Predict the Future

Believing that you can increase your investment returns by following the prognostications of certain gurus is a common mistake that some investors make. Many of us may want to believe that some experts can predict the future of the investment world. Believing in gurus makes it easier to accept the risk you know you're taking when trying to make your money grow. The sage predictions that you read in an investment newsletter or hear from an "expert" who is repeatedly quoted in financial publications make you feel protected — sort of like Linus and his security blanket.

Investment newsletter subscribers and guru followers would be better off buying a warm blanket instead — it has a lot more value and costs a whole lot less! No one can predict the future. If they could, they would be so busy investing their own money and getting rich that they wouldn't have the time and desire to share their secrets with you.

Investment newsletters

Many investment newsletters purport to time the markets, telling you exactly the right time to get into and out of certain stocks or mutual funds (or the financial markets in general). Such an approach is doomed to failure in the long run. By failure, we mean that this approach is not going to beat the tried-and-true strategy of buy and hold.

We see people paying hundreds of dollars annually to subscribe to all sorts of market-timing and stock-picking newsletters. One person we know, a lawyer, subscribed to several newsletters. When asked why, he said that their marketing materials claimed that if you followed their advice, you would make a 20-percent per year return on your money. But in the four years that Ken had followed their advice, he actually *lost* money, despite appreciating financial markets overall.

Before you ever consider subscribing to any investment newsletter, examine its historical track record. The newsletter's marketing materials typically hype the supposed returns that the publication's recommendations have produced. Sadly, newsletters seem to be able to make lots of bogus claims without suffering the timely wrath of securities regulators.

Don't get predictive advice from newsletters. If newsletter writers were so smart about the future of financial markets, they'd be making lots more money as money managers. The only types of investment newsletters and periodicals that you should consider subscribing to are those that offer research and information rather than predictions. We discuss the investment newsletters that fit the bill in the subsequent investment chapters.

Investment gurus

Investment gurus come and go. Some of them get their 15 minutes of fame on the basis of one or two successful predictions that someone in the press remembers (and makes famous). A classic example is a former market analyst at Shearson named Elaine Garzarelli.

Ms. Garzarelli became famous for predicting the stock market's plummet in the fall of 1987. Garzarelli's fund, Smith Barney Shearson Sector Analysis, was established just before the crash. Supposedly, Garzarelli's indicators warned her to stay out of stocks, which she did, and in doing so, she saved her fund from the plunge.

Shearson, being a money-minded brokerage, quickly motivated its brokers to sell shares in Garzarelli's fund. In addition to her having avoided the crash, it didn't hurt that Shearson brokers were being rewarded with a hefty 5-percent sales commission for selling her fund. By the end of 1987, investors had poured nearly $700 million into this fund.

In 1988, Garzarelli's fund was the worst-performing fund among funds investing in growth stocks. From 1988 to 1990, Garzarelli's fund underperformed the Standard & Poor 500 average by about 43 percent! In 1987 — the year of the crash — Garzarelli outperformed the S&P 500 by about 26 percent. So the amount she saved her investors by avoiding the crash was lost — along with more — in the years that followed. In fact, Garzarelli's performance was so dismal in the years following the crash that Shearson eventually fired her.

Despite her poor long-term track record, Garzarelli is still quoted as a market soothsayer. She now manages money privately and hawks investment newsletters. The following marketing hype, promoting her newsletter, recently appeared in a mailed brochure entitled "The Garzarelli Edge."

> "The proven, scientific system that has produced compounded yearly gains of 20.2% since 1982!"

> "Elaine Garzarelli has called every major turn in the Dow since 1982."

Now, if these comments were true, why did Garzarelli's investment fund perform so poorly, and why did Shearson fire her in the mid-1990s following numerous years of inaccurate predictions and the dismal performance of her mutual fund? We also find it humorous that the 20.2-percent return was reportedly "audited by a Big-6 accounting firm." Down in the fine print, however, it said, "Audit Pending" — probably with the same folks who audited Enron's financials (and went under)!

Every year, new gurus emerge. All it seems to take to leap into guru status these days is one right call or one good stock pick. In the mid- to late 1990s, for example, prognosticators who recommended one of the high-flying technology stocks were nearly vaulted to instant guru status as the stocks continued climbing.

Pundits who pitched investing in companies like Presstek and Iomega attracted fairly large followings as these stocks seemed to defy gravity and rational valuations while they rocketed ever skyward. Like Ms. Garzarelli, however, these stocks and their promoters were brought back to reality during the late 1990s when the stocks plummeted by more than 65 percent.

And, like other high-flying stocks and the pundits made famous by them, many investors weren't attracted to invest in Presstek and Iomega until nearly everybody was talking about them. By then, those stocks were peaking, and investors who bought them got clobbered.

Herb Greenberg, a former business writer for the *San Francisco Chronicle*, held a stock market contest. The contest was won by a group of 13-year-olds, because they put most of their money into Iomega while it was still heading up. Does this mean that these 13-year-olds are investing geniuses to whom we should look for guidance on the next hot stock? Of course not. Treat other pundits who happened to guess right the same way.

Commentators and experts who publish predictive newsletters and are interviewed in the media can't predict the future. Ignore the predictions and speculations of self-proclaimed gurus and investment soothsayers. The few people who have a slight leg up on everyone else aren't going to share their investment secrets — they're too busy investing their own money! If you have to believe in something to offset your fears, believe in good information and proven investment managers. And don't forget the value of optimism, faith, and hope — regardless of *what* or *whom* you believe in!

Leaving You with Some Final Advice

We cover a lot of ground in this chapter. In the remaining chapters in this part, we detail different investment choices and accounts, and how to build a champion portfolio. Before you move on, here are several other issues to keep in mind as you make important investing choices:

✔ **Don't invest based on sales solicitations.** Companies that advertise and solicit prospective customers aggressively with tactics such as telemarketing offer some of the worst financial products with the highest fees. Companies with great products don't have to reach their potential customers this way. Of course, all companies have to do some promotion. But the companies with the best investment offerings don't have to use the hard-sell approach; they get plenty of new business through the word-of-mouth recommendations of satisfied customers.

✔ **Don't invest in what you don't understand.** The mistake of not understanding the investments you purchase usually follows from the preceding no-no — buying into a sales pitch. When you don't understand an investment, odds are good that it won't be right for you. Slick-tongued brokers (who may call themselves financial consultants, advisers, or planners) who earn commissions based on what they sell can talk you into inappropriate investments. Before you invest in anything, you should know its track record, its true costs, and how easy it is to sell — also known as *liquidity*.

✔ **Minimize fees.** Avoid investments that carry high sales commissions and management expenses (usually disclosed in a prospectus). Virtually all investments today can be purchased without a salesperson. Besides paying unnecessary commissions, the bigger danger in investing through a salesperson is that you may be directed to a path that's not in your best interests. Management fees create a real drag on investment returns. Not surprisingly, higher-fee investments, on average, perform worse than alternatives with lower fees. High ongoing management fees often go toward lavish offices, glossy brochures, and skyscraper salaries, or toward propping up small, inefficient operations. Do you want your hard-earned dollars to support either of these types of businesses?

✔ **Pay attention to tax consequences.** Even if you never become an investment expert, you're smart enough to know that the more money you pay in taxes, the less you have for investing and playing with. See Chapter 11 for how tax-favoured retirement plans can help boost your investment returns. For investments outside registered retirement plans, you need to match the types of investments to your tax situation (see Chapter 12).

Chapter 8

Choosing Your Investment Vehicles

. . . .

In This Chapter

▶ Playing-it-"safe" investments: Bank and money market accounts and bonds

▶ Considering growth investments: Stocks, real estate, and small business

▶ Examining oddball investments: Precious metals, annuities, collectibles, and life insurance

. . . .

*I*n the investment world, you can place your money in many different types of investment vehicles. Decent investment vehicles work their way methodically around the racetrack, rarely deterred but also never at a fast rate. The best investment vehicles make their way through the course at a rapid clip, only occasionally slowed by a bump or detour. The worst investment vehicles sputter in fits and starts, and sometimes crash and burn in a flaming heap.

Which vehicle you choose for your investment journey depends on where you're going, how fast you want to get there, and what risks you're willing to take along the way. If you haven't yet read Chapter 8, please do so now. In it, we cover a number of investment concepts, such as the difference between lending and ownership investments, which will enhance your ability to choose among the common investment vehicles we discuss in this chapter.

Slow and Steady Investments

Everyone should have some money riding in stable, safe investment vehicles. For example, money that you have earmarked for your short-term bills, both expected and unexpected, should have two seatbelts on in the back seat of a Volvo family sedan. Likewise, if you're saving money for a home purchase within the next few years, you certainly don't want to risk that money on the roller coaster of the stock market.

The investment vehicles that follow are appropriate for money you don't want to put at great risk.

Transaction/chequing accounts

Transaction/chequing accounts are best used for depositing your monthly income and paying for your expenditures. If you want to have unlimited cheque-writing privileges and access to your money with an ABM card, chequing accounts at local banks are often your best bet. Make sure that you shop around for accounts that don't ding you $1 here for the use of an ABM, and $10 there for a low balance.

With interest rates as low as they are now, you want to focus on avoiding monthly service charges rather than chasing after a chequing account with a slightly higher interest rate.

If you don't need the convenience of an ABM on every other street corner — an option usually available through larger banks — you can generally get a better chequing account deal at a credit union or an alternative financial institution such as President's Choice Financial. Because you can easily obtain cash through ABM outlets, you may not need to do business with the Big City Bank that has branch offices at every intersection.

In any event, you should keep only enough money in the account for your monthly bill payment needs. If you consistently keep more than a few thousand dollars in a chequing account, get the excess out. You can earn more in a savings or money market account, which we describe in the following section.

Savings and money market accounts

Savings accounts are available at banks and a number of other institutions such as President's Choice Financial and ING Direct; money market funds are available through mutual fund companies. The major difference is that money market funds and the high-interest accounts offered by President's Choice Financial, ING Direct, and others generally pay a much better rate of interest. The interest rate paid to you, also known as the *yield,* fluctuates over time depending on the level of interest rates in the overall economy. In addition, the high-interest accounts typically have no transaction fees.

Most bank accounts are backed by the Canada Deposit Insurance Corporation (CDIC). We wouldn't suggest you give preference to a bank account just because your investment (your *principal*) is insured, and because of the psychological comfort some people derive from seeing branches of their bank on every second street corner.

The high-interest accounts offered by ING Direct and President's Choice Financial are also covered by CDIC insurance. Your money is just as safe as it is with a traditional bank, as long as you don't have more on deposit than the maximum insured by CDIC. And the lack of bricks-and-mortar outlets shouldn't bother you. In fact, not having the extra expenses of branches and tellers to serve you is a major reason why these companies can pay such high interest rates on your savings. You can reach President's Choice Financial by calling 1-888-8724-724 or on the Web at www.pcfinancial.com. ING Direct can be reached at 1-888-464-3232 or on the Web at www.ingdirect.ca.

For an easy way to find the lowest-cost way to do your banking, look in the consumer information section of Industry Canada's Web site at www.strategis. gc.ca for the Financial Services Charges Calculator. (The site also has an excellent credit card costs calculator.) This helpful online tool lets you compare what it will cost to bank with various financial institutions. It can even give you a precise total cost for the type of banking you do. Enter the number of different transactions you do a month — ABM withdrawals, debit card payments, deposits, automatic bill payments, and so forth — then tell the calculator which financial institution(s) you are interested in, and it estimates your monthly fees.

While money market funds are not covered by CDIC insurance they *are* regulated, and dozens of money market funds invest billions of dollars of individuals' and institutions' money. We haven't heard of the industry causing an individual to lose even a penny of principal. The risk difference versus a bank account is nil. General-purpose money market funds invest in safe, short-term bank guaranteed investment certificates (GICs), Government of Canada Treasury bills, provincial treasury bills, and corporate commercial paper (short-term debt), which is issued by the largest and most creditworthy companies. Money market fund investments generally must have an average maturity of less than 180 days. In the unlikely event that an investment in a money market fund's portfolio goes sour, the mutual fund company that stands behind the money market fund would almost certainly cover the loss.

If the lack of insurance on money market funds still spooks you, here's a way to get the best of both worlds: Select a money market fund that invests exclusively in Canadian government securities, which are virtually risk-free because they are backed by the full strength and credit of the federal government. These types of accounts typically pay around a quarter-percent less interest than other money market funds.

Bonds

When you invest in a bond, you effectively lend your money to an organization. When a bond is issued, it includes a specified maturity date at which time the principal will be repaid. Bonds are also issued at a particular interest rate, or what's known as a *coupon*. This rate is fixed on most bonds. So if, for example, you buy a five-year, 6-percent bond issued by Bombardier, you're lending your money to Bombardier for five years at an interest rate of 6 percent per year. Bond interest is usually paid in two equal, semi-annual instalments.

The overused guaranteed investment certificate (GIC)

A guaranteed investment certificate (GIC) is another type of bond that is issued by a bank. With a GIC, as with a real bond, you agree to lend your money to an organization (in this case, a bank) for a predetermined number of months or years. Generally, the longer you agree to lock up your money, the higher the interest rate you receive.

With most GICs, you pay a penalty for early withdrawal. If you want your money back before the end of the GIC's term, you'll get whacked with the loss of a number of months' worth of interest. Some GICs don't let you cash out early, period. Others may offer you the option of getting your money back before the GIC matures, but at the cost of a lower interest rate. Also, GICs generally don't tend to pay very competitive interest rates. You can usually beat the interest rate on shorter-term GICs (those that mature within a year or so) with the best money market mutual funds, which also give you access to your money without any penalty.

The value of a bond generally fluctuates with changes in interest rates. For example, if you're holding a bond issued at 5 percent, and rates increase to 7 percent on comparable, newly issued bonds, your bond decreases in value. (Why would anyone want to buy your bond at the price you paid if it yields just 5 percent, and 7 percent can be obtained elsewhere?)

Some bonds are tied to variable interest rates. For example, you can buy bonds that are adjustable-rate mortgages, on which the interest rate can fluctuate. As an investor, you're actually lending your money to a mortgage borrower — indirectly, you're the banker making a loan to someone buying a home.

Bonds differ from one another in the following major ways:

- ✔ **The type of institution to which you are lending your money:** There are bonds available from a wide range of sources, including the federal and provincial governments, mortgage holders, as well as corporations.

- ✔ **The credit quality of the borrower to whom you lend your money:** This refers to the probability that the borrower will pay you the interest and return your principal as agreed.

- ✔ **The length of maturity of the bond:** Bonds generally mature within 30 years. Short-term bonds mature within a few years, intermediate bonds within 7 to 10 years, and long-term bonds within 30 years. Longer-term bonds generally pay higher yields but fluctuate more with changes in interest rates.

Bonds are rated by major credit-rating agencies for their safety, usually on a scale where AAA is the highest possible rating. For example, high-grade corporate bonds (AAA or AA) are considered the safest (that is, most likely to pay you back). Next in safety are general bonds (A or BBB), which are still safe but just a little less so. Junk bonds (rated BB or lower), popularized by Michael Milken, are actually not all that junky; they're just lower in quality and have a slight (1 or 2 percent) probability of default.

Some bonds are *callable,* which means that the lender can decide to pay you back earlier than the previously agreed-upon date. This event usually occurs when interest rates fall and the lender wants to issue new bonds with a lower interest rate to replace the higher-rate bonds. To compensate you for early repayment, the lender typically gives you a small premium or bonus over what the bond is really worth.

Building Wealth with Ownership Vehicles

The three best legal ways to build wealth are to invest in stocks, real estate, and small business. We've found this to be true from observing many, many investors over the years.

Stocks

Stocks, which represent shares of ownership in a company, are the most common ownership investment vehicle. When companies go public, they issue shares of stock that people like you can purchase on the major stock exchanges, such as the Toronto Stock Exchange, New York Stock Exchange, and NASDAQ (National Association of Securities Dealers Automated Quotation system), or the *over-the-counter* market.

As the economy grows, and companies grow with it and earn greater profits, stock prices generally follow suit. Stock prices don't move in lockstep with earnings, but over the years the relationship is pretty close. In fact, the price–earnings ratio — which measures the level of stock prices relative to (or divided by) company earnings — of U.S. stocks has averaged approximately 15 during this century (although it's tended to be higher during periods of low inflation). A price–earnings ratio of 15 simply means that stock prices per share, on average, are selling at about 15 times those companies' earnings per share.

International stocks

Not only can you invest in company stocks that trade on Canadian stock exchanges, but you can also invest in stocks in the U.S. and overseas. Aside from folks with international business connections, why would the average citizen want to do so?

We can give you several reasons. First, many investing opportunities exist outside of Canada. If you look at the total value of all stocks outstanding worldwide, the value of Canadian shares is less than 3 percent of the total.

Another reason for investing in international stocks is that, when you confine your investing to Canadian securities, you miss a world of opportunities, not only because of business growth available in other countries but also because you get the opportunity to diversify your portfolio even further. International securities markets don't move in tandem with Canadian markets. During various Canadian stock market drops, some international stock markets drop less, while others actually rise in value.

Some people hesitate to invest in overseas securities for silly reasons. One column we came across in a big-city paper was entitled "Plenty of pitfalls in foreign investing: Timing is all in earning a decent return." The piece went on to say, "But as with sex, commuting and baseball, timing is everything in the stock market." Smart stock market investors know better than to try to time their investments. The piece also ominously warned, "Foreign stock markets have been known to evaporate overnight." We wish we could say the same for the jobs of some bone-headed financial journalists!

Others are concerned that overseas investing hurts the Canadian economy and contributes to a loss of Canadian jobs. We have some counterarguments. First, if *you* don't profit from the growth of economies overseas, someone else will. If there is money to be made, Canadians may as well be there to participate. Profits from a foreign company are distributed to all stockholders, no matter where they live. Dividends and stock price appreciation know no national boundaries.

Also, you must recognize that you already live in a global economy — making a distinction between Canadian and non-Canadian companies is no longer appropriate. Many companies that are headquartered in Canada also have overseas operations. Some Canadian firms derive a large portion of their revenue from their international divisions. Conversely, many firms based overseas also have Canadian operations. An increasing number of companies are worldwide operations. You don't get the full benefit of international investing by buying just large multinational companies headquartered in Canada. The overseas diversification advantage is obtained by investing in companies that trade on foreign exchanges.

Companies that issue shares (called *publicly held* companies) include automobile manufacturers, computer software producers, fast-food restaurants, hotels, magazine and newspaper publishers, supermarkets, wineries, zipper manufacturers, and everything in between! By contrast, some companies are *privately held,* which means that they have elected to have their shares owned by senior management (and sometimes a small number of affluent outside investors). The shares of privately held companies do not trade on a stock exchange, so folks like you (and us) can't buy shares in such firms.

Companies differ in what industry or line of business they're in and also in size. In the financial press, you often hear companies referred to by their *market capitalization,* which is the value of their outstanding stock (the number of total shares multiplied by the market price per share). When describing the sizes of companies, Bay Street and Wall Street have done away with such practical adjectives as big and small, and replaced them with expressions like *large cap* and *small cap* (where *cap* stands for capitalization). Such is the language of financial geekiness.

Investing in the stock market involves occasional setbacks and difficult moments (just like raising children or going mountain climbing), but the overall journey should be worth the effort. Over the past two centuries, the U.S. stock market (for which there is decades more data than the Canadian stock market) has produced an annual average rate of return of about 10 percent. However, the market, as measured by the Dow Jones Industrial Average, fell more than 20 percent during 16 different periods in the 20th century. On average, these periods of decline lasted less than two years. So if you can withstand a temporary setback over a few years, the stock market is a proven place to invest for long-term growth.

You can invest in stocks by making your own selection of individual stocks or by letting a mutual fund manager (discussed in Chapter 10) do it for you.

Discovering the relative advantages of mutual funds

Efficiently managed mutual funds offer investors of both modest and substantial means low-cost access to high-quality money managers. Mutual funds span the spectrum of risk and potential returns, from non-fluctuating money market funds (which are similar to savings accounts) to bond funds (which generally pay higher yields than money market funds but fluctuate with changes in interest rates) to stock funds (which offer the greatest potential for appreciation but also the greatest short-term volatility).

For most investors, mutual funds make better sense than individual securities. To illustrate, imagine the following scenario: You just bought your first home. It's an older, lived-in property with neon-yellow carpets that have accumulated 20-plus years of food spills and pet accidents. You want to tear out the yucky old carpet and install hardwood floors.

Imagine that you can either redo your flooring work yourself or pay a contractor just $200 to do it for you. You'd go with the contractor if you could hire him this cheaply. The only type of person who would choose to go it alone is someone who really enjoys this type of work. You're not going to be able to do a faster, better job than a full-time contractor if you do a decent job searching for a good one.

You should use this same line of thinking when considering how to invest in stocks and bonds. Investing in individual securities should be done only by those who really enjoy doing it. Mutual funds, if properly selected, are a low-cost, quality way to hire professional money managers.

Over the long haul, it's tough to beat talented full-time professional managers who are investing in securities of the same type and risk level. But, as with hiring a contractor, you need to do your homework to find a good money manager. Chapter 10 is devoted to mutual funds.

Investing in individual stocks

Our experience is that plenty of people choose to invest in individual securities because they think that they're smarter or luckier than the rest. We don't know you personally, but it's safe to say that, in the long run, your investment choices likely aren't going to outperform those of the better full-time investment professionals.

We notice a distinct difference between the sexes on this issue. Perhaps because of the differences in how people are raised, testosterone levels, or whatever, men tend to have more of a problem swallowing their egos and admitting that they're better off not selecting their own individual securities. Maybe the desire to be a stock picker is genetically linked to not wanting to ask for directions!

You should generally avoid investing in individual stocks. Success is difficult to attain, and the drawbacks and pitfalls are numerous:

- ✔ **You'll have to spend a significant amount of time doing research.** When you're considering the purchase of an individual security, you should know a lot about the company in which you're thinking about investing. Relevant questions to ask about the company include: What products does it sell? What are its prospects for future growth and profitability? How much debt does the company have? You need to do your homework not only before you make your initial investment but also on an ongoing basis for as long as you hold the investment. Research takes your valuable free time and sometimes costs money.

  Don't fool yourself or let others with a vested interest fool you into believing that picking and following individual companies and their stocks is simple, requires little time, and is far more profitable than investing in mutual funds.

- ✔ **Your emotions will probably get in your way.** Analyzing financial statements, corporate strategy, and competitive position requires great intellect and insight. However, those skills aren't nearly enough. Will you have the stomach to hold on after what you thought was a sure-win stock plunges 50 percent while the overall stock market holds steady or even climbs? Will you have the courage to dump such a stock if your new research suggests that the plummet is the beginning of the end rather than just a big bump in the road? When your money is on the line, emotions often kick in and undermine your ability to make sound long-term decisions. Few people have the psychological constitution to outfox the financial markets.

✔ **You're less likely to diversify.** Unless you have tens of thousands of dollars to invest in different stocks, you probably can't cost-effectively afford to develop a diversified portfolio. For example, when you're investing in stocks, you need to hold companies in different industries, different companies within an industry, and so on. By not diversifying, you unnecessarily add to your risk.

✔ **You'll face accounting and bookkeeping hassles.** When you invest in individual securities outside retirement plans, you must report those transactions on your tax return. Even if you pay someone else to complete your tax return, you still have the hassle of keeping track of statements and receipts.

Of course, you may find some people (often with a vested interest) who try to convince you that picking your own stocks and managing your own portfolio of stocks is easy and more profitable than investing in, say, a mutual fund. In our experience, such stock-picking cheerleaders usually fall into at least one of the following categories:

✔ **Newsletter writers:** Whether in print or on a Web site, you can find plenty of pundits who pitch the notion that professional money managers are just overpaid buffoons, and that you can handily trounce the pros with little investment of your time by simply putting your money into the pundits' stock picks. Of course, what these self-anointed gurus are really selling is either an ongoing print newsletter (which can run upward of several hundred dollars per year) or your required daily visitation of their advertising-stuffed Web sites. How else will you be able to keep up with their announced buy-and-sell recommendations? These supposed experts want you to be dependent on continually following their advice. Of course, you may be wondering, "Hey, if these pundits were such geniuses at picking the best stocks, why aren't they making piles of money just investing rather than selling their supposed brilliant insights on the cheap?" Go to the head of the class and don't waste your time and money following such pundits' picks! (We discuss investment newsletters in Chapter 8 and Web sites in Chapter 20.)

✔ **Book authors:** Go into any bookstore with a decent-sized investing section and you'll find plenty of books claiming that they can teach you a stock-picking strategy for beating the system. Never mind the fact that the author has no independently audited track record demonstrating his success! In Chapter 20, we present examples of such hucksters, including one investment group whose book publisher was successfully sued over hyping and distorting the group's actual investment success.

Individual stock dividend reinvestment plans

Many corporations allow existing shareholders to reinvest their dividends in more shares of stock without paying brokerage commissions. In some cases, companies allow you to make additional cash purchases of more shares of stock, also commission-free.

In order to qualify, you must first generally buy some shares of stock through a broker (although some companies allow the initial purchases to be made directly from them). Ideally, you should purchase these initial shares through a discount broker to keep your commission burden as low as possible. Some investment associations — including the Canadian ShareOwner Association (www.shareowner.ca) — also have plans

that allow you to buy one or just a few shares to get started.

We're not enamoured of these plans, because this type of investing is generally available and cost-effective only for investments held outside your RRSP or RRIF. You typically need to complete a lot of paperwork to invest in a number of different companies' stock. Life is too short to bother with these plans for this reason alone.

Finally, even with those companies that do sell shares directly without charging an explicit commission like a brokerage firm, you pay plenty of other fees. Many plans charge an upfront enrolment fee, fees for reinvesting dividends, and another fee when you want to sell.

✔ **Stockbrokers:** Some brokers steer you toward individual stocks for several reasons that benefit the broker and not you. First, as we discuss in Chapter 8, the high-commission brokerage firms can make handsome profits for themselves by getting you to buy stocks. Secondly, brokers can use changes in the company's situation to encourage you to then sell and buy different stocks, generating even more commissions. Lastly, as with newsletter writers, this whole process can lead you to become dependent on the broker, leaving you, well, broker!

Researching individual stocks can be more than a full-time job, and if you choose to take this path remember that you'll be competing against the professionals who do so on a full-time basis.

If you derive pleasure from picking and following your own stocks, or you want an opinion of some stocks you currently own, an excellent source of independent research for Canadian companies is the Canadian ShareOwner Association. A yearly membership costs $99 and gets you a subscription to *Canadian ShareOwner*. Published six times a year, the magazine offers updates on many stocks as well as in-depth assessments of two companies in each issue. The association also puts out a software program that helps you analyze stocks, with a focus on finding stocks that possess its two favourite qualities: steadily rising sales, and, more importantly, profit that's increasing even faster. The software costs $129. (You don't have to be a ShareOwner member to buy any of their products.) You can also purchase their database of some 7,000 Canadian and U.S. stocks. A one-year subscription that gets you the data on CD — with updated information sent out every two months — costs

$199. If you buy it together with the stock evaluation software, you can get the two products for a total of $299. You can subscribe and order publications and software products by calling 800-268-6881 or visiting www.shareowner.ca. Probably the best research reports available for U.S. stocks are from Value Line Investment Survey. This superb publication provides concise, user-friendly, single-page summaries of thousands of stocks. Libraries with good business sections often carry this publication. You can order a 10-week trial by calling Value Line at 800-833-0046. We also recommend that you limit your individual stock-picking to no more than 20 percent of your overall investments.

Income trusts

Income trusts have become an increasingly popular investment with Canadians looking for better steady payouts than what's available through traditional lending investments such as GICs and Canada Savings Bonds.

Despite this, income trusts aren't lending-type investments. While they may appear to be similar to bonds (except for the high yields), they're actually equity investments, and come with many of the risks that underlie investing in the stock market.

In general, with a traditional public company in which you can buy shares, the more profitable the company is, the higher the share price will rise. The company typically hangs on to its profit and uses it to grow or expand the business. Sometimes profitable companies will distribute some of the profits they earn to shareholders in the form of a dividend.

An *income trust* is simply a business that has changed its formal structure so that the bulk of its free cash flow is paid out directly to unitholders without the company having to pay tax on it, generally on a quarterly basis. These distributions are typically then taxable as income for investors at the investor's full marginal tax rate (see Chapter 6 for more information about taxes).

 Income trusts aren't another type of bond or GIC with much better returns. The dividends are dependent on the continuing health of the underlying business. Income trusts can and do run into trouble. Income trusts are an ownership investment or equity investment, with risks and rewards not dissimilar to those of common shares.

Just as there are good and bad businesses, there are good and bad income trusts. You can see this reflected in the various yields. Trusts built on companies in the power business traditionally offer yields at the lower end of the scale. This is because the businesses underlying them are seen as fairly stable and secure. At the other end you'll often find oil and gas trusts. The underlying businesses in the energy sector are vulnerable to changes in energy prices. Further, to keep paying out distributions, these companies must continually be discovering or acquiring new deposits to replace depleting reserves.

If you're considering investing in an income trust, accept a lower yield for investing in a business that can make money in both good and bad times, allowing it to maintain its distributions. Stick to trusts that pay out less than 100 percent of the cash the business generates. This ensures the management has a financial buffer, allowing them to run the business, invest where needed for the future, and maintain distributions.

Generating wealth with real estate

Over the generations, real estate owners and investors have enjoyed rates of return comparable to those produced by the stock market, thus making real estate another time-tested method for building wealth. However, like stocks, real estate goes through good and bad performance periods. Most people who make money investing in real estate do so because they invest over many years.

Buying your own home is the best place to start investing in real estate. The equity (the difference between the market value of the home and the amount you still owe on your home loan, or mortgage) in your home that builds over the years can become a significant part of your net worth. Among other things, this equity can be tapped into to help finance other important money and personal goals such as retirement, university, and starting or buying a business.

Throughout your adult life, owning a home should be less expensive than renting a comparable home. The reason: As a renter, your housing costs are fully exposed to inflation (unless you're the beneficiary of a rent-controlled dwelling). As a homeowner, the bulk of your housing costs — your monthly mortgage — are not exposed to inflation, except for the change in interest rates each time you renew your mortgage. And when you sell the home you live in, in most cases all the profits go directly to you without being taxed. See Chapter 14 to discover the best ways to buy and finance real estate.

Real estate: Not your ordinary investment

Besides providing solid rates of return, real estate also differs from most other investments in several other respects. Here's what makes real estate unique as an investment:

- ✔ **Usability:** You can't live in a stock, bond, or mutual fund (although we suppose you could glue together a substantial fortress with all the paper these companies fill your mailbox with each year). Real estate is the only investment you can use (living in or renting out) to produce income.

- ✔ **Land is in limited supply:** Last time we checked, the percentage of the Earth occupied by land wasn't increasing. And because humans like to reproduce, the demand for land and housing continues to grow. Consider the areas that have the most expensive real estate prices in the world — Hong Kong, Tokyo, Hawaii, San Francisco, and Manhattan. In these densely populated areas, virtually no new land is available for building new housing.

Comparing real estate and stocks

Real estate and stocks have historically produced comparable returns. Deciding between the two depends less on the performance of the markets than on you and your situation. Consider the following major issues when deciding which investment may be better for you:

✔ The first and most important question to ask yourself is whether you're cut out to handle the responsibilities that come with being a landlord. Real estate is a time-intensive investment. Investing in stocks can be time-intensive as well, but it doesn't have to be if you use professionally managed mutual funds (see Chapter 10).

✔ An often-overlooked drawback to investing in real estate is that you earn no tax benefits while you're accumulating your down payment. RRSPs (see Chapter 7) give you an immediate tax deduction as you contribute money to them. If you haven't exhausted your contributions to these plans, consider doing so before chasing after investment real estate.

✔ Ask yourself which investments you have a better understanding of. Some folks feel uncomfortable with stocks and mutual funds because they don't understand them. If you have a better handle on what makes real estate tick, you have a good reason to consider investing in it.

✔ Figure out what will make you happy. Some people enjoy the challenge that comes with managing and improving rental property; it can be a bit like running a small business. If you're good at it, and you have some good fortune, you can make money and derive endless hours of enjoyment.

Although few will admit it, some real estate investors get an ego rush from a tangible display of their wealth. Sufferers of this "edifice complex" can't obtain similar pleasure from a stock portfolio detailed on a piece of paper (although others have been known to boast of their stock-picking prowess).

✔ **Zoning shapes potential value:** Local government regulates the zoning of property, and zoning determines what a property can be used for. In most communities these days, local zoning boards are against big growth. This position bodes well for future real estate values. Also know that, in some cases, a particular property may not have been developed to its full potential. If you can figure out how to develop the property, you can reap large profits.

✔ **Leverage:** Real estate is also different from other investments because you can borrow a lot of money to buy it — up to 80 to 90 percent or more of the value of the property. This borrowing is known as using *leverage:* With only a small investment of 10 to 20 percent down, you're able to purchase and own a much larger investment. When the value of your real estate goes up, you make money on your investment and on all the money you borrowed. (In case you're curious, you can use leverage to buy stock and bond investments outside of registered plans through margin borrowing. However, you have to make a much larger "down payment" — about double to triple what's required when buying real estate.)

For example, suppose that you plunk down $50,000 to purchase a property for $200,000. If the property appreciates to $250,000, you make a profit of $50,000 (on paper) on your investment of just $50,000. In other words, you make a 100-percent return on your investment. But leverage cuts both ways. If your $200,000 property decreases in value to $150,000, you actually lose (on paper) 100 percent of your original $50,000 investment, even though the property value only drops 25 percent in value.

✔ **Hidden values:** In an efficient market, the price of an investment accurately reflects its true worth. Some investment markets are more efficient than others because of the large number of transactions and easily accessible information. Real estate markets can be inefficient at times. Information is not always easy to come by, and you may find an ultramotivated or uninformed seller. If you're willing to do some homework, you may be able to purchase a property below its fair market value (perhaps by as much as 10 to 20 percent).

Just as with any other investment, real estate has its drawbacks. For starters, buying or selling a property generally takes time and significant cost. Also, holding a property typically costs a good deal of ongoing money. When you're renting property, you discover first-hand the occasional headaches of being a landlord. And, especially in the early years of rental property ownership, the property's expenses may exceed the rental income, producing a net cash drain.

The best real estate investment options

Although real estate is in some ways unique, it's also like other types of investments in that prices are driven by supply and demand. You can invest in homes or small apartment buildings and then rent them out. In the long run, investment-property buyers hope that their rent income and the value of their properties will increase faster than their expenses.

When selecting real estate for investment purposes, remember that local economic growth is the fuel for housing demand. In addition to a vibrant and diverse job base, you want to look for limited supplies of both existing housing and land on which to build. When you identify potential properties in which you may want to invest, run the numbers to understand the cash demands of owning the property and the likely profitability. See Chapter 14 for help determining the costs of real estate ownership.

When you want to invest directly in real estate, residential housing — such as single-family homes or small multi-unit buildings — may be a straightforward and attractive investment for you. Buying properties close to "home" offers the advantage of allowing you to more easily monitor and manage what's going on. The downside is that you'll be less diversified — more of your investments will be dependent on your local economy.

If you don't want to be a landlord — one of the biggest drawbacks of investment real estate — consider investing in real estate through real estate investment trusts (REITs). REITs are diversified real estate investment companies that purchase and manage rental real estate for investors. A typical REIT invests in different types of property, such as shopping centres, apartments, and other rental buildings. You can invest in REITs either by purchasing them directly on the stock exchange or by investing in a real estate mutual fund (see Chapter 10) that invests in numerous REITs.

The worst real estate investments

Not all real estate investments are good; some aren't even real investments. The bad ones are characterized by burdensome costs and problematic economic fundamentals:

- **Limited partnerships:** You should avoid limited partnerships (LPs) sold through brokers and financial consultants. LPs are inferior investment vehicles. They're so burdened with high sales commissions and ongoing management fees that deplete your investment that you can do better elsewhere. The salesperson that sells you such an investment stands to earn a commission of up to 10 percent or more — so only 90 cents of each dollar get invested. Each year, LPs typically siphon off another several percent for management and other expenses. Most partnerships have little or no incentive to control costs. In fact, they have a conflict of interest that often causes them to charge more to enrich the managing partners.

  Unlike a mutual fund, you can't vote with your dollars. If the partnership is poorly run and expensive, you're stuck. LPs are illiquid, meaning they aren't readily convertible into cash without taking a substantial loss. You can't access your money until the partnership is liquidated, typically seven to ten years after you buy in.

  Brokers who sell LPs often tell you that, while your investment is growing at 20 percent or more per year, you get handsome dividends of 8 percent or so per year. Many of the yields on LPs have turned out to be bogus. In some cases, partnerships propped up their yields by paying back investors' principal (without telling them, of course). As for returns — well — most LP investors of a decade ago are lucky to have half their original investment left. The only thing limited about a limited partnership is its ability to make you money.

- **Timeshares:** Timeshares are another nearly certain money loser. With a timeshare, you buy a week or two of ownership, or usage, of a particular unit (usually a condominium in a resort location) per year. If, for example, you pay $8,000 for a week (in addition to ongoing maintenance fees), you're paying the equivalent of more than $400,000 for the whole unit, when a comparable unit nearby may sell for only $150,000. The extra mark-up pays the salespeople's commissions, administrative expenses, and profits for the timeshare development company.

People usually get enticed into buying a timeshare when they're enjoying a vacation someplace. They're easy prey for salespeople who want to sell them a souvenir of the trip. The "cheese in the mousetrap" is an offer of something free (for example, a free night's stay in a unit) for going through the sales presentation.

If you can't live without a timeshare, consider buying a used one. Many previous buyers, who more than likely have lost a good chunk of money, are trying to dump their shares (which should tell you something). In this case, you may be able to buy a timeshare at a fair price. But why commit yourself to taking a vacation in the same location and building at the same time each year? Many timeshares let you trade your weeks for other times and other places; however, doing so is a hassle — you're charged an extra fee, and your choices are usually limited to time slots that other people don't want (that's why they're trading them!).

✔ **Second homes:** The weekend getaway is a sometimes romantic notion and dream of many Canadians — a place you can escape to a couple of times a month. When your cottage or cabin is not in use, you may be able to rent it out and earn some income to help defray the expense of keeping it up.

REITs: Bricks-and-mortar mutual funds

Beyond owning your own home, another good way to invest in real estate is through a real estate investment trust *(REIT)*. Much like a mutual fund pools your money with that of other like-minded investors and buys a basket of investments within a certain category, a REIT assembles a portfolio of different properties. Typically, this may include apartments, shopping centres, offices, and other types of rental property. There are also REITs that hold hotels and even nursing homes. The REIT manages the property, collects rent, deducts its expenses, and then distributes most of the remaining profit to unitholders.

If you like the idea of rental property but don't want all the headaches, REITs are often a good choice. One way to think of a REIT is as a middleman that lets you be a landlord without all the associated hassles. The people managing the REIT scout the market, assess different properties, and decide which buildings to buy. They then manage the real estate, taking care of everything from repairs to finding new tenants.

The value of REIT units and the amount they pay out will be affected by the same factors that would affect you if you owned the properties directly. Rising vacancy rates, falling rental prices, and a shortage of quality, reasonably-priced buildings will make REIT prices as well as distributions suffer. Conversely, growing demand for limited rental space is positive for REIT investors.

REITs are generally less risky than other types of income trusts, such as oil and gas trusts or those involved in seasonal businesses. Also, many REITs have a large, diversified portfolio of buildings across the country, meaning they are less susceptible to downturns in one specific market or a particular region.

Units of REITs trade just like stocks on the major stock exchanges. They can be bought and sold through discount brokers and full-service brokerages.

If you can realistically afford the additional costs of a second (or vacation) home, we're not going to tell you how to spend your extra cash. But please don't make the all-too-common mistake of viewing a second home as an investment. The way most people use them, they're not. Most second-homeowners seldom rent out their property — they typically do so 10 percent or less of the time. As a result, second homes are usually money drains.

If you aren't going to rent out a second home most of the time, ask yourself whether you can afford such a luxury. Can you accomplish your other financial goals — saving for retirement, paying for the home in which you live, and so on — with this added expense? Keeping a second home is more of a consumption than an investment decision. Few people can afford more than one home.

Investing in small businesses

With what type of investment have more people built great wealth? If you said the stock market or real estate, you're wrong. The answer is small businesses. You can invest in small businesses by starting one yourself (and thus finding yourself the best boss you've probably ever had), buying an existing business, or investing in someone else's small business.

Launching your own enterprise

When you have self-discipline and a product or service you can sell, starting your own business can be both profitable and fulfilling. Consider first what skills and expertise you possess that you can use in your business. You don't need a "eureka-type" idea or invention to start a small business. Millions of people operate successful businesses that are hardly unique, such as dry cleaners, restaurants, tax preparation firms, and so on.

Begin exploring your idea by first developing a written business plan. Such a plan should detail what your product or service is going to be, how you're going to market it, who your customers and competitors are, and what the economics of the business are, including the start-up costs.

Of all the small-business investment options, starting your own business involves the greatest amount of work. Although you can do this work on a part-time basis in the beginning, most people end up running their business full-time — it's your new job, career, or whatever you want to call it.

We've both been running our own businesses for most of our working years, and neither of us would trade that experience for the corporate life. That's not to say that running our own businesses doesn't have drawbacks and down moments. But we've seen many people of varied backgrounds, interests, and skills succeed and be happy with running their own businesses.

In the eyes of most people, starting a new business is the riskiest of all small-business investment options. But if you're going into a business that utilizes your skills and expertise, the risk is not nearly as great as you may think. Many businesses can be started with little cash by leveraging your existing skills and expertise. You can build a valuable company and job if you have the time to devote. As long as you check out the competition and offer a valued service at a reasonable cost, the principal risk with your business comes from not doing a good job marketing what you have to offer. If you can market your skills, you're home free.

As long as you're thinking about the risks of starting a business, consider the risks of staying in a job you don't enjoy or that doesn't challenge or fulfill you. If you never take the plunge, you may regret that you didn't pursue your dreams.

Buying an existing business

If you don't have a specific product or service you want to sell, but you're skilled at managing and improving the operations of a company, buying a small business may be for you. Finding and buying a good small business takes much time and patience, so be willing to devote at least several months to the search. You may also need to enlist financial and legal advisers to help inspect the company, look over its financial statements, and hammer out a contract.

Although you don't have to go through the riskier start-up period if you buy a small business, you'll likely need more capital to buy an established enterprise. You'll also need to be able to deal with stickier personnel and management issues. The history of the organization and the way things work will predate your ownership of the business. If you don't like making hard decisions, firing people who don't fit with your plans, and coercing people into changing the way they do things, buying an existing business likely isn't for you.

Some people perceive buying an existing business as being safer than starting a new one. Buying someone else's business can actually be riskier. You're likely to shell out far more money upfront, in the form of a down payment, to buy an existing business. If you don't have the ability to run the business and it does poorly, you have more to lose financially. In addition, the business may be for sale for a reason — it may not be very profitable, it may be in decline, or it may generally be a pain in the neck to operate.

Good businesses don't come cheaply. If the business is a success, the current owner has already removed the start-up risk from the business, so the price of the business should be at a premium to reflect this lack of risk. When you have the capital to buy an established business and you have the skills to run it, consider going this route.

Investing in someone else's small business

Are you someone who likes the idea of profiting from successful small businesses but doesn't want the day-to-day headaches of being responsible for managing the enterprise? Then Investing in someone else's small business may be for you. Although this route may seem easier, few people are actually cut out to be investors in other people's businesses. The reason: Finding and analyzing opportunities isn't easy.

Are you astute at evaluating corporate financial statements and business strategies? Investing in a small, privately held company has much in common with investing in a publicly traded firm (as is the case when you buy shares), but it also has a few differences. One difference is that private firms aren't required to produce comprehensive, audited financial statements that adhere to certain accounting principles. Thus, you have a greater risk of not having sufficient or accurate information when evaluating a small private firm.

Another difference is that unearthing private small-business investing opportunities is harder. The best private companies that are seeking investors generally don't advertise. Instead, they find prospective investors through networking with people such as business advisers. You can increase your chances of finding private companies to invest in by speaking with tax, legal, and financial advisers who work with small businesses. You can also find interesting opportunities through your own contacts or experience within a given industry.

You shouldn't consider investing in someone else's business unless you can afford to lose all of what you're investing. Also, you should have sufficient assets so that what you're investing in small, privately held companies represents only a small portion (20 percent or less) of your total financial assets.

Off the Beaten Path: Investment Odds and Ends

The investments that we discuss in this section sometimes belong on their own planet (because they're not an ownership or lending vehicle). Here are the basics on these other common, but odd, investments.

Precious metals

Gold and silver have been used by many civilizations as currency or a medium of exchange. One advantage of precious metals as a currency is that they can't be debased by the government. With paper currency, such as Canadian dollars, the government can simply print more. This process can lead to the devaluation of a currency and inflation. It takes a whole lot more work to make more gold. Just ask Rumpelstiltskin.

Holdings of gold and silver can provide a so-called hedge against inflation. In the late 1970s and early 1980s, inflation rose dramatically in North America.

This largely unexpected rise in inflation depressed stocks and bonds. Gold and silver, however, rose tremendously in value — in fact, more than 500 percent (even after adjusting for inflation) from 1972 to 1980 (see Chapter 8). Such periods are unusual. Over many decades, precious metals tend to be lousy investments. Their rate of return tends to keep up with the rate of inflation but not surpass it.

When you want to invest in precious metals as an inflation hedge, your best option is to do so through mutual funds (see Chapter 10). Don't purchase precious metals futures. They're not investments; they're short-term gambles on which way gold or silver prices might head over a short period of time. You should also stay away from firms and shops that sell coins and bullion (not the soup, but bars of gold or silver). Even if you can find a legitimate firm (not an easy task), the cost of storing and insuring gold and silver is quite costly. You won't get good value for your money. We hate to tell you this, but the Gold Rush is over.

Annuities

Annuities are a peculiar type of insurance and investment product. They're a sort of savings-type account with slightly higher yields that are backed by insurance companies.

As with retirement plans, money placed in an annuity compounds without taxation until it is withdrawn. However, unlike RRSPs, you don't receive upfront tax breaks on contributions you make to an annuity. Annuities also tend to have much higher ongoing investment expenses— compared to other investments don't allow such tax deferral— which depress your returns. Consider an annuity only after you contribute the maximum you're allowed to your RRSP. (For more help on deciding whether to invest in an annuity, read Chapter 12.)

Collectibles

The collectibles category is a catch-all for antiques, art, autographs, baseball cards, clocks, coins, comic books, diamonds, dolls, gems, photographs, rare books, rugs, stamps, vintage wine, and writing utensils — in other words, any material object that, through some kind of human manipulation, has become more valuable to certain humans.

Notwithstanding the few people who discover on the *Antiques Road Show* that they own an antique of significant value, collectibles are generally lousy investment vehicles. Dealer mark-ups are enormous, maintenance and protection costs are draining, research is time-consuming, and people's tastes are quite fickle. All this for returns that, after you factor in the huge mark-ups, rarely keep up with inflation.

Buy collectibles for your love of the object, not for financial gain. Treat collecting as a hobby, not as an investment. When buying a collectible, try to avoid the big mark-ups by cutting out the intermediaries. Buy directly from the artist or producer if you can.

Life insurance with a cash value

Life insurance shouldn't be used as an investment, especially if you haven't exhausted your contributions to retirement plans. Life insurance that combines insurance protection with an account that has a cash value is often referred to as universal, whole, or variable life. Agents love to sell it for the high commissions.

The only common reason to consider buying cash-value life insurance is if you want the proceeds to help pay some or all of the taxes due on your death. This may help you ensure that some of your assets can be passed on intact to your heirs, rather than having to be sold to help pay your final tax bill. In this case, consider naming your estate as the beneficiary on your policy. This will ensure the insurance money is used for your tax bill. You need to look at your potential estate and the anticipated tax bill to decide if this is a benefit of value to your heirs. (See Chapter 16 for more on life insurance and why term life insurance is best for the vast majority of people.)

Chapter 9

Investing in Mutual Funds

· ·

In This Chapter

▶ Examining funds

▶ Checking out the different types of funds

▶ Choosing the best funds

▶ Evaluating your fund's performance

▶ Monitoring and selling your funds

· ·

*W*hen you invest in a mutual fund, an investment company pools your money with the money of many other like-minded individuals and invests it in stocks, bonds, and other securities. Think of it as a big investment club without the meetings! When you invest through a typical mutual fund, several hundred million to a billion dollars or more may be invested along with your money.

Understanding the Benefits of Mutual Funds

Mutual funds rank right up there with microwave ovens, DVDs, sticky notes, plastic wrap, and, of course, iPods as one of the best modern inventions. To understand how and why they can work for you, read on to discover the benefits you receive when you invest in mutual funds:

✔ **Professional management.** Mutual funds are managed by a portfolio manager and research team whose full-time job is to screen the universe of investments for those that best meet the stated objectives of the fund. The better ones call and visit companies, analyze companies' financial statements, and speak with companies' suppliers and customers. In short, the team does more work and research than you could ever hope to do in your free time.

Fund managers are typically graduates of the top business and finance schools in the country, where they learn the principles of portfolio management and securities valuation and selection. (Despite their time in the groves of academe, many of them do a good job of investing money.) The best fund managers typically have five or more years of experience in analyzing and selecting investments, and many measure their experience in decades rather than years.

✔ **Low cost.** The most efficiently managed stock mutual funds cost less than 2 percent per year in fees (bonds and money market funds cost much less). Because mutual funds typically buy or sell tens of thousands of shares of a security at a time, the percentage commissions these funds pay are generally far less than what you pay to buy or sell a few hundred shares on your own. In addition, when you buy a *no-load fund,* you avoid paying sales commissions (known as *loads*) on your transactions. We discuss these types of funds throughout this chapter.

✔ **Diversification.** Mutual fund investing enables you to achieve a level of diversification that is difficult to obtain without tens of thousands of dollars and a lot of time to invest. If you go it alone, you should invest money in at least 8 to 12 different securities in different industries to ensure that your portfolio can withstand a downturn in one or more of the investments. Proper diversification allows a mutual fund to receive the highest possible return at the lowest possible risk given its objectives. However, the most unfortunate investors during major stock market downswings have been individuals who had all of their money riding on only a few stocks that plunged in price by 90 percent or more.

✔ **Low cost of entry.** Most mutual funds have low minimum-investment requirements, especially if you're investing inside an RRSP. Even if you have a lot of money to invest, you should also consider mutual funds. Join the increasing numbers of companies and institutions (who have the biggest bucks of all) that are turning to the low-cost, high-quality money-management services that good mutual funds provide.

✔ **Audited performance records and expenses.** In their prospectuses, all mutual funds are required to disclose historical data on returns, operating expenses, and other fees. The securities regulators in each province oversee these disclosures for accuracy. Also, several organizations (such as GlobeFund and Morningstar, Inc.) provide monthly reporting on fund statistics, allowing comparisons of performance, risk, and many other factors.

✔ **Flexibility in risk level.** Among the different mutual funds, you can choose a level of risk that you're comfortable with and that meets your personal and financial goals. If you want your money to grow over a long period of time, you may want to select funds that invest more heavily in stocks. If you need current income and don't want investments that fluctuate in value as widely as stocks, you may choose more conservative bond funds. If you want to be sure that your invested principal doesn't drop in value (perhaps because you may need your money in the short term), you can select a money market fund.

TECHNICAL STUFF

The rise of the mutual fund industry

Just as computers replaced typewriters because they allowed for more efficient word processing, mutual funds have become a portfolio mainstay for many investors because they are easy to put to work and can make investing simpler and more straightforward. As for safety, mutual funds have a virtually zero risk of bankruptcy. Unlike banks and insurance companies (which have failed and will continue to fail), mutual funds have never failed — and probably won't fail in the future. The situation where the demand for money back *(liabilities)* exceeds the value of a fund's investments *(assets)* can't occur with a mutual fund.

The value of a fund fluctuates with the value of the securities in which it is invested. But this variation doesn't lead to the failure or bankruptcy of a mutual fund company. In contrast, hundreds of banks and dozens of insurance companies have failed in North America in recent decades. Banks and insurers can fail because their liabilities can exceed their assets. When a bank makes too many loans that go sour at the same time that depositors want their money back, the bank fails. Likewise, if an insurance company makes several poor investments or underestimates the number of claims that will be made by insurance policy holders, it too can fail.

And you don't have to worry about fund companies stealing your money. The specific securities in which a mutual fund is invested are held at a *custodian* — a separate organization independent of the mutual fund company. The employment of a custodian ensures that the fund management company can't embezzle your funds and use assets from a better-performing fund to subsidize a poor performer.

Exploring Various Fund Types

One of the major misconceptions about mutual funds is that they're all invested in stocks. They're not. Table 9-1 shows how the money currently invested in mutual funds breaks down.

As you can see, the majority of mutual fund money is *not* invested in stocks. When you hear folks talk about the "riskiness" of mutual funds, even in the media, you know that they're overlooking this fact: All mutual funds are not created equal. A mutual fund is simply a basket of investments. Just what kinds of investments are put in that basket can range from high-risk stocks to government-guaranteed, interest-paying Treasury bills. And some funds, such as money market funds, carry virtually *no* risk that your investment will decline in value.

When mutual fund companies package and market funds, the names they give their funds aren't always completely accurate or comprehensive. For example, a stock fund may not be *totally* invested in stocks. Twenty percent of it may be invested in bonds. Don't assume that a fund invests exclusively in Canadian companies, either — it may invest in international firms, as well.

The hazards of hedge funds

When you "hedge your bets," you're trying to limit your losses. In the financial world, *hedging* is typically done by making a second investment that will limit or counteract the loss if one's initial investment goes sour. For example, suppose you believed a stock was going to rise in value, but were concerned that certain events could cause its value to plummet. You could buy the stock, and also purchase *put options*, which would give you the right to sell the stock in the future at a set price. If the stock appreciated as you hoped, you would profit, although the money you spent buying the puts would be lost. On the other hand, if the stock price fell dramatically, the put options would allow you to sell the stock above its lower market price, giving you a profit that would offset the loss on the shares you actually owned. When this is done on a large scale with a number of different investments by a professional money manager, you get a *hedge fund*.

Hedge funds used to be a fringe investment of interest only to large pension funds, the super-rich, and those looking for the potential of huge returns who were willing to take large risks. However, in recent years hedge funds have begun to be marketed to mainstreet investors as mainstream investments, which in most cases they certainly aren't.

Part of the marketing drive is based on their supposed ability to earn positive returns even when the overall stock markets aren't advancing or are even falling. This comes from their so-called *market neutral* characteristic, meaning they are supposed to be unaffected by the overall performance of the stock markets. Unlike regular mutual funds, hedge fund managers don't only expect to make positive returns only by putting money into investments, they expect them to appreciate in value. Hedge funds can also bet against investments — making money

if they fall. Typically, they will do this by *selling short*. The fund sells stock it doesn't actually own to others at the going price. If the stock price does fall, the borrowed shares can then be replaced with lower priced shares bought on the open market. Think of it as the reverse of a normal transaction. An investor *going long* might buy a stock at $10, hoping that it would go to $15 for a profit of $5 a share. Someone shorting the same stock would first sell borrowed shares at $10. If the stock then fell to $5, they would replace the shares at that price, for a profit of $5.00.

It sounds good in practice, but in reality doesn't work out so neatly or profitably. No investment or approach to investing comes without risk. Hedge fund mangers can't eliminate all risks and still earn healthy returns. What they actually do is decide which risks they are willing to take, and then purchase insurance in the form of hedged positions to eliminate the risks they don't want to be exposed to.

Hedge funds have many other strikes against them:

- They attract hot money — money of aggressive investors who are quick to jump out of an investment where the returns are suffering and jump into an investment whose short-term numbers are above average. This puts a lot of pressure on hedge fund managers to "swing for the fences" — make big bets on short-term price movements to boost their returns — which adds to the risk and volatility.

- They're both aggressively managed and actively traded, which means that investors pay hefty fees to hedge fund managers. Typically, a hedge fund will charge 2% of fees under management, as well as taking 20% of any profits. To make matters worse, many retail investors end up being sold a collection of hedge funds as part of a "Fund of Funds," with additional fees attached.

✔ They often bring higher tax bills to investors, since they regularly ring up taxable capital gains.

You'll have a tough time picking good hedge funds: Is a hedge fund having impressive returns because of truly talented managers, or is it simply having a streak of good luck that may end at any time? Also, most hedge funds have short track records, making it tough to find those that have proven they are able to ring up good returns over the long haul. And those track

records can be deceiving, as many of the losers either fail or collapse.

Finally, you might want to heed the experience some 26,000 Canadians had with Portus Alternative Asset Management. Founded in 2002, Portus had been one of the country's fastest-growing hedge funds and had $800 million in assets when concerns over bookkeeping irregularities caused regulators to freeze its accounts in early 2005. Portus was actively promoted by many financial advisors due to the handsome fees they received. And in some cases, investors were told that Portus offered a low-risk investment with steady returns.

Table 9-1	How Mutual Fund Assets Are Invested
Fund Type	*Percentage of Total*
Mortgage	1%
Real estate	0.5%
Money market	9%
Dividend and income	11%
Balanced	21%
U.S. stocks	6%
Canadian stocks	23%
Bond and income	11%
Foreign stocks	16.5%
Foreign bond and income	1%

Note: If you haven't yet read Chapters 7 and 8, which provide an overview of investment concepts and vehicles, doing so will enhance your understanding of the rest of this chapter.

Money market funds

Money market funds are the safest type of mutual funds for those concerned about losing their invested dollars. Money market funds are like bank savings accounts in that the value of your original investment does not fluctuate. (For more background on money market funds, see Chapter 8.)

Money market funds have several advantages over bank savings accounts:

- ✔ The best money market funds have higher yields.
- ✔ They can be used inside as well as outside RRSPs and other registered savings plans.
- ✔ They are a handy parking place for money you have set aside to invest in other types of mutual funds but have yet to decide on. You earn a good return while doing your research or waiting for the right time. As with money you put into bank savings accounts, money market funds are suitable for money that you can't afford to see dwindle in value.

Bond funds

Bonds are IOUs. When you buy a newly issued bond, you typically lend your money to a corporation or government agency. A bond mutual fund is nothing more than a large group (pack, herd, gaggle, whatever) of bonds.

Bond funds usually invest in bonds of similar maturity (the number of years that elapse before the borrower must pay back the money you lend). The names of most bond funds include a word or two that provides clues about the average length of maturity of their bonds. For example, a short-term bond fund typically concentrates its investments in bonds maturing in the next two to three years. An intermediate-term fund generally holds bonds that come due within three to ten years. The bonds in a long-term fund usually mature in more than ten years.

In contrast to an individual bond that you buy and hold until it matures, a bond fund is always replacing bonds in its portfolio to maintain its average maturity objective. Therefore, if you know that you absolutely, positively must have a certain amount of your principal back on a particular date, individual bonds may be more appropriate than a bond fund.

Bond funds are useful when you want to live off dividend income or you don't want to put all your money in riskier investments such as stocks and real estate (perhaps because you plan to use the money soon).

Stock funds

Stock mutual funds, as their name implies, invest in stocks. These funds are often referred to as *equity funds*. Equity — not to be confused with equity in real estate — is another word for stocks. Stock mutual funds are often categorized by the type of stocks they primarily invest in.

Funds of funds

An increasing number of fund providers are responding to investors overwhelmed by the hundreds of funds available by offering a simplified way to construct a portfolio: a mutual fund that diversifies across numerous other mutual funds — or a *fund of funds*. When a fund of funds is done right, it helps focus fund investors on the important big-picture issue of asset allocation — how much of your investment money you put into bonds versus stocks.

Although the best funds of funds appear to deliver a high-quality, diversified portfolio of funds in one fell swoop, funds of funds are not all created equal and are not all worthy of your investment dollars. Some of the newer funds of funds developed by the larger fund companies are generally investor-friendly. Look for funds of

funds that don't add any extra fees for packaging together the individual funds.

Other funds of funds layer on high fees and merit a much more skeptical look. Some funds of funds charge annual operating expenses of 1 to 2 percent on top of the fees of the underlying mutual funds they invest in. When you add it all up, investing in mutual funds through these funds can siphon off a whopping 3 to 4 percent of your investment balances annually.

Remember that historical annual returns for stocks average just 10 percent. So paying 3 to 4 percent in fees gives away about 30 to 40 percent of your expected returns. Not surprisingly, in terms of performance the high-fee funds of funds have lagged far behind the market indexes.

Stock types are first defined by size of company (small, medium, or large). The total market value (capitalization) of a company's outstanding shares determines its size. Small- and mid-sized Canadian company stocks, for example, are usually defined as companies with total market capitalization of less than $500 million.

Stocks are further categorized as *growth* or *value*. Growth stocks are companies that are experiencing rapidly expanding revenues and profits, and typically have high stock prices relative to their current earnings or asset (book) values. These companies tend to reinvest most of their earnings back into their infrastructure to fuel future expansion. Thus, growth stocks typically pay little if any dividends.

Value stocks are at the other end of the spectrum. Value stock investors look for good buys. They want to invest in stocks that are cheaply priced in relation to the assets and profits of the company.

These categories are combined in various ways to describe how a mutual fund invests its money. One fund may focus on large-company growth stocks, while another fund may limit itself to small-company value stocks. Funds are further classified by the geographical focus of their investments: Canadian, U.S., international, worldwide, and so on (see the following section).

Balancing bonds and stocks: Hybrid funds

Hybrid funds invest in a mixture of different types of securities. Most commonly, they invest in bonds and stocks. These funds are usually less risky and volatile than funds that invest exclusively in stocks. In an economic downturn, bonds usually hold up in value better than stocks do. However, during good economic times when the stock market is booming, the bond portions of these funds tend to drag down their performance a bit.

Hybrid mutual funds are typically known as *balanced funds* or *asset allocation funds.* Balanced funds generally try to maintain a fairly constant percentage of investments in stocks and bonds. Asset allocation funds tend to adjust the mix of different investments according to the portfolio manager's expectations of the market. Of course, exceptions do exist — some balanced funds make major shifts in their allocations, whereas some asset allocation funds maintain a relatively fixed mix. You should note that most funds that shift money around instead of staying put in good investments rarely beat the market averages over a number of years.

Hybrid funds are a way to make fund investing simple. They give you instant diversification across a variety of investing options, rather than having to choose a stock fund and a bond fund, for example. They also make it easier for stock-skittish investors to invest in stocks while avoiding the high volatility of pure stock funds. Be warned, though, that this usually comes at a price in the form of higher expenses, which directly take away from your returns.

Canadian, U.S., international, and global funds

Unless they have words like *U.S., international, global, world,* or *worldwide* in their names, most funds focus their investments in Canada. But even funds without one of these terms attached may invest money internationally.

The only way to know for sure where a fund is currently invested (or where the fund may invest in the future) is to ask. You can start by calling the toll-free number of the mutual fund company you're interested in. A fund's annual report (which often can be found on the fund company's Web site) also details where the fund is investing.

When a fund has *international* in its name, it typically means that the fund can invest anywhere in the world except Canada. *Worldwide* or *global* generally implies that a fund invests anywhere in the world, including Canada. We generally recommend avoiding worldwide or global funds for two reasons. First, thoroughly following the financial markets and companies in so many parts of the world is difficult for a fund manager. Following financial markets and companies is hard enough to do solely in Canada or the United States or a specific international market. Second, most of these funds charge for high operating expenses — some in excess of 3 percent per year — which puts a drag on returns.

Index funds

Index funds are funds that can be (and are, for the most part) managed by a computer. An index fund's assets are invested to replicate an existing market index such as the Toronto Stock Exchange's S&P/TSX index, or the Standard & Poor's 500, an index of 500 large U.S. company stocks. Over long periods (ten years or more), index funds outperform about three-quarters of their peers! How is that possible? How can a computer making mindless, pre-dictable decisions beat an intelligent, creative, MBA-endowed portfolio manager with a crack team of research analysts scouring the market for the best securities? The answer is largely cost. The computer does not demand a high salary or need a big corner office. And index funds don't need a team of research analysts.

Most active fund managers can't overcome the handicap of high operating expenses that pull down their funds' rates of return. As we discuss later in this chapter, operating expenses include all the fees and profit that a mutual fund extracts from a fund's returns before the returns are paid to you. For example, the average Canadian stock fund has an operating expense ratio of around 2.5 percent per year. So a Canadian stock index fund with an expense ratio of just 1 percent per year has an advantage of 1.5 percent per year.

Socially responsible funds

Select mutual funds label themselves *socially responsible.* This term means different things to different people. In most cases, though, it implies that the fund avoids investing in companies whose products or services harm people or the world at large — tobacco manufacturers, for example. Because cigarettes and other tobacco products kill hundreds of thousands of people and add billions of dollars to health care costs, most socially responsible funds shun tobacco companies.

Socially responsible investing presents a couple of problems. For example, your definition of social responsibility may not match the definition offered by the investment manager who's running a fund. Another problem is that even if you can agree on what's socially irresponsible (such as selling tobacco products), funds aren't always as clean as you would think or hope. Even though a fund avoids tobacco manufacturers, it may well invest in retailers that sell tobacco products.

If you want to consider a socially responsible fund, review the fund's recent annual report that lists the specific investments the fund owns. Also consider giving directly to charities, and get a tax deduction, as well.

Another not-so-inconsequential advantage of index funds is that they can't underperform the market. Some funds do just that because of the burden of high fees and/or poor management. If you were unfortunate enough to have been involved in one of the loser mutual funds listed in Table 9-2 in the past ten years, you fared more than 9 percent worse per year in return than you would have if you had invested in a boring old index fund. (CIBC's U.S. Equity Index fund provided an average annual rate of return of +6.79 percent over the same time period.)

Table 9-2	U.S. Mutual Funds (Diversified) That Will Fetch a Stick
Fund	*Average Annual Rate of Return (10 Years)*
Investors U.S. Large Cap Growth	−2.84%
AIM American Growth	−2.64%

For money invested outside retirement plans, index funds have an added advantage: Lower taxable distributions are made to shareholders because less trading of securities is conducted and a more stable portfolio is maintained.

Yes, index funds may seem downright boring. When you invest in them, you give up the opportunity to brag to others about your shrewd investments that beat the market averages. On the other hand, with a low-cost index fund, you have no chance of doing much worse than the market (which more than a few mutual fund managers do). Sometimes index funds do get beaten by actively managed funds, particularly when the stock markets in general are falling. Actively managed funds may have some of their assets sitting in cash, which would hold its value when stock prices are dropping, while index funds usually have all their capital invested.

Index funds make sense for a portion of your investments, because beating the market is difficult for portfolio managers. The large banks, as well as some of the low- or no-load fund families, all offer index funds. In particular, TD's index eFunds — available only over the Internet — come with bargain-basement expenses starting as low as 0.30 percent.

Specialty (sector) funds

Specialty funds don't fit neatly into the previous categories. These funds are often known as sector funds, because they tend to invest in securities in specific industries.

In most cases, you should avoid investing in specialty funds. Investing in shares in a single industry defeats one of the major purposes of investing in mutual funds — diversification. Another good reason to avoid specialty funds is that they tend to carry much higher expenses than other mutual funds.

Specialty funds that invest in real estate or precious metals may make sense for a small portion (10 percent or less) of your investment portfolio. These types of funds can help diversify your portfolio because they can do better during times of higher inflation.

As for technology stocks, here's what we had to say about technology stock funds when the previous edition of this book was published in early 2001: "Be careful with technology funds, which were hot during the late 1990s and early 2000. Many of these stocks are selling at premium valuations. When you invest in diversified stock funds, you get plenty of exposure to the technology sector."

By 2003, technology stocks had plunged 80 percent in value. While they have since rebounded, many technology stocks are well below their late 1990s/early 2000s peak.

Selecting the Best Mutual Funds

When you go camping in the wilderness, you can do a number of things to maximize your chances for happiness and success. You can take maps to keep you on course, food for nourishment, proper clothing to stay dry and warm, and some first-aid gear to treat minor injuries. But regardless of how much advance preparation you do, you may have a problematic experience. You may take the wrong trail, trip on a rock and break your ankle, or lose your food to a tenacious bear that comes romping through camp one night.

And so it is with mutual funds. Although most mutual fund investors are rewarded for their efforts, you get no guarantees. You can, however, follow some simple, common-sense guidelines to help keep you on the trail and increase your odds of investment success and happiness. The issues in the following sections are the main ones you should consider.

Reading prospectuses and annual reports

Mutual fund companies produce information that can help you make decisions about mutual fund investments. Every fund is required to issue a *prospectus.* This legal document is reviewed and audited by securities regulators. Most of what's written isn't worth the time it takes to slog through it.

The most valuable information — the fund's investment objectives, costs, and performance history — is summarized in the first few pages of the prospectus. Make sure that you read this part. You can generally skip the rest, which is comprised mostly of tedious legal details.

Funds also produce *annual reports* that discuss how the fund has been doing and provide details on the specific investments a fund holds. If, for example, you want to know which countries an international fund invests in, you can find this information in the fund's annual report.

Keeping costs low

The charges you pay to buy or sell a fund, as well as the ongoing fund operating expenses, can have a big impact on the rate of return you earn on your investments. Many novice investors pay too much attention to a mutual fund's prior performance (in the case of stock funds) or to the fund's current yield (in the case of bond funds). Doing so is dangerous because a fund can inflate its return or yield in many (risky) ways. And what worked yesterday may flop tomorrow.

A study conducted by the Investment Company Institute in the U.S. confirms what we've long observed among fund buyers: Only 43 percent of fund buyers who were surveyed bothered to examine the fees and expenses of the fund they ended up buying. The majority of fund buyers — 57 percent, to be exact — didn't know what the funds were charging them to manage their money!

Fund costs are an important factor in the return you earn from a mutual fund. Fees are deducted from your investment. All other things being equal, high fees and other charges depress your returns. What are a fund's fees, you ask? Good question — read on to find the answers.

Eliminating loads

Loads are commissions paid to brokers who sell mutual funds. Loads typically range from 2 percent to as high as 6 or 7 percent of your investment. (An astonishing 73 percent of fund buyers surveyed by the Investment Company Institute didn't know whether the fund they bought charged a sales load!) Sales loads have two problems:

  ✔ **Sales loads are a needless cost that drags down your investment returns.** Because commissions are paid to the salesperson and not to the fund manager, the manager of a load fund doesn't work any harder and isn't any more qualified than a manager of a no-load fund. Common sense suggests, and studies confirm, that load funds perform *worse,* on average, than no-loads, when factoring in the load. And don't think that spotting a load fund is easy. Just as some jewellers flog fake diamonds on late-night TV commercials, increasing numbers of brokers and financial planners are selling bogus funds that appear to be no-loads but are not — they just hide the sales commission.

"Stay in this fund for five to seven years," the broker tells you, "and you don't have to pay the back-end sales that would normally apply upon sale of the investment." Although this claim may be true, the fund is probably also charging you high ongoing operating expenses (usually 1 percent more per year than true no-load funds) that the fund uses to pay the salesperson a hefty commission. So one way or another, the broker gets his pound of flesh (that is, his commission) from your investment dollars. These commissions that kick in when selling fund units are also referred to as *back-end loads and deferred sales charge,* or DSCs.

The problem with back-end loads is if you want to move your money out of these funds simply because you need the cash, or perhaps the managers that attracted you to them leave to work elsewhere, you are penalized if you sell your fund units.

✔ **The power of self-interest can bias your broker's advice.** Although this issue is rarely discussed, it's even more problematic than the issue of extra sales costs. Brokers who work for a commission are interested in selling you commission-based investment products; therefore, their best interests often conflict with your best interests.

Although you may be mired in high-interest debt or underfunding your retirement plan, some salespeople may never advise you to pay off your credit cards or put more money into your employer's pension plan. To get you to buy, they tend to exaggerate the potential benefits and obscure the risks and drawbacks of what they sell. They don't take the time to educate investors. We've seen too many people purchase investment products through brokers without understanding what they're buying, how much risk they're taking, and how these investments will affect their overall financial lives.

Invest in no-load (commission-free) funds. The only way to be sure that a fund is truly no-load is to look at the prospectus for the fund. Only there, in black and white and without marketing hype, must the truth be told about sales charges and other fund fees. When you want investing advice, hire a financial adviser on a fee-for-service basis (see Chapter 18), which can cost you less and minimize potential conflicts of interest.

If you want to buy a load fund — and there are some good choices available — remember that the load is the maximum, not the required, sales commission allowed. If you have enough business to offer them, some planners and brokers will sell you load funds at minimal cost, or even with no sales charge at all, because they receive ongoing commissions called *trailer fees* as long as you keep your money in a fund. If you do opt to pay commissions, be sure you're getting high quality, ongoing advice and expertise — after all, you're already paying for it!

Minimizing operating expenses

All mutual funds charge ongoing fees. The fees pay for the operational costs of running the fund — employees' salaries, marketing, servicing the toll-free phone lines, printing and mailing published materials, maintaining computers for tracking investments and account balances, accounting fees, and so on. Despite being labelled "expenses," the profit a fund company extracts for running the fund is added to the tab, as well.

The fund's operating expenses are quoted as an annual percentage of your investment and are essentially invisible to you, because they're deducted before you're paid any return. The expenses are charged on a daily basis, so you don't need to worry about trying to get out of a fund before these fees are deducted.

You can find a fund's operating expenses in the fund's prospectus. Look in the expenses section and find a line that says something like "Total Fund Operating Expenses." You can also call the fund's toll-free number and ask a representative.

Within a given sector of mutual funds (for example, money market, short-term bonds, or international stock), funds with low annual operating fees can more easily produce higher total returns for you. Although expenses matter on all funds, some types of funds are more sensitive to high expenses than others. Expenses are critical on money market mutual funds and very important on bond funds. Fund managers already have a hard time beating the averages in these markets; with higher expenses added on, beating the averages is nearly impossible.

With stock funds, expenses are a less important (but still significant) factor in a fund's performance. Don't forget that, over time, stocks average returns of about 10 percent per year. So if one stock fund charges 1 percent more in operating expenses than another fund, you're already giving up an extra 10 percent of your expected returns.

Some people argue that stock funds that charge high expenses may be justified in doing so if they generate higher rates of return. Evidence doesn't show that these stock funds actually generate higher returns. In fact, funds with higher operating expenses tend to produce lower rates of return. This trend makes sense, because operating expenses are deducted from the returns a fund generates.

In general, stick with funds that maintain low total operating expenses and don't charge loads (commissions). Both types of fees come out of your pocket and reduce your rate of return.

You have no reason to pay a lot for the best funds, as Table 9-3 shows. (In Chapters 11 and 12, we provide some specific fund recommendations as well as sample portfolios for investors in different situations.)

Table 9-3	Mutual Fund Operating Expense Ratios	
Fund Type	*Expense Ratio Range*	*Who Offers Good Ones*
Money market funds	0.4% to 0.75%	Legg Mason; McLean Budden; Phillips, Hager & North; Sceptre
Bond funds	0.5% to 1.6%	Altamira, Bank of Montreal, Bissett, Legg Mason, Mawer, Phillips, Hager & North, RBC, TD
Hybrid	1.9% to 2.5%	AIM, Bissett, CI, Mawer, Saxon
Canadian stock	0.3% to 2%	AGF, Bank of Montreal, Bissett, RBC, Saxon, Sceptre, TD
U.S. stock	0.3% to 2.5%	AIC, Chou Associates, CI, McLean Budden, RBC, TD
International stock	0.5% to 2.5%	CI, CIBC, Mawer, Trimark
Index	0.3% to 1.25%	TD (especially the low expense eFunds), Altamira, Bank of Montreal, CIBC, National Bank, RBC, Scotiabank

Evaluating historical performance

A fund's *performance,* or historical rate of return, is another factor to weigh when selecting a mutual fund. As all mutual funds are supposed to tell you, past performance is no guarantee of future results. An analysis of historical mutual fund performance proves that some of yesterday's stars turn into tomorrow's skid-row bums.

Many former high-return funds achieved their results by taking on high risk. Funds that assume higher risk should produce higher rates of return. But high-risk funds usually decline in price faster during major market declines. Thus, in order for a fund to be considered a best fund, it must consistently deliver a favourable rate of return given the degree of risk it takes.

When assessing an individual fund, compare its performance and volatility over an extended period of time (five or ten years will do) to a relevant market index. For example, compare funds that focus on investing in large Canadian companies to the S&P/TSX index. For large U.S. companies, look at the Standard & Poor's 500 index, and for funds that invest in U.S. stocks of all sizes to the Wilshire 5000 index. Indexes also exist for bonds, foreign stock markets, and almost any other type of security you can imagine.

Assessing fund manager and fund family reputations

Much is made of who manages a specific mutual fund. As Peter Lynch, the retired (and famous) former manager of the Fidelity Magellan fund, said, "The financial press made us Wall Street types into celebrities, a notoriety that was largely undeserved. Stock stars were treated as rock stars. . . ."

Although the individual fund manager is important, no fund manager is an island. The resources and capabilities of the parent company are equally important. Different companies have different capabilities and levels of expertise in relation to the different types of funds. When you're considering a particular fund — for example, the Barnum & Barney High-Flying Foreign Stock fund — examine the performance history and fees not only of that fund but also of similar foreign stock funds at the Barnum & Barney company. If Barnum's other foreign stock funds have done poorly, or Barnum & Barney offers no other such funds because it's focused on its circus business, those are strikes against its High-Flying fund. Also be aware that "star" fund managers tend to be associated with higher-expense funds to help pay their rock-star salaries.

Rating tax-friendliness

Investors often overlook tax implications when selecting mutual funds they plan on holding outside of their RRSP or Registered Retirement Income Fund (RRIF). Numerous mutual funds effectively reduce their shareholders' returns because of their tendency to produce more taxable distributions — that is, capital gains and dividends. (See the sections "Dividends" and "Capital gains" later in this chapter.)

Mutual fund capital gains distributions have a significant impact on an investor's after-tax rate of return. All mutual fund managers buy and sell stocks during the course of a year. Whenever a mutual fund manager sells securities, any gain or loss from those securities must be distributed to fund shareholders. Securities sold at a loss can offset securities sold at a profit.

When a fund manager has a tendency to cash in more winners than losers, investors in the fund receive a high amount of taxable gains. So, even though some funds can lay claim to producing higher total returns, after you factor in taxes, they actually may not produce higher total returns.

Choosing mutual funds that minimize capital gains distributions helps you defer taxes on your profits. By allowing your capital to continue compounding as it would in a retirement account, you receive a higher total return. When you're a long-term investor, you benefit most from choosing mutual funds that minimize capital gains distributions. The more years that appreciation can compound without being taxed, the greater the value to you as the investor.

 Investors who purchase mutual funds outside tax-sheltered retirement plans should also consider the time of year they purchase shares in funds. December is the most common month in which mutual funds make capital gains distributions. When making purchases late in the year, ask if and when the fund may make a significant capital gains distribution. Consider delaying purchases in such funds until after the distribution date.

Determining your needs and goals

Selecting the best funds for you requires an understanding of your investment goals and risk tolerance. What may be a good fund for your next-door neighbour may not necessarily be a good fund for you. You have a unique financial profile.

If you've already determined your needs and goals — terrific! If you haven't, refer to Chapter 2. Understanding yourself is a good part of the battle. But don't shortchange yourself by not being educated about the investment you're considering. If you don't understand what you're investing in and how much risk you're taking, you should stay out of the game.

Deciphering Your Fund's Performance

Odds are that when you look at a statement for your mutual fund holdings you're not going to understand it. Getting a handle on how you're doing is the hardest part. Most people want to know (and have a hard time figuring out) how much they made or lost on their investment.

You can't simply calculate your return by comparing the share price of the fund today to the share price you originally paid. Why not? Because mutual funds make distributions (of dividends and capital gains), which lead to your getting more shares of the fund.

Distributions create an accounting problem, because they reduce the share price of a fund. (Otherwise you could make a profit from the distribution by buying into it just before a distribution is made.) Therefore, over time, following just the share price of your fund doesn't tell you how much money you made or lost.

Imagine that the share price of your mutual fund is like a balloon with a small rock tied to the end of its string. The balloon (representing fund share price) struggles to rise, but the rock (representing fund distributions) keeps pulling down on it.

The only way to figure out exactly how much you made or lost on your investment is to compare the total value of your holdings in the fund today with the total dollar amount you originally invested. If you invested chunks of money at various points in time, and you want to factor in the timing of your various investments, this exercise becomes more complicated. (Check out our investment software recommendations in Chapter 19 if you want your computer to help you crunch the numbers.)

The total return of a fund is the percentage change of your investment over a specified period. For example, a fund may tell you that, in 2005, its total return was 15 percent. Therefore, if you invested $10,000 in the fund on the last day of 2004, your investment would be worth $11,500 at the end of 2005. To find out a fund's total return, you can call the fund company's toll-free number, visit the company's Web site, or read the fund's annual report.

The following three components make up your total return on a fund:

- Interest and dividends
- Capital gains distributions
- Share price changes

Interest and dividends

Both bonds and stocks can pay interest. A second source of income is dividends paid out by stocks a fund holds. When an interest or dividend distribution is made, you can receive it as cash (which is good if you need money to live on) or as more shares in the fund. In either case, the share price of the fund drops by an amount to offset the payout. So if you are hoping to strike it rich by buying into a bunch of funds just before they pay out, don't bother. You'll just end up paying more in income taxes.

If you hold your mutual fund outside a retirement plan, both interest and dividend distributions are taxable income. You'll have to pay tax on your gains whether you receive them as cash or use them to buy more units of the fund.

Interest is taxed at your full marginal tax rate. Dividends, however, are taxed at a much lower rate thanks to the dividend tax credit. As a result, dividend funds are a good bet if you are investing to earn income outside of a tax-sheltered plan such as an RRSP. (See Chapter 6 for more on how different types of investments are taxed.) The approximate tax rates on dividends are as follows: Dividends are taxed at 7 percent for those in the 24 percent marginal tax bracket and 19 percent for those in the 34-percent marginal tax bracket. For higher-income earners in the 41-percent marginal tax bracket dividends are taxed at 26 percent, and for those in the 45-percent bracket the dividend tax rate is 31 percent.

Capital gains

When a mutual fund manager sells a security in the fund, net gains realized from that sale (the difference from the purchase price) must be distributed to you as a capital gain. Typically, funds make one annual capital gains distribution in December, but distributions can be paid multiple times per year.

As with a dividend distribution, you can receive your capital gains distribution as cash or as more shares in the fund. In either case, the share price of the fund drops to offset the distribution.

For funds held outside retirement plans, your capital gains distribution is taxable. As with dividends, capital gains are taxable whether or not you reinvest them in additional shares in the fund. If you want to avoid making an investment in a fund that is about to make a capital gains distribution, check with the fund to determine when capital gains are distributed. Capital gains distributions increase your current-year tax liability for investments made outside of retirement plans. (We discuss this concept in more detail in Chapter 12.)

Share price changes

You also make money with a mutual fund when the unit price increases. This occurrence is just like investing in a stock or piece of real estate. If the mutual fund is worth more today than it was when you bought it, you made a profit (on paper, at least). In order to realize or lock in this profit, you need to sell your shares in the fund.

There you have it. Here are the components of a mutual fund's total return:

```
Dividends and interest distribution + Capital gains +
          Share price changes = Total return
```

Following and Selling Your Funds

How closely you follow your funds is up to you, depending on what makes you happy and comfortable. We don't recommend tracking the unit prices of your funds (or other investments, for that matter) on a daily basis; it's time-consuming and nerve-racking, and it can make you lose sight of the long-term picture. When you track your investments too closely, you're more likely to panic when times get tough. And with investments held outside of retirement plans, every time you sell an investment at a profit you get hit with taxes.

A monthly or quarterly check-in is more than frequent enough for following your funds. Many publications carry total return numbers over varying periods so that you can determine the exact rate of return you're earning.

Trying to time and trade the markets so that you buy at lows and sell at highs rarely works. Yet an entire industry of investment newsletters, hotlines, online services, and the like purport to be able to tell you when to buy and sell. Don't waste your time and money on such nonsense. (See Chapter 9 for more info about gurus and newsletters.)

You should consider selling a fund when it no longer meets the criteria mentioned in the section "Selecting the Best Mutual Funds" earlier in this chapter. If a fund underperforms its peers for at least a two-year period, or if a fund jacks up its management fees, it may be a good time to sell. But if you do your homework and buy good funds from good fund companies, you shouldn't have to do much trading.

Finding and investing in good funds isn't rocket science. Chapters 11 and 12 recommend some specific mutual funds using the criteria discussed earlier in this chapter.

Chapter 10

Registered Retirement Savings Plans

. . . .

In This Chapter

▶ Looking at the benefits of RRSPs

▶ Figuring out how to boost your contributions

▶ Considering your options for when your RRSP matures

. . . .

*F*or most Canadians, putting money into an RRSP is the most effective, easy, and efficient way to save for retirement and reduce the tax they pay. To make the most out of RRSPs, though, you need to understand not only how to use them, but also what they are and why they offer numerous benefits. The phrase Registered Retirement Savings Plan, or RRSP, is perhaps the single best-known financial term in the country. Unfortunately, it's also often one of the most misunderstood. For example, many people think of an RRSP as an investment. In fact, it's a special holding account or holding place in which you can place most generally available Canadian and foreign investments.

 Putting money into an RRSP is, for most people, the most effective, easy, and efficient way to save for retirement and reduce the tax they pay. To make the most out of RRSPs, though, you need to understand not only how to use them, but also what they are and how they offer numerous benefits.

How RRSPs Work

The word *Registered* in Registered Retirement Savings Plan means you have made an agreement with the government. By "registering" your retirement savings plan with the government, you agree to put money away for your retirement and not spend it. In return, the government gives you two valuable benefits:

> ✔ Money that you contribute to your RRSP is deductible from your taxable income. This means that any income that you contribute to your savings plan is not taxed.
>
> ✔ The government lets the savings in your RRSP grow tax-free. Any profits your RRSP investments earn are not taxable until you collapse your plan and withdraw the funds.

The combined benefits of tax-deductible contributions and tax-deferred growth combine to supercharge your retirement savings. Here's a look at the powerful impact they can have on your ability to save for the future.

The benefit of tax-deferred contributions

Money that you contribute to an RRSP can be deducted from your income before your income tax is calculated for the year. For instance, say you made $50,000 and contributed $5,000 to your RRSP. If you claimed that $5,000 as a deduction on your tax return, your income tax would be calculated as if you had made only $45,000 that year.

Suppose that you're in a 41-percent tax bracket, which means that the government takes 41 cents of the last dollar you earn. If you contribute $1,000 to your RRSP, you save yourself $410 in tax. So the *real* out-of-pocket cost of a $1,000 contribution is only $590. In other words, contributing $1,000 to your RRSP really only leaves you short $590 in after-tax money you can put your hands on.

As shown in Table 10-1, the tax savings from contributing to an RRSP are substantial, regardless of your tax bracket.

Table 10-1	Short-Term Benefits of Tax-Deductible RRSP Contributions			
Where	*Investment Amount*	*Tax Rate*	*Tax Reduction*	*After-Tax Cost in Dollars*
Outside RRSP	$5,000	All	$0	$5,000
Inside RRSP	$5,000	24%	$1,200	$3,800
Inside RRSP	$5,000	34%	$1,700	$3,300
Inside RRSP	$5,000	41%	$2,050	$2,950
Inside RRSP	$5,000	45%	$2,250	$2,750

The benefits of tax-deductible contributions increase over time. Suppose that you're 35 and invest $5,000 of your salary this year outside an RRSP. Assuming that, given your province's tax rate, you're in a combined federal and provincial tax bracket of 40 percent, the Canada Revenue Agency would first take $2,000 in tax, leaving you with $3,000. You invest that $3,000 in a mutual fund that earns a 10-percent compound return. After 30 years, you would have amassed a tidy $52,000. (This doesn't take into account the taxes you would likely have to pay each year on the distribution of capital gains, dividends, and interest, which would further reduce your average compound return outside an RRSP.)

Now, how would the numbers look if you had contributed that money to your RRSP? Because the Canada Revenue Agency doesn't take any tax off your contributions, you can invest the full $5,000. Right away, that puts you $2,000 ahead. (In the real world, of course, you would have had the tax already taken off your income as it was earned. But you would then receive a $2,000 tax rebate for your $5,000 contribution, so, at the end of the day, the real cost is only $3,000.)

If you invest that $5,000 in the same mutual fund inside an RRSP earning an average 10-percent compound return for 30 years, you're left with $87,000, or almost $35,000 more than you would have if you had put the money in a mutual fund. Table 10-2 shows just how valuable a tax-sheltered RRSP contribution can be to the long-term growth of your savings.

Table 10-2 Long-Term Payoff of Tax-Favoured RRSP Contributions			
Where	*Savings*	*Available for Investment (with 10-percent growth)*	*Value in 30 Years*
Inside RRSP	$5,000	$5,000	$87,000
Outside RRSP	$5,000	$3,000	$52,000

As Table 10-2 demonstrates, the message is simple: The more money you invest to begin with, the more money you end up with for any given investment.

Tax-deferred compound growth

If you put your money into an RRSP, any profits you earn with that money aren't taxed until you take the money out of your plan. Over time, the tax-free compounding leads to faster and faster growth of your retirement savings.

Tax-free compound growth occurs when interest and earnings on investments aren't taxed, so the full value is added to the original amount. This new, larger amount then earns further gains, which again are added to, or *compounded with,* your investments. Over time, this compounding leads to exponential growth. Just how well does compound growth work? A good guideline to remember is the "Rule of 72." Take 72, divide it by your rate of return, and the result is the approximate number of years it will take for your investment to double in value. For example, an investment earning 7 percent will double in about ten years.

Maximizing Your RRSP Savings

You need only follow two basic rules to turn your RRSP into a real moneymaker:

- ✔ Begin contributing as early as you can in life, and
- ✔ Try to maximize your RRSP's returns.

Starting an RRSP early in life

Your RRSP needs a good, long runway to get off the ground, but once it takes flight it will gain altitude quickly. The real value in starting as early in life as possible is not simply the total amount of the extra contributions you manage to put in. It's that the longer you have money in an RRSP, the more time your savings have to compound.

Take someone who starts an RRSP when she is 28, making annual $2,000 contributions each year until she's 65. If she puts her money into a family of mutual funds that earns an average return of 10 percent, the total accumulation would be about $660,000.

Getting motivated to make RRSP contributions

Looking at the benefits of an RRSP contribution is often an excellent way to stem your appetite for a large expense that you may desperately want but not necessarily need. Say, for example, that you were able to put $6,000 every year into your RRSP and earned an average return of 9 percent. After 30 years, you would have accumulated an impressive $817,845.

But what if you put in only $4,500 annually, using the extra $1,500 to give yourself a week in the sun? Your total would still be a respectable $613,384. But look at it another way. Indulging yourself a little today will cost you more than $200,000 in your retirement. Are your sunfests really worth having $200,000 less when you retire?

But she could have accumulated that same amount if she had begun putting $2,000 a year into an RRSP when she was 21 — and contributed for only seven years (see Table 10-3).

Even if you're just 25 and have only $1,000 to spare, put it in an RRSP! If you earn an average of 10 percent a year, you'll have an extra $45,000 in your plan when you retire at 65.

Table 10-3	The Money-Earning Potential of Starting an RRSP When You're Young			
Annual Contribution	*Age Beginning*	*Age Ended*	*Total Years*	*Final Value at Age 65*
$2000	21	27	7	$664,000
$2000	28	65	37	$660,000

Note: Table 10-3 assumes a 10-percent annual rate of return.

Examples like the previous one are commonly used to sell the benefits of putting money into an RRSP from an early age. The problem is that if you *aren't* young, these examples can be unsettling. If you didn't find out about the benefits of RRSPs when you were young or didn't have money to contribute, you likely find it dispiriting to realize the tax savings and compound growth you missed out on. Whatever you do, don't let that stop you from taking action today. To rework that old cliché, today is the first day of the rest of your financial life!

Increasing your returns

Choosing appropriate investments is critical in maximizing the growth of your RRSP. And the more years you have before you have to collapse your plan, the larger the impact of boosting your returns by even just 1 or 2 percent.

Say you contribute $5,000 a year to your plan for 30 years, and you earn an average return of 8 percent. The final value of your plan would be just over $566,000.

But consider the results if you had taken a little more time in choosing your RRSP investments and you had managed to earn 9 percent a year — just 1 percent more. In 30 years' time, your plan would be worth more than $681,000.

By improving your fund's performance by only 1 percent, you would end up with an extra $115,000! (See Table 10-4.)

Table 10-4	The Payoff from Profitable Investing: How a $5,000 Annual Contribution Will Grow	
Value at Growth Rate of . . . *Years*	*8%*	*9%*
5	$29,333	$29,924
10	$72,433	$75,965
30	$566,416	$681,538

Do you find it tough to come up with anywhere near your maximum allowable contribution when the RRSP deadline comes around? Try an automatic deduction plan. You can tell your financial institution or RRSP holder to take a certain amount out of your bank account every few weeks — for example, when your paycheque comes in. You likely won't miss the money, and you'll be surprised at how much more you can put away.

Understanding the Contribution Rules

As long as you are 69 years or younger and you have received income from a job, running a business, or even net rental income — that is, as long as you've received *earned income* — you generally can contribute to an RRSP. There is no minimum age requirement. Even a child can have an RRSP, as long as he or she has earned income.

Checking out the contribution limits

There are three factors that determine the maximum you can contribute to your RRSP in any year.

✔ **The absolute maximum amount that any one can contribute in any one year:** The maximum for the 2005 tax year is $16,500, and for 2006, $18,000. After 2006, the absolute maximum amount will be *indexed*, meaning it will be increased at the same rate as the cost of living is rising.

If you don't contribute the full amount you're allowed to in a given year — or don't make a contribution at all — the unused portion can be carried ahead and used in later years. For example, if you were allowed to contribute $7,000 this year and only contributed $5,000, you would have $2,000 of what's called *unused contribution room* to use in the future. If the next year your income meant that you could contribute

$10,000, the total amount you could contribute to your RRSP in that year would be $12,000 — the $2,000 of allowable contributions brought forward from the previous year, and the $10,000 allowable contribution for the current year. In the jargon of RRSPs, this amount is not called your allowable contribution, but your *contribution room*.

✔ **Your income:** The most you can contribute to your RRSP in any year is also limited to 18 percent of your earned income from the previous year, up to certain maximum amounts (see the sidebar "What's earned income?" for more information about what qualifies as earned income). For example, the most you could contribute in the 2006 tax year would be 18 percent of your 2005 earned income.

✔ **Whether you're a member of a company pension plan or a deferred profit sharing plan:** The government makes an estimate of the value of the pension you earned in the previous year. This amount, called your *pension adjustment (PA)* is subtracted from whichever is lower, the dollar maximum contribution allowable, or 18 percent of your earned income, to arrive at the most you can put into your RRSP.

TECHNICAL STUFF

What's earned income?

Now, you probably quite naturally believe that when it comes to your income, you've earned *all* of it — but the government has other ideas. When determining what qualifies as your "earned income," certain types of earnings are excluded.

Earned income includes only income sources such as these:

✔ Salary

✔ Net self-employment income

✔ Bonuses and commissions

✔ Net business income

✔ Taxable alimony, maintenance, and child-support payments you receive

✔ Net rental income

✔ Royalties

✔ Disability pension received under the Canada Pension Plan or Quebec Pension Plan

✔ Employee profit sharing plan income

✔ Unemployment benefits

✔ Some types of taxable employment incomes, including disability and sick benefits

The following *reduce* your earned income:

✔ Deductible alimony, maintenance, and child-support payments you make

✔ Most deductible employment-related expenses, including travel expenses and union dues

✔ Rental losses

✔ Union or professional dues

Finally, there are many types of income that are simply excluded from your earned income. In addition to most income from investments, including interest, dividends, and capital gains, you may not include pension benefits, retiring allowances or severance pay, death benefits, or money received from an RRSP, RRIF, or deferred profit-sharing plan.

In the spring or summer of each year, Canada Revenue Agency sends all taxpayers a Notice of Assessment for the previous year. Your contribution limit for the current year is included on the statement. For example, if you've filed your 2005 tax return, you'll find your allowable contribution for 2006 on your assessment statement, which you should receive in the first half of 2006.

Review your allowable maximum contribution to ensure that the government has come up with the right figure. If Canada Revenue Agency is too high and you overcontribute, you may risk having to pay a penalty. If the figure is too low, your plan will suffer because you won't have maximized your contribution.

Calculating your allowable contribution

To begin with, realize that the government puts absolute maximums on how much people, regardless of their situations, can contribute each year.

If you don't have a company pension plan, the most you can contribute in any given year, then, is the lowest of

✔ The annual maximum amount for that year (see the previous section), or

✔ 18 percent of your earned income in the previous year

(If no one in your family has a company pension plan, you can skip this next section. Those with plans, please stay with the program.)

If you belong to a pension plan or deferred profit-sharing plan (DPSP), the government further scales back the amount it lets you contribute. The thinking is that because you have alternative sources of retirement income, you shouldn't get the full tax break allotted to people without pensions.

The government reduces your otherwise maximum allowable contribution by the value attributed for the contributions that both you and your employer make to your pension or deferred profit-sharing plan. This figure is called your *pension adjustment*, or *PA factor*. How that figure is arrived at depends on the type of plan you belong to.

Your pension adjustment is then subtracted from 18 percent of your earned income to arrive at your RRSP limit. Your pension adjustment is listed on your T4 slip, which you should receive from your employer before the end of every February. In general, the higher your pension the larger your pension adjustment and the lower your maximum allowable contribution.

The contribution deadline

For any given tax year, you can make a contribution any time up to — and including — the 60th day in the next year. The last day you were allowed to contribute for the 2005 tax year, for example, was March 1, 2006. You could have contributed as early as January 1, 2005, of course. The only exception is that in the year in which you turn 69, you must contribute to your plan before December 31.

The only positive thing that can be said about leaving your contribution to the last minute is that it's probably good for an adrenaline rush. But consider this: If you plan ahead and make your contributions well in advance, you'll likely earn enough in extra interest over the years to pay for hours of heart-stopping bungee jumping and skydiving when you retire.

Every February, many people dash around trying to get their RRSP contribution in before the deadline. Rushed contributions, however, are usually made without considering investment options.

If you can't avoid making your contribution at the last minute, put off making any major investment decisions. Consider putting your money into a money market mutual fund or other cash-like investment, and then moving your money into better-performing investments when you have the time and energy to consider your options. By carefully assessing your RRSP investments, you can greatly boost the value of your plan, which translates directly into thousands of dollars more income to live on during retirement.

If you belong to a defined-benefit pension plan

With a defined-benefit pension plan, the amount you receive when you retire is based upon your years of service and your income level. If you belong to this kind of plan, your pension adjustment (PA factor) is based on a calculation of the future value attributed to your pension of your previous year of employment. Your maximum contribution for 2006, for example, would be 18 percent of your 2005 earned income to a maximum of $18,000, less your 2005 PA factor.

If you belong to a money-purchase pension plan

Your pension adjustment under this kind of pension plan is the total combined amount put into your pension by both you and your employer for the previous year. Your maximum contribution for 2006, for example, would be 18 percent of your 2005 earned income to a maximum of $18,000, less all the 2005 pension contributions (PA factor).

If you belong to a deferred profit-sharing plan

If your employer contributes money to a deferred profit-sharing plan on your behalf, your pension adjustment equals the total of the contributions made (up to the maximum allowable DPSP contribution) for the previous year. For example, your 2006 maximum would be 18 percent of your 2005 earned income to a maximum of $18,000, minus your 2005 PA factor.

Withdrawing money from your RRSP

You don't have to be retired to access the funds in your plan. You are allowed to withdraw money out of your RRSP whenever you like. When you do, though, the government will want to collect the taxes it had earlier forgone on your contributions.

When you withdraw money from your RRSP, the plan holder is required to withhold taxes on your withdrawals. As of 2005, the rates in all provinces (except Quebec) were 10 percent on amounts up to $5,000, 20 percent on the next $10,000, and 30 percent on withdrawals of more than $15,000. In Quebec, the withholding rates were 21 percent of amounts up to $5,000, 30 percent on any amount between $5,000 $15,000, and 35 percent on withdrawals of $15,000 and higher.

(When you do your income tax return, you have to declare your withdrawals as income in the year you took the money out of your plan. For most people, that will mean an additional tax bill because the withholding rates in most cases are lower than the marginal tax rate.)

The withholding tax rates are calculated on each individual withdrawal. If you do need to get at your RRSP funds, take out separate withdrawals of no more than $5,000 each time to minimize the amount of withholding tax.

Getting support from spousal RRSPs

A spousal RRSP can help reduce your household's future tax bill if you are married or living common-law and you anticipate there will be a big gap between your income and your spouse's income when you both retire.

Pensions and your contribution limits

Sometimes, pension benefits under a defined benefit pension plan are improved retroactively. If this happens, your RRSP contribution limit may be further reduced by a *past service pension adjustment* (PSPA).

On the other hand, you may find your contribution limits increased. For example, you may work for a company that has a pension plan. As a result, your RRSP contribution limits will be reduced by your pension adjustment. However, you may leave the company before you fully earn the rights to those benefits — before they *vest*. To give you back some of the RRSP contribution room that had been taken away because of the supposed pension benefits you were due to receive, you will get a *pension adjustment reversal* (PAR). A PAR increases your allowable RRSP contribution in the year you leave that particular job.

A *spousal RRSP* is simply a special kind of RRSP to which one spouse makes the contributions and is able to claim the tax deduction. However, the money then belongs to the other spouse. (While this change in official ownership worries some potential contributing partners, it shouldn't. In most cases the money in RRSPs is simply counted as part of your combined assets and divided equally between you and your spouse if you get separated or divorced.) A spousal RRSP allows you to move some future income out of the hands of the person in the higher tax bracket, and into the hands of the spouse with the lower retirement income, and therefore the lower tax bracket.

You need to know some specific rules. The total contributions made by a spouse to both his or her own plan and a spousal RRSP can't exceed that individual's allowable maximum individual contribution. In addition, there are restrictions to prevent the higher-earning spouse contributing to a spousal plan, claiming the deduction against income that is taxed at a high marginal rate, and then the lower-earning spouse removing the money from the plan and having it taxed at their lower marginal rate. If you contribute to a spousal plan, the money immediately belongs to your spouse. However, if he or she withdraws any of that contribution in that year or during the next two calendar years, the withdrawal is treated as if you had earned it, and taxed at your marginal rate. (This rule does not apply if you and your spouse are separated or divorced.)

Also, you have to close down your RRSP by the end of the year in which you turn 69. But if you have earned income in any year, that still earns your RRSP contribution room. If your spouse is 69 or younger, you can contribute to a spousal RRSP and claim a deduction.

Getting to Know the Different Types of RRSPs

While the names don't make complete sense, you'll often hear three different types of RRSP being pitched — *guaranteed, mutual funds,* and *self-directed* or *brokerage-house* RRSPs. The names are often partly dictated by the financial institution that is offering them. (You can get an RRSP just about anywhere — your local bank, trust company, brokerage house, insurance company, credit union, or mutual fund company.) Here's how to interpret what the different names mean.

Guaranteed RRSPs

Guaranteed plans are really just RRSPs in which you put your money into investments where your principal is protected, such as guaranteed investment certificates (GICs). When you do so, you lend your money to a bank or other financial institution in return for regular interest payments. Guaranteed plans pay fixed returns, and your money, if invested in GICs, is usually protected by the Canada Deposit Insurance Corporation's deposit protection.

Mutual fund RRSPs

The second basic type of RRSP is an investment in mutual funds. There are two benefits to mutual fund RRSPs. First, by using funds, you can invest your money in stocks and bonds, which over the long haul will handily beat the returns from guaranteed investments. Second, if you set up an RRSP with a mutual fund company, you can diversify your savings by putting them into several different types of funds with the same company. Some mutual fund companies charge an annual trustee fee ranging from $25 to $50 a year for RRSP accounts.

Self-directed and brokerage-house RRSPs

The third type of RRSP includes self-directed plans and RRSPs you open with brokerage houses. This type of plan allows you to invest in a wide range of securities. In addition to GICs and mutual funds, you can invest in individual stocks and bonds and a wide range of other securities.

You can set up a self-directed plan with most investment dealers and discount brokerages. Some of these companies charge an annual fee, which typically runs around $100. Some institutions are willing to reduce or eliminate their fees for self-directed plans. The discount brokerages run by the big banks and trust companies often waive the first-year fee for new plans. If you do have to pay a fee, make sure that you pay it out of your regular savings, not out of the funds in your plan.

Closing Down Your RRSP

You must close out, or *mature,* your RRSP by the end of the year during which you turn 69. You can make a final contribution to your plan in that year; however, instead of having 60 days into the next year to get your money in, the deadline for your final contribution is December 31.

Deciding just when to fold your plan and what to do with your funds are two of the most important financial decisions you'll ever make. Time your moves correctly and make some astute choices, and you'll find you have a much larger financial comfort zone than you expected. However, if you make your decisions at the last minute without doing your homework, you may find that your lack of attention costs you in terms of a lower standard of living.

Can I have more than one plan?

You aren't limited to a specific number of RRSPs. You could, for example, open up a handful of RRSPs, each investing in different types of investments, with different companies. There are drawbacks to having several plans, however.

The paperwork can be burdensome, and it can become a real chore to follow your investments. If you invest with a number of different mutual fund companies, the trustee fees can start to add up.

While you can close out your RRSP earlier than the year in which you celebrate your 69th birthday, the best strategy for most people is to leave your RRSP intact for as long as you're allowed. This is almost always the case if you decide to turn it into a *Registered Retirement Income Fund* (RRIF). If you choose to go the *annuity* route, collapsing your plan a year or two early can make sense. If interest rates are relatively high, you can lock in a higher-than-average return.

Wrapping up your RRSP: Your three options

You have three basic options to choose from when your RRSP matures. You can simply cash out — take all the money right out of your RRSP and do what you will with it. If you do, the Canada Revenue Agency will treat the sum total of your plan as taxable income in that year. The resulting tax bill will lop off anywhere from one-third to half of your retirement savings, right then and there. Ughh!

Far more practical is using the funds to buy an annuity by handing over your money to a financial institution (usually an insurance company), which then pays out regular sums to you for a period of time that you choose. This can be as short as ten years or as long as the rest of your life.

The third, and often best, choice is to convert your RRSP into another sort of registered plan that continues to enjoy tax-deferred compounding. The only condition of these accounts, called Registered Retirement Income Funds (or RRIFs), is that you take out a certain minimum amount every year.

You aren't limited to choosing one of these three options. You can choose to split your RRSP funds and use two or even all three of these different strategies.

To make the right decision for your individual circumstances, you have to consider a lot more than simply how much cash flow each option will bring in. Each strategy has its own specific tax burden and a different schedule on when those tax bills will come due to consider. Further, you need to decide how much control you want to have over how your funds are invested, and whether you want to have access to your funds. Finally, each option offers different levels of estate or survivorship protections.

Registered Retirement Income Funds (RRIFs)

An RRIF is similar in many ways to an RRSP. An RRIF allows your money to continue to grow tax-deferred, and you can invest your funds in most of the eligible RRSP investments, from money market funds to individual stocks. Also, as with an RRSP, you can have one, two, or a handful of different RRIFs.

The only difference between an RRIF and an RRSP is that you aren't allowed to put any money into your RRIF. Instead, you're required to take out a certain minimum amount each year.

These payments must start the year after you set up your RRIF. You can choose monthly, quarterly, semi-annual, or annual payments. What's more, you don't have to take your payments in cash. You can move any investment out of your RRIF without selling it. However, you must pay tax on the fair market value at the time of the withdrawal, just as if it had been taken out as income.

The main benefit of an RRIF is that you continue to have control over how and where your money is invested. This control gives you the best chance of earning healthier returns on your money. In particular, it allows you to invest in equities and bonds.

RRIFs also let you have a say about how much income you have. As long as you withdraw the required minimums, you can take out as little or as much as you wish in any given year. If you suddenly come into some money, you can leave your RRIF essentially untouched and keep ringing up tax-free growth. If you have a medical emergency, you can quickly get your hands on as much as you need at the time.

RRIFs are usually a good choice if you:

- Enjoy managing your money.
- Have an indexed company pension plan that guarantees you a basic level of income.
- Don't immediately need to start drawing on your funds. Another advantage of RRIFs is that you can convert them to an annuity at any time, whereas an annuity is for life: Once you sign up for an annuity, there's no changing your mind. Further, with an RRIF you have a lot more control over what happens to your money at your death.

Minimum RRIF withdrawals

Before 1993, you were required to have withdrawn all your money from your RRIF by the time you were 90. The rules changed in 1992 to allow you to maintain your RRIF as long as you live. If you opened an RRIF before 1993, your minimum withdrawals are determined by the pre-1993 rules until you hit 78 or, if you have a younger spouse, when he or she turns 78.

Your minimum withdrawals are a percentage of the market value of your RRIF at the end of the previous year. The requirement for each year is determined by your age on January 1 of that year (see Table 10-5).

Table 10-5	Minimum RRIF Withdrawals	
Age RRIF	**Opened before 1993**	**RRIF Opened 1993 and Later**
64	3.85%	3.85%
65	4.00%	4.00%
66	4.17%	4.17%
67	4.35%	4.35%
68	4.55%	4.55%
69	4.76%	4.76%
70	5.00%	5.00%
71	5.26%	7.38%
72	5.56%	7.48%
73	5.88%	7.59%
74	6.25%	7.71%
75	6.67%	7.85%
76	7.14%	7.99%
77	7.69%	8.15%
78	8.33%	8.33%
79	8.53%	8.53%
80	8.75%	8.75%
81	8.99%	8.99%
82	9.27%	9.27%

(continued)

Table 10-5 *(continued)*

Age RRIF	Opened before 1993	RRIF Opened 1993 and Later
83	9.58%	9.58%
84	9.93%	9.93%
85	10.33%	10.33%
86	10.79%	10.79%
87	11.33%	11.33%
88	11.96%	11.96%
89	12.71%	12.71%
90	13.62%	13.62%
91	14.73%	14.73%
92	16.12%	16.12%
93	17.92%	17.92%
94 and up	20.00%	20.00%

Annuities

When you use your RRSP funds to buy an annuity, you transfer your RRSP funds over to a financial institution (usually an insurance company), which then pays them back to you a little bit at a time. You don't pay tax on any RRSP funds at the time you turn them into an annuity. The regular payments from the annuity, though, are taxable and treated by the Canada Revenue Agency as "pension" income. If you have no other pension income, up to $1,000 of the annuity payments will qualify for the Pension Income Tax Credit.

The biggest decision when buying an annuity is the length of time you want your payments to run for. One option is to pick a specific number of years, such as 5, 10, or 20. At the end of the specific time, your payments end and your annuity is fully depleted. Another choice is a *life annuity,* which provides you with payments for the rest of your life, while a *joint-life annuity* continues payments as long as you or your spouse is still alive.

If you select a life annuity, the size of your payments depends on your age and sex. Men tend to die at an earlier age than women do, so life annuity payments for males are generally higher because the funds have to last for fewer years. And, obviously, the younger you are the smaller your payments will be because (we hope) your payments will have to stretch far into the future.

You can also add a couple of wrinkles to your annuity. If you choose a life annuity, even if you die the very next week the insurance company gets to keep all the money. But if you choose a *guaranteed annuity,* you ensure that if you die before a certain number of years have passed the payments will continue and will go to your beneficiaries. You can also choose to have your payments increase gradually from year to year. Such *indexed annuities* help your income keep up with inflation.

Just how much your funds will pay you, how long you want them to continue, and the options you want are all put through complex calculations by the technical climbers of the accounting world, actuaries. Once you decide on your options, your payments can be calculated by using the statistics of how long you're likely to live and the likelihood of your dying at various ages. (Don't ask to see these numbers, because you probably don't want to know.) After you select your options, they can never be changed; they will remain in place until the annuity contract ends with your death or, if you chose the spousal survivor option, when your spouse dies.

This means that options such as indexing and guarantees all come at a price. Because these features mean that the insurance company will in all likelihood have to pay out more money, your regular payments will be lower than if you chose to go with a basic, stripped-down *defined-term annuity*.

Annuities are usually best if you:

- ✔ Have small retirement savings that absolutely need to last a number of years, especially if you're young and your family has a history of living a long time.

- ✔ Must have the peace of mind that comes with knowing just how much you have to live on.

- ✔ Don't want to have to make ongoing decisions about how to invest your money.

On the flip side of these advantages are several drawbacks, including these:

- ✔ You lose all control of your savings.

- ✔ Your rate of return is fixed when you buy your plan and will likely be lower than what you could earn investing in good mutual funds. If the investment world suddenly becomes littered with far more profitable options, you'll just have to lump it.

- ✔ If you don't accept lower payments in return for an indexed annuity, you may be faced with having less buying power over the years if inflation takes off.

- ✔ If you don't take out a guarantee, or you die after the guarantee period expires, your family or other beneficiaries won't get anything on your death.

Unlocking locked-in RRSPs and retirement accounts

If you leave a company in which you were a member of a pension plan, you may have earned the right to your pension benefits. However, you may not be allowed to gain access to those benefits due to the pension regulations (*locking-in* legislation). In this case, your pension benefits may be transferred to a special type of RRSP called a *locked-in RRSP* or *locked-in retirement account* (*LIRA*). Withdrawals from the locked-in account are usually subject to the same rules as the pension plan. For example, you may only be able to actually take control of the money within ten years of the retirement age specified in the pension plan.

The largest drawback to annuities is that you lose all input in how your money is invested and in how much it earns for you. You also have to accept lower initial payments if you want your annuity to increase with the cost of living.

Even then, you are still limited in what you can do. One choice is to use the money to purchase an annuity. A second option is to convert the funds into a special Registered Retirement Income Fund (RRIF) called a *life income fund,* or *LIF.* Like an RRIF, you have to withdraw a set minimum as a percentage of the funds in your LIF every year. However, unlike an RRIF, on which there are no maximums, a LIF has a ceiling on how much you can withdraw each year as well. Another rule that makes an LIF more restricted than an RRIF is that when you turn 80 you have to take the money inside your LIF and buy a life annuity. Some provinces have recognized that this is an unneeded rule, and have introduced *locked-in retirement income funds,* or *LRIFs*. These work much like LIFs. The big difference is that with an LRIF, there is no requirement to purchase an annuity at age 80.

Chapter 11

Investing in Retirement Plans

. . . .

In This Chapter

▶ Determining how to allocate money in RRSPs and retirement plans

▶ Looking at investments to avoid in RRSPs and retirement plans

▶ Moving your retirement plan to a new firm

. . . .

This chapter helps you decide how to invest money you currently hold inside — or plan to contribute to — an RRSP or other retirement plan.

When compared to the often-overwhelming world of investing outside retirement accounts, investing inside tax-sheltered retirement plans — RRSPs, RRIFs, and company plans — is less complicated for two reasons:

✔ **The range of possible retirement plan investments is more limited.** Direct investments, such as real estate and investments in small, privately owned companies, are not generally available or accessible in most retirement plans.

✔ **When you invest in a tax-sheltered retirement plan, your returns aren't taxed as you earn them.** Money inside retirement plans compounds and grows without taxation. You generally pay taxes on these funds only when you withdraw money from the account. (Direct transfers to registered retirement plans at another investment firm are not withdrawals, so they're not taxed.) So when you choose an investment for your retirement plan, don't rack your brain over dividends and capital gains; save all that worry for the money you invest in non-retirement accounts.

Allocating Your Money in Retirement Plans

With good reason, people are concerned about placing their retirement plan money in investments that can decline in value. You may feel that you're gambling with dollars intended for the security of your golden years.

Most working folks need to make their money work hard in order for it to grow fast enough to provide this security. This involves taking some risk; you have no way around it. Luckily, if you have 15 to 20 years or more before you need to draw on the bulk of your retirement plan assets, time is on your side. As long as the value of your investments has time to recover, what's the big deal if some of your investments drop a bit over a year or two? The more years you have before you're going to retire, the greater your ability to take risk.

The section on asset allocation in Chapter 7 can help you decide how to divide your money among different investment options based on your time frame and risk tolerance.

Understanding the difference between an RRSP and the investments inside your RRSP

Investments and account types are different issues. People sometimes get confused when discussing the investments they make in retirement plans, especially RRSPs. Often, they don't realize that you can have an RRSP at a variety of financial institutions (for example, a mutual fund company or brokerage firm). At each financial institution, you can choose among the firm's investment options for putting your RRSP money to work.

No-load, or commission-free, mutual fund and discount brokerage firms are your best bet for establishing an RRSP. For more specifics, see our recommendations in Chapter 9.

Prioritizing retirement contributions

When you have access to various retirement plans, prioritize which account you're going to use first by determining how much each gives you in return. Your first contributions should be to employer-based plans that match your contributions. After that, contribute to any other employer plan that allows tax-deductible contributions or to an RRSP. After you contribute as much as possible to tax-deductible plans, consider an annuity (see the section on annuities later in this chapter).

Allocating money when your employer selects the investment options

In some company-sponsored plans, you're limited to the predetermined investment options your employer offers. In the following sections, we discuss typical investment options for employer-sponsored plans in order of increasing risk and, hence, likely return. Then we follow with examples of how to allocate your money across the different types of common employer retirement plan options.

Money market/savings accounts

For regular contributions that come out of your paycheque, the money market or savings account option makes little sense. Some people who are skittish about the stock and bond markets are attracted to money market and savings accounts because they can't drop in value. However, the returns are low . . . so low that you have a great risk that your investment will not stay ahead of, or even keep up with, inflation and taxes (which are due upon withdrawal of your money from the retirement plan).

Don't be tempted to use a money market fund as a parking place until the time that you think stocks and bonds are cheap. In the long run, you won't be doing yourself any favours. As we discuss in Chapter 7, timing your investments to attempt to catch the lows and avoid the peaks is impossible. If you can figure out how to do that, you're wasting your time in your current occupation: You can make a fortune as a professional money manager.

You may need to keep money in the money market investment option if you utilize the borrowing feature that some retirement plans allow. Check with your employee benefits department for more details. After you retire, you may also want to use a money market to hold money you expect to withdraw and spend within a year or so.

Bond mutual funds

Bond mutual funds (which we describe in Chapter 9) invest in a mixture of typically high-quality bonds. Bonds pay a higher rate of interest or dividends than money funds. Depending on whether your plan's option is a short-term or long-term fund (maybe you have more than one type), the bond fund's current yield is probably a percentage or two higher than the money market fund's yield.

Bond funds carry higher yields than money market funds, but they also carry greater risk, because their value can fall if interest rates increase. However, bonds tend to be more stable in value than stocks.

Aggressive, younger investors should keep a minimum amount of money in bond funds. Older folks who want to invest conservatively can place more money in bonds (see the asset allocation discussion in Chapter 7).

Guaranteed investment certificates (GICs)

GICs are backed by a bank, trust company, or insurance company, and they typically quote you a rate of return projected anywhere from six months to five or more years forward. The positive return is, as the name implies, guaranteed — so you don't have the uncertainty that you normally face with bond or stock investments.

The attraction of these investments is that your account value does not fluctuate (at least, not that you can see). Financial institutions normally invest your money mostly in bonds and maybe a bit in stocks. The difference between what these investments generate and what they pay in interest is profit to the issuer. A GIC's yield is usually comparable to that of a bond fund.

For people who hit the eject button the moment that a bond fund slides a bit in value, GICs are soothing to the nerves. And they're certainly higher yielding than a money market or savings account.

Like bonds, however, GICs don't give you the opportunity for long-term growth. Over the long haul, you should earn a better return in a mixture of bond and stock investments. In GICs, you pay for the peace of mind of a guaranteed return with lower long-term returns.

Balanced mutual funds

Balanced mutual funds invest primarily in a mixture of stocks and bonds. This one-stop-shopping concept makes investing easier and smooths out fluctuations in the value of your investments — funds investing exclusively in stocks or in bonds make for a rougher ride. These funds are solid options and, in fact, can be used for a significant portion of your retirement plan contributions. One drawback is that balanced funds often come with relatively high management expense fees. Refer to Chapter 9 to find out more about balanced funds.

Stock mutual funds

Stock mutual funds invest in stocks, which often provide greater long-term growth potential but also wider fluctuations in value from year to year. Some companies offer a number of different stock funds, including funds that invest overseas. Most people should have a healthy helping of stock funds. See Chapter 9 for an explanation of the different types of stock funds as well as for details on how to evaluate a stock fund.

Shares in the company you work for

Some companies offer employees the option of investing in the company's stock. We generally advocate avoiding this option for the simple reason that your future income and other employee benefits are already riding on the success of the company. If the company hits the skids, you may lose your job and your benefits. You certainly don't want the value of your retirement plan to depend on the same factors.

Recall the hubbub from the early 2000s, when companies such as Enron went under and their employees lost piles of money in their retirement savings plans. Enron's bankruptcy in and of itself shouldn't have caused direct problems for those who had money tied up in Enron's pension plan. The problem was that Enron required employees to hold substantial amounts of Enron company stock. Thus, when the company tanked, employees lost their jobs as well as much of their retirement savings.

If you think that your company has its act together and the stock is a good buy, investing a portion of your retirement plan funds is fine — but no more than 25 percent. Now, if your company is on the verge of hitting it big, and the stock is soon to soar, you'll of course be kicking yourself for not putting more of your money into the company's shares. But when you place a big bet on your company's stock, be prepared to suffer the consequences if the shares tank. Don't forget that lots of smart investors track companies' prospects, so odds are that the current value of your company's shares is fair.

Some employers offer employees the option to buy company shares at a discount, sometimes as much as 15 percent, when compared to its current market value. If your company offers a discount on its shares, take advantage of it When you sell the stock as your employer's plan allows (usually after a certain holding period), you should be able to lock in a decent profit.

Some asset allocation examples

Using the methodology that we outline in Chapter 7 for allocating money, Table 11-1 shows a couple of examples of how people in different employer plans may choose to allocate their retirement investments among the plan's options.

Please note that making allocation decisions is not a science. Use the formulas in Chapter 7 as a guideline.

Table 11-1	Allocating Company Pension Plan Investments		
Risk	*25-Year-Old, Aggressive*	*45-Year-Old, Moderate Risk*	*60-Year-Old, Moderate Risk*
Bond fund	10%	35%	50%
Balanced fund (50% stock/ 50% bond)	10%	0%	0%
Blue-chip/larger company stock fund(s)	30–40%	25–30%	25%
Smaller company stock fund(s)	20%	15%	10%
International stock fund(s)	20–30%	20–25%	15%

Allocating money in RRSPs

With RRSPs, you get to select the investment options as well as the allocation of money among them.

International investing and your RRSP

Up to 2005, there was a longstanding rule that limited the amount of your RRSP you were allowed to invest in foreign investments. Thankfully, the government abolished this limitation in 2005.

The rule made it difficult to maximize your foreign exposure and yet not go over your limit. If you exceeded the allowable maximum, you were hit with penalties on the excess. More to the point, the rule meant that Canadians had to choose from a much smaller range of possible investments for the somewhat nebulous interests of the country, which were supposedly being served by keeping most of your RRSP funds invested in Canadian securities.

Prior to the rule change, many mutual fund companies had found a way for investors to stay under the foreign content limit, but have more than the allowable maximum invested in non-Canadian investments. They did this with *clone funds*. These were funds built to mirror the performance of funds invested in foreign securities, yet set up in such a way that you could put an unlimited percentage of your RRSP into them without transgressing the rules.

In essence, fund companies took a fund that would normally qualify as foreign content and, using advanced financial instruments, make the fund qualify as Canadian content. You essentially got a fund that mirrored the return of the non–RRSP friendly version of the fund, but the fund didn't eat up any of your 30-percent foreign content limit. They were foreign funds in an RRSP rules-friendly wrapper. However, these funds usually had a higher management fee compared to the regular version of the fund. At their peak, there were more than 200 of these clone funds on the market.

With the end of the restrictions on foreign content, fund companies began to close down their clone funds. Investors were generally allowed to swap the units they had in these clone funds for units in the non-clone version of the same foreign fund, gaining from the non-clone's lower expenses. If your units have not been transferred to a non-clone fund, contact the fund company and ask what steps you need to take to move your money into the regular, lower-fee fund or funds.

While the ending of the foreign content restrictions makes administering your RRSP easier and lets you choose from a much larger universe of potential investments, don't simply assume you should abandon Canadian securities. In recent years the Canadian stock market has been a strong performer. In addition, the Canadian dollar has been doing well. If you had money invested in U.S. securities, your returns would have been decreased by the drop of the U.S dollar against the loonie. Many so-called Canadian companies also have built-in international exposure to the rest of the world. Companies like Bombardier, for example, sell to many countries around the world. Finally, Canada is home to both mining companies and many oil and gas companies. There is a growing belief that commodities should do well over the next several years. In particular, as demand for oil increases and the supply falls, conditions look favourable for companies in the oil sector.

In the sections that follow, we give some specific recipes that you may find useful for investing at some of the premier investment companies. To establish an RRSP at one of these firms, simply pick up your telephone, dial the company's toll-free number, and ask the representative to mail you an account application. You can also have the company mail you background information on specific mutual funds. (If you're less patient, and you're a fan of the Internet, many investment firms provide downloadable account applications. However, downloading an application can be a tedious process, especially if you also need other information such as investment prospectuses and annual reports.)

Note. We recommend a conservative portfolio and an aggressive portfolio for each firm. We use the terms *conservative* and *aggressive* in a relative sense. Because some of the funds we recommend do not maintain fixed percentages of their different types of investments, the actual percentage of stocks and bonds that you end up with may vary slightly from the targeted percentages. Don't sweat it.

When you have more than one fund choice, you can pick one or split the suggested percentage among them. If you don't have enough money today to divide your portfolio up as we suggest, you can achieve the desired split over time as you add more money to your RRSP's.

Here are some examples of how you might allocate your money among different funds offered by two of our recommended fund companies.

Franklin Templeton Investments

The following two Franklin Templeton (1 800-897-7282; www.templeton. ca) recommendations are for a conservative mix and an aggressive mix, respectively.

A conservative portfolio with 50-percent stocks, 50-percent bonds

If you don't want to risk too much, try this:

- ✓ Bissett Canadian Equity — 20 percent
- ✓ Bissett Bond — 35 percent
- ✓ Bissett Canadian Balanced — 15 percent
- ✓ Templeton Global Balanced — 15 percent
- ✓ Templeton Growth — 15 percent

An aggressive portfolio with 80-percent stocks, 20-percent bonds

If you can afford to be aggressive, try this:

- ✓ Bissett Large Cap Equity — 30 percent
- ✓ Bissett Small Cap — 5 percent
- ✓ Bissett Dividend Income — 10 percent
- ✓ Templeton Growth — 25 percent
- ✓ Templeton Global Smaller Co. — 10 percent
- ✓ Bissett Bond — 20 percent

Phillips, Hager & North

The following two Phillips, Hager & North (1-800-661-6141; www.phn.com) recommendations are for a conservative mix and an aggressive mix, respectively.

A conservative portfolio with 50-percent stocks, 50-percent bonds

If you don't want to risk too much, try this:

- ✔ PH&N Canadian Equity — 15 percent
- ✔ PH&N Bond — 35 percent
- ✔ PH&N Balanced — 30 percent
- ✔ PH&N Dividend — 10 percent
- ✔ PH&N Global Equity Portfolio — 10 percent

An aggressive portfolio with 80-percent stocks, 20-percent bonds

If you can afford to be aggressive, try this:

- ✔ PH&N Canadian Equity — 30 percent
- ✔ PH&N Canadian Growth — 10 percent
- ✔ PH&N Dividend — 10 percent
- ✔ PH&N U.S. Equity — 15 percent
- ✔ PH&N Global Equity — 15 percent
- ✔ PH&N Bond — 20 percent

Self-directed or discount brokerage portfolios

You don't have to set up your RRSP with one particular mutual fund company. Discount brokerages offer self-directed RRSPs in which you can choose from a huge range of investments — including mutual funds. When you buy through discount brokerages, you can buy hundreds of different mutual funds without paying transaction fees. However, there may be a charge for switching funds or selling within a certain period. Here is a suggested conservative portfolio and an aggressive portfolio using a basket of funds from different fund companies.

A conservative portfolio with 50-percent stocks, 50-percent bonds

If you don't want to risk too much, try this:

✔ Elliot and Page, Bissett Canadian Equity, or RBC O'Shaughnessy Canadian Equity — 25 percent.

✔ Mawer World Investment — 15 percent

✔ AGF International Value — 10 percent

✔ Altamira Bond or TD Canadian Bond — 35 percent

✔ RBC Global Bond — 15 percent

An aggressive portfolio with 80-percent stocks, 20-percent bonds

If you can afford to be aggressive, try this:

✔ Sceptre Equity or Legg Mason Canadian Growth — 30 percent

✔ Saxon Small Cap — 10 percent

✔ GBC Canadian Growth — 10 percent

✔ Fidelity Growth America — 15 percent

✔ RBC O'Shaughnessy U.S. Value — 15 percent

✔ Altamira Bond or TD Canadian Bond — 20 percent

Index funds and exchange-traded funds

Don't forget that the majority of mutual funds fail to match the returns rung up by the general markets. If the low-cost investing appeals to you, consider building your own portion using low-cost index funds and *exchange-traded funds* (ETFs). ETFs are traded like stocks, but they are designed to mirror the returns of different indexes. For example, the S&P/TSX 60 Index Participation iUnits matches the return of the S&P/TSX 60 index.

Should I use one investment firm, or more?

The firms we recommend in this chapter offer a large enough variety of investment options, managed by different fund managers, that you can feel comfortable concentrating your money at one firm. Discovering the nuances and choices of just one firm rather than several and having fewer administrative hassles are the advantages of a focused approach.

If you like the idea of spreading your money around, you may want to invest through a number of different firms. With a discount brokerage account (see Chapter 7), you can have your cake and eat it too. You can diversify across different mutual fund companies through one brokerage firm. However, you may have to pay small transaction fees on some of your purchases and sales of funds.

You can purchase all of these products through most brokerages. If you buy them online, TD offers a line of "e" index funds with extremely low management expense ratios (MERs). ETFs are provided by Barclays Global Investors Canada (their ETFs are called *iUnits*) as well as Vanguard.

Discount brokers

As we discuss in Chapter 7, a discount brokerage account can allow you centralized, one-stop shopping and the ability to hold mutual funds from a variety of leading fund companies. Some funds are available without transaction fees, although most of the better funds require you to pay a small transaction fee when you buy funds through a discount broker. The reason: The discounter is an intermediary between you and the fund companies. You have to weigh the convenience of being able to buy and hold funds from multiple fund companies in a single account versus the lower cost of buying funds directly from their providers. A $25 to $30 transaction fee can gobble a sizeable chunk of what you have to invest, especially if you're investing smaller amounts.

Among brokerage firms or brokerage divisions of mutual fund companies, for breadth of fund offerings and competitive pricing we like BMO InvestorLine (888-776-6886; www.bmoinvestorline.com), TD Waterhouse (800-465-5463; www.tdwaterhouse.ca.com), and E*Trade Canada (888-872-3388; www.etrade.ca).

Inappropriate Retirement Plan Investments

Some investments are simply inappropriate for retirement plans. The basic problem stems from otherwise intelligent folks forgetting, ignoring, or simply not knowing that retirement plans are sheltered from taxation; you want to maximize this benefit by selecting investment vehicles that would otherwise be taxed.

Annuities

Annuities are peculiar investment products. They are contracts that are backed by an insurance company. If you, the annuity holder (investor), die during the so-called accumulation phase (that is, prior to receiving payments from the annuity), your designated beneficiary is guaranteed to receive the amount of your contribution. In this sense, annuities look a bit like life insurance.

Annuities, like RRSPs, allow your capital to grow and compound without taxation. You defer taxes until withdrawal. Unlike an RRSP that has an annual contribution limit, you can deposit as much as you want into an annuity in any year — even a million dollars or more if you have it!

Although annuities can be considered as retirement vehicles, they have no place inside retirement plans. Annuities allow your investment dollars to compound without taxation. In comparison to other investments that don't allow such tax deferral annuities carry much higher annual operating expenses, which depresses your returns.

Purchasing an annuity inside an RRSP is a bit like wearing a belt and suspenders together. Either you have a peculiar sense of style, or you're spending too much time worrying about your pants falling down. In our experience, many people who mistakenly invest in annuities inside retirement plans have been misled by investment salespeople.

Unlike contributions to employer-sponsored plans and your RRSP, contributions to an annuity aren't tax-deductible. Contributing to an annuity, however, may make sense if you have exhausted contributions to those plans.

Also, annuities make more sense if you expect to leave the money compounding in the annuity for at least 15 years. It typically takes this long for the benefits of tax-deferred compounding to outweigh the higher annuity fees and treatment of all withdrawn annuity earnings at the higher ordinary income tax rates. If you're close to or are actually in retirement, tax-friendly investments made outside of retirement plans (discussed in Chapter 12) are usually preferable.

Limited partnerships

Limited partnerships (LPs) are treacherous, high-commission, high-cost (and hence low-return) investments sold through investment salespeople. Part of their supposed allure, however, is the tax benefits they generate. But when you buy and hold a limited partnership in a retirement account, you lose the ability to take advantage of many of the tax deductions. The illiquidity of LPs may also mean that you can't make withdrawals when needed. These are just some of the many reasons to avoid investing in limited partnerships. (For more reasons, see Chapter 8.)

For more details about other investment options and the best places to purchase annuities, see Chapter 12, where we discuss investing money outside of retirement plans.

Transferring Retirement Plans

With the exception of plans maintained by your employer that limit your investment options, you can move your money held in RRSPs or RRIFs (registered retirement income funds) to almost any major investment firm or mutual funds company. Moving the money is pretty simple; if you can fill out a couple of short forms and send them back in a postage-paid envelope, you can transfer an account. The investment firm to which you are transferring your account does the rest.

Transferring accounts you control

Here's a step-by-step list of what you need to do to transfer a retirement savings plan to another investment firm. Even if you're working with a financial adviser, you should be aware of this process (called a *direct trustee to trustee transfer*) to ensure that no hanky-panky takes place on the adviser's part.

1. **Decide where you want to move the account.** We recommend several investment companies in this chapter, along with some sample portfolios within those firms. You may also want to consult the latest edition of our other book, *Investing For Canadians For Dummies*.

2. **Obtain an account application and asset transfer form.** Call the toll-free number of the firm you're transferring the money to and ask for an account application and asset transfer form for the type of account you're transferring. You can also visit the firm's Web site, but for this type of request we think most people find it easier to speak directly with someone.

   Important note: Ask for the form for the same type of account you currently have at the company from which you are transferring the money. You can determine the account type by looking at a recent account statement — it should appear near the top of the form or in the section with your name and address. If you can't figure out the account type on a cryptic statement, call the firm where the account is currently held and ask a representative to tell you what kind of account you have.

   Another important note: Never, ever sign over assets such as cheques and security certificates to a financial adviser, no matter how trustworthy and honest he or she may seem. The adviser could bolt with them quicker than you can say "Bonnie and Clyde." Transfers should not be completed this way. Besides, you'll find it easier to handle the transfer by following the information we provide in this section.

3. **Complete and mail the account application and asset transfer form.** Completing these for your new investment firm opens your new account and authorizes the transfer.

You shouldn't take possession of the money in your retirement plan when moving it over to the new firm. The tax authorities impose huge penalties if you perform a transfer incorrectly. For instance, if you make the mistake of withdrawing your investments from an RRSP during the transfer process, the full amount gets included in your taxable income for that year, and you'll have to pay tax on it at your marginal tax rate. Let the company to which you're transferring the money do the transfer for you. If you have questions or problems, the firm(s) to which you're transferring your account has armies of capable employees waiting to help you. Remember, these firms know that you're transferring your money to them, so they should roll out the red carpet.

4. **Figure out which securities you want to transfer and which need to be liquidated.** Transferring existing investments in your account to a new investment firm can sometimes be a little sticky. Transferring such assets as cash (money market funds) or securities that trade on any of the major stock exchanges is not a problem.

If you own publicly traded securities, transferring them as-is (also known as transferring them "in kind") to your new investment firm is better, especially if the firm offers discount brokerage services. You can then sell your securities through that firm more cheaply.

If you own mutual funds unique to the institution you're leaving, check with your new firm to see if it can accept them. If not, you need to contact the firm that currently holds them to sell them.

GICs are tricky to transfer. Ideally, you should send in the transfer forms several weeks or so before the GIC matures — few people do this. If the GIC matures soon, call the bank and tell it that when the GIC matures you would like the funds to be invested in a savings or money market account that you can access without penalty when your transfer request lands in the bank's mailbox. Note that for investments you are liquidating, you need to leave the proceeds inside the RRSP so as not to trigger a tax bill.

5. **Let the firm from which you're transferring the money know that you are doing so. (This step is optional.)** If the place you're transferring the money from doesn't assign a specific person to your account, you can definitely skip this step. When you're moving your investments from a brokerage firm where you dealt with a particular broker, deciding whether or not to follow this step can be more difficult.

Most people feel obligated to let their representative know that they're moving their money. In our experience, calling the person with the "bad news" is usually a mistake. Brokers or others who have a direct financial stake in your decision to move your money will try to sell you on staying. Some may try to make you feel guilty for leaving, and some may even try to bully you.

Writing a letter may seem like the coward's way out, but writing usually makes leaving your broker easier for both of you. You can polish what you have to say, and you don't put the broker on the defensive. Although we don't want to encourage lying, not telling the whole truth may be an even better idea. Excuses, such as you have a family member in the investment business who will manage your money for free, may help you avoid an uncomfortable confrontation.

Then again, telling an investment firm that its charges are too high or that it misrepresented and sold you a bunch of lousy investments may help the firm improve in the future. Don't fret too much — do what's best for you and what you're comfortable with. Brokers are not your friends. Even though the broker may know your kids' names, your favourite hobbies, and your birthday, you have a business relationship with him.

Transferring your existing assets typically takes a month to complete. If the transfer is not completed within one month, get in touch with your new investment firm to determine the problem. If your old company isn't cooperating, call a manager there to help get the ball rolling.

The unfortunate reality is that an investment firm will cheerfully set up a new account to accept your money on a moment's notice, but it will drag its feet, sometimes for months, when the time comes to relinquish your money. To light a fire under the behinds of the folks at the investment firm, tell a manager at the old firm that you're going to send a letter to the provincial securities regulator if it doesn't complete your transfer within the next week.

Moving money from an employer's plan

When you leave a job, particularly if you're retiring or being laid off after many years of service, money-hungry brokers and financial planners probably will be on you like a pack of bears on a tree leaking sweet honey. If you seek financial help, tread carefully — Chapter 17 helps you avoid the pitfalls of hiring such assistance.

When you leave a job, you're confronted with a slightly different transfer challenge: If you've earned the right to some or all of your pension benefits (called vesting), you have the option of moving them into a special account called a locked-in retirement account (LIRA). In some provinces, these are called locked-in RRSPs. (As long as your employer allows it, you may be able to leave your money in your old employer's plan. Evaluate the quality of the investment choices using the information we provide in this part of the book.)

Never take personal possession of money from your employer's retirement plan. If you want to transfer your pension funds, simply inform your employer of where you want your money to be sent. Prior to doing so, you should establish an appropriate account at the investment firm you intend to use. Then tell your employer's benefits department where you would like your retirement money transferred. You can send your employer the Canada Revenue Agency forms and lock-in agreement (if required) that have been signed by the investment firm's retirement account trustee. These forms will contain the investment firm's mailing address and your account number.

Chapter 12

Investing Outside Retirement Plans

· ·

In This Chapter

▶ Taking advantage of frequently overlooked investment options

▶ Factoring taxes into your investment decisions

▶ Bolstering your emergency reserves

▶ Recommended long-term investments

· ·

*I*n this chapter, we discuss investment options for money held *outside* retirement plans, and we include some sample portfolio recommendations. Chapter 11 reviews investments for money *inside* retirement plans. This distinction may seem somewhat odd — it's not one that is made in most financial books and articles. Thinking of these two types of investments differently can be useful.

✔ **Investments held outside retirement plans are subject to taxation.** You have a whole range of different investment options to consider when taxes come into play.

✔ **Money held outside retirement plans is more likely to be used sooner than funds held inside retirement plans.** Why? Because you'll generally have to pay far more in income taxes to access money inside rather than outside retirement plans.

✔ **Funds inside retirement plans have their own nuances.** For example, when you invest through your employer's retirement plan, your investment options are usually limited to a handful of choices. And special rules govern transfer of your retirement plan balances.

Getting Started

Suppose that you have some money sitting around in a bank savings account or money market mutual fund. Your money is earning a small amount of interest, but you want to invest it more profitably. You need to remember two things about investing this type of money:

> ✔ **Earning a little is better than losing 20 to 50 percent or more.** Just talk to anyone who bought a lousy investment. Be patient. Educate yourself before you invest.
>
> ✔ **To earn a higher rate of return, you must be willing to take more risk.** In order to earn a better rate of return, you need to consider investments that fluctuate in value — of course, the value can drop as well as rise.

You approach the vast sea of investment options and start stringing up your rod to go fishing. You hear stories of people catching big ones — cashing in big on stocks or real estate that they bought years ago. Even if you don't have delusions of grandeur, you'd at least like your money to grow faster than the cost of living.

But before you cast your investment line, consider the following frequently overlooked ways to put your money to work and earn higher returns without as much risk. These options may not be as exciting as hunting the big fish out there, but they should easily improve your financial health.

Paying off high-interest debt

Many folks have credit card or other consumer debt that costs more than 10 percent per year — sometimes much more — in interest. Paying off this debt with savings is like putting your money in an investment with a guaranteed return that's equal to the rate you're paying on the debt.

For example, if you have credit card debt outstanding at 14-percent interest, paying off that loan is the same as putting your money to work in an investment with a sure 14-percent annual return. Remember that the interest on consumer debt is not tax-deductible, so you would actually need to earn *more* than 14 percent investing your money elsewhere in order to net 14 percent after paying taxes. (Refer to Chapter 4 for more details if you're still not convinced.)

Paying off some or all of your mortgage may make sense, too. This financial move isn't as clear, because the interest rate is lower than it is on consumer debt.

Taking advantage of tax breaks

Make sure that you take advantage of the *terrific* tax benefits offered by an RRSP or other retirement plan. If you work for a company that offers to match your contributions to a retirement savings plan, try to fund it at the highest level you can manage.

If you need to save money outside retirement plans for shorter-term goals (for example, to buy a car or a home), then, by all means, save money outside retirement plans. But remember that investing money outside retirement plans doesn't provide you with tax deductions. It also requires greater thought and consideration, because your investments can produce taxable distributions.

Understanding Taxes on Your Investments

When you invest money outside of a retirement plan, money distributed to you on your investments — such as interest, dividends, and capital gains — is exposed to taxation. Too many folks (and too many of their financial advisers) ignore the tax impact of their investment strategies. You need to pay attention to the tax implications of your investment decisions *before* you invest your money.

Consider a person with a moderate income who is in a 34-percent tax bracket (federal plus provincial taxes combined) and who keeps extra cash in a bond paying 3 percent interest. If she pays 34 percent of her interest earnings in taxes, she ends up making just 2 percent. If she weren't using that money as an emergency fund, she might consider putting it into a dividend-producing investment, such as a dividend mutual fund. The effective tax rates on dividend income are much lower than that for interest income. For someone in a 34-percent tax bracket, the effective tax rate on dividends is about 19 percent, so her taxes would be 44 percent less than what she would pay on interest income.

If the changes proposed by the Liberals in 2005 have since become law, dividends are now taxed at even lower rates. Those in the 34% tax bracket pay tax of just a few percent on dividend income, depending on the province in which they live. For those in the top marginal tax rate, the effective tax on dividend income falls to around 21% to 23%, down from 32.5%.

In the sections that follow, we give specific advice about investing your money while keeping an eye on taxes.

Fortifying Your Emergency Reserves

In Chapter 2, we explain the importance of keeping sufficient money in an emergency reserve account. From such an account, you need two things:

- ✔ **Accessibility:** When you need to get your hands on the money for an emergency, you want to be able to do so quickly and without penalty.

✔ **Highest possible return:** You want to get the highest rate of return possible without risking your principal. This doesn't mean that you should simply pick the money market or savings option with the highest yield, because other issues such as taxes are a consideration. What good is earning a slightly higher yield if you pay a lot more in taxes?

Bank and credit union accounts

When you have a few thousand dollars or less, your best and easiest path is to keep this excess savings in a local bank or credit union. Look first to the institution where you keep your chequing account.

Keeping this stash of money in your chequing account, rather than in a separate savings account, makes financial sense if the extra money helps you avoid monthly service charges when your balance occasionally dips below the minimum. Compare the service charges on your chequing account with the interest earnings from a savings account.

For example, suppose that you're keeping $2,000 in a savings account to earn 1 percent interest, versus earning no interest on your chequing account money. Over the course of a year, you earn $20 interest on that savings account. If you incur a $9 per month service charge on your chequing account, you pay $108 per year. So, keeping your extra $2,000 in a chequing account may be better if it keeps you above a minimum balance and erases that monthly service charge. (However, if you're more likely to spend the extra money in your chequing account, keeping it in a separate savings account where you won't be tempted to spend it may be better.)

High-interest savings accounts

Another good choice for your savings or emergency funds is a high-interest savings account. This relatively new type of account is a good and often superior alternative to money market funds.

In many cases, high-interest savings accounts offer similar returns to what you would earn in a money market account. In addition, you can often set them up in conjunction with a chequing account. You can also arrange to have your paycheque deposited directly.

Unlike money market funds, there is no minimum deposit required — you also don't have to worry about getting dinged with commissions, charges, or fees for withdrawing your money within a certain time frame of making a deposit. Another big plus is that, unlike a money market fund, you can get at your money at any time of day, as long as your money has been in the account the required number of days. Most of these accounts allow you to access your cash simply by using a bank card at an ABM.

There are two reasons why high-interest accounts can pay such a high rate of return. The first is that they don't have to support a chain of bricks-and-mortar outlets like the large banks do. Much of your communication and transactions with the company that holds your high-interest-rate account will be by mail, phone, and over the Internet. Second, the companies that offer high-interest accounts use them as a way to win over new customers, and then sell you on other products that they may offer. These can include GICs, chequing accounts, and even mortgages. However, you are under no obligation to buy any other products if they don't suit your needs and aren't competitive with your other options.

Dealing with a company that doesn't have any actual branches in your neighbourhood or town may be somewhat unnerving. However, your money is generally just as safe as if it were in a traditional savings account. Just be sure to check that, like the two companies mentioned below, the institution is a member of the CDIC, an insurance program that protects your savings up to $60,000. We recommend a few high-interest savings accounts below.

President's Choice Financial

Loblaw Companies Limited took its well-known President's Choice brand of food products, hooked up with Canadian Imperial Bank of Commerce, and developed the President's Choice Financial line of financial products, which now includes banking accounts, mortgages, GICs, and insurance.

The President's Choice Financial Interest First savings account is a stripped-down affair that doesn't include a bank card or ABM access to your funds. Instead, access is provided through an accompanying chequing account that comes with a bank card. You use the chequing account to deposit and withdraw funds, and move money from the chequing account into the savings account to earn the best return. To move money from one account to another, you simply give your instructions to the company over the phone, by mail, or using the Internet. You can also make deposits to the savings account and transfer funds using an ABM.

The savings account interest rate is usually comparable to the best money market mutual funds. The chequing account has tiered interest rates. If your balance is only a few hundred dollars, you'll make next to nothing. However, the rates rise along with your balance. If you have more than $10,000 in your chequing account, for instance, there's no need to use the savings account at all because the chequing account will generally pay essentially the same rate.

You can use the bank card without getting nicked for fees at any CIBC bank machine. You can also use the card at any other ABM, but you'll have to pay the Interac transaction fee. A President's Choice Financial chequing account can also be used to pay bills, which you can arrange to have done automatically.

ING Direct

ING Direct is part of the Amsterdam-based ING Group. ING's Investment Savings Account typically pays the same rate as one-year GICs, far beyond what you would earn in a regular savings account.

There is no minimum balance required, and there are no fees. The only restriction you'll face is that you have to wait five days after making a deposit before you can withdraw those funds. Interest is earned daily on your balances, and compounded monthly. You also get a bank card with your account. While it can be used to withdraw money at any ABM, there is a transaction fee each time you use the card. However, ING has installed its own machines in Canadian Tire stores, and you can use those machines at no charge.

Money market mutual funds

Money market funds, a type of mutual fund (see Chapter 10), are just like bank savings accounts — but better, in most cases. The best money market funds pay higher yields than bank savings accounts.

The amount of operating expenses deducted before payment of dividends is the single biggest determinant of yield. All other things being equal (which they usually are with different money market funds), lower operating expenses translate into higher yields for you. With interest rates as low as they have been in recent years, seeking out money market funds with the lowest operating expenses is now more vital than ever.

The other types of fund investing you have the option to do at the fund company where you establish a money market fund is another factor that may be important when choosing a money market fund. Doing most or all of your fund shopping (money-market and otherwise) at one or two good fund companies can reduce the clutter in your investing life; chasing after a slightly higher yield offered by another company is sometimes not worth the extra paperwork and administrative hassle. On the other hand, there's no reason why you can't invest in funds at multiple firms (as long as you don't mind the extra paperwork), using each for its relative strengths.

Most mutual fund companies don't have many local branch offices, so you may have to open and maintain your money market mutual fund through the fund's toll-free phone line and the mail. Distance has its advantages. Because you can conduct business by mail, the Internet, and the phone, you don't need to go schlepping into a local branch office to make deposits and withdrawals.

Despite the distance between you and your mutual fund company, you can usually have money transferred to your local bank on any business day, as well as having the fund company simply mail you a cheque. Don't fret about a deposit being lost in the mail; it rarely happens, and no one can legally cash a cheque made payable to you anyway. Just be sure to endorse the cheque with the notation "for deposit only" under your signature.

For that matter, driving or walking to your local bank isn't 100-percent safe. Imagine all the things that could happen to you or your money en route to the bank. You could slip on a banana peel, drop your deposit down a sewer grate, get mugged or kidnapped, walk into a bank holdup and get taken hostage, or get run over by a bakery truck.

In the sections that follow, we recommend good money market mutual funds.

Recommended money market mutual funds

- ✔ Beutel Goodman Money Market (800-461-4551; www.beutel-can.com)

- ✔ Elliot & Page Money (888-588-7999; www.manulife.ca)

- ✔ Legg Mason T-Bill Plus (800-565-6781; www.leggmasoncanada.com)

- ✔ Mackenzie Sentinel Cash Management (800-387-0614; www.mackenziefinancial.com)

- ✔ Mawer Canadian Money Market (800-889-6248; www.mawer.com)

- ✔ McLean Budden Money Market (800-884-0436; www.mcleanbudden.com)

- ✔ Phillips, Hager & North Money Market (800-661-6141; www.phn.com)

- ✔ Saxon Money Market (888-287-2966; www.saxonfunds.com)

- ✔ Sceptre Money Market (800-265-1888; www.sceptre.ca)

- ✔ TD Canadian Money Market (866-567-8888; www.tdcanadatrust.com/mutualfunds)

Recommended T-bill money market mutual funds

Canadian Treasury bill (T-bill) money market funds are appropriate if you prefer a fund that invests solely in government-issued debt, which has the safety of government backing. Note that some of these funds are permitted to invest in other money market securities. Call the specific fund to ensure it is 100-percent in T-bills before you invest, if the additional security is important to you.

- ✔ Altamira T-Bill (800-263-2824; www.altamira.com)

- ✔ Franklin Templeton Treasury Bill (800-387-0830; www.templeton.ca)

- ✔ RBC Canadian T-Bill (800-769-2599; www.rbcfunds.com)

- ✔ TD Canadian T-Bill (866-567-8888; www.tdcanadatrust.com/mutualfunds)

Investing Money for the Longer Term

Important note: This section (together with its recommended investments) assumes that you have a sufficient emergency reserve stashed away and are taking advantage of tax-deductible registered retirement plan contributions. (Please see Chapter 3 for more on these goals.)

Which investments you should consider depends on how comfortable you are with risk. But your choice of investments should also be suited to how much *time* you have until you plan to use the money. We're not talking about investments you won't be able to sell on short notice if necessary (most of them you can). Investing money in a more volatile investment is riskier if you need to liquidate it in the short term.

For example, suppose that you're saving money for a down payment on a house and are about one to two years away from having enough to make your foray into the real estate market. If you had put this "home" money into the stock market near the beginning of one of the stock market's 20 to 50 percent corrections, you'd have been a mighty unhappy camper. You would have seen a substantial portion of your money *vanish* in short order and your home dreams put on hold.

Defining your time horizons

The different investment options in the remainder of this chapter are organized by time frame. All the recommended investment funds that follow assume that you have *at least* a several-year time frame, and are *no-load* (commission-free) mutual funds. Mutual funds can be sold on any business day, usually with a simple phone call. Funds come with all different levels of risk, so you can choose funds that match your time frame and desire to take risk. (Chapter 10 discusses all the basics of mutual funds.)

The recommended investments are also organized by your tax situation. (If you don't know your current tax bracket, be sure to review Chapter 6.) Following are summaries of the different time frames associated with each type of fund:

> ✓ **Short-term investments:** These investments are suitable for a period of a few years — perhaps you're saving money for a home or some other major purchase in the near future. When investing for the short-term, look for liquidity and stability — features that rule out real estate on one hand and stocks on the other. Recommended investments include shorter-term bond funds, which are higher-yielding alternatives to money market funds. If interest rates increase, these funds drop

slightly in value — a couple of percent or so (unless rates rise tremendously). We also discuss treasury bonds and guaranteed investment certificates (GICs) later in this chapter.

- ✓ **Intermediate-term investments:** These investments are appropriate for more than a few years but less than ten years. Investments that fit the bill are intermediate-term bonds and well-diversified hybrid funds (which include some stocks as well as bonds).

- ✓ **Long-term investments:** If you have a decade or more for investing your money, you can consider potentially higher-return (and therefore riskier) investments. Stocks, real estate, and other growth oriented investments can earn the most money if you're comfortable with the risk involved.

Allocating assets for the long haul

Asset allocation refers to the process of figuring out what portion of your wealth you should invest in different types of investments. You often (and most appropriately) practise asset allocation with retirement accounts, because this money is earmarked for the long term. Ideally, more of your saving and investing should be conducted through tax-sheltered retirement plans. These accounts generally offer the best way to lower your long-term tax burden (see Chapter 7 for details).

Bond funds

Bond funds pay taxable distributions (mostly interest) that generally are taxed at your full marginal tax rate. Just like interest earned from a savings account, you have to pay tax on any interest generated by bond funds each year, whether the interest is distributed to you or reinvested in your fund. As a result, you're far better off holding bond funds inside your RRSP, where the interest isn't taxed and the full amount of your earnings can be reinvested.

Here are some of our favourite bond funds:

- ✓ **Short-term:** TD Short-Term Bond, TD Mortgage Income (800-386-3757; www.tdwaterhouse.ca); National Bank Mortgage (800-263-2824; www.nbc.ca); Phillips, Hager & North Short Term Bond and Mortgage (800-661-6141; www.phn.com) Scotia Mortgage Income (800-268-9269; www.scotiabank.com; Fidelity Canadian Short Term Bond (800) 263-4077; www.fidelity.ca); CIBC Canadian Short-Term Bond Index (800-465-3863; www.cibc.com)

- ✓ **Long-term:** Altamira Bond (800-263-4769; www.altamira.com); TD Canadian Bond; Phillips, Hager & North; Beutal Goodman Income (800-461-4551, www.beutal-can.com); McLean Budden Fixed Income (800-884-0436, www.mcleanbudden.com)

Guaranteed investment certificates (GICs)

For many decades, *guaranteed investment certificates* (GICs) have been a popular investment for folks with some extra cash that isn't needed in the near future. With a GIC, you get a higher rate of return than you get on a bank savings account. And unlike bond funds, your principal does not fluctuate in value.

Compared to bonds, however, GICs have a couple of drawbacks:

- ✔ In a GIC, your money is not accessible unless you cough up a fairly big penalty — typically six months' interest. With a no-load (commission-free) bond fund, you can access your money without penalty — whether you need some or all of your money next week, next month, or next year.

- ✔ A good deal of your earnings on GICs usually end up in Canada Revenue Agency's hands. Unless you hold them in your RRSP, the interest earned on a GIC is taxed at your full marginal tax rate, the same rate as your salary.

In the long run, you should earn more — perhaps 1 to 2 percent more per year — and have better access to your money in bond funds than in GICs.

One final piece of advice: Don't buy GICs simply for the CDIC (Canada Deposit Insurance Corporation) insurance. Much is made, particularly by bankers, of the CDIC insurance that comes with bank GICs. The lack of this insurance on high-quality bonds shouldn't be a big concern for you. High-quality bonds rarely default; even if a fund held a bond that defaulted, it would probably represent only a tiny fraction (less than 1 percent) of the value of the fund, having little overall impact.

Besides, the CDIC itself is no Rock of Gibraltar. Banks have failed, and will continue to fail. Yes, you are insured if you have less than $100,000 in a bank. However, if the bank crashes, you may have to wait a long time and settle for less interest than you thought you were getting. You're not immune from harm, CDIC or no CDIC.

If the insurance you receive through the CDIC allows you to sleep better, you can invest in T-bills (see "Bond funds" earlier in this chapter), which are government-backed bonds.

Stock funds

Selected tax-friendly stock funds are appropriate if you don't want current income. TD (800-386-3757; www.tdwaterhouse.ca) offers a good range of tax-friendly index funds. Alternatively, you can invest in a wider variety of diversified stock funds inside an annuity (see the following section).

Dividend funds

Dividend funds, which come with terrific tax savings built in, are often a good choice if you want regular income from an investment outside your RRSP. These funds invest primarily in the preferred shares of Canadian companies, as well as in common shares that usually pay regular dividends.

The income you receive from the fund will benefit from the dividend tax credit, which means that you pay a lower tax rate on dividend income than on regular interest income.

Inflation-indexed bonds

Like a handful of other nations, the government of Canada offers *inflation-indexed* government bonds. Because a portion of the return on these bonds is pegged to the rate of inflation, the bonds offer investors a safer type of bond investment option.

To understand the relative advantages of an inflation-indexed bond, take a brief look at the relationship between inflation and a normal bond. When an investor purchases a normal bond, he's committing himself to a fixed yield over a set period of time — for example, a bond that matures in 10 years and pays 6 percent interest. However, changes in the cost of living (inflation) are not fixed, so they're difficult to predict.

Suppose that an investor put $10,000 into a regular bond in the 1970s. During the life of his bond, he would've unhappily watched escalating inflation. During the time he held the bond, and by the time his bond matured, he would've witnessed the erosion of the purchasing power of his $600 of annual interest and $10,000 of returned principal.

Enter the inflation-indexed bond. Say that you have $10,000 to invest, and you buy a 10-year, inflation-indexed bond that pays you a real rate of return (this is the return above and beyond the rate of inflation) of, say, 2 percent. This portion of your return is paid out in interest. The other portion of your return is from the inflation adjustment to the principal you invested. The inflation portion of the return gets put back into principal. So if inflation were running at about 2 percent, as it has in recent years, your $10,000 of principal would be indexed upward after one year to $10,200. In the second year of holding this bond, the 2-percent real return of interest would be paid on the increased ($10,200) principal base.

If inflation skyrocketed and was running at, say, 8 percent rather than 2 percent per year, your principal balance would grow 8 percent per year and you'd still get your 2-percent real rate of return on top of that. Thus, an inflation-indexed bond investor would not see the purchasing power of his invested principal or annual interest earnings eroded by unexpected inflation.

Inflation-indexed bonds can be a good investment for conservative bond investors who are worried about inflation, as well as taxpayers who want to hold the government accountable for increases in inflation. The downside: Inflation-indexed bonds can yield slightly lower returns, because they're less risky compared to regular bonds.

The only drawback to dividend income funds is that they have a higher risk than other fixed-income funds that invest in bonds or mortgages. Also, some funds broaden their investments to include common stocks that have lower yields in the hope of using capital gains to boost their performance. The main purpose of an income fund, though, is strong after-tax returns, so be sure to find a fund that invests almost exclusively in preferred shares or common stocks with regular, strong dividends.

Recommended dividend mutual funds

- BMO Dividend (800-665-7700; www.bmo.com)
- Phillips Hager & North Dividend Income (800-661.6141; www.phn.com)
- RBC Dividend (800-463-3863; www.rbcfunds.com)
- Scotia Dividend Income (800-268-9269; www.scotiabank.com)

Annuities

As we discuss in Chapter 9, *annuities* are accounts that are partly insurance but mostly investment. You should consider contributing to an annuity only after you exhaust contributions to all your available retirement accounts. Because annuities carry higher annual operating expenses than comparable mutual funds, you should consider them only if you plan to leave your money invested, preferably for 15 or more years. Even if you leave your money invested for that long, the tax-friendly funds discussed in the previous sections of this chapter can allow it to grow without excessive annual taxation.

Real estate

Real estate can be a financially and psychologically rewarding investment. It can also be a money pit and a real headache if you buy the wrong property or get a "tenant from hell." (We discuss the investment particulars of real estate in Chapter 9, and the nuts and bolts of buying real estate in Chapter 14.)

Small-business investments

Investing in your own business or someone else's established small business can be a high-risk but potentially high-return investment. The best options are those you understand well. See Chapter 9 for more information about small-business investments.

Chapter 13

Investing for Education Expenses

● ●

In This Chapter

▶ Understanding the financial aid system

▶ Looking at the best and worst ways to save for university and college

▶ Exploring education investment options

▶ Calculating how much you need to save

▶ Finding ways to pay for university or college when the time comes

● ●

*I*f you're like most parents (or potential future parents), just turning to this chapter makes you anxious. Such trepidation is understandable. According to much of what you see in the news about the cost of university or college, if costs keep rising at the current rate you'll have to spend tens of thousands of dollars to give your youngster a quality post-secondary education.

Whether you're about to begin an education investment plan, or you've already started saving, your emotions may lead you astray. The hype about education costs may scare you into taking a path that is less financially beneficial than others that are available. Your worries will likely be particularly troublesome if your children are close to university-going age. But quality education for your child doesn't have to — and probably won't — cost you as much as those gargantuan projections suggest.

Neglecting RRSPs: A Big Mistake

You want what's best for your children. As a parent, that's a given. Not only do you want to be able to provide good learning opportunities for them when they are young, but you also want to give them choices. When little Dweezil and Moon Unit fill out their university applications, you don't want to have to say that you can't afford to send them to their dream school.

We know you're going to think that our advice sounds selfish. But consider this reality: You have to provide for your own financial security before saving for your child. Let us explain.

If you're a frequent flyer, think back to your most recent trip by airplane. Remember what the flight attendants instructed you to do in an emergency? In the event of a loss of air pressure that necessitates the use of oxygen masks, put your own oxygen mask on *first.* Only then should you help your children with their oxygen masks.

Consider for a moment why airlines recommend this approach. Although your instinct may be to ensure that your children are safe before taking care of yourself, by taking care of yourself first, you're stronger and better able to help your children.

Similarly, in regard to your personal finances, you need to take care of yourself first. You should save and invest through an RRSP or other retirement savings plan that gives you significant tax benefits.

Take care of your long-term financial needs first (for example, by saving through an RRSP). By doing so, you strengthen your financial health, which better enables you in the long run to help your kids with their educational expenses. (See Chapters 6 and 11 to learn how to reduce your taxes and save for retirement.)

How Will You Pay for Education Expenses?

If you concentrate today on contributing to your RRSP or company pension plan and paying down your mortgage, you'll have a number of options when your kids graduate from high school. If you've paid down some — or all — of your mortgage, you can borrow against the paid-up value of your home (your *home equity*), usually at or near the lowest interest rate available (the *prime rate*).

You'll also already have some strong momentum and compounding going on if you've been building up your retirement savings. You've also established a savings habit. When your kids get close to university age, you can divert your RRSP or other retirement plan contributions to help pay their education costs. When they graduate, you can easily resume your RRSP contributions.

You can even take advantage of the allowable RRSP contributions you missed out on because you're allowed to carry forward unused contributions indefinitely. (Canada Revenue Agency tracks this for you. You'll find a summary on the income tax return assessment notice you receive every year.) This will leave you in much better financial shape than if you had forgone contributions to your RRSP or company retirement savings plan when you were younger in order to start an educational savings program.

Further, when your kids are ready to go to university you'll likely be in your peak earning years, so some extra funds will probably be available.

Estimating the cost of university or college

University or college can cost a lot. The total price tag — including tuition, fees, books, supplies, room, board, and transportation — will vary substantially from school to school. The total average annual cost is currently running around $8,000 to $10,000 a year. If you have younger children, you'll be interested to hear that some estimates put the cost of a four-year degree, including tuition and living costs, at close to $100,000 by 2020. Ouch!

Is all this expense worth it? Although many critics of higher education claim that the cost shouldn't be rising faster than inflation and that costs can and should be contained, denying the value of going to university or college is hard. Whether you're considering a local community college, your friendly local university, or a selective high-end business school, investing in education is usually worth the effort and the cost.

An *investment* is an outlay of money for an expected profit. Unlike a car that depreciates in value each year that you drive it, an investment in education yields monetary, social, and intellectual profit. A car is more tangible in the short term, but an investment in education (even if it means borrowing money) gives you more bang for your buck in the long run.

Universities and colleges are now finding themselves somewhat subject to the same types of competition that companies confront. As a result, some schools are trying to clamp down on rising costs. As with any other product or service purchase, it pays to shop around. You can find good values — schools that offer competitive pricing *and* provide a quality education.

Setting realistic savings goals

If you have money left over *after* taking advantage of retirement plans, by all means try to save for your children's post-secondary education.

Be realistic about what you can afford for education expenses given your other financial goals, especially saving for retirement (refer to Chapter 2). Being able to personally pay anything approaching the full cost of a university or college education is a luxury of the affluent. If you're not a high-income earner, consider trying to save enough to pay a third or, at most, half of the cost. You can make up the balance through loans, your child's employment before and during school, and the like.

Use Table 13-1 to help get a handle on how much you should be saving for college.

Table 13-1	How Much to Save for University or College*
Figure Out This	*Write It Here*
1. Cost of the school you think your child will attend.**	$_____
2. Percentage of costs you'd like to pay (for example, 20% or 40%).	×_____%
3. Line 1 times line 2 is the amount you'll pay (in today's dollars).	= $ _____
4. Number of months until your child reaches university or college age.	÷ _____ months
5. Line 3 divided by line 4 is the amount to save per month (today's dollars).***	= $ _____ / month

* Don't worry about correcting the overall analysis for inflation. This worksheet takes care of that through the assumptions made on the returns of your investments as well as the amount that you save over time. This way of doing the calculations works because you assume that the money you're saving will grow at the rate of inflation of education costs. (In the happy event that your investment return exceeds the rate of university or college inflation, you end up with a little more than you expected.)
** The average cost of a four-year university education today is about $40,000.
*** The amount you need to save (calculated in line 5) needs to be increased once per year to reflect the increase in university or college inflation — 5 or 6 percent should do.

How to Save for Education Expenses

If you have sufficient funds to take care of your other needs, such as contributing to an RRSP, terrific! You can also start putting money away for your children's post-secondary education.

Just as important as the investments you choose is the way in which you organize your savings efforts. Two basic ways to set up an effective savings plan for post-secondary education expenses exist.

The first option is a *Registered Education Savings Plan* (RESP). For many people, an RESP is a great way to save, thanks in part to a generous government grant program.

The second option is to use an *in trust account*. Under this arrangement, you put money into a special account and invest it on your child's behalf. If there is a good chance that your children may not attend university or college, this may be a better choice.

Registered Education Savings Plans (RESPs)

You can put up to $4,000 a year for each child into an RESP. The total lifetime contribution limit per child is $42,000. You're allowed to contribute money for up to 21 years, but the plan must be closed down within 25 years of being set up.

Money that you contribute to an RESP isn't tax deductible, but any gains inside the plan aren't taxed. When your child is ready to go to school, money from the plan can be taken out tax-free and used for a variety of education-related expenses.

In the past, a major drawback to RESPs was that if your child didn't go to a post-secondary institution, you forfeited the earnings. They either had to go to another child, to an educational institution, or, in the case of pooled or "scholarship" RESPs, to other children in the program.

The rules have been relaxed, though, and you can now transfer up to $50,000 of earnings from an RESP to your RRSP or your spouse's RRSP, as long as you have the contribution room available. Any earnings that can't be transferred in this way can still be moved out of the RESP, but they're taxed at your marginal tax rate plus an additional 20-percent penalty. You can take out your original contributions — your principal — without any penalties or restrictions. Also, you can open a family plan, into which you can make contributions for several children. If one of the children in the plan chooses not to pursue a post-secondary education, both the money you've contributed to the plan for that child, as well as any gains it has rung up, can be used by the other children in the plan.

The big kicker that makes RESPs truly worthwhile, though, is the RESP grant. The official name is the *Canada Education Savings Grant*, or CESG. Under the CESG program, the government will make a contribution to the RESP of 20 percent of the first $2,000 of contributions you make in a year, up to a maximum grant of $400 per year per child. The grant is available in every year the child is 17 or under on December 31.

If you don't contribute enough in any year to get the full $400 grant, you can earn the unused portion in later years. However, the maximum CESG per beneficiary each year is capped at whichever is lower, $800 or 20 percent of any unused RESP room. The total lifetime maximum you can receive under this program is $7,200.

How scholarship RESPs work —
And often don't pay!

Scholarship RESPs are offered by a number of organizations, including the Canadian Scholarship Trust and the Children's Education Trust of Canada.

The traditional offerings were pooled funds. Your contributions were pooled with those of other considerate parents and grandparents and invested in safe but low-earning investments, such as T-bills, Canada Savings Bonds, and mortgages. These types of RESPs have three major strikes against them.

First, because they invest in guaranteed investments, their rate of return is much lower than your money could earn in a broadly based conservative international equity mutual fund. To ride out the ups and downs of the equity markets, you should generally be able to leave your money invested for seven to ten years. If you start an RESP when your child is born, you have more than enough time — two to three times, in fact — to be able to benefit from the long-term higher returns offered by stocks (unless, of course, you have a little genius on your hands who will toddle off to university before he's old enough to baby-sit).

The second drawback is highlighted by the word scholarship, which these plans usually feature in big, bright letters in their marketing materials. Don't let this fool you. A true scholarship is something your child earns on his or her own by earning high grades, by excelling at a particular subject or sport, or by developing an interest or expertise in a particular area. The only justification for calling the payout from these plans a scholarship is that some children in the plans receive more than the combined value of their families' contributions and the earnings on that money. The reason? Well, with traditional "pooled" plans, if your child doesn't go to a qualifying educational institution you forfeit all the earnings on your money — you get back only your original contributions, and the interest is distributed among the other children in the plan who do go on to university or college.

Finally, these pooled plans typically have lots of costs and fees that can really add up. Those can include a sales charge, often disguised by the cute name "enrolment fee," as well as deposit charges, trustee and administration fees, and so on.

Now that the RESP rules have changed to allow you to get back the earnings on your contributions (either by transferring them to your RRSP or by paying a hefty tax), the scholarship-type fund providers have come up with a new offering. In addition to their traditional "pooled" funds, most offer individual accounts, where your contributions earn interest for your child alone. If your child doesn't use the money to go to school, then you can claim the earnings. Although this makes them somewhat more attractive, you still have to deal with the many administrative charges, and your contributions are still typically invested in guaranteed investments, limiting the growth of your savings.

If you don't contribute the maximum $4,000 allowed per child in a year, you don't carry forward that unused contribution amount as you do with an RRSP. In the case of an RESP, it's use it or lose it.

The grant rates for lower- and middle-income families were enhanced in 2005. For families with incomes of $35,000 or less, the first $500 on RESP contributions earns a 40-percent CESG; families with incomes between $35,000 and $70,000 earn a 30-percent CESG on the first $500. The maximum CESG payable each year was also increased to accommodate the enhanced grants.

In order to qualify for the grant, the RESP beneficiary must be a resident of Canada, be age 17 or under, and also have a social insurance number. SINs can take several weeks to obtain. Contact Human Resources and Skills Development Canada for an application.

You'll find two basic types of RESPs. The first are so-called "scholarship" plans. Because these plans are limited to mostly guaranteed investments, the rate of return on your plan is mediocre. Read the sidebar "How scholarship RESPs work — And often don't pay!" to see how you can end up actually losing all the gains earned on your contributions.

A much better choice is self-directed or mutual fund RESPs. You can open these with most brokerage and mutual fund firms, often at no charge. A self-directed or mutual fund RESP allows you to choose from a wide range of investments. If you start an RESP when your children are still in diapers, these plans are a much better choice because they allow you to benefit from the larger earnings potential of equities and equity mutual funds.

In-trust accounts

Also known as informal trusts, *in-trust accounts* allow you to save money for your child's future and have a portion of your earnings compound tax-free. These accounts also go by the name *ITF* (which stands for "in trust for") *account.* The account is "in trust" because minors can't enter into financial contracts. There are no restrictions on contributions to an in-trust account. You can put in as much or as little you wish at any time.

Once money is inside an informal trust, it belongs to the child. All profits on investments inside the trust are taxed. The person who contributes the money pays taxes on the dividends and income, but the child is responsible for paying taxes on any capital gains. Because most children have insufficient income to actually have to pay any tax, that portion of the account can compound tax-free. Because of this, the best investments for an in-trust account, especially if there are many years left before the child will need the money, are equity mutual funds, where most of the profits are in the form of capital gains.

Tapping your RRSP to pay university or college expenses

Under the federal government's Lifelong Learning Plan, you can tap your RRSP to help finance a post-secondary education or full-time training for either yourself or your spouse. You can withdraw up to $10,000 a year from your RRSP for four years. The maximum amount you can withdraw over that time is capped at $20,000.

Much like the RRSP Home Buyer's Plan (which we discuss in Chapter 15), there are several drawbacks to using your RRSP to fund an education. While the withdrawals are not taxed, you have to repay the money to your RRSP in equal instalments over ten years. The first payment has to be made within 60 days after the end of the fifth year after your first withdrawal.

Any repayments not made are included in the taxable income of the person who made the withdrawal. In addition, you will likely find it difficult to repay what you've taken out for education expenses as well as continue your regular contributions. In that case, you will have to be able to get by on less if you have been factoring your tax rebate from a regular RRSP contribution into your cash flow, since your repayments don't earn you a deduction. Further, borrowing money from your plan, as well as delaying new contributions while you repay those funds, will significantly reduce the long-term growth of your retirement savings.

If you set up an in-trust account and contribute only Child Tax Benefit payments, the above tax rules don't apply. All the gains, whether they're in the form of capital gains, interest, or dividends, are taxed to the child.

The big drawback to informal trusts is that when the child turns 18, the money and all the profits legally become hers to spend as she wishes. There are no rules about what the money must be spent on, so your child could use it for purposes other than an education, such as starting his or her own small business. Although you can hope that little Johnny or Jenny will spend the money wisely, there's nothing you can do if, on the day of his 18th birthday, Johnny empties his account and buys a convertible.

Certain steps are involved in setting up an in-trust account. When you open the account you must clearly delineate the role of everybody involved. The person who puts money into the account is known as the "settler" or contributor. The law requires that a different person have the responsibility of overseeing how the money is invested (the trustee) on behalf of the child (the beneficiary). When you set up an account, ensure that you use the proper phrasing: your name (if you are the trustee) followed by "in trust for" and then your child's name.

Loans, Grants, and Scholarships

Now you may be wondering how you'll come up with the money to pay for education expenses even if you stash money into retirement plans and manage to put some away into an RESP. We don't have just one correct solution, because how you'll help pay for your child's university or college costs depends on your own unique situation. However, even if you have available cash that can be directed to pay the school bills as they come in you will probably have to borrow some money.

Government student loans program

The largest source of student loans is the Canada Student Loan Program (CSLP). Run by the federal government in conjunction with the provinces, the program provides loans to university and college students. The provinces administer the loans through their own separate student aid offices.

Each province also has its own loan scheme that's rolled in with the CSLP. (You can find out more by following the link to your province's student loan program at www.canlearn.ca.) Students generally make only one combined application to receive loans from both programs, although interest and conditions on the federal loan and the provincial loan differ slightly. To qualify, students must be citizens or permanent residents of Canada, attend an institution recognized by the program, and meet the criteria for being either part-time or full-time students. Students must also live in a province that participates in the Canada Student Loans Program (if your province doesn't, it will run its own distinct loans programs to which the federal government contributes).

Regardless of where they're going to go to school, your kids must apply to the province in which they live. Applications can be obtained from any university or college or by calling your provincial student loans program. Find the number in the blue pages of your telephone book.

Part of the assessment of your application involves examining your entire family's income. The assessment is based solely on cash flow — assets don't come into the picture at all. As a result, it doesn't pay to neglect contributing to your RRSP or company retirement savings plan, or paying down your mortgage.

The loan programs demand that parents assist in paying the education costs of any dependent children. Even if parents absolutely refuse to assist their children, their ability to pay will still be taken into account when the application is assessed. In order not to be classified as a dependant, a child must have graduated from high school at least four years earlier or have been in the workforce for at least 24 months.

If the loan is approved, your children should go to the financial aid office when they enrol at their university or college. They'll be given some loan documents, which they can then take to the bank of their choice. (The loans are administered through the big banks, but the provincial and federal governments guarantee them.) A number of credit unions and *caisses populaires* are also approved student loan providers. The maximum amount available varies depending on which province the student lives in.

The federal and provincial governments pay the interest on the debt until the student either graduates or withdraws. At that point, the federal government stops paying its share of the interest, and the student is responsible for the debt. Some of the provinces, however, will continue to pay the debt costs on their part of the loan for an additional six months.

The interest rate on the two components is calculated differently. The rate on the federal part of the loan is fixed once a year at a percentage or so above the best rates offered by financial institutions (the prime rate). The provinces tend to use a floating rate. For example, a province might charge prime plus 1 percent on its loans, with the rate rising and falling along the going prime rate.

Even though the federal government stops paying the interest on its portion of the combined loan at graduation, students aren't required to start repaying the federal or provincial component of their loan until six months after graduation. Generally, this due date falls on November 1. At that time, students must negotiate a schedule with their bank. While students are largely free to choose whatever repayment time frame they like, both the federal and provincial loans must be completely paid off within 114 months (ten years minus six months). After the student signs agreements for the two separate loans, most institutions will consolidate the debts and work out a single payment schedule.

Once upon a time, many students saw these loans as giveaways because the government didn't seem all that interested in collecting from people who walked away from their obligations. Those days are long gone. Both Ottawa and the provinces have become aggressive in tracking down delinquents and getting their money back. The federal government can even take what it's owed out of the tax refunds of those who are behind on their payments. Worse yet, many past-due student loans are now routinely handed over to collection agencies, and the students end up with a nick on their credit rating.

Bankruptcy is also now much less of a reasonable option if a student's post-school debt becomes unbearable. In addition to the negative impact it will have on the student's credit rating, the rules surrounding student bankruptcy have been tightened. In the past, a student loan would not be discharged in a bankruptcy if the student filed for bankruptcy within two years of being in school. However, changes to the bankruptcy rules in 1998 mean that a student would now have to have been out of school for a minimum of ten years before filing for bankruptcy to have his or her student loans discharged.

Canada Access Grants

Started in 2005, the Canada Access Grants program offers grants to low-income students and students with permanent disabilities. The grants do not have to be repaid, but are considered as taxable income.

To qualify, the student must be in the first year of a program at a qualifying institution, and it must be his or her first time studying at the post-secondary level. All the eligibility requirements for a Canada Student Loan must also be met. The student must be enrolled in a program that is a minimum of two years in length, and that will lead to a certificate, degree, or diploma.

The student must also be considered a dependent student, which means he or she cannot be married, in a common-law relationship, or a single parent. Also, the student cannot have children living with him or her or be separated, divorced, or widowed. You are also not considered a dependent student if you have been out of high school for at least four years, if you haven't attended high-school or a post-secondary institution for 12 consecutive months on at least two occasions, if you are a Crown ward or former Crown ward who has not been adopted, or if both of your parents are deceased.

The amount of the grant is the lowest of three amounts:

- 50 percent of your tuition,
- $3,000, or
- The amount of Canada Student Loan you would otherwise be able to receive.

The word "otherwise" is used here because if you receive a Canada Access Grant the amount of your Canada Student Loan is reduced by a corresponding amount.

For the 2005–2006 loan period, the threshold net family income for families with up to three children was $35,5959. For families with four children the amount was $39,912. An accompanying provincial grant may also be available, depending on the province in which you live.

Tips for getting loans, grants, and scholarships

A number of grant programs are available through schools and the government as well as through independent sources. Employers, banks, credit unions, and community groups also offer grants and scholarships.

Many scholarships and grants don't require any extra work on your part — simply apply for financial aid through universities and colleges. Other programs need seeking out — check directories and databases at your local library, your child's school counselling department, and university and college financial aid offices. Also try local organizations, churches, employers, and so on. You have a better chance of getting scholarship money through these avenues.

Post-secondary scholarship search services are generally a waste of money; in some cases, they're scams. Some of these services charge up to $100 just to tell you about scholarships that either you're already being considered for or that you aren't even eligible for.

Your child can work and save money during high school and university. In fact, if your child qualifies for financial aid he or she may be expected to contribute a certain amount to education costs from savings and from employment during the school year or summer breaks. Besides giving your child a stake in his or her own future, this training encourages sound personal financial management down the road.

Students who support a spouse or child or who have a disability can also often obtain nonrepayable grants. Disabled students can get up to several thousand dollars a year in grants from the Canada Student Loan program, as well as grants from their province, depending on where they live.

Investing Education Funds

Financial companies pour millions of dollars into advertising for investment and insurance products that they claim are best for making your money grow for your little gremlins — er, children. Don't get sucked in by these ads.

What makes for good and bad investments in general applies to investments for educational expenses, too. Stick with basic, proven, lower-cost investments. (Chapter 8 explains what you generally need to look for and beware of.) The following sections focus on considerations specific to investing for post-secondary education.

Good investments: No-load mutual funds and exchange-traded funds

As we discuss in Chapter 9, the professional management and efficiency of the best no-load mutual funds makes them a tough investment to beat. Exchange-traded funds (ETFs), which give you the return of an associated index and offer razor-thin management fees, are also an attractive investment choice. Chapters 11 and 12 provide recommendations for investing money in funds both inside and outside tax-sheltered retirement plans.

Gearing the investments to the time frame involved until your children will need to use the money is the most important issue with these investments. The closer your child gets to attending university or college and using the money saved, the more conservatively the money should be invested.

Bad investments

Life insurance policies that have cash values are some of the most oversold investments for funding university costs. Here's the usual pitch: "Because you need life insurance to protect your family, why not buy a policy that you can borrow against to pay for your child's education?"

The reason why you shouldn't invest in this type of policy to fund university or college costs is because you're better off contributing to an RRSP, which gives you an immediate tax deduction — a benefit that saving through life insurance doesn't offer. Because life insurance that comes with a cash value is more expensive, parents are also more likely to make a second mistake — not buying enough coverage. If you need and want life insurance, you're better off buying lower-cost term life insurance (see Chapter 16).

Another poor investment for university or college expenses is one that fails to keep you ahead of inflation, such as savings or money market accounts. You need your money to grow so that you can afford education costs down the road.

Prepaid tuition plans should generally be avoided. Some U.S. schools have developed plans that allow you to pay costs at a specific school (calculated for the age of your child). The allure of these plans is that, by paying today, you eliminate the worry of not being able to afford rising costs in the future.

This logic doesn't work for several reasons. Odds are quite high that you don't have the money today to pay in advance. If you have that kind of extra dough around, you're better off using it for other purposes (and you're not likely to worry about rising costs anyway). You can invest your own money — that's what the school's going to do with it anyway.

Besides, how do you know which university or college your child will want to attend and how long it may take him or her to finish? Coercing your child into the school you've already paid for is a sure ticket to long-term problems in your relationship.

Overlooked investments

Too often, we see parents knocking themselves out to make more money so that they can afford to buy a bigger home, purchase more expensive cars, take more exotic vacations, and send their kids to expensive (and therefore supposedly better) private schools. Sometimes families want to send younger children to costly preschools and private elementary schools, too. Families stretch themselves with outrageous mortgages or complicated living arrangements so that they can get into neighbourhoods with top-rated public schools or send their kids to expensive private elementary schools.

The best school in the world for your child is his or her own home. The reason why many people we know (including both of us) have been able to attend top educational institutions is that our concerned parents worked hard — not just at their jobs, but at spending time with the kids when they were growing up. Rather than working to make more money (with the best of intentions to buy educational games or trips, or send the kids to better schools), try focusing more attention on your kids. In our humble opinion, you can do more for your kids by spending more time with them.

We see parents scratching their heads about their child's lack of academic interest and achievement — they blame the school, TV, or society at large. These factors may contribute to the problem, but education begins in the home. Schools can't do it alone.

Living within your means not only allows you to save more of your income but it also frees up more of your time for raising and educating your children. Don't underestimate the value of spending time with your kids and giving them your attention.

Chapter 14

Investing in Real Estate

· ·

In This Chapter

▶ Choosing between buying and renting

▶ Determining how to finance your real estate purchase

▶ Finding a great property

▶ Working successfully with a real estate agent

▶ Making a solid offer

▶ Handling issues after you buy

· ·

*B*uying a home or investing in real estate can be rewarding. On the other hand, owning real estate can be a real pain in the posterior, because purchasing and maintaining property can be time-consuming, emotionally draining, and financially painful.

Perhaps you're looking to escape your rented apartment and buy your first home. Or maybe you're interested in cornering the local real estate market and making millions in investment property. In either case, you can learn many lessons from real estate buyers who have travelled before you.

Note: Although this chapter focuses primarily on real estate in which you're going to live — otherwise known by those in the trade as *owner-occupied property* — much of what this chapter covers is relevant to real estate investors. For additional information on buying *investment real estate* — property that you rent out to others — see Chapter 8.

Deciding Whether to Buy or Continue Renting

You may be tired of moving from rental to rental. Perhaps your landlord doesn't adequately keep up the place, or you have to ask permission to hang a picture on the wall. You may desire the financial security and rewards that seem to come with home ownership. Or maybe you just want a place to call your own.

Any one of these reasons is a good enough one to *want* to buy a home. But you should take stock of your life and your financial health *before* you decide to buy, so that you can decide whether you still want to buy a home and how much you can really afford to spend. You need to ask yourself some bigger questions.

Assessing your timeline

From a financial standpoint, you really shouldn't buy a place unless you can anticipate being there for at least three years (preferably five or more). Buying and selling a property entails a lot of expenses, including the cost of getting a mortgage inspection, moving costs, and real estate agents' commissions. To cover these transaction costs plus the additional costs of ownership, a property needs to appreciate about 10 to 15 percent.

If you need or want to move in a couple of years, counting on this kind of appreciation is risky. If you're fortunate, and you happen to buy before a sharp upturn in housing prices, you may get it. If you're not fortunate, you'll probably lose money on the deal.

Some people are willing to invest in real estate even when they don't expect to live in it for long and would consider turning their home into a rental. Doing so can work well financially in the long haul, but don't underestimate the responsibilities that come with being a landlord. Also, most people need to sell their first home in order to tap all the cash that they have in it so that they can buy the next one.

Determining what you can afford to buy

Although buying and owning your own home can be a wise financial move in the long run, it's a major purchase that can send shock waves through the rest of your personal finances. You'll probably have to take out a mortgage — really just a loan secured by the property you're buying — where the payments are spread out, or *amortized* (typically over 25 years), to finance your purchase. The home you buy will need maintenance over the years. Owning a home is a bit like running a marathon: Just as you have to be in good physical shape to successfully run a marathon, you have to be in good financial health when you buy a home. For as long as you own the home, you'll be paying for something or another all the time.

We've seen too many people fall in love with a home and make a rash decision without taking a hard look at the financial ramifications. Take stock of your overall financial health (especially where you stand in terms of retirement planning) *before* you buy property or agree to a particular mortgage. Don't let the financial burdens of a home control your financial future.

To determine how much a potential home buyer can borrow, lenders look primarily at annual income; they pay no attention to a borrower's overall financial situation. Even if you don't have money tucked away into retirement savings, or you have several children to clothe, feed, and help put through university, you still qualify for the same size loan as other people with the same income (assuming equal outstanding debts).

So don't trust a lender when he tells you what you can afford according to some formulas the bank uses to determine what kind of a credit risk you are. Only you can figure out how much you can afford, because only you know what your other financial goals are and how important they are to you.

Here are some important financial questions that no lender will ask or care about but that you should ask yourself before buying a home:

- ✔ Are you saving enough money monthly to reach your retirement goals?
- ✔ How much do you spend (and want to continue spending) on fun things such as travel and entertainment?
- ✔ How willing are you to budget your expenses in order to meet your monthly mortgage payments and other housing expenses?
- ✔ How much of your children's expected university educational expenses do you want to be able to pay for?

The other chapters in this book can help you answer these important questions. Chapter 2 in particular will help you think through saving for important financial goals.

Many new homeowners run into financial trouble because they don't know their spending needs and priorities, and they don't know how to budget for them. Some of these owners have trouble curtailing their spending despite the large amount of debt they just incurred; in fact, some spend even more for all sorts of home furniture and remodelling expenditures. Many people prop up their spending habits with credit. For this reason, a surprisingly large percentage — some studies say about half — of people who borrow additional money against their home equity use the funds to pay consumer debts.

Calculating how much lenders will allow you to borrow

Mortgage lenders want to know your ability to repay the money you borrow, as well as the likelihood that you're going to repay it. So you have to pass a few tests that calculate the maximum amount the lender is willing to lend you. For a home in which you will reside, lenders total up your monthly housing expenses. They define your housing costs as

Mortgage Payment + Property Taxes + Insurance

Lenders typically loan you up to about 30 to 32 percent of your monthly gross (before taxes) income for the housing expense. This is known as the *gross debt-service ratio*. If you're self-employed, it's a lot more complicated. Lenders will often want to see your financial statements and your income tax returns from the last several years, and many decide on a case-by-case basis.

Lenders also consider your other debts when deciding how much to lend you. These other debts diminish the funds available to pay your housing expenses. Lenders add the amount you need to pay down your other consumer debts (auto loans, credit cards) to your monthly housing expense. The monthly total costs of these debt payments plus your housing costs typically cannot exceed 40 percent. This assessment is called the *total debt-service ratio*.

One general guideline says that you can borrow up to three times (or two and one-half times) your annual income when buying a home. But this rule is a really rough estimate. The maximum that a mortgage lender will loan you depends on interest rates. If rates are low (as they have been during much of the past decade), the monthly payment on a mortgage of a given size will also be relatively lower. Lower interest rates make buying real estate more affordable.

Table 14-1 gives you a ballpark idea of the maximum amount you may be eligible to borrow. Multiply your gross annual income by the number in the second column to determine the approximate maximum you may be able to borrow. For example, if you're getting a mortgage with a rate around 7 percent, and your annual income is $50,000, multiply 3.5 by $50,000 to get $175,000 — the approximate maximum mortgage allowed.

Table 14-1	What's the Approximate Maximum You Can Borrow?
When Mortgage Rates Are	*Multiply Your Gross Annual Income* By This Figure to Estimate the Maximum You May Be Able to Borrow*
4%	4.6
5%	4.2
6%	3.8
7%	3.5
8%	3.2
9%	2.9
10%	2.7
11%	2.5

*If you're self-employed, this is your net income (after expenses, but before taxes).

Comparing the cost of owning versus renting

The cost of owning a home is an important financial consideration for many renters. Some people assume that owning costs more. In fact, owning a home doesn't have to cost a truckload of money; it may even cost less than renting.

On the surface, buying a place seems a lot more expensive than renting. You're probably comparing your monthly rent (measured in hundreds of dollars to more than $1,000, depending on where you live) to the purchase price of a property, which is usually a much larger number — perhaps $150,000 to $500,000 or more. When you consider a home purchase, you're forced to think about your housing expenses in one huge chunk rather than in small monthly instalments (like a rent cheque).

Tallying up the costs of owning a place can be a useful and not-too-complicated exercise. To make a fair comparison between ownership and rental costs, you need to figure what it will cost on a *monthly basis* to buy a place you desire versus what it will cost to rent a *comparable* place. The worksheet in Table 14-2 enables you to do such a comparison. *Note:* In the interest of reducing the number of variables, all this "figuring" assumes a fixed-rate mortgage. (For more info on mortgages, see "Financing Your Home" in this chapter.)

Also, we ignore what economists call the *opportunity cost of owning.* In other words, when you buy, the money you put into your home can't be invested elsewhere, and the forgone investment return on that money, say some economists, should be considered a cost of owning a home. We choose to ignore this concept for two reasons. First, and most importantly, we don't agree with this line of thinking. When you buy a home, you're investing your money in real estate, which historically has offered solid long-term returns (see Chapter 8). And secondly, we have you ignore opportunity cost because it greatly complicates the analysis.

Table 14-2	Monthly Expenses: Renting versus Owning
Figure Out This	*Write It Here* *($ per Month)*
1. Monthly mortgage payment (see "Mortgage")	$_____
2. Plus monthly property taxes (see "Property taxes")	+ $_____
3. Equals total monthly mortgage plus property taxes	= $_____
4. Plus insurance ($30 to $150/mo., depending on property value)	+ $_____
5. Plus maintenance (1% of property cost divided by 12 months)	+ $_____
6. Equals total costs of owning (add lines 3, 4, and 5)	= $_____

Now compare Line 6 in Table 14-2 with the monthly rent on a comparable place to see which costs more — owning or renting.

Mortgage

To determine the monthly payment on your mortgage, simply multiply the relevant number (or multiplier) from Table 14-3 by the size of your mortgage expressed in thousands of dollars (divided by 1,000). For example, if you're taking out a $100,000, 8-percent mortgage amortized over 25 years, you multiply 100 by 6.32 for a $632 monthly payment.

Table 14-3	Your Monthly Mortgage Payment Multiplier	
Interest Rate	*15-Year Amortization*	*25-Year Amortization*
5.0%	7.88	5.82
5.5%	8.14	6.10
6.0%	8.40	6.40
6.5%	8.66	6.70
7.0%	8.93	7.00
7.5%	9.21	7.32
8.0%	9.49	7.63
8.5%	9.77	7.96
9.0%	10.05	8.27
9.5%	10.34	8.61
10.0%	10.62	8.94
10.5%	10.92	9.29
11.0%	11.21	9.62
11.5%	11.51	9.97
12.0%	11.81	10.32

Property taxes

You can ask a real estate person, mortgage lender, or your local assessment office what your annual property tax bill would be for a house of similar value to the one you are considering buying. Divide this amount by 12 to arrive at your monthly property tax bill.

Recognizing advantages to renting

Renting has its advantages. Some of the financially successful renters we've seen include people who pay low rent, either because they made housing sacrifices or they live in a rent-controlled building. If you're consistently able to save 10 percent or more of your earnings, you're probably well on your way to achieving your future financial goals.

As a renter, you can avoid worrying about or being responsible for fixing up the property — that's your landlord's responsibility. You also have more financial and psychological flexibility as a renter. If you want to move, you can generally do so a lot easier as a renter than you can as a homeowner.

Having a lot of your money tied up in your home is another problem that you don't face when renting over the long haul. Some people enter their retirement years with a substantial portion of their wealth in their homes. As a renter, you can have all your money in financial assets that you can tap into more easily.

Considering the long-term costs of renting

When you crunch the numbers to find out what owning rather than renting a comparable place may cost you on a monthly basis, you may discover that owning isn't as expensive as you thought. Or you may find that owning costs a bit more than renting. This discovery may tempt you to think that, financially speaking, renting is cheaper than owning.

Be careful not to jump to conclusions. Remember that you're looking at the cost of owning versus renting *today*. What about 5, 10, or 30 years from now? As an owner, your biggest monthly expense — the mortgage payment — doesn't rise steadily, it fluctuates, and only if interest rates are at a different level when one mortgage term expires and you renew. If interest rates are higher or lower when your mortgage term expires and you renew your loan, your payments will rise — or fall — accordingly. Your property taxes, homeowner's insurance, and maintenance expenses — which are generally far less than your mortgage payment — are the items that increase with the cost of living.

When you rent, however, your entire monthly rent is subject to the vagaries of inflation. Living in a rent-controlled unit, where the annual increase allowed in your rent is capped, is the exception to this rule. Rent control does not eliminate price hikes, it just limits them.

Suppose that you are comparing the costs of owning a home that costs $200,000 to renting that same home for $1,200 a month. Table 14-4 compares the cost of owning the home to your rental costs over 25 years. The comparison assumes that you take out a mortgage loan equal to 75 percent of the cost of the property at a fixed interest rate of 7.5 percent, meaning your mortgage payments would be $1,097 (rounded up to $1,100) and that the rate of inflation of your homeowner's insurance, property taxes, maintenance (which for the ownership example starts off at $450 a month), and rent is 4 percent per year.

Table 14-4	Cost of Owning versus Renting over 25 Years	
Year	*Ownership Cost per Month*	*Rental Cost per Month*
1	$1,550	$1,200
5	$1,626	$1,404
10	$1,740	$1,708
20	$2,048	$2,528
25	$2,253	$3,076

As you can see in Table 14-4, in the first few years owning a home costs a little more than renting it. In the long run, however, owning becomes less expensive, because more of your rental expenses increase with inflation. And don't forget that you're building equity in your property as a homeowner; that equity will be quite substantial by the time you have your mortgage paid off.

You may be thinking that if inflation doesn't rise 4 percent per year, renting could end up being cheaper. This is not necessarily so. Suppose that inflation didn't exist. Your rent wouldn't escalate, but home ownership expenses wouldn't either. And, with no inflation, you could probably refinance your mortgage at a rate lower than 7 percent. If you do the math, owning would still cost less in the long run with lower inflation, but the advantage of owning is less than during periods of higher inflation.

Financing Your Home

After you look at your financial health, figure out your timeline, and compare renting costs to owning costs, you need to confront the tough task of obtaining a hunk of debt to buy a home (unless you're independently wealthy). A mortgage loan from a bank or other source makes up the difference between the cash you intend to put into the purchase and the agreed-upon selling price of the real estate.

Understanding the different types of mortgages

Like other financial products, there are many different features you can choose from when it comes to picking your mortgage. The differences can be important or trivial, expensive or cost-free. We'll begin with the big differences.

When selecting your mortgage, there are three main features you need to become familiar with. The first is the total amount of time you want to take to pay your loan back. This is called the *amortization*. The second is the term that your mortgage agreement runs for. This typically will range from six months to five years or more. The second factor to consider is whether the interest rate is fixed for the term of your loan, or whether it fluctuates with the general level of interest rates. We help you understand your choices on these two fronts in the sections below.

Ideally, you should weigh the pros and cons of each mortgage type and decide what's best for your situation before you go out to purchase a piece of real estate or refinance a loan.

In the real world, most people ignore this advice. The excitement of purchasing a home tends to cloud one's judgment. Our experience has been that few people look at their entire financial picture before making major real estate decisions. You may end up with a mortgage that could someday seriously overshadow your delight in your little English herb garden out back.

Consider the issues that we discuss in this section before you decide which kind of mortgage is right for you.

Understanding amortization — How long you'll take to pay off your home loan

When you take out a consumer loan to buy, for example, a car, you have to decide how long you will take to pay the money back. Say you choose four years. Over that time, you'll have to pay back the full amount you originally borrowed, plus interest. After the four years is up, you'll have paid your lender all the money you borrowed, and all the interest on the borrowed funds.

Mortgages are essentially home loans, but they differ in one significant way. When your mortgage payments are calculated, you can choose the number of years over which you want to stretch out the repayment of the principal, with your interest costs being calculated over that period and included in your regular payments. The number of years you choose to spread your home loan out over is called the *amortization*. This is the period used to calculate your monthly payments, given the interest rate you accept.

Most mortgages in Canada are amortized over 25 years. You can, however, choose a shorter or sometimes longer period. These typically range from 5 to as much as 40 years.

Understanding your mortgage term

The length of the amortization you choose is distinct and separate from the *term*. The term is the length of time you want your loan agreement with a particular lender to run. When the term expires, your loan expires. You can choose to sign up for another loan for whatever term you like, either with the same lender or a different financial institution. You can pay off some of or your entire mortgage at that point if you have the money available. You can even alter the amortization at that point.

For instance, you could take out a mortgage with the total cost spread out — amortized — over 25 years, with the actual mortgage agreement lasting for only two years. When those two years are up, you could renew your mortgage and change the loan arrangement. This time, for instance, you could decide to choose a shorter amortization of just 15 years, but sign up for a five-year term.

Comparing short-term and long-term mortgages

In general, you can choose a term of anywhere from six months or a year to five years. Some lenders also offer seven- and ten-year terms. Generally, the longer the term you choose, the higher your interest rate. Lenders charge you more as a way to protect themselves should rates rise. The longer your term, the longer you have a lower rate locked in, and the more the lender loses out on what they could make off you if you had to renew earlier at a higher interest rate.

A short term, such as a six-month or one-year agreement, means that you have to renew much more frequently, putting you at the mercy of current interest rates. If rates have moved up by the time your term ends and you have to renew, your monthly payments will also be higher. If rates stay level, though, your payments will be less than what they would be with a longer-term mortgage, which generally comes with a higher interest rate. Of course, if rates have fallen when you come to renew, you'll be even further ahead.

Should you choose a short-term or long-term mortgage?

When choosing your term, you are making a trade-off. If you choose a short term, you risk having rates rise between now and your next renewal date. If you go long and rates don't rise, you pay more than you need to.

Selecting a long term (four to five years or longer) guarantees your payments for that entire period, often an important consideration for those who are on tightly controlled budgets. This approach is often a good choice if you are in the early years of home ownership. Once you're locked in, you know exactly how much your mortgage will cost for years to come. You don't have to make any new decisions about your home loan for a long time. And your heart won't jump every time interest rates do. But this peace of mind comes at a price.

Five-year rates, for example, typically range anywhere from 1 percent to more than 3 percent higher than six-month rates. You pay a kind of insurance premium to protect yourself against the possibility of higher rates in the future. Ask yourself if the cost is worth it. Often, you'll find that both the financial and security risks of going short are not as great as you think.

Longer terms are also worth considering if you're just starting out, or you find your finances stretched to the limit. If an unexpected jump in rates would push your payments beyond what you can comfortably handle, then lock in at a rate you know you can afford for several years.

When is it generally wise to consider a shorter term? When rates are at historical all-time highs. Remember, the reason for going long is to lock in a rate that protects you from renewing at an even higher rate. Otherwise, everyone would select a short term. Sure, it's hard to know if rates have peaked. But by staying short, you can quickly capture the gains when rates fall back down again.

If you choose a short term, you'll have to take your chances at the mortgage rate roulette wheel more often. If you can handle the uncertainty — both psychologically and financially — you'll be rewarded by rates that are consistently lower than long-term rates. Making decisions more often also allows you to fine-tune your strategy and gives you more opportunity to reduce your principal.

Be warned, however, that interest rates fluctuate. If they jump quickly, they can just as easily fall back to where they started or even lower. The moral of the story is don't base your decisions on short-term movements. Make sure that you have enough of a financial cushion to afford the higher payments that you'll have to make if rates have risen by the time your renewal date rolls around.

Assessing your best option

Your decision depends on your ability to live with risk. Staying short means more uncertainty, but you're almost certain to have lower mortgage costs unless rates keep marching up without coming back down. Choose long and you may sleep better, but you pay a premium for those worry-free nights.

If you're still unsure about which route to follow, don't worry. It's something that everybody goes through. Next time you're at a party, just start asking people about the choices they've made with their mortgages. You're bound to hear all sorts of tales about thousands of dollars lost or saved.

Open and closed mortgages

When you choose a *closed* mortgage, you're stuck with the terms of the deal until your loan agreement ends, or matures. You can refinance only if your lender lets you, and often that can involve paying stiff penalties. The upside of a closed mortgage is that, because the lender knows it can depend on your regular payments, your rates are lower.

Growing competition, however, has forced lenders to build in ways for you to pay off significant portions of your loan even within a closed mortgage. For example, the right to pay off 10 percent of your initial principal amount on each anniversary of your agreement is common.

In contrast to a closed mortgage, an *open* mortgage allows you to pay off part or all of the loan at any time without penalty. That can be a valuable option if you expect to come into a substantial sum of money or if you know you'll sell your home shortly. By completely paying off an open mortgage, you effectively terminate your contract with the lender. An open loan gives you flexibility to adapt your loan to changes in your financial picture or the economic situation. You have to pay more for this feature, usually a percent or so.

If falling rates are too tough to resist, but you want something less risky than a variable rate (which we describe in the next section), consider a fixed open mortgage. Your rate is guaranteed, but if rates fall to an even more attractive level you can lock in at that point without any penalty. If you want to play the interest game, this allows you to keep your options open while still protecting you should rates go up instead of down. It's usually not worth paying the premium that lenders charge for open mortgages, though, and you have other options.

Today's numerous prepayment options allow you to pay down significant sums during the life of your mortgage. In addition, more and more homeowners opt for shorter and shorter terms. Simply rolling over six-month terms, for example, can be a sensible strategy. At the end of each term, you're free to pick whatever term you like, from whatever lender you want, if you meet the lender's basic requirements. You also have the option of paying off any amount of your principal that you choose.

Otherwise, however, if you're trying to take advantage of low or falling rates, there is now a much better alternative available, called a six-month convertible. We talk more about convertible mortgages later in this chapter.

Understanding fixed- and variable-rate mortgages

If you choose a _fixed-rate mortgage,_ your payments don't change during your mortgage term. You lock in an interest rate that's fixed for the entire length of your term. With a fixed-rate mortgage, there's nothing complicated to track, and there's no uncertainty. If you like getting your daily newspaper delivered at the same time every day, you're gonna like fixed-rate mortgages.

In contrast to a fixed-rate mortgage, a _variable-rate mortgage_ (sometimes referred to as an _adjustable mortgage_) carries an interest rate that (no surprise here!) varies. Usually tied to the lender's prime rate, it moves, jumps, rises, falls, and otherwise can't sit still, just like a fidgeting child.

The return for putting up with this volatility is that the rate is usually the lowest available at any point in time. Variable rates generally are set at, or slightly above, the lender's prime rate, and they rise and fall accordingly.

Some lenders offer protection from soaring rates by putting an absolute ceiling on how high your rate can go. You pay a slightly higher rate for a capped variable, usually around 1 percent above that of a regular variable.

If rates are on their way up, you're better off locking in to a fixed-rate mortgage before the rates go any higher. And if rates are going down, you should select a variable rate and go along for the ride. So some people ask, "Shouldn't the likelihood of interest rates going up or down determine whether I take a fixed-rate or variable-rate mortgage?"

Good question. The problem is that there really is no accurate way to predict which way rates are going. If you feel strongly that rates are likely to fall and you prefer the variable option, you should understand the risks involved. A rise in interest rates can mean that at some point your monthly payment won't even cover the interest cost of your loan. If this happens, the outstanding interest is added to your balance. Once that figure hits about 105 to 110 percent of the original loan amount, you can expect to hear from your lender. You'll either have to make a lump-sum payment against your principal or lock in to a fixed term.

If you decide that a variable-rate mortgage is the way to go, you also have to pass some extra tests. Due to their volatility, variable-rate mortgages often have lower lending limits. Many lenders won't let you borrow more than 70 percent of your property's appraised value. In some cases, you must also select an amortization period of 20 years or less.

Convertible mortgages

While the bells and whistles of *convertible mortgages* vary from lender to lender, the basic principle remains the same. You get a mortgage with a term of six months — or sometimes a year — typically with the same interest rate available for fixed mortgages for the same term. This is generally the best mortgage rate available.

At any point during the term of your convertible mortgage, you can "convert" your mortgage to a different term; you can also choose between an open or closed loan.

The benefit of a convertible mortgage is that it allows you to avoid paying a premium for longer-term fixed rates. You're also protected against rapidly rising rates because you can lock in at any time, rather than having to wait until your term expires or paying a hefty penalty. If rates should suddenly move up, you can simply lock in a longer-term rate. Meanwhile, you also save yourself the extra premium for an open mortgage.

If rates are falling, you can lock in the lower rates at any point. It often pays to simply ride out the term and, if rates are still falling at that point, to just sign up for another six-month convertible.

The important point with a convertible loan is to check the fine print for specific conditions. One institution, for example, allows you to convert only to a five-year term. Even if you let the six months elapse, you're automatically signed up. In essence, this is really a 5½ year mortgage, with the possibility of lower rates for a maximum of the first six months.

Most lenders allow you to convert at any time to any term you wish. The only across-the-board restriction is that you can't convert during the term to another six-month convertible. The other drawback to convertibles is that if you want to renew part way through the six months, you can't change lenders. That means losing some bargaining power, which can cost you a quarter or a half percentage point.

Variables are variable in another way: No other type of mortgage differs so much from lender to lender. Every aspect, from the terms available to whether you can pay the loan off early, varies widely depending on the institution. It's important to ask specific questions about any variable mortgage — and make sure that the answers are there on paper — before signing on the dotted line.

There's a relatively unpromoted player on the mortgage scene that can save you from having to decide whether the potential savings from lower rates is worth all this worry. It's called a *convertible mortgage,* and it's one of the best-kept secrets in the mortgage game. A convertible loan offers many of the benefits of a variable-rate mortgage, with very little downside. For more information, see the sidebar on "Convertible mortgages."

Shopping for mortgages

The following sections cover what you need to know when shopping for fixed-rate mortgages.

Understanding other lender fees

Lenders often tack on all sorts of other upfront fees when processing your loan. You need to know the total of all lender fees so that you can compare different mortgages and determine how much completing your home purchase is going to cost you.

Lenders can nickel and dime you with a number of different fees. Here are the main culprits:

- **Application and processing fees:** Most lenders charge several hundred dollars to complete your paperwork and process it through their underwriting (loan evaluation) department. The justification for this fee is that if your loan is rejected or you decide not to take it, the lender needs to cover the costs. Some lenders return this fee to you upon closing if you go with their loan (after you're approved).

- **Credit report:** Some lenders may charge a modest fee to pay for the cost of obtaining a copy of your credit report. This report tells the lender whether you've been naughty or nice to other lenders in the past. If you have problems on your credit report, clean them up before you apply (see "Increasing your approval chances" in this chapter).

- **Appraisal:** The property for which you're borrowing money needs to be valued. If you default on your mortgage, your lender doesn't want to get stuck with a property worth less than you owe. For most residential properties, the appraisal cost is typically several hundred dollars.

Get a written itemization of charges from all lenders you are seriously considering so that you can more readily compare different lenders' mortgages, and so that you have no surprises when you close on your loan. And to minimize your chances of throwing money away on a loan for which you may not qualify, ask the lender if you may not be approved for some reason. Be sure to disclose any problems you're aware of on your credit report or with the property.

Avoiding the down-payment blues

When you buy a home, ideally you want to make a down payment of at least 25 percent of the purchase price of the property. Why? Because you can generally qualify for the most favourable terms on a mortgage with such a down payment, and you can avoid the added cost of mortgage insurance. Mortgage insurance protects lenders against losing money in the event you default on your loan, and can cost several hundred dollars per year on a typical mortgage.

Many people don't have the equivalent of 25 percent or more of the purchase price of a home so that they can avoid paying private mortgage insurance. Here are a number of solutions for coming up with that 25 percent faster or buying with less money down:

- **Go on a spending diet.** One sure way to come up with a down payment is to raise your savings rate by slashing your spending. Take a tour through Chapter 5 to find strategies for cutting back on your spending.

- **Consider lower-priced properties.** Some first-time home buyers have expectations that are too grand. Smaller properties and ones that need some work can help keep down the purchase price and, therefore, the required down payment.

- **Find partners.** You can often get more home for your money when you buy a building in partnership with one, two, or a few people. Make sure that you write up a legal contract to specify what is going to happen if a partner wants out.

- **Seek reduced-down-payment financing.** Some lenders will offer you a mortgage even though you may be able to put down only as little as 5 to 10 percent of the purchase price. You can't be as picky about properties because not as many are available under these terms — many need work or haven't yet sold for other reasons.

  Some property owners or developers may be willing to finance your purchase with as little as 5 to 10 percent down. You can't be as picky about properties, because not as many are available under these terms — many need work or haven't been sold yet for other reasons.

- **Get assistance from family members.** If your parents, grandparents, or other relatives have money dozing away in a savings account or GIC, they may be willing to lend (or even give) you the down payment. You can pay them an interest rate that's higher than the rate they're currently earning but lower than what you'd pay to borrow from a bank — a win/win situation for both of you. Lenders generally ask if any portion of the down payment is borrowed and will reduce the maximum amount they are willing to loan you accordingly.

- **Obtain a high-ratio mortgage.** If you have a down payment of at least 5 percent of the purchase price, you can obtain a high-ratio mortgage from most lenders. However, you're required to buy special mortgage insurance. If your application is approved, your lender will generally organize this for you. The insurance is provided either by the Canada Mortgage and Housing Corporation (CMHC), which is run by the federal government, or GE Capital. The insurance is there to protect your lender — not you — in case you fail to meet your payments.

Your down payment determines your insurance rate, which can run from 0.5 percent to 2.9 percent. You pay the premium only once — when you take out your mortgage. You're required to insure the entire loan, not just the difference between your down payment and the 25 percent required for a conventional loan. On a $100,000 mortgage, an insurance rate of 2.5 would mean paying $2,500 in insurance. If you don't have the money, you can ask your lender to add the insurance premium to your loan. Of course, that means you'll likely end up paying twice or three times that amount back over the life of the mortgage once all the interest costs are added in.

In general, your down payment has to come out of your own pocket. But CMHC's Flex Down option allows you to get the money for the down payment from a variety of sources. The money can be borrowed from family members, or obtained from a financial institution as a loan or through a cashback program. The major restriction is that the money has to come from a party that is at arm's length to the transaction. This means, for instance, you can't get the money from the builder of the property. While it would seem that borrowing the full amount would be a sign you've set your sights too high given your financial fitness, there are circumstances where the Flex Down option may make sense. For instance, say you have recently graduated from a university program such as medical school and have already entered the working world. You likely haven't had the opportunity to start putting away any savings, yet can probably look forward to many decades of an income that is far above the average. To qualify, you'll still need to have a healthy financial profile, including a good credit rating.

The RRSP Home Buyers' Plan

You can borrow up to $20,000 from your RRSP to buy a house without paying any extra taxes or penalties under the federal government's Home Buyers' Plan.

For hopeful home buyers, the plan can be useful, but it is by no means perfect. The plan has a number of strict conditions and some potentially big costs, too. It's vital that you understand all the specifics, despite their positively desert-like aridity. Knowing what you're getting into now can save you a lot of financial worries down the road.

One important restriction is that neither you nor your spouse is allowed to make a contribution to your RRSP in the year that you withdraw funds under the plan. The government doesn't want people to put money into their plan, get the tax break, and then draw on the same funds to use as part of a down payment. If you've been making regular contributions to your RRSP, and you've been building the tax refund into your budget, you need to prepare for this loss in cash flow.

Repayment rules

There are strict rules governing how quickly you have to repay the money you've borrowed from your RRSP. You must repay the money into your RRSP within 16 years. The minimum you have to repay each year starting with the second year after you make your withdrawal is the equivalent of ¹⁄₁₅ of the amount borrowed.

Keep in mind those payments aren't considered RRSP contributions, and you don't get any tax write-offs for them. And if you miss a payment or part of a payment, the government treats that money as if you had withdrawn it directly from your RRSP. The sum is included as part of your income for that year, and you have to pay tax on it. Ouch!

If you're currently finding it tough to put money into your RRSP, it will be twice as hard if you use your retirement funds for a down payment. Before you can even think of making a fresh contribution, you have to replace the required portion of the borrowed funds for that year. If that leaves you unable to make a direct RRSP contribution for that year, you miss out on a big tax break and a large tax refund. You also forgo the tax-free compound growth you could have earned from that new contribution.

Loss of potential growth in your RRSP

By taking money out, you lose all the potential growth from those funds as long as that money isn't in your plan. The younger you are, the higher the cost is to you. Unfortunately, the only way to understand the dangers this option poses for your RRSP is to do battle with a few numbers.

Suppose that you're 30 and that you borrow $18,000 from your plan to buy a home. You have to repay $1,200 a year, or $100 a month, for the next 15 years. The alternative would have been to borrow the money, say, as a second mortgage. If you borrowed the money at 10 percent and spread the loan over 15 years, the monthly payments would be $193.50. So the extra cost of borrowing the money from a bank or trust company instead of your RRSP is $93.50 a month.

But you have to balance that off against the gains possible by leaving that $18,000 in your RRSP. Earning an average of 10 percent a year, in 40 years that money would grow to more than $800,000. By comparison, if it were left in for 35 years, it would be worth just over $500,000.

This is an extreme example, but it amply demonstrates the true cost of borrowing "free" from your RRSP. The actual cost depends on how old you are and how quickly you're able to repay the borrowings. In general, if you're over 40 the price may not be too steep. In addition, if you use the plan to buy a home and it appreciates steadily, the growth on the value of your house will offset some of the forgone growth in your RRSP. You may be able to get the best of both worlds by borrowing from your RRSP and repaying the loan quickly, say in the first three or four years after you have settled into your new home.

In general, you're probably better off borrowing the money, even if that means taking out a second mortgage or a high-ratio mortgage. Just make sure that you can afford the higher interest rate charges or the mortgage insurance premium.

Should you consider faster mortgage payoff?

The appeal of paying off your mortgage sooner is enticing. So if you can afford the higher payments on your mortgage, you'd be silly not to make them, right? Not so fast. You're really asking whether you should pay off your mortgage slowly or more quickly. And the answer isn't simple — it depends.

You need to think through this decision, despite the fact that entire books have been written extolling the virtues of owning your home without mortgage debt as soon as possible. Those books come complete with endless rows and columns of numbers so that you can look up how much you save through a faster payback.

If you have the time and inclination (and a good financial calculator), you can calculate how much interest you can save or avoid through a faster payback. We have a friendly word of advice about spending hours crunching numbers: *don't.* You can make this decision by considering some qualitative issues.

Consider alternative uses for savings

First, think about *alternative uses* for the extra money you'd be throwing into the mortgage paydown. What's best for you depends on your overall financial situation and what else you can do with the money. If you would end up blowing the extra money at the racetrack or on an expensive car, pay down the mortgage. That's a no-brainer.

But suppose that you take the extra $100 or $200 per month that you were planning to add to your mortgage payment and contribute it to an RRSP instead. That step may make financial sense. Why? Because contributions to RRSPs (discussed in Chapter 7) are tax-deductible.

When you add an extra $200 to your mortgage payment to pay off your mortgage faster, you get no tax benefits. Zero, nada, zippo! When you dump that $200 into an RRSP, you get to subtract that $200 from the income on which you pay taxes. If you're paying 40 percent in federal and provincial income taxes, you shave $80 (that's $200 multiplied by 40 percent) off your tax bill.

In fact, choosing between putting more money into your RRSP or paying down your mortgage involves a lot of serious number-crunching. The results depend on your mortgage rate, how many years you have left before your mortgage is paid off, as well as the return you'll earn in your RRSP. Because of all these variables — some of which are hard to nail down — a good compromise is to maximize your RRSP contributions and to take the tax refund that the contributions earn you and put it down against your mortgage.

Cut your costs at renewal time

No matter how long your mortgage is amortized for, your actual contract with your lender expires at the end of each term. When you renew, you're really entering into an entirely new agreement. This gives you complete flexibility to change any or all of the terms of your mortgage, from payment levels and the amortization period to the frequency of instalments. You can even change lenders if you wish.

A few months before your renewal date, shop around for guaranteed rate offers from a handful of lenders. Sixty- and sometimes ninety-day guarantees are common. Getting your renewal rate guaranteed in advance protects you from sudden increases in rates before your renewal. You can also use the guarantee to negotiate better rates from your current mortgage company. If it won't match the competition, you're free to transfer your mortgage to another financial institution.

Finding the best lender

As with other financial purchases, you can save a lot of money by shopping around. It doesn't matter whether you shop around on your own or hire someone to help you. Just do it!

On a 25-year, $150,000 mortgage, for example, getting a mortgage that costs 0.5 percent less per year saves you about $14,000 in interest over the life of the loan (given current interest rates). That's enough to buy a decent car! On second thought, save it!

Shopping for a lender on your own

In most areas, you can find many mortgage lenders. Although having a large number of lenders to choose from is good for competition, it also makes shopping a chore.

Large banks whose names you recognize from their advertising usually don't offer the best rates. Make sure that you check out some of the smaller lending institutions in your area, as well. Include alternative lenders such as President's Choice Financial and ING Direct in your search.

Real estate agents can also refer you to lenders with whom they've previously done business. These lenders may not necessarily offer the most competitive rates — the agent simply may have done business with them in the past.

The Internet is a good place to get an initial idea of what rates are being offered. You can find charts summarizing the rates from dozens of lenders at www.cannex.com. Others sites offering charts of rates include www.canadamortgage.com and www.themortgage.com. The major banks and other lenders all post their rates on their Web site.

You can also look in the real estate section of one of the larger weekend newspapers in your area for charts of selected lender interest rates. These tables are by no means comprehensive or reflective of the best rates available. In fact, many of them are sent to newspapers for free by firms that distribute mortgage information to mortgage brokers. Use the tables as a starting point by calling the lenders who list the best rates.

Hiring a mortgage broker

Insurance agents peddle insurance, real estate agents sell real estate, and mortgage brokers deal in mortgages. The terms of the loan obtained through a broker are generally the same as the terms you obtain from the lender directly.

Mortgage brokers get paid a percentage of the loan amount — typically 0.5 to 1 or 2 percent. This commission is negotiable, especially on larger loans that are more lucrative. Ask a mortgage broker what his cut is. Many people don't ask for this information, so some brokers may act taken aback when you inquire. Remember, it's your money!

The chief advantage of using a mortgage broker is that the broker can shop among lenders to get you a good deal. If you're too busy or disinterested to shop around for a good deal on a mortgage, a competent mortgage broker can probably save you money. A broker can also help you through the tedious process of filling out all those horrible documents lenders demand before giving you a loan. And if you have credit problems or an unusual property, a broker may be able to match you up with a hard-to-find lender who is willing to offer you a mortgage.

When evaluating a mortgage broker, be on guard for those who are lazy and don't continually shop the market looking for the best mortgage lenders. Some brokers place their business with the same lenders all the time, and those lenders don't necessarily offer the best rates. Also watch out for salespeople who earn big commissions pushing certain loan programs that are not in your best interests. These brokers aren't interested in taking the time to understand your needs and discuss your options. Thoroughly check a broker's references before you do business with him or her.

Even if you plan to shop on your own, talking to a mortgage broker may still be worthwhile. At the very least, you can compare what you find with what brokers say they can get for you. Just be careful. Some brokers tell you what you want to hear and then aren't able to deliver when the time comes.

When a mortgage broker quotes you a really good deal, make sure that you ask who the lender is. (Most brokers refuse to reveal this information until you pay the few hundred dollars to cover the appraisal and credit report.) You can check with the actual lender to verify the interest rate the broker quotes you and make sure that you're eligible for the loan.

Increasing your approval chances

A lender can take several weeks to complete your property appraisal and an evaluation of your loan package. When you're under contract to buy a property, having your loan denied after waiting several weeks can mean that you lose the property as well as the money you spent applying for the loan and having the property inspected. Some property sellers may be willing to give you an extension, but others won't.

Here's how to increase your chances of having your mortgage approved:

✔ **Get your finances in shape before you shop.** You're not going to have a good handle on what you can afford to spend on a home until you whip your personal finances into shape. Do so before you begin to make offers on properties. This book can help you. If you have consumer debt, get rid of it — the more credit card, auto loan, and other consumer debt you rack up, the less mortgage you qualify for. In addition to the high interest rate and the fact that it encourages you to live beyond your means, you now have a third reason to get rid of consumer debt. Hang on to the dream of owning a home and plug away at paying off consumer debts.

✔ **Clear up credit report problems.** Late payments, missed payments, or debts that you never bothered to pay can come back to haunt you. If you think that you have problems on your credit report, get a copy before you apply for a mortgage. The major credit bureaus are Equifax (800-465-7166; www.equifax.ca) and TransUnion (866-525-0262; www.tuc.ca). These credit bureaus generally charge about $15 for a copy of your report.

Mistakes crop up on credit reports. The only way to fix them, unfortunately, is to get on the phone with the credit bureaus and start squawking. If specific creditors have reported erroneous information, call them too. If the customer service representatives you talk with are no help, dash off a nice letter to the president of each company. If you have bona fide problems documented on your credit report, try explaining them to your lender. If the lender is unsympathetic, try calling other lenders. Tell the lenders your credit problems upfront, and see if you can find one that is willing to give you a loan. Mortgage brokers (see the previous section) can also help you shop for lenders who are willing to offer you a loan despite credit problems.

✔ **Get preapproved or prequalified.** When you get *prequalified,* a lender speaks with you about your financial situation and then calculates the maximum amount they're willing to lend you based on what you tell them. *Preapproval* is much more in-depth and includes a lender's actual review of your financial statements. Although neither requires a lender to actually make you a mortgage loan, preapproval means more, especially in qualifying you financially in the eyes of a seller. Just be sure not to waste your time and money getting preapproved if you're not really ready to get serious about buying.

✔ **Be upfront about problems.** The best defence against loan rejection is to avoid it in the first place. You can sometimes head off potential rejection by disclosing to your lender anything that may cause a problem before you apply for the loan. That way, you have more time to correct problems and find alternate solutions.

✔ **Work around low/unstable income.** When you've been changing jobs or you're self-employed, your recent economic history may be as unstable as a communist country trying out capitalism. Making a larger down payment is one way around this problem. If you put down 30 to 45 percent or more, you may be able to get a no–income verification loan. You may try getting a co-signer, such as a relative or good friend. As long as they aren't borrowed up to their eyeballs, they can help you qualify for a larger loan than you can get on your own. Be sure that all parties understand the terms of the agreement, including who is responsible for monthly payments!

✔ **Consider a backup loan.** You certainly should shop among different lenders, and you may even want to apply to more than one for a mortgage. Although applying for a second loan means additional fees and work, it can increase your chances of getting a mortgage if you're attempting to buy a difficult-to-finance property, or if your financial situation makes some lenders leery. Also be sure to disclose to each lender what you're doing — the second lender to pull your credit report will see that another lender has been there already.

Finding the Right Property and Location

Shopping for a home can be fun. You get to peek inside other people's refrigerators and closets. But for most people, finding the right house at the right price can take a lot of time. When you're buying with partners or a spouse (or children, if you choose to share the decision-making with them), it can also entail a lot of compromise. A good agent (or several who specialize in different areas) can help with the legwork. The following sections cover the main things you need to consider when shopping for a home to call your own.

Condo, town house, co-op, or detached home?

Some people's image of a home is a single-family dwelling — a stand-alone house with a lawn and white picket fence. In some areas, however — particularly in higher-cost neighbourhoods — you find *condominiums* (you own the unit and a share of everything else), *town homes* (attached or row houses), and *cooperatives* (you own a share of the entire building).

The allure of such higher-density housing is that it's generally less expensive. In some cases, you don't have to worry about some of the general maintenance, because the owner's association (which you pay for, directly or indirectly) takes care of it.

If you don't have the time, energy, or desire to keep up a property, shared housing may make sense for you. You generally get more living space for your dollar and it may also provide you with more security than a stand-alone home.

As investments, however, single-family homes generally do better in the long run. Shared housing is easier to build and hence easier to overbuild; on the other hand, single-family houses are harder to put up because more land is required. But most people, when they can afford it, still prefer a stand-alone home.

With that being said, you should remember that a rising tide raises all boats. In a good real estate market, all types of housing appreciate, although single-family homes tend to do better. Shared housing values tend to increase the most in densely populated urban areas with little available land for new building.

From an investment-return perspective, if you can afford a smaller single-family home instead of a larger shared-housing unit, buy the single-family home. Be especially wary of buying shared housing in suburban areas with lots of developable land.

Casting a broad net

You may have an idea about the type of property and location you're interested in or think you can afford before you start your search. You may think, for example, that you can afford only a condominium in the neighbourhood you want. But if you take the time to check out other communities, you may be surprised to find one that meets most of your needs and also has affordable single-family homes. You'd never know about this community, though, if you narrowed your search too quickly.

Even if you've lived in an area for a while and think that you know it well, look at different types of properties in a number of areas before you start to narrow your search. Be open-minded, and figure out which of your many criteria for a home you *really* care about. You may have to be flexible on some of your preferences.

Finding out actual sale prices

Don't look at just a few of the homes listed at a particular price and then get depressed because they're all dogs or you can't afford what you really want. Before you decide to renew your apartment lease, remember that properties often sell for less than the price at which they are listed.

Find out what the places you look at eventually sell for. Doing so gives you a better sense of what you can really afford as well as what places are really worth. Ask the agent or owner who sold the property what the sales price was, or contact the town's assessors' office for information on how to obtain property sales price information.

Researching the neighbourhood and area

Even (and especially) if you fall in love with a house at first sight, go back to the neighbourhood at different times of the day and on different days of the week. Travel between your prospective new home and your place of business during commute hours to see how long your commute will really take. Knock on a few doors and meet your potential neighbours. You may discover, for example, that a flock of chickens lives in the backyard next door, or that the street and basement flood every other winter.

What are the schools like? Go visit them. Don't rely on statistics about test scores. Talk to parents and teachers. What's really going on at the school? Even if you don't have kids, the quality of the local school has direct bearing on the value of your property. Is crime a problem? Call the local police department. Will future development be allowed? If so, what type? Talk to the municipal planning department. What are your property taxes going to be? Is the property located in an area susceptible to major risks, such as floods, mudslides, fires, or earthquakes? Consider these issues even if they're not important to you, because they can affect the resale value of your property.

When you buy a home, you're stuck with it. Make sure that you know what you're getting yourself into *before* you buy.

Working with Real Estate Agents

When you buy (or sell) a home, you're probably going work with a real estate agent. Real estate agents earn their living on commission. As such, their incentives, which are different from yours, can be at odds with what's best for you.

Real estate agents don't hide the fact that they get a cut of the deal. Property buyers and sellers generally understand the real estate commission system. We credit the real estate profession for calling its practitioners "agents" instead of coming up with some silly obfuscating title such as "housing consultants."

A top-notch real estate agent can be a significant help when you purchase or sell a property. On the other hand, a mediocre, incompetent, or greedy agent can be a real liability. Real estate agents don't have as bad a reputation as used-car salespeople, but they still don't have a very good reputation. The following sections help you sort the good from the bad.

Recognizing real estate agents' conflicts of interest

Real estate agents, because they work on commission, face numerous conflicts of interest. Some agents may not even recognize the conflicts in what they're doing. The following list presents the most common conflicts of interest that you need to watch out for.

- ✔ Because agents work on commission, it costs them when they spend time with you and you don't buy or sell. They want you to complete a deal, and they want that deal as soon as possible — otherwise, they don't get paid. Don't expect an agent to give you objective advice about what you should do given your overall financial situation. Examine your overall financial situation before you decide to begin working with an agent.

- ✔ Because real estate agents get a percentage of the sales price of a property, they have a built-in incentive to encourage you to spend more. Adjustable-rate mortgages (see "Financing Your Home" in this chapter) allow you to spend more, because the interest rate starts at a lower level than that of a fixed-rate mortgage. Thus, real estate agents are far more likely to encourage you to take an adjustable. But adjustables are a lot riskier — you need to understand these drawbacks before signing up for one.

- ✔ Agents often receive a higher commission when they sell listings that belong to other agents in their office. Beware. Sometimes the same agent represents both the property seller and the property buyer in the transaction — a real problem. Agents who are holding open houses for sale may try to sell to an unrepresented buyer they meet at the open house. There's no way one person can represent the best interests of both sides.

✔ Since agents work on commission and get paid a percentage of the sales price of the property, many are not interested in working with you if you can't or simply don't want to spend a lot. Some agents may reluctantly take you on as a customer and then give you little attention and time. Before you hire an agent, check references to make sure that he works well with buyers like you.

✔ Real estate agents typically work a specific territory. As a result, they usually can't objectively tell you the pros and cons of the surrounding region. Most won't admit that you may be better able to meet your needs by looking in another town (or some other part of town) where they don't normally work. Before you settle on an agent (or an area), spend time figuring out the pros and cons of different territories on your own. If you want to seriously look in more than one area, find agents who specialize in each area.

✔ If you don't get approved for a mortgage loan, your entire real estate deal will unravel. So some agents may refer you to a more expensive lender who has the virtue of high approval rates. Be sure to shop around — you can probably get a loan more cheaply. Be especially wary of agents who refer you to mortgage lenders and mortgage brokers who pay agents referral fees. Such payments clearly bias a real estate agent's "advice."

✔ Home inspectors are supposed to be objective third parties who are hired by prospective buyers to evaluate the condition of a property. Some agents may encourage you to use a particular inspector with a reputation of being "easy" — meaning he may not "find" all the house's defects. Remember, it's in the agent's best interest to seal the deal, and the discovery of problems may sidetrack that accomplishment.

✔ Some agents, under pressure to get a house listed for sale, agree to be accomplices and avoid disclosing known defects or problems with the property. In most cover-up cases, it seems, the seller doesn't explicitly ask an agent to help cover up a problem, the agent just looks the other way or avoids telling the whole truth. Never buy a home without having a home inspector look it over from top to bottom.

Looking for the right qualities in real estate agents

When you hire a real estate agent, you want to find someone who is competent and with whom you can get along. Working with an agent costs a lot of money — so make sure that you get your money's worth.

Buyer's brokers

An increasing number of agents are marketing themselves as buyer's brokers. Supposedly, these brokers represent your interests as a property buyer exclusively.

Legally speaking, buyer's brokers may sign a contract saying that they represent your — and only your — interests. Before this enlightened era, all agents contractually worked for the property seller.

The title "buyer's broker" is one of those things that sounds better than it really is. Agents who represent you as buyer's brokers still get paid only when you buy. And they still get paid on commission as a percentage of the purchase price. So they still have an incentive to sell you a piece of real estate; and the more expensive it is, the more commission they make.

Interview several agents. Check references. Ask agents for the names and phone numbers of at least three clients they worked with in the past six months (in the geographical area in which you are looking). You should look for the following traits in any agent you work with:

- **Full-time employment.** Some agents work in real estate as a second or even third job. Information in this field changes constantly. The best agents work at it full-time so that they can stay on top of the market.

- **Experience.** Hiring someone with experience doesn't necessarily mean looking for an agent who's been kicking around for decades. Many of the best agents come into the field from other occupations, such as business or teaching. Some sales, marketing, negotiation, and communication skills can certainly be picked up in other fields, but experience in buying and selling real estate does count.

- **Honesty and integrity.** You're trusting your agent with a lot. If your agent doesn't level with you about what a neighbourhood or particular property is really like, you suffer the consequences.

- **Interpersonal skills.** An agent has to be able to get along not only with you but also with a whole host of other people who are typically involved in a real estate deal: other agents, property sellers, inspectors, mortgage lenders, and so on. An agent doesn't have to be Mr. or Ms. Congeniality, but he or she should be able to put your interests first without upsetting others.

- **Negotiation skills.** Putting a real estate deal together involves negotiation. Is your agent going to exhaust all avenues to get you the best deal possible? Be sure to ask the agent's references how well the agent negotiated for them.

> ✔ **High quality standards.** Sloppy work can lead to big legal or logistical problems down the road. If an agent neglects to recommend an inspection, for example, you may be stuck with undiscovered problems after the deal is done.

Agents sometimes market themselves as *top producers,* which means that they sell a relatively large volume of real estate. This title doesn't count for much for you, the buyer. It may be a red flag for an agent who focuses on completing as many deals as possible. When you're buying a home, you need an agent who has the following additional traits:

> ✔ **Patience.** When you're buying a home, the last thing you want is an agent who tries to push you into making a deal. You need an agent who is patient and willing to allow you the necessary time it takes to get educated and make the best decision for yourself.

> ✔ **Local market and community knowledge.** When you're looking to buy a home in an area in which you're not currently living, an informed agent can have a big impact on your decision.

> ✔ **Financing knowledge.** As a buyer (especially a first-time buyer or someone with credit problems), you should look for an agent who knows which lenders can best handle your type of situation.

Buying real estate requires somewhat different skills than selling real estate. Few agents can do both equally well. No law or rule says that you must use the same agent when you sell a property as you do when you buy a property. Don't feel obliged to sell through the agent who worked with you as a buyer, just because he sends you holiday cards every year asking how your garden is growing. Remember, he works on commission.

Putting Your Deal Together

After you do your homework on your personal finances, discover how to choose a mortgage, and research neighbourhoods and home prices, you'll hopefully be ready to close in on your goal. Eventually you'll find a home you want to buy. Before you make that first offer, though, you need to understand the importance of negotiations, inspections, and the other elements of a real estate deal.

Negotiating 101

When you work with an agent, the agent usually handles the negotiation process. But you need to have a plan and strategy in mind — otherwise, you may end up overpaying for your home. Here are some recommendations for getting a good deal:

- **Never fall in love with a property.** If you have money to burn, and you can't imagine life without the home you just discovered, then pay what you will. Otherwise, always remind yourself that other good properties are out there. Having an actual backup property in mind never hurts.

- **Find out about the property and owner before you make your offer.** How long has the property been on the market? What are its flaws? Why is the owner selling? For example, if the seller is moving because she got a job in another town where she's about to close on a home purchase, she may be eager to get her money out of the home and may be willing to reduce the price. The more you understand about the property that you want to buy and the seller's motivations, the better able you will be to draft an offer that meets both parties' needs.

- **Get comparable sales data to support your price.** Too often, home buyers and their agents pick a number out of the air when making an offer. But if the offer has no substance behind it, the seller will hardly be persuaded to lower his asking price. Pointing to recent and comparable home sales to justify your offer price strengthens your case.

- **Remember that price is only one of several negotiable items.** Sometimes sellers get fixated on selling their homes for a certain amount. Perhaps they want to get at least what they paid for it several years ago. You may be able to get a seller to pay for certain repairs or improvements, or to offer you an attractive loan without all the extra loan fees that a bank would charge. Likewise, the real estate agent's commission is negotiable, too.

Inspecting before you buy

When you buy a home, you may be making one of the biggest (if not *the* biggest) purchases of your life. Unless you build homes and do contracting work, you probably have no idea what you're getting yourself into when it comes to furnaces and termites.

Games real estate agents play to get a deal done

The thirst for commission brings out the worst in some agents. They tell you fibs to motivate you to buy on the seller's terms. Saying that other offers are coming in on the property you're interested in is one common fib. Or they say that the seller already turned down an offer for X dollars because he is holding out for a higher offer.

The car dealer trick — blaming the office manager for not allowing them to reduce their commission — is another tactic. Be sure to spend the time needed to find a good agent and to understand an agent's potential conflicts of interest (see the section on agents in this chapter).

Spend the time and money to locate and hire good inspectors and other experts to evaluate the major systems and potential problem areas of the home. Areas that you want to check include:

- ✔ Overall condition of the property
- ✔ Electrical, heating, and plumbing systems
- ✔ Foundation
- ✔ Roof
- ✔ Pest control and dry rot
- ✔ Seismic/slide/flood risk

Inspection fees often pay for themselves. When problems that you weren't aware of are uncovered, the inspection reports give you the information you need to go back and ask the property seller to fix the problems or reduce the purchase price of the property to compensate you for correcting the deficiencies yourself.

As with other professionals whose services you retain, you need to make sure that you interview at least a few inspection companies. Ask which systems they inspect and how detailed a report they are going to prepare for you (ask for a sample copy). Ask them for names and phone numbers of three people who used their service within the past six months.

Never accept a seller's inspection report as your only source of information. When a seller hires an inspector, he may hire someone who won't be as diligent and critical of the property. What if the inspector is buddies with the seller or the agent selling the property? By all means, review the seller's inspection reports if available, but get your own, as well.

And here's one more inspection for you to do: The day before you close on the purchase of your home, do a brief walk-through of the property to make sure that everything is still in good order and that all the fixtures, appliances, curtains, and other items that were to be left per the contract are still there. Sometimes sellers (and their movers) "forget" what they are supposed to leave, or try to test your powers of observation.

After You Buy

After you buy a home, you'll make a number of important decisions regarding your castle (or shoe box) over the months and years ahead. This section discusses the key issues you need to deal with as a homeowner and tells what you need to know to make the best decision for each of them.

Refinancing your mortgage

Three reasons motivate people to *refinance* — obtaining a new mortgage to replace your old one. One is obvious — to save money because interest rates have dropped. Refinancing also can be a way to raise capital for some other purpose. Or, you can use refinancing to get out of one type of loan and into another. The following sections can help you to decide on the best option in each case.

Refinancing options

Lower rates look very appealing when you look at how much more money would stay in your bank account every month by cutting your mortgage payments. That's hard cash you could put toward other purposes or use to pay down your principal.

If you have an open mortgage, of course, you can renew whenever current rates are more attractive. Find a new term you're comfortable with and sit back and count your savings. Better yet, keep your payments at the previous level and use the drop in rates to take years off your mortgage. And remember: When you refinance, you terminate your deal with your current lender. You're free to shop around your mortgage to other lenders. Or you could get a few offers to use as leverage to get your current lender to chop a quarter or even half a percent off its published rates.

Most mortgages, however, are closed. And although your lender may be willing to allow you to refinance early, it will want to be compensated for some — or all — of its losses. After all, if you want to refinance to reduce your rate from 11 percent to 8 percent, the banks aren't exactly going to leap at the chance to make 3 percent less on your loan, now are they?

The first step is to get your mortgage agreement out and read the fine print. Growing competition means that some lenders have made it easier for you to get out of your current loan. But this is a marketing edge they don't particularly want to tout unless they have to. After all, if you don't read your agreement and simply assume that you're stuck paying higher rates than you may need to, you don't really expect banks and trust companies to bring that to your attention — do you?

The three months' interest penalty

Your mortgage agreement may allow you to refinance your loan by paying the equivalent of three months' interest on your outstanding balance. By law, any mortgage with a term longer than five years also becomes open on the fifth anniversary, with the same three-month penalty applying.

Although they don't widely promote the fact, several of the big banks now also allow you to refinance under the same terms at any point after the third anniversary of your present agreement. But remember, it's unlikely that your lenders will alert you to the money you could be saving.

Whether the three-month penalty is worth paying is different in every case. It depends on the difference between your existing rate and what current rates are as well as on how much remains in your principal. Your best bet is to ask your lender to work the numbers out for you. The lender may not be that happy about doing so, but you should get the answers you need.

The interest-rate differential (IRD) penalty

The most common penalty is something called the *interest-rate differential* (IRD). The IRD is the value today of the income the lender gives up by allowing you to refinance.

Say you're paying 10 percent and have two years left in your term. Your lender calculates how much it can make by taking the balance of your loan and lending it out elsewhere. Then it will ask you to make up the difference so that it can break even on the deal. The problem is that paying the IRD leaves you breaking even as well. The money you save with lower rates will be wiped out by the compensation you'll have to pay.

Another potential problem is that nobody can say with certainty where interest rates are headed. You lose out if rates fall and are lower at the end of your present term. If that happens, you've gone through an awful lot of tedious paperwork only to be locked in at a higher term than you would be paying if you had simply sat tight.

Mortgage life insurance

Shortly after you buy a home or close on a mortgage, you start getting mail from all kinds of organizations that keep track of publicly available information about mortgages. Most of these organizations want to sell you something, and they don't tend to beat around the bush.

"What will your dependants do if you meet with an untimely demise and they are left with a gargantuan mortgage?" they ask. In fact, this is a good financial-planning question. If your family is dependent on your income, can they survive financially if you and your income disappear from life as we know it?

Don't waste your money on mortgage life insurance. You may need life insurance to provide for your family and help meet large obligations such as mortgage payments or educational expenses for your children. But mortgage life insurance is typically grossly overpriced. (Check out Chapter 16 for advice about term life insurance.) You should consider mortgage life insurance only if you have a health problem and the mortgage life insurer does not require a physical examination. Be sure to compare it with term life options.

Is getting a reverse mortgage a good idea?

An increasing number of homeowners are finding, particularly in their later years of retirement, that they lack cash. The home in which they live is usually their largest asset. Unlike other investments, such as bank accounts, bonds, or stocks, a home does not provide any income to the owner unless he or she decides to rent out a room or two.

A *reverse mortgage* allows a homeowner who's low on cash to tap into home equity. For an elderly homeowner, tapping into home equity can be a difficult thing to do psychologically. Most people work hard to feed a mortgage month after month, year after year, until it is finally all paid off. What a feat and what a relief after all those years!

Taking out a reverse mortgage, well, *reverses* this process. Each month, the reverse mortgage lender sends you a cheque that you can spend on food, clothing, travel, or whatever suits your fancy. The money you receive each month is really a loan from the bank against the value of your home, which makes the monthly cheque free from taxation. A reverse mortgage also allows you to stay in your home and use its equity to supplement your monthly income.

The main drawback of a reverse mortgage is that it can diminish the estate that you may want to pass on to your heirs or use for some other purpose. Also, some loans require repayment within a certain number of years. The fees and the effective interest rate you're charged to borrow the money can be quite high.

Because some loans require the lender to make monthly payments to you as long as you live in the home, lenders assume that you will live many years in your home so they won't lose money when making these loans. If you end up keeping the loan for only a few years because you move, for example, the cost of the loan is extremely high.

 You may be able to create a reverse mortgage within your own family network. This technique can work if you have family members who are financially able to provide you with monthly income in exchange for ownership of the home when you pass away.

You also have some other alternatives to tapping the equity in your home. Simply selling your home and buying a less expensive property (or renting) is one alternative. Generally, any profit you make on the sale of the home you live in is not taxable.

Selling your house

The day will someday come when you want to sell your house. If you're going to sell, make sure that you can afford to buy the next home you desire. Be especially careful if you're a trade-up buyer — that is, if you're going to buy an even more expensive home. All of the affordability issues discussed at the beginning of this chapter apply. You need to also consider the following issues.

Selling through an agent

When you're selling a property, you want an agent who can get the job done efficiently and for as high a price as possible. As a seller, you need to seek agents who have marketing and sales expertise, and are willing to put in the time and money necessary to sell your house. Don't necessarily be impressed by an agent who works for a large company. What matters more is what the agent is going to do to market your property.

When you list your house for sale, the contract you sign with the listing agent includes specification of the commission to be paid if the agent is successful in selling your house. In most areas of the country, agents usually ask for a 6-percent commission. In an area that has lower-cost housing, they may ask for 7 percent.

Regardless of what an agent says is "typical," "standard," or "what my manager requires," *always* remember that commissions are negotiable. Because the commission is a percentage, you have a much greater possibility of getting a lower commission on a higher-priced house. If an agent makes 6 percent selling both a $200,000 house and a $100,000 house, the agent makes twice as much on the $200,000 house. Yet selling the higher-priced house does not take twice as much work. (Selling a $400,000 house certainly doesn't take four times the effort of selling a $100,000 house.)

If you live in an area with higher-priced homes (above $250,000), you have no reason to pay more than a 5-percent commission. For expensive properties ($500,000 and up), a 4-percent commission may be reasonable. You may find, however, that your ability to negotiate a lower commission is greatest when an offer is on the table. Because you don't want to give other agents (working with buyers) a reason not to sell your house, have your listing agent cut his take rather than reduce the commission that you advertise you're willing to pay to an agent who brings you a buyer.

In terms of the length of the listing sales agreement you make with an agent, three months is reasonable. When you give an agent a listing that is too long (6 to 12 months), the agent may simply toss your listing on the the multiple listing website and expend little effort to sell your property. Practically speaking, you can fire your agent whenever you want, regardless of the length of the listing agreement. But a shorter listing may be more motivating for your agent.

Selling without a real estate agent

You may be tempted to sell without an agent so that you can save the commission that's deducted from your house's sale price. If you have the time, energy, and marketing experience, you can sell your house without an agent and possibly save some money.

The major problem with attempting to sell your house on your own is that you generally can't list it in the *multiple listing service* (MLS). While you can browse through MLS listings, both in print and on the web (www.mls.ca), only brokers can use it to advertise properties for sale. which only real estate agents can do. Some people say (and we concur) that the MLS functions as an effective near-monopoly over the selling of houses. And if you're not listed in the MLS, many potential buyers will never know that your house is for sale. Agents who are working with buyers don't generally look for or show their clients properties that are for sale by owner.

Besides saving you time, a good agent can help ensure that you're not sued for failing to disclose the known defects of your property. If you decide to sell your house on your own, make sure that you have access to a legal adviser who can review the contracts.

Should you keep your home until prices go up?

Many homeowners are tempted to hold on to their properties (when they need to move) if the property is worth less than when they bought it or if the real estate market is soft. Renting out your property is probably not worth the hassle, and holding on to it is probably not worth the financial gamble. If you need to move, you're better off, in most cases, selling your house.

You may reason that, in a few years, the real estate storm clouds will clear and you'll be able to sell your property at a much higher price. Here are three risks associated with this line of thinking:

✔ You can't know what's going to happen to property prices in the next few years. They may rebound, but they can stay the same or drop even further. A property generally needs to appreciate at least a few percent per year just to make up for all the costs of holding and maintaining it.

✔ If you've never been a landlord, don't underestimate the hassle and headaches associated with this job.

✔ If you convert your home into a rental property, and it appreciates in value, you're going to have to pay capital gains tax on your profit when you sell it. This tax wipes out much of the advantage of having held on to the property until prices recovered.

If you would realize little cash from selling, *and* you lack other money to come up with the down payment to purchase your next property, you have good reason for holding on to a home that has plunged in value.

Should you keep your home as investment property if you move?

Converting your home into rental property is worth considering if you need or want to move. Don't consider doing so unless it really is a long-term proposition (ten or more years). As discussed in the preceding section, selling rental property has tax consequences.

If you want to convert your home into an investment property, you have an advantage over someone who is looking to buy an investment property, because you already own your home. Locating and buying investment property takes time and money. You also know what you have with your current home. If you go out and purchase a property to rent, you're starting from scratch.

If your property is in good condition, consider what damage renters may do to it — few renters will take care of your home the way that you will. Also consider whether you're cut out to be a landlord. For more information, read the section on real estate as an investment in Chapter 9.

Part IV

Insurance: Protecting What You've Got

The 5th Wave — By Rich Tennant

"Frankly sir, issuing you reasonably priced auto insurance isn't going to be easy given the number of crashes you've been involved in."

In this part . . .

We show you how to obtain the right kind of insurance to shield you from the brunt of unexpected major expenses and protect your assets and future earnings. Just because insurance is boring, it doesn't mean that you can ignore it! We reveal which types of insurance you do and do not need, what to include and what not to include in your policies, and how much of which things you should insure. Plus, we help you face other creepy but important stuff such as wills, probate, and estate planning.

Chapter 15

Insurance: Getting What You Need at the Best Price

· ·

In This Chapter

▶ Understanding our three laws of buying insurance

▶ What to do if you're denied coverage

▶ Getting your claim paid

· ·

*U*nless you work in the industry (by choice), you may find insurance to be a dreadfully boring topic. Most people associate insurance with disease, death, and disaster, and would rather do just about anything other than review or spend money on insurance. But because you don't want to deal with money hassles when you're coping with catastrophes — illness, disability, death, fires, floods, earthquakes, and so on — you must take care of insurance well before you need it.

Insurance is probably the least understood and least monitored area of personal finance. Studies by the U.S. non-profit National Insurance Consumer Organization show that more than nine in ten people purchase and carry the wrong types and amounts of insurance coverage. Our own experience in speaking with people about the type of insurance they have and should have confirms this statistic. Most people are overwhelmed by all the jargon in sales and policy statements. As a result, people get insurance from the wrong companies, pay more than is necessary for their policies, or get insured through companies with poor customer service reputations.

Discovering Our Three Laws of Buying Insurance

We know your patience and interest in finding out about insurance may be limited, so we boil the subject down to three fairly simple but powerful concepts that can easily save you thousands of dollars over the rest of your insurance-buying years. And while you're saving money, you can still get the coverage you need in order to avoid a financial catastrophe.

Law 1: Insure for the big stuff, not the small stuff

Imagine, for a moment, that you're offered a chance to buy insurance that reimburses you for the cost of a magazine subscription in the event that the magazine folds and you don't get all the issues you paid for. Because a magazine subscription doesn't cost much, we don't think you'd buy that insurance.

What if you could buy insurance that pays for the cost of a restaurant meal if you get food poisoning? Even if you're splurging at a fancy restaurant, you don't have a lot of money at stake, so you'd probably decline that coverage, as well.

The point of insurance is to protect against losses that would be financially catastrophic to you, not to smooth out the bumps of everyday life. The previous examples are silly, but some people buy equally foolish policies without knowing it. In the following sections, we tell you how to get the most appropriate insurance coverage for your money. We start off with the "biggies" that are worth every penny you pay in premiums, and then we work down to some insurance options that are less worthy of your dollars.

Buy insurance to cover financial catastrophes

You should insure against what could be a huge financial loss for you or your dependants. The price of insurance isn't cheap, but it is relatively small in comparison to the potential total loss from a financial catastrophe.

The beauty of insurance is that it spreads risks over millions of other people. Should your home burn to the ground, paying the rebuilding cost out of your own pocket probably would be a financial catastrophe. If you have insurance, the premiums paid by you and all the other homeowners collectively can easily pay the bills.

Think for a moment about what your most valuable assets are. (No, they're not your dry wit and your charming personality.) Also consider potential large expenses.

> ✔ During your working years, your most valuable asset is probably your future earnings. If you were disabled and unable to work, what would you live on? Long-term disability insurance exists to help you handle this type of situation. If you have a family that is financially dependent on your earnings, how would your family manage if you died? Life insurance can fill the monetary void left by your death.

✔ If you're a business owner, what would happen if you were sued for $1 million for negligence in some work that you messed up? Liability insurance can bail you out.

✔ In this age of soaring medical costs, you can easily rack up significant bills in short order. You may need extended medical health insurance coverage that covers you for expenses your provincial plan doesn't. (See Chapter 16 for more on health insurance.)

Psychologically, buying insurance coverage for the little things that are more likely to occur is tempting. You don't want to feel like you're wasting your insurance dollars. You want to get some of your money back, darn it! You're more likely to get into a fender bender with your car or have a package lost in the mail than you are to lose your home to fire or suffer a long-term disability. But if the fender bender costs $500 (which you end up paying out of your pocket because you took our advice to take a high deductible), it isn't going to be a financial disaster.

On the other hand, if you lose your ability to earn an income because of a disability, or if you're sued for $1 million and you're not insured against such catastrophes, you'll not only be extremely unhappy but you'll also face financial ruin. "Yes, but what are the odds," we hear people rationalize, "that I'll suffer a long-term disability or that I'll be sued for $1 million?" We agree that the odds are quite low, but the risk is there. The problem is that you just don't know what, or when, bad luck may befall you.

And don't make the mistake of thinking that you can figure the odds any better than the insurance companies can. The insurance companies predict the probability of your making a claim, large or small, with a great deal of accuracy. They employ armies of number-crunching actuaries to calculate the odds of bad things happening and the frequency of current policyholders making particular types of claims. The companies then price their policies accordingly.

So buying (or not buying) insurance based on your perception of the likelihood of needing the coverage is foolish. Insurance companies aren't stupid; in fact, they're ruthlessly smart! When insurance companies price policies, they look at a number of factors to determine the likelihood of your filing a claim. Take the example of auto insurance. Who do you think will pay more: a single male, age 20, living the fast life in a high-crime city, driving a macho, turbo sports car, and who has received two speeding tickets in the past year; or a couple in their 40s, living in a low-crime area, driving a four-door sedan, and having a clean driving record?

Take the highest deductible you can afford

Most insurance policies have _deductibles_ — the maximum amount you must pay, in the event of a loss, before your insurance coverage kicks in. On many policies, such as auto and homeowner's/renter's coverage, most folks opt for a $100 to $250 deductible.

Here are two benefits to taking a higher deductible:

- ✔ **You save premium dollars.** Year in and year out, you can enjoy the lower cost of an insurance policy with a high deductible. You may be able to shave 15 to 20 percent off the cost of your policy. Suppose, for example, that you can reduce the cost of your policy by $150 per year by raising your deductible from $250 to $1,000. That $750 worth of coverage is costing you $150 per year. Thus, you'd need to have a claim of $1,000 or more every five years — highly unlikely — to come out ahead. If you are that accident-prone — guess what — the insurance company will crank up your premiums.

- ✔ **You don't have the hassles of filing small claims.** If you have a $300 loss on a policy with a $100 deductible, you need to file a claim to get your $200 (the amount you're covered for after your deductible). Filing an insurance claim can be an aggravating experience that takes hours. In some cases, your claim may be denied even after you've jumped through all the necessary hoops.

When you have low deductibles, you may file more claims (although this doesn't necessarily mean that you'll get more money). After filing more claims, you may be rewarded with higher premiums — in addition to the headache you get from preparing all those blasted forms! Filing too many claims may even cause cancellation of your coverage!

Avoid small-potatoes policies

A good insurance policy can seem expensive. A policy that doesn't cost much, on the other hand, can fool you into thinking that you're getting something for next to nothing. Policies that cost little also cover little — they're priced low because they aren't covering large potential losses.

The following are examples of common, "small-potatoes" insurance policies that are generally a waste of your hard-earned dollars. As you read through this list, you may find examples of policies that you bought and that you feel paid for themselves. We can hear you saying, "But I collected on that policy you're telling me not to buy!" Sure, getting "reimbursed" for the hassle of something being lost or going wrong is comforting. But consider all such policies that you bought or may buy over the course of your life. You're not going to come out ahead in the aggregate — if you did, insurance companies would lose money! These policies aren't worth the cost relative to the small potential benefit. On average, insurance companies pay out just 60¢ in benefits on every dollar collected. Many of the following policies pay you back even less — around 20¢ in benefits (claims) for every insurance premium dollar spent:

- ✔ **Extended warranty and repair plans.** Isn't it ironic that right after the salesperson persuades you to buy a television, computer, or car — in part by saying how reliable the goods are — he tries to convince you to spend more money to insure against the failure of the item? If the product is so good, why do you need such insurance?

Extended warranty and repair plans are expensive and unnecessary insurance policies. Product manufacturers' warranties typically cover any problems that occur in the first three months to a year. After that, paying for a repair out of your own pocket won't be a financial catastrophe. Reputable manufacturers often fix problems or replace the product without charge after a warranty has expired (within a reasonable time period).

✔ **Home warranty plans.** A third-party new-home warranty is for most buyers mandatory in Ontario, Quebec, and British Columbia. In other provinces, it was still optional in 2005. If your real estate agent or the seller of a home wants to pay the cost of a home warranty plan for you, turning down the offer would be ungracious. (As grandma would say, you shouldn't look a gift horse in the mouth.) But don't buy this type of plan for yourself, unless you're required to by provincial regulations. In addition to requiring some sort of fee (around $50) if you need a contractor to come out and look at a problem, home warranty plans limit how much they'll pay for problems.

Your money is much better spent on hiring a competent inspector to uncover problems and fix them *before* you buy the home. If you're buying a house, you should expect to spend money on repairs and maintenance. Buying insurance for the smaller repairs and maintenance is a waste of money.

✔ **Dental insurance.** If your employer pays for dental insurance, take advantage of it. But you generally shouldn't pay for this coverage on your own. Dental insurance generally covers a couple of teeth cleanings each year and limits payments for more expensive work.

✔ **Credit life and credit disability policies.** *Credit life policies* pay a small benefit if you die with an outstanding loan. *Credit disability policies* pay a small monthly income in the event of a disability. Banks and their credit card divisions usually sell these policies. Some companies sell insurance to pay off your credit card bill in the event of your death or disability.

The cost of such insurance seems low, but that's because the potential benefits are relatively small. In fact, given what little insurance you're buying, these policies are usually extraordinarily expensive. If you need life or disability insurance, purchase it. But get enough coverage, and buy it in a separate, cost-effective policy (see Chapter 16 for more details).

If you're in poor health, and you can buy these insurance policies without a medical evaluation, you represent an exception to the "don't buy it" rule. In this case, these policies may be the only ones to which you have access — another reason why these policies are expensive. If you're in good health, you're paying for the people with poor health who can enrol without a medical examination and who undoubtedly file more claims.

✔ **Insuring packages sent in the mail.** You buy a $40 gift for a friend, and when you go to the post office to ship it, the friendly postal clerk asks if you want to insure it. For a few bucks, you think, "Why not?" Canada Post rarely loses or damages things. Go spend your money on something else — or better yet, invest it.

✔ **Contact lens insurance.** The things that people in this country come up with to waste money on just astound us. Contact lens insurance really does exist! The money goes to replace your contacts if you lose or tear them. Lenses are cheap. Don't waste your money on this kind of insurance.

✔ **"Little stuff" riders.** Many policies that are worth buying, such as auto and disability insurance, have all sorts of riders added on. These *riders* are extra bells and whistles that insurance agents and companies like to sell because of the high profit margin they provide (for *them*). On auto insurance policies, for example, you can buy a rider for a few bucks per year that pays you $25 each time your car needs to be towed. Having your vehicle towed isn't going to bankrupt you, so it isn't worth insuring against.

Likewise, small insurance policies that are sold as add-ons to bigger insurance policies are usually unnecessary and overpriced. For example, you can buy some disability insurance policies with a small amount of life insurance added on. If you need life insurance, purchasing a sufficient amount in a separate policy is less costly.

Law 11: Buy broad coverage

Purchasing insurance coverage that is too narrow is another major mistake people make. Such policies often seem like cheap ways to put your fears to rest. For example, instead of buying life insurance, some folks buy flight insurance at an airport self-service kiosk. They seem to worry more about their mortality when getting on an airplane than they do when getting into a car. If they die on the flight, their beneficiaries collect. But should they die the next day in an auto accident or get some dreaded disease — which, statistically, is far more likely than going down in a jumbo jet — the beneficiaries don't collect anything from flight insurance. Buy life insurance (broad coverage to protect your loved ones financially in the event of your death no matter how you die), not flight insurance (narrow coverage).

The medical equivalent of flight insurance is cancer insurance. Older people, who are fearful of having their life savings depleted by a long battle with this dreaded disease, are easy prey for unscrupulous insurance salespeople pitching this narrow insurance. If you get cancer, cancer insurance pays the bills. But what if you get heart disease, diabetes, AIDS, or some other disease? Cancer insurance won't pay the costs, including any portion not covered by your province's health plan, if you are a member.

Our fears in life are natural and inescapable; they're also often arbitrary and irrational. Although we may not have control over the emotions that our fears invoke, we must often ignore those emotions in order to make rational insurance decisions. In other words, getting shaky in the knees and sweaty in the palms when boarding an airplane is okay, but letting your fear of flying cause you to make poor insurance decisions is not okay, especially when those decisions affect the lives of your loved ones.

You can't possibly predict what's going to happen to you. Buy the broadest possible coverage.

Examining our misperceptions of risks

How high do you think your risks are for expiring prematurely if you're exposed to toxic wastes or pesticides, or if you live in a dangerous area that has a high murder rate? Well, actually, these risks are quite small when compared to the risks you're subjecting yourself to when you get behind the wheel of a car or light up yet another cigarette.

ABC reporter John Stossel was kind enough to share the results of a study done for him by physicist Bernard Cohen. In the study, Cohen compared different risks. Cohen's study showed that our riskiest behaviours are smoking and driving. Smoking whacks an average of seven years off a person's life, whereas driving a car results in a bit more than half a year of life lost, on average. Toxic waste shaves an average of one week off an American's life span.

To buy the proper insurance, you need to know what's risky and what isn't. Unfortunately, you can't buy a formal insurance policy to protect yourself against all of life's great dangers and risks. But that doesn't mean that you must face these dangers as a helpless victim. Simple changes in behaviour can help you improve your security.

Personal health habits are a good example of the types of behaviour you can change. If you're overweight, and you eat fatty, high-cholesterol foods, drink excessively, and don't exercise, you're asking for trouble, especially during post–middle age. Engage in these habits, and you dramatically increase your risk of heart disease and cancer.

So does this mean that we should all eat bean sprouts, stay out of cars, and cease being concerned about toxic waste? No. But you should understand the consequences of your behaviours before you engage in them, and minimize your risks accordingly.

You can buy all the types of traditional insurance that we recommend in this book and still not be well-protected, for the simple reason that you're overlooking uninsurable risks. But just because you can't buy formal insurance to protect against some dangers, it doesn't mean that you can't drastically reduce your exposure to such risks by modifying your behaviour. For example, you can't buy an auto insurance policy that protects your personal safety against drunk drivers, who are responsible for thousands of deaths every year. In fact, in Canada there are about 1,300 deaths annually due to drunk drivers. However, you can choose to drive a safe car, practise safe driving habits, and minimize driving on the roads during the late evening hours and on major holidays when drinking is prevalent (such as New Year's Eve, July 1st, Labour Day, and so on).

Law 111: Shop around and consider buying direct

Whether you're looking at auto, home, life, disability, or other types of coverage, some companies may charge double or triple the rates that other companies charge for the same coverage. The companies that charge the higher rates may not be better about paying claims, however. You may even end up with the worst of both possible worlds — high prices *and* lousy service.

Most insurance is sold through agents and brokers who earn commissions based on what they sell. The commissions, of course, tend to bias what they recommend you buy. A study done by Cummins and Weisbart, cited in Andrew Tobias's book *Invisible Bankers,* confirms this bias: "48% of the time, an agent's decision on where to place a customer's business was based on which insurer paid the highest commission."

Not surprisingly, policies that pay agents the biggest commissions also tend to be more costly. In fact, insurance companies compete for the attention of agents by offering bigger commissions. If you browse through magazines and other publications targeted to insurance agents, you'll often see ads in which the largest text is the commission percentage offered to agents who sell the advertiser's products.

Besides the attraction of policies that pay higher commissions, agents also get hooked, financially speaking, to companies whose policies sell frequently. After an agent sells a certain amount of a company's insurance policies, he or she is rewarded with higher commission percentages on any future sales. Just as airlines bribe frequent fliers with mileage bonuses, insurers bribe agents with fatter commissions.

Shopping around is a challenge not only because most insurance is sold by agents working on commission but also because insurers set their rates in mysterious ways. Every company has a different way of analyzing how much of a risk you are; one company may offer low rates to you but not to your cousin, and vice versa.

Despite the obstacles, several strategies exist for obtaining low-cost, high-quality policies. The following tips offer smart ways to shop for insurance.

Employer and other group plans

When you buy insurance as part of a larger group, you generally get a lower price because of the purchasing power of the group. Most of the health and disability policies that you can access through your employer are less costly than equivalent policies that you can buy on your own.

Choosing your insurers carefully

In addition to the price of the policy and the insurer's reputation and track record for paying claims, an insurer's financial health is important to consider when choosing a company. If you faithfully pay your premium dollars year after year, you're going to be upset if the insurer goes bankrupt right before you have a major claim.

Insurance companies can fail just like any other company, and dozens do in a typical year. A number of organizations evaluate and rate, with some sort of letter grade, the financial viability and stability of insurance companies. The major rating agencies include A. M. Best Canada, Dominion Bond Rating Service, Moody's, and Weiss.

The rating agencies' letter-grade system works just the way it does in high school: A is better than B or C. Each company uses a different scale. Some companies have AAA as their highest rating, and then AA, A, BBB, BB, and so on. Others use A, A–, B+, B, B–, and so on. Just as some teachers grade more easily, some firms, such as A. M. Best, have a reputation for giving out a greater number of high grades. Other firms, such as Weiss, are tough graders. Unlike in school, however, you want the tough critics when researching where to put your money and future security.

Just as getting more than one medical opinion is a good idea, getting two or three financial ratings can give you a better sense of the safety of an insurance company. Stick with companies that are in the top two — or, at worst, three — levels on the different rating scales.

You can obtain current rating information about insurance companies, free of charge, by asking your agent for a listing of the current ratings. If you're interested in a policy sold without the involvement of an agent, you can request the current ratings from the insurer itself.

Although the financial health of an insurance company is important, it's not as big a deal as some insurers (usually those with the highest ratings) and agents make it out to be. Just as financially unhealthy banks are taken over and merged into viable ones, sickly insurers usually follow a similar path under the direction of insurance regulators.

With most insurance company failures, claims still get paid. The people who had money invested in life insurance or annuities with the failed insurer are the ones who usually lose out. Even then, you typically get back 80¢ to 90¢ on the dollar of your account value with the insurer, but you may have to wait years to get it.

Likewise, many occupations have professional associations through which you may be able to obtain lower-cost policies. Not all associations offer better deals on insurance — compare their policy features and costs with other options.

Life insurance is the one exception to the rule that group policies offer better value than individual policies. Group life insurance plans usually aren't cheaper than the best life insurance policies that you can buy individually. However, group policies may have the attraction of convenience (ease of enrolment and avoidance of lengthy sales pitches from life insurance salespeople). Group life insurance policies that allow you to enrol without a medical evaluation are probably going to be more expensive, because such plans attract more people with health problems who can't get coverage on their own. If you're in good health, you should definitely shop around for life insurance (see Chapter 16 to find out how).

Insurance agents who want to sell you an individual policy can come up with 101 reasons why buying from them is preferable to buying through your employer or some other group. In most cases, agents' arguments for buying an individual policy from them include a lot of self-serving marketing hype. In some cases, agents tell outright lies (which are hard to detect if you're not insurance-savvy).

One valid issue that agents will raise is that, if you leave your job, you'll lose your group coverage. Sometimes that may be true. For example, if you know that you're going to be leaving your job to become self-employed, securing an individual disability policy before you leave your job makes sense. However, the company that runs your employer's health insurance plan may allow you to buy an individual policy when you leave.In the chapters that follow, we explain what you need to find in the policies you're looking for so that you can determine whether a group plan meets your needs. In most cases, group plans, especially through an employer, offer good benefits. So as long as the group policy is cheaper than a comparable individual policy, you'll save money buying through the group plan.

The straight scoop on commissions and how insurance is sold

The commission paid to an insurance agent is never disclosed through any of the documents or materials that you receive when buying insurance. This information ought to be disclosed by insurers and agents, just as sales charges on mutual funds are disclosed through a prospectus.

The only way you can know what the commission is on a policy and how it compares with other policies is to ask the agent. Nothing is wrong or impolite about asking. After all, your money pays the commission. You need to know whether a particular policy is being pitched harder because of its higher commission.

Commissions are typically paid as a percentage of the first year's premium on the insurance policy. (Many policies pay smaller commissions on subsequent years' premiums.) With life and disability insurance policies, for example, a 50-percent commission on the first year's premium is not unusual. With life insurance policies that have a cash value, commissions of 80 to 100 percent of your first year's premium are possible. Commissions on health insurance are lower, but generally not as low as commissions on auto and homeowner's insurance.

Insurance without sales commissions

Buying policies from the increasing number of companies that are selling policies directly to the public without the insurance agent and the agent's commission is your best bet for getting a good insurance value. Just as you can purchase no-load mutual funds directly from an investment company without paying any sales commission (see Chapter 10), you also can buy no-load insurance. Be sure to read Chapter 16 for more specifics on how to buy insurance direct.

Annuities, investment/insurance products traditionally sold through insurance agents, are also now available directly to the customer, without sales commission.

Dealing with Insurance Problems

When you seek out insurance or have insurance policies, sooner or later you're bound to hit a roadblock. Although insurance problems can be among the more frustrating in life, in the following sections we explain how to successfully deal with the more common obstacles.

Knowing what to do if you're denied coverage

Just as you can be turned down when you apply for a loan, you can also be turned down when applying for insurance. With medical, life, or disability insurance, a company may reject you if you have an existing medical problem (a pre-existing condition) and are therefore more likely to file a claim. When it comes to insuring assets such as a home, you may have difficulty getting coverage if the property is deemed to be in a high-risk area.

Here are some strategies to employ if you're denied coverage:

- ✔ **Ask the insurer why you were denied.** Perhaps the company made a mistake or misinterpreted some information that you provided in your application. If you're denied coverage because of a medical condition, find out what information the company has on you and determine whether it's accurate.

- ✔ **Request a copy of your medical information file.** Many people don't know that, just as you have a credit report file that details your use (and misuse) of credit, you also have a medical information report. You can request a current copy of your medical information file (which typically highlights only the more significant problems over the past seven years, not your entire medical file or history) by writing to the Medical

Information Bureau at 330 University Avenue, Suite 501, Toronto, Ontario, M5G 1R7. You can call them at 416-597-0590. If you find a mistake on your report, you have the right to request that it be fixed. However, the burden is on you to prove that the information in your file is incorrect. Proving that your file is incorrect can be a major hassle — you may even need to contact physicians you saw in the past, because their medical records may be the source of the incorrect information.

✓ **Shop other companies.** Just because one company denies you coverage, it doesn't mean that all insurance companies will deny you coverage. Some insurers better understand certain medical conditions and are more comfortable accepting applicants with those conditions. Most insurers, however, charge higher rates to people with blemished medical histories than they do to people with perfect health records, but some companies penalize you less than others. An agent who sells policies from multiple insurers, called an *independent agent,* can be helpful, because he or she can shop among a number of different companies.

✓ **Find out about provincial high-risk pools.** If you're turned down for health or property insurance, check with your provincial department of insurance (see the "Government" section of your local phone directory). A number of provinces act as the insurer of last resort and provide insurance for those who can't get it from insurance companies. Provincial high-risk pool coverage is usually bare bones, but it beats going without any coverage.

✓ **Check for coverage availability before you buy.** If you're considering buying a home, for example, and you can't get coverage, the insurance companies are trying to tell you something. What they are effectively saying is, "We think that property is so high-risk, we're not willing to insure it even if you pay a high premium."

Getting your due on claims

In the event that you suffer a loss and file an insurance claim, you may hope that your insurance company is going to cheerfully and expeditiously pay. Given all the money that you shelled out for coverage, and all the hoops you jumped through to get approved for coverage in the first place, that's a reasonable expectation.

However, for various reasons your claim may not be covered under the terms of the policy. At a minimum, the insurer wants documentation and proof of your loss. Other people who have come before you have been known to cheat, so insurers won't simply take your word, no matter how honest and ethical you are.

In other cases, the insurance company may jerk you around. Some companies view paying claims as an adversarial situation and take a "negotiate tough" stance. Thinking that all insurance companies are going to pay you a fair and reasonable amount unless you make your voice heard is a mistake.

The tips that we discuss in the next section help you ensure that you get paid what your policy entitles you to.

Documenting your assets and case

When you're insuring assets, such as your home and its contents, having a record of what you own can be helpful if you need to file a claim. The best offence is a good defence. If you keep records of valuables and can document their cost, you should be in good shape.

A videotape is the most efficient record for documenting your assets, but a handwritten list detailing your possessions works, too. Just remember to keep this record someplace away from your home — if your home burns to the ground, you'll lose your documentation, too!

If you're robbed or are the victim of an accident, get the names, addresses, and phone numbers of witnesses. Take pictures of property damage and solicit estimates for the cost of repairing or replacing whatever has been lost or damaged. File police reports when appropriate, if for no other reason than to bolster your documentation for the insurance claim.

Preparing your case

Filing a claim should be viewed the same way as preparing for a court trial or a tax audit. Any information you provide verbally or in writing can and will be used against you to deny your claim. First, you should understand whether your policy covers your claim (this is why getting the broadest coverage possible helps). Unfortunately, the only way to find out whether the policy covers your claim is to read it. Policies are hard to read because they use legal language in non-user-friendly ways.

A possible alternative to reading your policy is to call the claims department and, *without* providing your name, ask a representative whether a particular loss (such as the one that you just suffered) is covered under its policy. You have no need to lie to the company, but you have no need to tell the representative who you are and that you're about to file a claim, either. Your call is informational so that you can understand what your policy covers. Some companies are not willing to provide detailed information, however, unless a specific case is cited.

After you initiate the claims process, keep records of all conversations and all copies of the documents you gave to the insurer's claims department. If you have problems down the road, this "evidence" may bail you out.

For property damage, you should get at least a couple of estimates from reputable contractors. Demonstrate to the insurance company that you're trying to shop for a low price, but don't agree to use a low-cost contractor without knowing that he or she can do quality work.

Approaching your claim as a negotiation

To get what you're owed on an insurance claim, you must approach the filing of most claims for what they are — a negotiation that is often not cooperative. And the bigger the claim, the more your insurer will play the part of adversary.

A number of years ago, when Eric filed a homeowner's insurance claim after a major rain and wind storm significantly damaged his backyard fence, he was greeted on a weekday by a perky, smiley adjuster. When the adjuster entered his yard and started to peruse the damage, her demeanour changed dramatically. She had a combative, hard-bargainer type attitude that he last witnessed when he worked on some labour–management negotiations during his days as a consultant.

The adjuster stood on his back porch, a good distance away from the fences that had been blown over by wind and crushed by two large trees, and said that his insurer preferred to repair damaged fences rather than replace them. "With your deductible of $1,000, I doubt this will be worth filing a claim for," she said.

The fence that had blown over, she reasoned, could have new posts set in concrete. Because he had already begun to clean up some of the damage for safety reasons, he presented to her some pictures of what the yard looked like right after the storm; she refused to take them. She took some measurements and said that she'd have a settlement cheque sent out in a couple of days. The settlement she faxed was for $1,119 — nowhere near what it would cost to fix the damage that was done.

Practising persistency

When you take an insurance company's first offer and don't fight for what you're due, you may be leaving a lot of money on the table. To make Eric's long fence-repair story somewhat shorter, after *five* rounds of haggling with the adjusters, supervisors, and finally managers, he was awarded payment to replace the fences and clean up most of the damage. Even though all the contractors he contacted recommended that the work be done this way, the insurance adjuster discredited their recommendations by saying, "Contractors try to jack up the price and recommended work once they know an insurer is involved."

His final total settlement came to $4,888, more than $3,700 higher than the insurer's first offer. Interestingly, his insurer backed off its preference for repairing the fence when the contractor's estimates for doing that work exceeded the cost of a new fence.

Eric was disappointed with the behaviour of that insurance company. But his homeowner's insurance company was not unusual in its adversarial strategy. And to think that this insurer at the time had one of the better track records for paying claims!

Enlisting support

If you're doing your homework, and you're not making progress with the insurer's adjuster, ask to speak with supervisors and managers. This is the strategy Eric had to use to get the additional $3,700 that was needed to get things back to where they were before the storm.

The agent who sold you the policy may be helpful in preparing and filing the claim. A good agent can help increase your chances of getting paid — and getting paid sooner. If you're having difficulty with a claim for a policy obtained through your employer or other group, speak with the benefits department or a person responsible for interacting with the insurer. These folks have a lot of clout, because the agent and/or insurer doesn't want to lose the entire account.

If you're having problems getting a fair settlement from the insurer of a policy you bought on your own, try contacting your provincial dispute resolution group. You can find the phone number under "Insurance" in the blue pages of your phone book or possibly in your insurance policy.

Hiring a public adjuster who, for a percentage of the payment (typically 5 to 10 percent) can negotiate with insurers on your behalf is another option.

When all else fails, and you have a major claim at stake, try contacting a lawyer who specializes in insurance matters. You can find these specialists in the yellow pages of your phone directory under "Lawyers." Expect to pay around $150 or more per hour. Look for a lawyer who is willing to negotiate on your behalf, help draft letters, and perform other necessary tasks on an hourly basis without filing a lawsuit. Your provincial insurance departments, the local bar association, or other legal, accounting, or financial practitioners also may be able to refer you to someone.

The possible headache of filing a claim is another reason to take the highest insurance deductibles you're comfortable with. Remember that you buy insurance to protect against large losses, not small ones. With a high deductible and a small loss, you'll save yourself some haggling.

Chapter 16

Insurance on You: Life, Disability, and Health

· ·

In This Chapter

▶ Checking out life insurance

▶ Looking into disability insurance

▶ Considering an overlooked form of personal insurance

· ·

Multiply your typical annual income by the number of years you plan to continue working — you come up with a pretty big number, don't you (unless you're in or near retirement)? That dollar amount equals what is probably your most valuable asset — your ability to earn an income. You need to protect this asset by purchasing some insurance on you.

This chapter explains the ins and outs of buying insurance to protect your income: life insurance in case of death, and disability insurance in case of an accident or severe medical condition that prevents you from working. We tell you what coverage you should have, where to look for it, and what to avoid.

In addition to protecting your income, you also need to insure against financially catastrophic expenses. We're not talking about December's credit card bill; you're on your own with that one. We're talking about the type of bills that are racked up from a major surgery and a multi-week stay in the hospital. Medical expenses today can make even the most indulgent shopping sprees look dirt-cheap. To protect yourself from potentially astronomical medical bills, you also need to assess whether you need to buy health insurance beyond what you may receive through a provincial health insurance plan.

Providing for Your Loved Ones: Life Insurance

You generally need life insurance only when other people depend on your income. The following types of people typically don't need life insurance to protect their incomes:

- Single people
- Working couples who could maintain an acceptable lifestyle if one of the incomes disappeared
- Independently wealthy people who don't need to work
- Retired people who are living off their retirement nest egg
- Minor children (are you financially dependent upon your children?)

If others are either fully or partly dependent on your paycheque (usually a spouse and/or children) you should buy life insurance, especially if you have major financial commitments such as a mortgage or years of child-rearing ahead. You may also want to consider life insurance if an extended family member is currently or likely to be dependent on your future income.

Determining how much life insurance to buy

Determining how much life insurance to buy is as much a subjective decision as it is a quantitative decision. We've seen some worksheets that are incredibly long and tedious (some are worse than your tax returns). There's no need to get fancy. If you're like us, your eyes start to glaze over if you have to complete 20-plus lines of calculations. Figuring out how much life insurance you need doesn't have to be that complicated.

The main purpose of life insurance is to provide a lump-sum payment to replace the deceased person's income. You need to ask yourself how many years of income you want to replace. Table 16-1 provides a simple way to figure how much life insurance you need to consider purchasing. To replace a certain number of years of income, simply multiply the appropriate number in the table by your annual after-tax income.

Table 16-1	Life Insurance Calculation
Years of Income to Replace	*Multiply Annual After-Tax Income* By*
5	4.5
10	8.5
20	15
30	20

*You can roughly determine your annual after-tax income by getting out last year's tax return and subtracting the federal, provincial, and other payroll deductions you paid from your gross employment income.

Another way to determine the amount of life insurance to buy is to think about how much you will need to pay for major debts or expenditures, such as your mortgage, other loans, and university for your children. For example, suppose that you want your spouse to have enough of a life insurance death benefit to be able to pay off your mortgage and half of your children's university education. Simply add your mortgage amount to half of your children's university or college costs (refer to Chapter 13 for approximate numbers) and then buy that amount of life insurance.

Looking at the Canada Pension Plan's survivor benefits

If you're covered, the Canada Pension Plan (or Quebec Pension Plan) can provide *survivor benefits* to your spouse and children. However, if your surviving spouse is working and earning even a modest amount of money, he or she is going to get little if any survivor benefits.

If you're already receiving your own CPP retirement pension or disability benefits, your survivor benefits will be combined with what you are already receiving into one monthly payment. This new combined total amount can't exceed the maximum retirement pension. If you are receiving a disability benefit, the total, once your survivor benefits are added in, can't exceed the maximum disability benefit.

The Guaranteed Income Supplement (GIS) and Allowance benefits are calculated using a couple's combined income. If you are receiving these benefits and your spouse or common-law partner dies, the monthly payments will be recalculated using your own income. If you start receiving a CPP survivor benefit, that is included in your income for the purposes of calculating your eligibility for GIS or Allowance benefits in the following year.

What you will get as a survivor benefit depends on many factors, including whether your spouse was receiving a CPP retirement or disability pension, how long and how much they had paid into the plan, and your spouse's age when they died.

Children of a contributor to the CPP may also be eligible for payments called the CPP Children's Benefit. If a child is under the age of 18, the benefit is normally paid to the parent. The monthly benefit is a flat amount, which in 2004 was around $192 a month. Children between the ages of 18 and 25 who are attending school full-time are also eligible, as are part-time students in certain cases.

TIP

Some couples choose to split one of their CPP payments as a way to balance out their income and thus reduce their household's overall tax bill. This has no impact on the surviving spouse's benefits. If one spouse dies, the survivor benefits are calculated as if the splitting (officially called *assigning*) of benefits never took place.

INVESTIGATE

Human Resources and Skills Development Canada (HRSDC) can tell you how much your survivors will receive per month in the event of your death. You can find this information online at www.hrsdc.gc.ca/en/isp/cpp/survivor.shtml, or you can request what you need by mail, by visiting a local HRSDC office, or by calling 1-800-277-9914.

You should factor this benefit into the amount of life insurance that you calculate in Table 16-1. For example, suppose that your annual after-tax income is $15,000, and HRSDC provides a survivor benefit of $8,000 annually. Therefore, for the purposes of Table 16-1, you should determine the amount of life insurance needed to replace $7,000 annually ($15,000 – $8,000), not $15,000.

Comparing term life insurance to cash value life insurance

We're going to tell you how you can save hours of time and thousands of dollars. Ready? *Buy term life insurance.* (The only exception is if you have a high net worth — several million bucks or more — in which case you may want to consider other options. See the estate-planning section in Chapter 17.) If you've already figured out how much life insurance to purchase, and this is all the advice you need to go ahead, you can skip the rest of this section and jump to the "Buying term insurance" section that follows.

If you want the details behind our recommendation for term insurance, the following information is for you. Or maybe you heard (and have already fallen prey to) the sales pitches from life insurance agents, most of whom love selling cash value life insurance because of its huge commissions.

"Other" life insurance

Contemplating the possibility of your untimely demise is surely depressing. You'll likely feel some peace of mind when purchasing a life insurance policy to provide for your dependants.

However, let's take things a step further. Suppose that you (or your spouse) pass away. Do you think that simply buying a life insurance policy will be sufficient "help" for the loved ones you leave behind? Probably not. Surely your contribution to your household involves far more than being a breadwinner.

For starters, you should make sure that all of your important financial documents — investment account and RRSP/RRIF statements, insurance policies, employee benefits materials, small-business accounting records, and so on — are kept in one place (such as a file drawer) that your loved ones know about.

Do you have a will? See Chapter 17 for more details on wills and other estate-planning documents.

You may also want to consider providing a list of key contacts — such as whom you recommend calling (or what you recommend reading) in the event of legal, financial, or tax quandaries.

So, in addition to trying to provide financially for your dependants, you also need to take some time to reflect on what else you can do to help point them in the right direction on matters you normally handle. With most couples, it's natural for one spouse to take more responsibility, say, for money management. That's fine; just make sure to talk about what's being done so that in the event that the responsible spouse dies, the surviving person knows how to jump into the driver's seat.

If you have kids (and even if you don't), you may want to give some thought to philosophical leave-behinds for your loved ones. These leave-behinds can be something like a short note telling them how much they meant to you and what you'd like them to remember about you.

We're going to start with some background. Despite the variety of names that marketing departments have cooked up for policies, life insurance comes in two basic flavours:

- ✔ **Term insurance.** This insurance is pure life insurance. You pay an annual premium for which you receive a predetermined amount of life insurance protection. If the insured person passes away, the beneficiaries collect; otherwise, the premium is gone.

- ✔ **Cash value insurance.** All other life insurance policies (whole, universal, variable, and so on) combine life insurance with a supposed savings feature. Your premiums do not pay only for life insurance; some of your dollars are also credited to an account that grows in value over time, assuming you keep paying your premiums. On the surface, this sounds potentially attractive. People don't like to believe that all their premium dollars are being tossed away.

  But cash value insurance has a big catch. For the same amount of coverage (for example, for $100,000 of life insurance benefits), cash value policies cost you anywhere from four to ten times (yes, 1,000 percent) more than comparable term policies.

Insurance salespeople know the buttons to push to get you interested in buying the wrong kind of life insurance. In the following sections we give you some of the typical arguments they make for purchasing cash value polices, followed by our perspective on each one.

"Cash value policies are all paid up after x years. You don't want to be paying life insurance premiums for the rest of your life, do you?"

Agents who pitch cash value life insurance present projections that imply that after the first ten or so years of paying your premiums, you don't need to pay more premiums to keep the life insurance in force. The only reason you may be able to stop paying premiums is if you pour so much extra money into the policy in the early years of payment. Remember that cash value life insurance costs four to ten times as much as term insurance.

Imagine that you're currently paying $500 a year for auto insurance, and an insurance company comes along and offers you a policy for $4,000 per year. The representative tells you that after 10 years, you can stop paying and still keep your same coverage. We're sure that you wouldn't fall for this sales tactic, but many people do when they buy cash value life insurance.

You also need to be wary of the projections, because they often include unrealistic and lofty assumptions about the investment return that your cash balance can earn. When you stop paying into a cash value policy, the cost of each year's life insurance is deducted from the remaining cash value. If the rate of return on the cash balance is not sufficient to pay the insurance cost, the cash balance declines, and eventually you receive notices saying that your policy needs more funding to keep the life insurance in force.

"You won't be able to afford term insurance when you're older."

As you get older, the cost of term insurance increases because the risk of dying rises. But life insurance is not something you need all your life! It's typically bought in a person's younger years when financial commitments and obligations outweigh financial assets. Twenty or thirty years later, the reverse should be true.

When you retire years from now, you won't need life insurance to protect your employment income, because there won't be any to protect! You may need life insurance when you're raising a family and/or you have a substantial mortgage to pay off, but by the time you retire, the kids should be out on their own (you hope!), and the mortgage should be paid down.

In the meantime, term insurance saves you a tremendous amount of money. For most people, it takes 20 to 30 years for the premium they're paying on a term insurance policy to finally catch up to (equal) the premium they've been paying all along on a comparable amount of cash value life insurance.

"You can borrow against the cash value at a low rate of interest."

Such a deal! It's your money in the policy, remember? If you deposited money in a savings or money market account, how would you like to pay for the privilege of borrowing your own money back? Borrowing on your cash value policy is potentially dangerous: You increase the chances of the policy exploding on you — leaving you with nothing to show for your premiums.

"Your cash value grows tax-deferred."

Ah, a glimmer of truth at last. The cash value portion of your policy grows without taxation until you withdraw it, but if you want tax deferral of your investment balances, you should first take advantage of your RRSP. An RRSP gives you an immediate tax deduction for your current contributions in addition to growth without taxation until withdrawal. The money you pay into a cash value life policy gives you no upfront tax deductions. (See Chapter 7 for details on retirement plans.)

Life insurance tends to be a mediocre investment. The insurance company quotes you an interest rate for the first year only; after that, most companies pay you what they want. If you don't like the future interest rates, you can be penalized for quitting the policy. Would you ever invest your money in a bank account that quoted an interest rate for the first year only and then penalized you for moving your money within the next seven to ten years?

"Cash value policies are forced savings."

Many agents argue that a cash value plan is better than nothing — at least it's forcing you to save. This line of thinking is silly, because so many people drop cash value life insurance policies after just a few years of paying into them because of their high cost.

You can accomplish "forced savings" without using life insurance. You can arrange to have money automatically transferred from your chequing account into your RRSP, for example. Your employer may also offer the option of having contributions to an RRSP or company pension plan come from your paycheque — and it doesn't take a commission! You can also set up monthly electronic transfers from your bank chequing account to automatically invest in mutual funds (see Chapters 7 and 9).

Making your decision

Insurance salespeople aggressively push cash value policies because of the high commissions that insurance companies pay them. Commissions on cash value life insurance range from 50 to 100 percent of your first year's premium. An insurance salesperson, therefore, can make *four to ten times more money* (yes, you read that right) selling you a cash value policy than he can selling you term insurance.

Ultimately, when you purchase cash value life insurance, you pay the high commissions that are built into these policies. As you can see in the policy's cash value table, you don't get back any of the money that you dump into the policy if you quit the policy in the first two to three years. The insurance company can't afford to give you any of your money back in those first few years because so much of it has been paid to the selling agent as commission. That's why these policies explicitly penalize you for withdrawing your cash balance within the first seven to ten years.

Because of the high cost of cash value policies relative to the cost of term, you're more likely to buy less life insurance coverage than you need — that's the sad part of the insurance industry's pushing of this stuff. *The vast majority of life insurance buyers need more protection than they can afford to buy with cash value coverage.*

Cash value life insurance is the most oversold insurance and financial product in the history of the financial services industry. Cash value life insurance makes sense for a small percentage of people, such as small-business owners who own a business worth more than several million dollars and don't want their heirs to be forced to sell their business to pay estate taxes in the event of their death. (See "Considering the purchase of cash value life insurance," later in this chapter.)

Purchase low-cost term insurance and do your investing separately. Life insurance is rarely a permanent need; over time, you can reduce the amount of term insurance you carry as your financial obligations lessen and you accumulate more assets.

Buying term insurance

Term insurance policies have several features to choose from. We cover the important elements of term insurance in this section so that you can make an informed decision about purchasing it.

Choosing how often your premium adjusts

As you get older, the risk of dying increases, so the cost of your insurance goes up. Term insurance can be purchased so that your premium adjusts (increases) annually or every 5, 10, 15, or 20 years. The less frequently your premium adjusts, the higher the initial premium and its incremental increases will be.

The advantage of a premium that locks in for, say, 15 years is that you have the security of knowing how much you'll be paying each year for the next 15 years. You also don't need to go through medical evaluations as frequently to qualify for the lowest rate possible.

The disadvantage of a policy with a long-term rate lock is that you pay more in the early years than you do on a policy that adjusts more frequently. In addition, you may want to change the amount of insurance you carry as your circumstances change. You throw money away when you dump a policy with a long-term premium guarantee before its rate is set to change.

Policies that adjust the premium every five to ten years offer a happy medium between price and predictability.

Ensuring guaranteed renewability

Guaranteed renewability, which is standard practice on the better policies, guarantees that the policy can't be cancelled because of poor health. Don't buy a life insurance policy without this feature unless you expect that your life insurance needs will disappear when the policy is up for renewal.

Investigating guaranteed renewal rates

When assessing the costs of different policies, what really matters is the overall amount you'll pay for your coverage for all the years that you'll require life insurance. Be sure that the premiums you'll pay each time you renew are guaranteed and laid out term by term in your policy. To evaluate different policies, have the agent do a present-value comparison of the total amount you'll pay in premiums over the period you estimate you'll require life insurance. This figure represents what a policy would cost if you had to pay for all your years of coverage in a single payment today.

Deciding where to buy term insurance

There are a number of sound ways to obtain high-quality, low-cost term insurance. You may choose to buy through a local agent — because you know her, or because you prefer to buy from someone close to home. However, you should invest a few minutes of your time getting quotes from one or two of the following sources to get a sense of what's available in the insurance market. Gaining familiarity with the market can prevent an agent from selling you an overpriced, high-commission policy.

Here are some sources for high-quality, low-cost term insurance (be sure to also ask any groups, professional associations, or business organizations you belong to about low-cost term insurance offerings):

- **Blue Cross** (You can find a phone number for Blue Cross in your province on the Web site, www.bluecross.ca)
- **Canadian Automobile Association** (877-942-4222; www.caa.ca)
- **RBC Insurance** (866-223-7113; www.rbcinsurance.ca)
- **TD Insurance** (877-397-4187; www.tdcanadatrust.com/tdinsurance/)

Insurance agency quotation services provide proposals from the highest-rated, lowest-cost companies available. Like other agencies, the services receive a commission if you buy a policy from them, which you're under no obligation to do. They ask your date of birth, whether you smoke, and how much coverage you want. (See Chapter 19 for information on how to use your computer when making life insurance decisions.)

Here are some sources for obtaining quotes from a variety of insurance providers:

- ✔ www.insurancehotline.com
- ✔ www.kanetix.ca
- ✔ www.lifeinsurancequote.com
- ✔ www.term10quotes.com
- ✔ www.termcanada.ca

Getting rid of cash value life insurance

If you were snookered into buying a cash value life insurance policy, and you want to part ways with it, go ahead and do so. *But don't cancel the coverage until you first secure new term coverage.* When you need life insurance, you don't want to leave open a period when you're not covered (Murphy's Law says *that's* when disaster will strike).

Ending a cash value life insurance policy has tax consequences. For most of these policies, you must pay tax on the amount you receive in excess of the premiums you paid over the life of the policy. If you want to withdraw the cash balance in your life insurance policy, consider checking with the insurer or a tax adviser to clarify what the tax consequences may be.

Considering the purchase of cash value life insurance

Don't expect to get objective information from anyone who sells cash value life insurance. Beware of insurance salespeople masquerading under the guise of self-anointed titles, such as estate-planning specialists or financial planners.

As we discuss earlier in the chapter, purchasing cash value life insurance may make sense if you expect your death to leave your estate and heirs with a big tax bill. However, cash value life insurance is just one of numerous ways to reduce taxes that will come due when you die. (See the section on estate planning in Chapter 17.)

If you want to obtain some cash value life insurance, make sure that you avoid local insurance agents, especially while you're in the learning stage. Agents aren't as interested in educating as they are in selling (big surprise). Besides, the best cash value policies can be obtained free of most (or all) sales commissions when you buy them direct from the provider. The money saved on commissions is reflected in a much higher cash value for you — up to several thousand dollars' worth.

Preparing for the Unpredictable: Disability Insurance

As with life insurance, the purpose of disability insurance is to protect your income. The only difference is that, with disability insurance, you're protecting the income for yourself (and perhaps also your dependants). If you're completely disabled, you still have living expenses but you probably can't earn employment income.

We're referring to long-term disabilities. If you throw out your back while reliving your athletic glory days, and you wind up in bed for a couple of weeks, it won't be as much of a disaster to your finances as it is to your ego! What would be a financial disaster, however, is if you were disabled in such a way that you couldn't work for several years.

Most large employers offer disability insurance to their employees. Many small-company employees and all self-employed people are left to fend for themselves without disability coverage. Being without disability insurance is a risky proposition, especially if, like most working people, you need your employment income to live on.

If you're married, and your spouse earns a large enough income that you can make do without yours, you may want to consider skipping disability coverage. The same is true if you've already accumulated enough money for your future years (in other words, you're financially independent). Keep in mind, though, that your expenses may go up if you become disabled and require specialized care.

For most people, dismissing the need for disability coverage is easy. The odds of suffering a long-term disability seem so remote — and they are. But if you meet up with bad luck, disability coverage can relieve you (and possibly your family) of a major financial burden.

Most disabilities are caused by medical problems, such as arthritis, heart conditions, hypertension, and back/spine or hip/leg impairments. Some of these ailments occur with advancing age, but more than one-third of all disabilities are suffered by people under the age of 45. The vast majority of these medical problems cannot be predicted in advance, particularly those caused by random accidents.

If you think that you have good disability coverage through government programs, you'd better think again:

- ✔ **Government benefits.** In general, you must have paid into the Canada Pension Plan or Quebec Pension Plan in order to receive CPP/QPP disability benefits for at least four of the six years leading up to the point at which you became disabled. To qualify, your disability must be severe, which means it prevents you from doing not only your former job but also any job on a regular basis. The disability must also be prolonged, meaning it is expected to last at least a year or be likely to result in death. CPP/QPP disability payments are quite low because they are intended to provide only for basic, subsistence-level living expenses. In 2005, for example, the maximum CPP disability payment was $1,010.23 a month. The average (in the fall of 2004) was $749.

- ✔ **Workers' compensation.** Worker's compensation (if you have such coverage through your employer) pays you benefits if you're injured on the job, but it doesn't pay any benefits if you become disabled away from your job. You need coverage that pays regardless of where and how you are disabled.

Determining how much disability insurance you need

You need enough disability coverage to provide you with sufficient income to live on until other financial resources become available. If you don't have much saved in the way of financial assets, and you want to continue with the lifestyle supported by your current income if you suffer a disability, get enough disability coverage to replace your entire monthly take-home (after-tax) pay.

The benefits you purchase on a disability policy are quoted as the dollars per month you receive if disabled. So if your job provides you with a $2,000-per-month income after payment of taxes, seek a policy that provides a $2,000-per-month benefit.

If you pay for your disability insurance, the benefits are tax-free (but hopefully you won't ever have to collect them). If your employer picks up the tab your benefits are taxable, so you need a higher amount of benefits.

In addition to the monthly coverage amount, you also need to select the duration of time you want a policy to pay you benefits. You need a policy that pays benefits until you reach an age where you become financially self-sufficient.

For most people, that's around age 65. If you anticipate needing your employment income past your mid-60s, you may want to obtain disability coverage that pays you until a later age.

On the other hand, if you crunched some numbers (see Chapter 3), and you expect to be financially independent by age 55, you can get a policy that pays benefits up to that age — it'll cost you less than one that pays benefits until age 65. If you're within five years of being financially independent or able to retire, five-year disability policies are available, too. You may also consider such short-term policies when you're sure that someone (for example, a family member) can support you financially over the long term.

Identifying other features you need in disability insurance

Disability insurance policies have many confusing features. Here's what to look for — and look *out* for — when purchasing disability insurance:

- **Definition of disability.** An *own-occupation* disability policy provides benefit payments if you can't perform the work you normally do. Some policies pay you only if you're unable to perform a job for which you are *reasonably trained*. Other policies revert to this definition after a few years of being own-occupation.

  Own-occupation policies are the most expensive, because there's a greater chance that the insurer will have to pay you. The extra cost may not be worth it unless you're in a high-income or specialized occupation, and you'd have to take a significant pay cut to do something else (and you wouldn't be happy about a reduced income and the required lifestyle changes).

- **Non-cancellable and guaranteed renewable.** These features guarantee that your policy can't be cancelled because of poor health conditions, and that you have the right to renew it. With policies that require periodic physical exams, you can lose your coverage just when you're most likely to need it.

- **Waiting period.** This is the "deductible" on disability insurance — the lag time between the onset of your disability and the time you begin collecting benefits. As with other types of insurance, you should take the highest deductible (longest waiting period) that your financial circumstances allow. The waiting period significantly reduces the cost of the insurance and eliminates the hassle of filing a claim for a short-term disability. The minimum waiting period on most policies is 30 days. The maximum waiting period can be up to one to two years. Try a waiting period of three to six months if you have sufficient emergency reserves.

- **Residual benefits.** This option pays you a partial benefit if you have a disability that prevents you from working full time.

✔ **Cost-of-living adjustments (COLAs).** This feature automatically increases your benefit payment by a set percentage or in accordance with changes in inflation. The advantage of a COLA is that it retains the purchasing power of your benefits. A modest COLA, such as 4 percent, is worth having.

✔ **Future insurability.** A clause that many agents encourage you to buy, future insurability allows you to buy additional coverage, regardless of health. For most people, paying for the privilege of buying more coverage later is not worth it if the income you earn today fairly reflects your likely long-term earnings (except for cost-of-living increases). Disability insurance is sold only as a proportion of your income. You may benefit from the future insurability option if your income is artificially low now and you're confident that it will rise significantly in the future. (For example, you just got out of medical school and you're earning a low salary while being enslaved as a resident.)

✔ **Insurer's financial stability.** As we discuss in Chapter 15, you should choose insurers that will be here tomorrow to pay your claim. But don't get too hung up on the stability of the company; benefits are paid even if the insurer fails, because the province or another insurer will almost always bail the unstable insurer out.

Deciding where to buy disability insurance

The best place to buy disability insurance is through your employer or professional association. Unless these groups have done a lousy job shopping for coverage, group plans offer a better value than disability insurance you can purchase on your own. Just make sure that the group plan meets the specifications discussed in the preceding section.

Don't trust an insurance agent to be enthusiastic (or even honest) about the quality of a disability policy your employer or other group is offering. Agents have a huge conflict of interest when they criticize these options, because your group insurance cuts them out of the picture.

Tread carefully when purchasing disability insurance through an agent. Some agents try to load down your policy with all sorts of extra bells and whistles to pump up the premium along with their commission.

If you buy disability insurance through an agent, try to use a process called *list billing*. With list billing, you sign up with several other people for coverage at the same time and are invoiced together for your coverage. It can knock up to 15 percent off an insurer's standard prices. Ask your insurance agent how list billing works.

Other types of "insurance" for protecting your income

Life insurance and disability insurance replace your income if you die or suffer a disability. But you may also see your income reduced or completely eliminated if you lose your job. Although no formal insurance exists to protect you against the forces that can cause you to lose your job, you can do some things to reduce your exposure to such risk:

✔ Make sure that you have an emergency reserve of money that you can tap into if you lose your job. (Chapter 2 offers specific guidelines for deciding how much money is right for you.)

✔ Attend to your skills and professional development on a continual basis. Not only does upgrading your education and skills ensure that you'll be employable if you have to look for a new job, but it may also help you keep your old job and earn a higher income.

Getting Care for the Road: Travel Medical Insurance

An emergency ward or doctor's waiting room likely isn't on your list of must-sees when you head out of the country. But you simply can't predict whether a visit to a medical facility will end up being part of your itinerary when you leave our home and native land.

If you head out of Canada on vacation, for business, or even just for a day-shopping trip across the border, you need to ensure you are properly insured against unexpected medical expenses. Without sufficient *travel medical coverage,* an accident or illness that strikes while you are out of Canada could severely damage your financial health.

As long as you belong to your province's health care plan, you already have some coverage outside of Canada. However, each provincial plan covers you only up to certain levels, with maximums established for various procedures and other medical costs. The amounts that provincial plans will pay have been shrinking, though, and what your provincial health plan pays might be only a fraction of the final bill.

Don't blindly assume that you're adequately covered if you have a premium credit card that trumpets medical coverage. The eligibility requirements can be highly confusing, and the rules are regularly changed. With some premium cards, for instance, you're covered for only a certain number of days for each trip you make. You may be covered for trips up to 21 days in length, for instance, so if you're injured on the 22nd day, your card company won't pay any of the medical expenses.

If you're travelling on company business, it's wise to check with your benefits department before you leave. While most corporations provide medical insurance for employees who are travelling on business, the policies can be complicated and can leave you exposed. For instance, you may be covered during the week while you're on company business, but not if you choose to stay over for the weekend to enjoy a little skiing at a nearby resort. Should you break your leg on the slopes, you may find you're responsible for any bills because company policy doesn't cover injuries sustained on personal time.

Buying travel medical insurance

Be sure to take a look at your family's overall need. Many providers now offer plans that will cover your family. If you travel a lot, check into annual plans, which cover you up to a maximum number of days outside the country over 12 months.

Here are some sources for low-cost travel medical insurance:

- **Belair Direct** (888-280-9111; www.belairdirect.com)
- **Canadian Automobile Association** (Call toll-free directory assistance at 1-800-555-1212 for the toll-free number for your province, or visit www.caa.ca)
- **Ingle Health** (800-360-3234; www.ingle-health.com)
- **TD Insurance** (800-293-4941; www.tdcanadatrust.com/tdinsurance)
- **T.I.C. Trent Health** (800-379-9628; www.trenthealth.com)

Looking at Long-Term Care Insurance

Insurance agents who are eager to earn a hefty commission will often tell you that *long-term care insurance* (LTC) is the solution to your concerns about an extended stay in a nursing home. Don't get your hopes up. Policies are complicated and filled with all sorts of exclusions and limitations. On top of all that, they're expensive, too.

The decision to purchase LTC insurance is a trade-off. Do you want to pay several thousand dollars annually to guard against the possibility of a long-term stay in a nursing home? If you live into or past your mid-80s, you can end up paying more than $50,000 to $100,000 or more on an LTC policy (not to mention the lost investment earnings on these insurance premiums).

People who end up in a nursing home for years on end may come out ahead financially when buying LTC insurance. Many people who stay in a nursing home are there for less than a year, though, because they either pass away or move out. One study puts the average length of stay in a long-term care facility at under three years.

Provincial health plans will cover only a portion of long-term care costs, generally requiring you to pay a fixed amount that can range from around $12,000 to $25,000 or more a year.

If you have relatives or a spouse who will likely care for you in the event of a major illness, you should generally *not* waste your money on nursing-home insurance. You can also bypass this coverage if you have and don't mind using retirement assets to help pay nursing-home costs. Even if you do deplete your assets, there may be government assistance available, However, this will usually cover only basic accommodation. To find out what assistance may be available to you, contact your province's ministry of health.

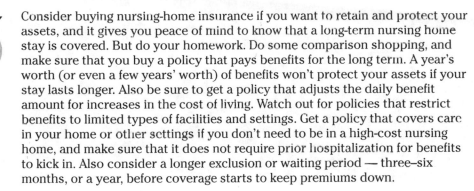

Consider buying nursing-home insurance if you want to retain and protect your assets, and it gives you peace of mind to know that a long-term nursing home stay is covered. But do your homework. Do some comparison shopping, and make sure that you buy a policy that pays benefits for the long term. A year's worth (or even a few years' worth) of benefits won't protect your assets if your stay lasts longer. Also be sure to get a policy that adjusts the daily benefit amount for increases in the cost of living. Watch out for policies that restrict benefits to limited types of facilities and settings. Get a policy that covers care in your home or other settings if you don't need to be in a high-cost nursing home, and make sure that it does not require prior hospitalization for benefits to kick in. Also consider a longer exclusion or waiting period — three–six months, or a year, before coverage starts to keep premiums down.

Discovering the Most Overlooked Form of Insurance

You buy health insurance to cover large medical expenses, disability insurance to replace your income in the event of a long-term disability, and perhaps life insurance to provide money to those dependent on your income in the event of your death. Many people buy all the right kinds of personal insurance, spending a small fortune over the course of their lives. Yet they overlook the obvious, virtually free protection: taking care of themselves.

If you work at a desk all day and use many of life's modern conveniences, you may end up being a contender for Canadian Idle. Odds are that you've heard of most of these methods of enhancing longevity and quality of life, but if you're still on the couch, the advice apparently didn't sink in.

So, for you sofa spuds, here are seven healthful tips:

- ✔ Don't smoke.
- ✔ Drink alcohol in moderation, if you drink at all.
- ✔ Get plenty of rest.
- ✔ Exercise regularly.
- ✔ Eat a healthy diet (see Chapter 5 for diet tips that can save you money and improve your health).
- ✔ Get regular checkups to detect medical, dental, and vision problems.
- ✔ Take time to smell the roses.

Chapter 17

Covering Your Assets

· ·

In This Chapter

▶ Checking out homeowner's/renter's insurance

▶ Considering automobile insurance

▶ Looking at umbrella insurance

▶ Planning your estate

· ·

*I*n Chapter 16, we discuss the importance of protecting your future income from the possibilities of disability, death, or large, unexpected medical expenses. But you also need to insure major assets that you acquired in the past: your home, your car, and your personal property.

You need to protect these assets for two reasons:

▶ **Your assets are valuable.** If you were to suffer a loss, replacing the assets with money out of your own pocket could be a financial catastrophe.

▶ **A lawsuit could drain your finances.** This reason is less well-known. If someone were injured or killed in your home or because of your car, a lawsuit could be even more financially devastating than an outright loss of the asset.

Protecting Where You Live

When you buy a home, most lenders require you to purchase homeowner's insurance. But even if they don't you're wise to do so, because your home and the personal property within it are worth a great deal and would cost a bundle to replace.

As a renter, damage to the building in which you live is not your immediate financial concern (assuming, of course, you haven't purposely caused the damage yourself), but you still have personal property you may want to insure. You also have the possibility (albeit remote) that you can be sued by someone who is injured in your rental.

When shopping for a homeowner's or renter's policy, you need to consider the important features that we cover in the following sections.

Dwelling coverage: The cost to rebuild

How much would you have to spend to *rebuild* your home if it were completely destroyed in a fire, an attack of locusts, or whatever? The cost to rebuild should be based on the size (square footage) of your home. Neither the purchase price nor the size of your mortgage should determine how much *dwelling coverage* you need.

If you're a renter, you don't need dwelling coverage. If you're a condominium owner, find out whether the coverage the condo association bought for the entire building is sufficient.

Be sure that your homeowner's policy includes a *guaranteed replacement cost* provision. This useful feature ensures that the insurance company will rebuild the home even if the cost of construction is more than the policy coverage. If the insurance company underestimates your dwelling coverage, it has to make up the difference.

Unfortunately, insurers define guaranteed replacement cost differently. Some companies pay for the full replacement cost of the home, no matter how much it ends up costing. Other insurers set limits. For example, some insurers may only pay up to 25 percent more than the dwelling coverage on your policy. Ask your insurer how it defines guaranteed replacement cost.

If you have an older property that doesn't meet current building standards, consider buying a *rider* (supplemental coverage to your main insurance policy that costs extra money) that pays for code upgrades. This rider covers the cost of rebuilding your home to comply with current building codes that may be more stringent than when your home was built. Ask your insurance company what your basic policy does and does not cover. Some companies include a certain amount (for example, 10 percent of your dwelling coverage) for code upgrades in the base policy.

Personal property coverage: For your things

On your homeowner's policy, the amount of personal property coverage is typically derived from the amount of dwelling coverage you carry. Generally, you get personal property coverage that is equal to 50 to 75 percent of the dwelling coverage. This amount is usually more than enough.

We're not fans of buying riders to cover jewellery, computers, furs, and other somewhat costly items that may not be fully covered by typical homeowner's policies. Ask yourself if the out-of-pocket expense from the loss of such items would constitute a financial catastrophe. Unless you have tens of thousands of dollars worth of jewellery or computer equipment, skip such riders.

Some policies come with *replacement cost guarantees* that pay you the cost to replace an item. This payment can be considerably more than what the used item was worth before it was damaged or stolen. When this feature is not part of the standard policy sold by your insurer, you may want to purchase it as a rider, if available.

As a renter or condominium owner, you need to choose a dollar amount for the personal property you want covered. Tally it up instead of guessing — the total cost of replacing all your personal property may surprise you.

Make a list of your belongings — or even better, take pictures or make a video — with an estimate of what they're worth. Keep this list updated; you'll need it if you have to file a claim. Keeping receipts for major purchases may also help your case. No matter how you document your belongings, don't forget to keep the documentation somewhere besides your home — otherwise, it could be destroyed along with the rest of your house in a fire or other disaster.

Liability insurance: Coverage for hurting others

Liability insurance protects you financially against lawsuits that may arise if someone gets injured on your property, including wounds inflicted by the family pit bull or terrible tabby. (Of course, you should keep Bruno restrained when guests visit — yes, even your in-laws.) At a minimum, get enough liability insurance to cover your financial assets — covering two times your assets is better. Buying extra coverage is inexpensive and well worth the cost.

The probability of being sued is low, but if you *are* sued, and you lose, you could end up owing big bucks. If you have substantial assets to protect, you may want to consider an umbrella, or excess liability, policy. (See "Protecting Against Mega-Liability: Umbrella Insurance," later in this chapter.)

Liability protection is one of the side benefits of purchasing a renter's policy — you protect your personal property as well as insure against lawsuits. (But don't get careless with your banana peels just because you have liability insurance!)

Flood and earthquake insurance: Protection from Mother Nature

You want to purchase the broadest possible coverage when buying any type of insurance (see Chapter 15). The problem with homeowner's insurance is that it's not comprehensive enough — it doesn't typically cover losses due to earthquakes and floods. You must buy such disaster coverage piecemeal.

If an earthquake or flood struck your area and destroyed your home, you'd be out tens (if not hundreds) of thousands of dollars without proper coverage. Yet many people don't carry these important coverages, often as a result of some common misconceptions:

- ✓ **"Not in my neighbourhood."** Many people mistakenly believe that earthquakes occur only in California and Japan. We wish this were true for those of you who live in the True North, but it's not. Vancouver is built on a major fault line, and known (though not very active) fault lines lie in eastern Canada, including the Ottawa—Hull region. The cost of earthquake coverage is based on insurance companies' assessment of the risk of your area and property type, so you shouldn't decide whether to buy insurance based on how small you think the risk is. The risk is already built into the price.

  Floods can also be a very real and potentially financially devastating hazard, as those who lived in southern Alberta when the Red Deer River overflowed its banks in 2005 found out. Floods have also caused extensive and costly damage in many other parts of the country, including Quebec, Ontario, and Manitoba. Like earthquakes, floods are not a covered risk in standard homeowner's policies, so you need to purchase a flood insurance rider. Check with your current insurer or with the insurers recommended in this chapter.

- ✓ **"The government will bail me out."** The vast majority of government financial assistance is obtained through low-interest loans. Loans, unfortunately, need to be repaid, and the money comes out of your pocket. Even if you do receive government money with no strings attached, it may be a long time in coming and likely won't come anywhere near to covering all of your losses.

- ✓ **"In a major disaster, insurers would go bankrupt anyway."** This is highly unlikely given the reserves insurers are required to keep and the fact that the insurance companies reinsure — that is, they buy insurance to back up the policies they write.

People who have little equity in their property and are willing to walk away from the property and the mortgage in the event of a major quake or flood may consider not buying earthquake or flood coverage. Keep in mind that doing so damages your credit report, because you're essentially defaulting on your loan.

You may be able to pay for much of the cost of earthquake or flood insurance simply with the money you'll save on premiums by raising the deductibles (discussed in the next section) on the main part of your homeowner's/renter's insurance and other insurance policies (such as auto insurance). You can more easily afford the smaller claims, not the big ones. If you think flood or earthquake insurance is too costly, compare those costs with the costs you may have to incur to completely replace your home and personal property. Buy this insurance if you live in an area that has a chance of being affected by these catastrophes. To help keep the cost of earthquake insurance down, consider taking a 10-percent deductible. Most insurers offer deductibles of 5 or 10 percent of the cost to rebuild your home. Ten percent of the rebuilding cost is a good chunk of money. But losing the other 90 percent is what you want to insure against.

Deductibles: Your cost with a claim

As we discuss in Chapter 15, the point of insurance is to protect against catastrophic losses, not the little losses. By taking the highest deductibles you're comfortable with, you save on insurance premiums year after year, and you don't have to go through the hassle of filing small claims.

Special discounts

You may qualify for special discounts. Companies and agents that sell homeowner's and renter's insurance don't always check to see if you're eligible for discounts. After all, the more you spend on policy premiums, the more money they make! If your property has a security system, you're older, or you have other policies with the same insurer, you may qualify for a lower rate. Don't forget to ask.

Buying homeowner's or renter's insurance

Each insurance company prices its homeowner's and renter's policies based on its own criteria. So the lowest-cost company for your friend's property may not be the lowest-cost company for you. You have to shop around at several companies to find the best rates. The following list features companies that historically offer lower-cost policies for most people and have decent track records regarding customer satisfaction and the payment of claims:

- ✔ BelairDirect (800-268-8551 or www.belairdirect.com). Belair is a division of ING Direct.

- ✔ Certas Direct Insurance (formerly CIBC Insurance) (888-275-2422 or www.certasinsurance.com)

✔ DirectProtect (800-810-4990 or www.directprotect.com)

✔ e-Insurers (800-565-5386 or www.e-insurers.com)

✔ President's Choice Financial (888-633-2303 or www.pcinsurance.ca)

✔ RBC Insurance (800-769-2526 or www.rbcinsurance.ca)

✔ TD Insurance (800-338-0218 or www.tdbank.ca/tdinsurance)

Don't worry that some of these companies require you to call a toll-free number for a price quote. This process saves you money, because these insurers don't have to pay commissions to local agents hawking their policies. These companies usually have local claims representatives to help you if and when you have a claim.

A number of the previously named companies sell other types of insurance (for example, life insurance). But don't assume that if they offer the best value in home (or auto) insurance, their other offerings are as competitively priced.

Some provincial insurance departments conduct surveys to determine the insurers' prices and tabulate complaints received. Look under "Insurance" in the blue pages (the government section) of your local phone directory, or visit the Canadian Council of Insurance Regulators Web site at www.ccir-ccrra.org to find links to the regulators that oversee each province's insurance companies.

Auto Insurance 101

Over the course of your life, you'll probably spend tens of thousands of dollars on auto insurance. Much of the money people spend on auto insurance is not spent where it's needed most. In other cases, the money is simply wasted. Look for the following important features when searching for an auto insurance policy.

Bodily injury/property damage liability

As with homeowner's liability insurance, auto liability insurance provides insurance against lawsuits. Accidents happen, especially with a car. Third-party liability coverage has two components. The bodily injury liability part covers you if your vehicle injures someone else. Property damage liability insurance covers you against damage caused by your vehicle to someone else's property.

Coping with teen drivers

If you have a teenage driver in your household, you're going to be spending a lot more on auto insurance (in addition to worrying a lot more). Try to keep your teenager out of your car as long as possible — this is the best advice we can offer.

If you allow your teenager to drive, you can take a number of steps to avoid spending all of your take-home pay on auto insurance bills:

✔ Make sure that your teen does well in school. Some insurers offer discounts if your child is a strong academic achiever and has successfully completed a driver's education class.

✔ Get price quotes from several insurers to see how adding your teen driver to your policy affects the cost.

✔ Have your teenager share in the costs of using the car. If you pay all the insurance, gas, and maintenance bills, your teenager won't value the privilege of using your "free" car.

Of course, letting your teen drive shouldn't just be about keeping your insurance bills to a minimum. Auto accidents are the number-one cause of death for teens. So, before you let your teen drive, be sure to educate him or her about the big risks of driving and the importance of not riding in a car driven by someone who's intoxicated or sleep deprived. Also be sure that your teen drives in safe cars.

This coverage is a provincial requirement, but the amounts are quite low — $50,000 to $200,000, depending on your province. (Typically your premiums for the two coverage components are broken out, but there is one single combined figure for your total liability coverage.)

Make sure that you have at least enough to cover your assets. Preferably, your coverage should be two to five times your assets. Also, don't forget that your future earnings, which are an asset, can be garnished in a lawsuit.

Uninsured or underinsured motorist liability

When you're in an accident with another motorist, and he doesn't carry his own liability protection (or doesn't carry enough), *uninsured or underinsured motorist coverage* allows you to collect for lost wages, medical expenses, and pain and suffering incurred in the accident.

If you already have comprehensive health and long-term disability insurance, uninsured or underinsured motorist liability coverage is largely redundant, but it is generally still required.

To provide a death benefit to those financially dependent on you in the event of a fatal auto accident, buy term life insurance (see Chapter 16).

Deductibles

To keep your auto insurance premiums down and eliminate the need to file small claims, take the highest deductibles you're comfortable with. (Most people should consider a $500 to $1,000 deductible.) On an auto policy, two deductibles exist: *collision* and *comprehensive*. Collision applies to claims arising from — you guessed it — collisions. (Note that if you have collision coverage on your own policy, some policies allow you to bypass collision coverage when you rent a car. However, read through your policy or ask the person who sold the policy to you to find out for sure.) Comprehensive applies to other claims for damages not caused by collision (for example, a window broken by vandals).

As your car ages and loses its value, you can eventually eliminate your comprehensive and collision coverages altogether. The point at which you do this is up to you. Insurers won't pay more than the book value of your car, regardless of what it costs to repair or replace it. Remember that the purpose of insurance is to compensate you for losses that are financially catastrophic to you. For some people, this amount may be as high as $5,000 or more — others may choose $1,000 as their threshold point.

Special discounts

You may be eligible for special discounts on auto insurance. Don't forget to tell your agent or insurer if your car has a security alarm, air bags, or anti-lock brakes. If you're older, or you have other policies or cars insured with the same insurer, you may also qualify for discounts. And make sure that you're given appropriate "good driver" discounts if you've been accident- and ticket-free in recent years.

And here's another idea: *Before* you buy your next car, call insurers and ask for insurance quotes for the different models you're considering. The cost of insuring a car should factor into your decision of which car you buy, because the insurance costs represent a major portion of your car's ongoing operating expenses.

Driving safely: Overlooked auto insurance

A pipe bomb explodes in a crowded park and kills a person. An airplane crashes and several dozen people die.

Such tragic events are well-covered by our media, but the number of deaths that make the front pages of our newspapers pales in comparison to the approximately 3,500 people who die on Canada's roads every year.

We're not suggesting that our national media should start reporting every automobile fatality. Even 24 hours of daily CNN coverage probably couldn't keep up with all the accidents on our roads. But the real story with auto fatalities lies not in the who, what, and where of specific accidents but in the why. When we ask the why question, we see how many of them are preventable.

No matter what kind of car you drive, you can and should drive safely. Stay within the speed limits and don't drive while intoxicated or tired, or in adverse weather conditions. Wear your seat belt — a U.S. Department of Transportation study found that 60 percent of auto passengers killed were not wearing their seat belts. And don't try to talk on your cell phone and write notes on a pad of paper attached to your dashboard while balancing your coffee cup between your legs!

You can also greatly reduce your risk of dying in an accident by driving a safe car. You don't need to spend buckets of money to get a car with desirable safety features. The *Consumer Reports* annual auto-buying guide and Phil Edmonston's annual *Lemon-Aid* car guides contain lots of good information on individual car model safety.

Little-stuff coverage to skip

Auto insurers have dreamed up all sorts of riders, such as towing and rental car reimbursement. On the surface, these riders appear to be inexpensive. But they're expensive given the little amount you'd collect from a claim and the hassle of filing.

Riders that waive the deductible under certain circumstances make no sense, either. The point of the deductible is to reduce your policy cost and eliminate the hassle of filing small claims.

Accident benefits coverage replaces some of your income that is lost due to an accident, and pays for some other medical expenses. If you and your passengers are covered by a provincial health plan and you have disability insurance, this rider coverage isn't usually necessary, especially if you are also covered by an extended health benefit plan. However, almost all provinces require you to carry a minimum level of this type of coverage.

Roadside assistance, towing, and rental car reimbursement coverage pay only small dollar amounts, and they aren't worth buying. In fact, if you belong to an automobile club, you may already have some of these coverages.

Buying auto insurance

You can use the homeowner's insurers list we present earlier in this chapter to obtain quotes for auto insurance. You may get a small discount if you buy both your automobile and home insurance from the same company. Also, university alumni associations, as well as organizations such as the Canadian Automobile Association, often offer competitive rates for both automobile and property insurance.

Protecting Against Mega-Liability: Umbrella Insurance

Umbrella insurance (which is also referred to as *excess liability insurance*) is additional liability insurance that is added on top of the liability protection on your home and car(s). If, for example, you have $1 million in liability insurance on both your property and auto insurance, you could buy a $2-million umbrella liability policy for around $200 per year to add to the existing liability insurance that you have on your home and car. This is a small cost for big protection. Each year, thousands of people suffer lawsuits of more than one million dollars related to their cars and homes.

Insuring your assets: Investment insurance

Insurance companies don't sell policies that protect the value of your investments, but you can shield your portfolio from many of the dangers of a fickle market through diversification.

If all of your money is invested in bank accounts or bonds, you're exposed to the risks of inflation, which can erode your money's purchasing power. Conversely, if the bulk of your money is invested in one high-risk stock, your financial future could go up in smoke if that stock explodes.

Chapter 9 discusses the benefits of diversification and tells you how to choose investments that do well under different conditions. Chapter 10 discusses why mutual funds are powerful investment vehicles that make diversification easy and cost-effective.

Umbrella insurance is generally sold in increments of one million dollars. So how do you decide how much you need if you have a lot of assets? As with other insurance coverages, you should have at least enough liability insurance to protect your assets, and preferably enough to cover twice the value of those assets.

Purchasing umbrella insurance through your existing homeowner's or auto insurance company is usually necessary.

You Can't Take It with You: Planning Your Estate

Estate planning is the process of determining what will happen to your assets after you die. Thinking about your mortality in the context of insurance may seem a bit odd. But the time and cost of various estate-planning manoeuvres is really nothing more than buying insurance: You're ensuring that, after you die, everything will be taken care of as you wish and taxes will be minimized. Thinking about estate planning in this way can help you better evaluate whether certain options make sense at particular points in your life.

Depending upon your circumstances, you may eventually want to contact a lawyer who specializes in estate-planning matters. However, educating yourself first about the different options is worth your time. More than a few lawyers have their own agendas (increased fees) about what you should do, so be careful. And most of the estate-planning strategies that you're likely to benefit from don't require hiring a lawyer.

Wills, living wills, and medical powers of attorney

When you have children who are minors (dependants), a *will* is a necessity. The will names the guardian to whom you entrust your children if both you and your spouse die. Should you and your spouse both die without a will (called *intestate*), your province (the courts and social-service agencies) decides who will raise your children. Therefore, even if you can't decide at this time who you want to raise your children, you should *at least* appoint a trusted guardian who can decide for you.

Having a will makes good sense even if you don't have kids, because it gives instructions on how to handle and distribute all your worldly possessions. When you die without a will, your province decides how to distribute your money and other property, according to provincial law. Therefore, your friends, distant relatives, and favourite charities will probably receive nothing.

Without a will, your heirs are legally powerless, and the province may appoint a public executor to supervise the distribution of your assets at a fee of around 5 percent of your estate. A bond typically must also be posted at a cost of several hundred dollars.

A living will and a medical power of attorney are useful additions to a standard will. A *living will* tells your doctor what, if any, life-support measures you prefer. A *medical (or health care) power of attorney* grants authority to someone you trust to make decisions regarding your medical care options.

The simplest and least costly way to prepare a will, a living will, and a medical power of attorney is to use a high-quality, user-friendly software program (see Chapter 19). You may then want to have a lawyer go over them for you to ensure you've covered all the bases and the documents are legally sound. Be sure to give copies of these documents to the guardians and executors named in the documents.

You don't need a lawyer to make a legal will. Most lawyers, in fact, prepare wills and living trusts using software packages! What makes a will valid is that two people witness your signing it.

If preparing the will yourself seems overwhelming, you can (besides hiring a lawyer) use a paralegal typing service to help you prepare the documents. These services generally charge 50 percent or less than what a lawyer charges.

Avoiding probate through living trusts

Because of our quirky legal system, even if you have a will some or all of your assets must go through a court process known as *probate*. *Probate* is the legal process for administering and implementing the directions in a will.

Probate can be a lengthy, expensive hassle for your heirs — with fees ranging as high as 1.5 percent of the value of the estate, depending on your province. In addition, your assets become a matter of public record as a result of probate.

Property and assets that are owned in joint tenancy generally pass to heirs without having to go through probate. If you have designated a beneficiary, proceeds from an RRSP, RRIF, or insurance policy also do not require probate. Your family home, joint bank account, and other assets should also not be subject to probate if you register their ownership as "joint and survivor." Most other assets pass through probate.

A *living trust* effectively transfers assets into a trust. You control those assets, and you can revoke the trust whenever you desire. The advantage of a living trust is that, upon your death, assets can pass directly to your beneficiaries without going through probate.

Living trusts are likely to be of greatest value to people who meet the following criteria:

- ✔ Age 60 or older
- ✔ Single
- ✔ Assets worth more than $1 million that must pass through probate (including real estate, non-retirement plans, and small businesses)

As with a will, you do *not* need a lawyer to establish a legal and valid living trust. (See our software recommendations in Chapter 19.) Legal fees for establishing a living trust can range from $700 to $2,000 and higher. Hiring a lawyer is of greatest value to people with large estates (see the next section) who do not have the time, desire, and expertise to maximize the value derived from estate planning.

Note: Living trusts keep assets out of probate but have nothing to do with minimizing capital gains taxes triggered by your death.

Planning your estate to minimize taxes triggered by your death

While Canada doesn't have estate taxes like the U.S., your death will likely result in one final tax bill, and a potentially large one! When you die, the government taxes your assets such as stocks, real estate, and so on as if you had sold them all at their fair market value at the time of your death. If those assets are worth more than their purchase price, the result will generally be a taxable capital gain.

The key exception to this rule is if you leave your assets to your spouse, including a common-law spouse. In this case, the assets simply transfer tax-free to your spouse. When he or she in turn dies, the difference between the original purchase price and the market value at that time will be used to calculate any taxable gains. The rule also doesn't apply if you leave your assets to a spousal trust.

Assets in registered plans such as an RRSP or RRIF are treated as regular income in the year that you die. To avoid this, name your spouse as the beneficiary of any RRSPs or RRIFs. Your spouse can then transfer the assets to his or her own RRSP or RRIF.

Whether you need to do some planning to reduce the tax bill that will arise when you die depends on several issues. How much of your assets you're going to use up during your life is the first and most important issue you need to consider. This amount depends on how much your assets grow over time, as well as how rapidly you spend money. During retirement, you'll (hopefully) be utilizing at least some of your money.

We've seen too many affluent individuals worry throughout their retirement how taxes will impact their estate. If your intention is to leave your money to your children, grandchildren, or a charity, why not start giving while you're still alive so that you can enjoy the act? There are no limitations on the amount of money you can give away to adult family members other than your spouse. By giving away money, you reduce your estate and, therefore, the amount of money that may be subject to tax.

If you give assets to your spouse while you are living, you'll be subject to the attribution rules. If you give money or investments, such as stocks or bonds, the government attributes any income or loss or any capital gains (or losses) back to you. If you give your children or others assets beyond cold hard cash, there may also be a tax bill to pay. If you give away assets, Canada Revenue Agency deems that you have sold those assets at their market value. Any difference between what you paid and the value at the time you gave them away will be deemed a taxable capital gain.

In addition to gifting, establishing in your will that a trust will be set up when you die — a *testamentary trust* — can also help reduce taxes. With a testamentary trust, you can choose to have some or all of your assets transferred to the trust when you die, with your intended heirs named as the beneficiaries.

The advantage of a testamentary trust is that it's taxed as if it were a separate individual. As a result, it can take advantage of our graduated tax rates. For example, say you had assets that would earn $25,000 a year. If you left those assets directly to an heir, that income would be added to his or her existing yearly income, and might get taxed at the top marginal tax bracket of around 45 percent. On the other hand, if it belonged to a trust that same income would be taxed at the lowest tax rate of around 24 percent. In addition to set-up fees trusts have other costs, including trustee fees, along with the need to file a tax return for the trust each year.

Cash-value life insurance is another estate planning tool. Unfortunately, it's a tool that is overused. People who sell cash value insurance — that is, insurance salespeople and others masquerading as financial planners — too often advocate life insurance as the one and only way to deal with minimizing taxes due upon your death. Other methods for reducing taxes are often superior, because they don't require wasting money on life insurance.

Small-business owners whose businesses are worth $1 million or more may want to consider cash-value life insurance under specialized circumstances. If you lack the necessary additional assets to pay expected taxes and you don't want your beneficiaries to be forced to sell the business, you can buy cash-value life insurance to pay expected taxes.

Part V
Where to Go for More Help

The 5th Wave   By Rich Tennant

"It's really quite an entertaining piece of software. There's roller coaster action, suspense and drama, where skill and strategy are matched against winning and losing. And I thought managing our budget would be dull."

In this part . . .

We help you sift through the morass of financial resources competing for your attention and dollars. Many people who call themselves financial planners claim to be able to make you rich, but we show you how you may end up poorer if you don't choose an adviser wisely. We also cover software and Internet resources and name the best of the bunch. Finally, we discuss how to benefit from the financial coverage in print and on the air, as well as how to sidestep the problematic advice in these media.

Chapter 18

Working with Financial Planners

In This Chapter

▶ Taking a journey through financial planner–land

▶ Checking out your financial management options

▶ Determining whether you need help from a financial planner

▶ Understanding why it's hard to find good financial help

▶ Looking for a good financial planner

▶ Interviewing financial planners before you hire them

> The financial planning business has two problems. One is credibility, and the other is conflict of interest.
>
> — *Fortune* magazine

> Financial planners often end up being wolves in sheep's clothing with hidden agendas to sell mutual funds, for example, or life insurance.
>
> — *Consumer Reports*

*H*iring a competent, ethical, and unbiased financial planner or adviser to help you make and implement financial decisions can be money well spent. But if you pick a poor adviser or someone who really isn't a financial planner but a salesperson in disguise, your financial situation can get worse instead of better. So before we talk about the different types of help to hire, we're going to take a little journey with Alice to give you an idea of what you may find yourself up against in the land of financial planners.

Alice in Financial Planner–Land

This true story tells the sorry tale of Alice and her quest for sound financial advice. She struck out the first four times she sought financial help. Her story illustrates many of the pitfalls you may face when trying to find a good financial planner.

Alice's (mis)adventures

First, on the recommendation of her accountant, Alice called a financial consultant who was a certified financial planner (CFP) at a well-known investment (brokerage) firm. Alice explained that she wanted a conservative investment, but the broker sold her a mutual fund that, unbeknownst to Alice, primarily held *aggressive growth* (volatile) stocks.

After buying the fund and getting her first account statement a few days later, Alice noticed that the fund contained several thousand dollars less than she had invested. The broker told her that he earns a 4 percent commission and assured her that she need not concern herself with it because the fund paid him and it wouldn't affect her investment.

After a little investigation, Alice discovered that the fund had, in fact, paid the broker out of her investment — a hefty 6.5-percent commission. Thus, the broker not only lied about where the commission dollars came from (all such commissions come from the investors' money), but he also understated the size of his commission.

Alice, who was understandably steamed, called the regulatory agency; after she jumped through many hoops, the brokerage firm coughed up nearly $2,000 for the broker's fib about the commission amount.

Thinking that perhaps men and women simply don't communicate well, Alice then turned to a female financial planner on the recommendation of a friend. The planner told Alice, "Women need to stick together." Then she promptly tried to sell Alice a limited partnership that, according to the planner, was *sure* to return upward of 20 to 40 percent per year.

Alice took a gander at the *prospectus* — a delightfully long document, written by lawyers — that contains detailed information about an investment and the firm offering it. She saw in black and white on page 2 that the partnership paid the selling broker a 10-percent sales commission (which, she now knew, would be deducted from her investment).

Because Alice is a conscientious investor, she did more research in financial books and magazines and found out that limited partnerships are also handicapped by high, ongoing management fees. Alice did not return the dozen or so follow-up calls ("to see how you are doing") from her "sister" financial planner. Fortunately, she passed on the partnership.

Alice wanted to find out more about investing before her next attempt to get help, so she enrolled in an "adult education class" at a local college. Alice, a student eager to learn, attended all the classes but soon felt only more confused. Her teacher said that the world of finance and investments is *very, very complicated.* Unless, of course, you're a financial expert.

What credentials qualify a financial adviser?

It seems that everywhere you turn today, more and more people carry credentials after their names. We have certified lactation consultants, certified foot reflexologists, and registered dieticians.

Among salespeople, especially in the financial services industry, the use of dubious credentials and self-anointed and misleading titles is rampant. Stockbrokers are no longer called stockbrokers — they're "financial consultants" and "financial advisers." Some life insurance agents now call themselves "estate planning specialists." Next thing you know, when you visit an auto dealer, you'll speak with a certified transportation consultant, and when you buy your next home, it will be through a certified housing consultant rather than a real estate agent.

Speaking of certified, the last few years saw some significant changes to the meaning behind the most common financial planning designations and what they mean. In 2002, a new association called Advocis was formed by a merger of two of the main financial planning groups in Canada. One, the Canadian Association of Financial Planners, was home to many RFPs (Registered Financial Planners), the designation that we felt had the highest standards by far at the time. The other group involved in the merger was the Canadian Association of Insurance and Financial Advisors (CAIFA). The new group, Advocis, in essence became the home to those with the far more common — and far less difficult to attain — Certified Financial Planner (CFP) designation.

The CFP used to be somewhat meaningless. It was easy to attain since standards were low, eligibility requirements easy to meet, testing far from rigorous, and policing all but non-existent. However, the CFP designation, administered by the Financial Planning Standards Council, now has somewhat higher standards. The exam is more difficult to pass, and must be written in a proper, supervised setting. In order to be licensed a planner must disclose any past or pending litigation. They also must agree to abide by the FPSC code of ethics, and also grant the FPSC the right to enforce the code. Another welcome change is that the licensing body is now auditing some members every year.

However, the standards could still do with some further upgrading. Currently, would-be CFPs aren't required to prepare a financial plan and have it assessed, which would be a useful test of a planner's ability to apply their knowledge to the real world.

Unfortunately, many people with CFPs work on commission and are employed by securities and insurance brokerage firms, so in most cases they're not really financial planners so much as salespeople with a credential. Most of the rest sell ongoing money management services.

If you're interested in hiring financial help, be sure to read the "Interviewing Financial Advisers: Asking the Right Questions" section later in this chapter, where we detail questions you should ask financial advisers before hiring them and tell you how to make sense of all the credential gobbledygook.

If you enlist a CFP be sure he or she prepares a letter of engagement, which should state in clear terms how he or she is being paid, which is now part of their practise standards.

The "teacher" told the class that he was just such an expert. He offered a free, one-hour consultation to all his students at the end of his "course." During her free session, Alice was told that she should invest in an annuity. Investigation, however, revealed (you guessed it) high sales commissions and management fees.

Alice was also uncomfortable because planner number three didn't inquire about other aspects of her situation, and he seemed intent only on selling her an annuity. She later found out that an annuity didn't make sense for her because she was in a low tax bracket and nearly retired.

At this point, most people would probably buy a good financial book or put their money in a mattress or the next best place — their local bank — but Alice really wanted to talk to someone about her money issues and ideas.

After listening to a financial planner on a radio call-in program, Alice had the planner mail his background materials to her. In addition to a certified financial planning credential, *this* planner had a seemingly endless list of other, lofty-sounding credentials, such as BSCE, LLB, and MBA.

Alice, who was quite wary of sales commissions by now, also liked the sound of the planner's fee: $350 for his time to help with her investment decisions and to discuss her financial questions. Partway through their two-hour, $350 consultation, however, planner number four tried to persuade Alice to hire him as an ongoing manager of her money. For just $2,000 per year (commissions and management fees were extra), he would trade her in and out of investments based on his economic analyses and expert prognostications.

That seemed like a lot of money to Alice (who had $150,000 to invest), and she did not like the thought of turning over her money to someone who could move it around among various investments without her approval. Besides, she was interested in finding out more about finance, and this "planner" kept telling her how complicated it is to make investing and other financial decisions. Alice declined planner number four's sales pitch for managing her investments, whereupon the moody planner stormed out of her house, complaining that she had wasted his time (for which he had a $350 cheque in hand for a mere two hours!).

Learning from Alice's journey

Alice's case highlights four major problems that people often encounter when hiring financial help:

- First, you absolutely, positively *must* do your homework before hiring any financial adviser. Despite enthusiastic recommendations from her accountant and a friend, Alice ended up with bad advice from biased advisers.

✔ Second, the financial planning and brokerage fields are minefields for consumers. The fundamental problem is the enormous conflict of interest that is created when "advisers" sell products that earn them sales commissions. Selling ongoing money management services, as Alice found out from the last "adviser," creates a conflict of interest as well.

As an analogy, imagine that you have flu symptoms. Would you be comfortable seeing a physician who didn't charge for office visits but instead made money only by selling you drugs? Maybe you don't *need* the drugs — or at least not so many expensive ones. Maybe what you really need is Mom's chicken soup and ten hours of sleep.

What's truly amazing about Alice's situation is that none of the so-called financial planners ever bothered to ask about her insurance and debt situation. As it turns out, Alice not only lacked adequate homeowner's insurance but she also had some relatively high-interest consumer debt that none of the "planners" ever asked about — probably because paying off her debt would've diminished the funds that Alice would have available for investment.

✔ Third, some financial advisers like to make things far more complicated than they need to be, and they're generally not interested in educating you. As others have observed, financial planning is hardly the only occupation guilty of this. As author George Bernard Shaw put it, "All professions are conspiracies against the laity."

The more you know, and the more you understand that investing and other financial decisions needn't be complicated, the more you realize that you don't need to spend gobs of money (or any money at all) on financial planners and advisers. When you look in the mirror, you see the person who has your best interests at heart and is your best financial adviser.

✔ Fourth, don't place all your faith in credentials. Some credentials are meaningless. And while others can provide you with some degree of comfort, you still need to do your own homework, and often ask some direct questions in order to find an adviser who truly is looking after your interests, not his or her own.

Finally, in case you're wondering, Alice did happily invest her money in a nice portfolio of commission-free mutual funds (see Chapter 10), which have been performing just swimmingly for her over the years.

Surveying Your Financial-Management Options

Everyone has three basic choices when it comes to managing money: You can do nothing, you can do it yourself, or you can hire someone to help you.

Doing nothing

The *do-nothing* approach has a large following (and you thought you were the only one!). People who fall into this category may be leading terribly exciting, interesting lives, and are therefore too busy to attend to something as mundane as dealing with their personal finances. Or they may be leading terribly mundane lives but are too busy fantasizing about more-appealing ways to spend their time. For both types, everything from a major UFO sighting to taking out the garbage captures their imagination more than thinking about financial management.

But the dangers of doing nothing are many. Problem areas, when left to themselves, get worse. Putting off saving for retirement or ignoring your build-up of debt eventually comes back to haunt you. If you don't carry adequate insurance, accidents can be devastating. Fires in the west, flooding in the prairies, and even ice storms in Ontario and Quebec show how precarious living in paradise actually is.

If you've been following the do-nothing approach all your life, you're now officially promoted out of it! You bought this book to find out more about personal finance and make changes in your money matters, right? So take control and keep reading!

Doing it yourself

The do-it-yourselfers learn enough about financial topics to make informed decisions on their own. Doing anything yourself, of course, requires you to invest some time in learning the basic concepts and keeping up with changes. For some, personal financial management becomes a challenging and absorbing interest. Others focus on what they need to do to get the job done efficiently.

The idea that you're going to spend endless hours on your finances if you direct them yourself and make your own decisions is a myth. The hardest part of managing money for most people is catching up to where they should be and correcting past mistakes. After you get things in order, which you can easily do with this book as your companion, you shouldn't have to spend more than an hour or two working on your personal finances every few months (unless a major issue, like a real estate purchase, comes up).

Some people in the financial advice business like to make what they do seem so complicated, comparing it to brain surgery! Their argument goes, "You wouldn't perform brain surgery on yourself, so why would you manage your money yourself?" Well, to this we say, "Personal financial management ain't brain surgery — not even close." You can manage on your own. In fact, you can do a better job than most advisers. Why? Because you're not subject to their conflicts of interest, and you care the most about your money.

Hiring financial help

Realizing that you need to hire someone to help you make and implement financial decisions can be a valuable insight. A few hours and several hundred dollars to hire a competent professional can be time and money well spent, even if you have a modest income or assets. But you need to know what your money is buying.

Financial planners or advisers make money in one of three ways:

- ✔ They earn commissions based on the sales of financial products.
- ✔ They can charge a percentage of the assets they're investing.
- ✔ They can charge by the hour.

As you can see from Alice's journey into this area at the beginning of this chapter, hiring financial assistance can be anything but a tea party. The following sections help you differentiate among the three main types of financial planners.

Commission-based planners

Most commission-based planners don't really function as planners, advisers, or counsellors at all — they're salespeople. Many *stockbrokers* and *insurance brokers* are now called *financial consultants* or *financial service representatives* in order to glamourize the profession and obscure how they're compensated. Ditto for insurance salespeople calling themselves *estate planning specialists*.

A stockbroker referring to himself as a financial consultant is like a Honda dealer calling himself a transportation consultant. A Honda dealer is a salesperson who makes a living selling Hondas — period. He's definitely not going to tell you nice things about Ford, Chrysler, or Toyota cars — unless, of course, he happens to sell those, too. He also has no interest in educating you about money-saving public-transit possibilities!

As we discuss earlier in this chapter, salespeople and brokers can have an enormous self-interest when they push certain products, particularly those products that pay generous commissions. Getting paid on commission tends to skew their recommendations toward certain strategies (such as buying investment or life insurance products) and cause them to ignore or downplay other aspects of your finances. For example, they'll gladly sell you an investment rather than persuade you to pay off your debts that carry high interest rates.

Table 18-1 gives you an idea of the commissions that a financial planner/salesperson can earn by selling particular financial products.

Table 18-1	Financial Product Commissions
Product	*Commission*
Life Insurance ($250,000, age 45):	
Term life	$150 to $600
Universal/whole life	$1,000 to $2,500
Disability Insurance:	
$4,000/month benefit, age 35	$350 to $1,300
Investments ($20,000):	
Mutual funds	$200 to $1,200
Limited partnerships	$1,400 to $2,000
Annuities	$1,000 to $1,800

Percentage-of-assets-under-management advisers

This compensation system removes the incentive to sell you products with high commissions and initiate lots of transactions (to generate more of those commissions).

The fee-based system is often better for consumers than product-pushers working on commission, but is not a guarantee of unbiased financial planning help. First off, suppose that you're trying to decide whether to invest in stocks, bonds, or real estate. A planner who earns her living managing your money may not recommend real estate, because that will deplete your investment capital. The planner may not recommend paying down your mortgage for the same reason — she'll claim that you can earn more investing your money (with her help, of course) than it will cost you to borrow.

Fee-based planners are often generally only interested in managing the money of those who have already accumulated a fair amount of it — which rules out most people.

Hourly-based advisers

In many cases, your best bet for professional help with your personal finances is an adviser who charges for his time. Because he doesn't sell any financial products, his objectivity is maintained. He doesn't perform money management, so he can help you make comprehensive financial decisions with loans, retirement planning, and the selection of good investments, including real estate, mutual funds, and small business.

Hiring someone who is incompetent is the primary risk you face when select-ing an hourly-based planner. So be sure to check references and find out enough about finances on your own to discern between good and bad finan-cial advice. Another risk comes from not clearly defining the work to be done and the approximate total cost of the planner's service before you begin. You should also review some of the other key questions that we outline in the "Interviewing Financial Advisers: Asking the Right Questions" section later in this chapter.

A drawback of an entirely different kind occurs when you don't follow through on the recommendations of your adviser. You paid for her work, but you didn't act on it, so you didn't capture its value. If part of the reason that you hired the planner in the first place was that you're too busy or not inter-ested enough to make changes to your financial situation, then you should look for this type of support in the services you buy from the planner.

If you just need someone to act as a sounding board for ideas or to recom-mend a specific strategy or product, you can hire an hourly-based planner for one or two sessions of advice. You save money doing the legwork and imple-mentation on your own. Just make sure that the planner is willing to give you specific advice so that you can properly implement the strategy.

Private investment management

If you have a substantial amount of savings to invest — typically $250,000 or more — a sometimes-overlooked but often good choice is *private investment management* (also called *private asset management*). When you choose to have your money managed in this way, the investment company assesses your goals, and then typically allocates your money between its various in-house funds. You don't pay a separate management expense fee on each indi-vidual fund. Rather, you are charged a fixed percentage based on the total amount you invest with the firm.

Many firms provide this service. Some of them, including Phillips, Hager, & North Investment Management (www.phn.com), Mawer Investment Management (www.mawer.com), and Integra Investment Management (www.integra.com), also offer funds to regular retail investors through full-service and discount brokerages. (Retail investors who invest in any of these firm's funds in this way pay the set management fee that is associated with each fund they invest in.)

Having an initial meeting with such companies won't cost you anything, and typically they will assign an adviser to you who will discuss your goals and suggest various investment approaches. Since these companies typically don't heavily market themselves, nor are the companies trying to provide investment product for every possible customer, the number of funds they offer will typically be quite small, generally ranging anywhere from around 5 to 20 funds or so. While this number is often dwarfed by the dozens — and sometimes hundreds — of funds run by the large fund companies, you still should have access to the major sectors of the market (Canadian bonds and stocks, as well as U.S. and foreign securities).

One of the benefits of using a private money manager is individual attention. At minimum, you will be paired with an adviser who will typically have a lot more training and experience than the typical front-line helper at a regular mutual fund company. The adviser will likely meet with you on a semi-annual or annual basis, and also be available for consultation when needed. Once you agree to a plan, your money is portioned out amongst the company's individual funds according to your goals and need for income.

Beyond this personal attention, a major attraction of private money managers is their low cost, particularly when compared to regular off-the-shelf mutual funds. The fee you pay is typically a flat percentage of the money you invest with the company, regardless of how you allocate it amongst the firm's funds. Generally, fees start at around 1.5%. Most private money managers fees work on a sliding scale. The more money you give them to manage, the lower the fee.

Deciding Whether to Hire a Financial Planner

If you're like most people, you don't need to hire a financial planner, but you may benefit from hiring help.

The good reasons you have for hiring a financial planner can be similar to the reasons you have for hiring someone to clean your home or do your taxes. If you're too busy, you don't enjoy doing it, or you're terribly uncomfortable making decisions on your own, using a planner for a second opinion makes good sense. And if you shy away from numbers and bristle at the thought of long division, a good planner can help you.

How a good financial planner can help

The following list gives you a rundown of some of the important things a competent financial planner can assist you with.

- ✔ **Identifying problems and goals:** Many otherwise intelligent people have a hard time being objective about their financial problems. They may ignore their debts or have unrealistic goals and expectations given their financial situations and behaviours. And many are so busy with other aspects of their lives that they never take the time to think about what their financial goals are. A good financial planner can give you the objective perspective you need.

Surprisingly, some people are in a better financial position than they thought they were in relation to their goals. Good counsellors really enjoy this aspect of their jobs — good news is easier and much more fun to deliver.

✔ **Identifying strategies for reaching your financial goals:** Your mind may be a jumble of various plans, ideas, and concerns, along with a cobweb or two. A good counsellor can help you sort out your thoughts and propose alternative strategies for you to consider as you work to accomplish your financial goals.

✔ **Setting priorities:** You may be doing dozens of things to improve your financial situation, but making just a few key changes will likely have the greatest value. Identifying the changes that fit your overall situation and that won't keep you awake at night is equally important. Good planners help you prioritize.

✔ **Saving research time and hassle:** Even if you know what major financial decisions are most important to you, doing the research can be time-consuming and frustrating if you don't know where to turn for good information and advice. A good planner does research to match your needs to the best available strategies and products. So much lousy information on various financial topics is out there that you can easily get lost, discouraged, sidetracked, or swindled. A good adviser can prevent you from making a bad decision based on poor or insufficient information.

✔ **Purchasing commission-free financial products:** When you hire a planner who charges for her time, you can easily save hundreds or thousands of dollars by avoiding the cost of commissions in the financial products you buy. Purchasing commission-free is especially valuable when it comes to purchasing investments and insurance.

✔ **Providing an objective voice for major decisions:** When you're trying to figure out when to retire, how much to spend on a home purchase, and where to invest your money, you're faced with some big decisions. Getting swept up in the emotions of these issues can cloud your perspective and objectivity. A competent and sensitive adviser can help you cut through the cloud and provide you with sound counsel.

✔ **Helping you to just do it:** Deciding what you need to do is not enough — you have to actually do it, too. And although you can use a planner for advice and then make all the changes on your own, a good counsellor can help you follow through with your plan, as well. After all, part of the reason you hired the adviser in the first place may be that you're too busy or uninterested to manage your finances.

✔ **Mediating:** If you have a spouse or partner, financial decisions can produce real fireworks — particularly financial decisions involving the extended family. Although a counsellor can't be a therapist, a good one can be sensitive to the different needs and concerns of each party and can try to find middle ground on the financial issues you're grappling with.

✔ **Making you money and allowing you peace of mind:** The whole point of professional financial planning is to help you make the most of your money and plan for and attain your financial and personal goals. In the process, the financial planner should show you how to enhance your investment returns; reduce your spending, taxes, and insurance costs; increase your savings; improve your insurance coverage for catastrophes; and achieve your financial-independence goals. Putting your financial house in order should take some weight off your mind — like that clean, light-headed feeling you get after a haircut.

Why financial planners aren't for everyone

Finding a good financial planner isn't easy, so make sure that you *want* to hire an adviser before you venture out in search of a competent one.

You should also consider your personality type before you decide to hire help. Our experience has been that some people (believe it or not) enjoy the research and number-crunching. If this sounds like you, or if you're not really comfortable taking advice, you may be better off doing your own homework and creating your own plan.

Likewise, if you are dealing with an esoteric tax or legal matter, you may be better off hiring a good professional who specializes in that specific field rather than a financial planner.

The Frustrations of Finding Good Financial Planners

Overwhelmed consumers like Alice (see "Alice in Financial Planner–Land" earlier in this chapter for Alice's story), especially those in low- and middle-income brackets, have few attractive options when hiring financial help. The vast majority of the people who call themselves *financial planners* and *financial consultants* sell products and work on commission, which, as Alice found out, can often create enormous conflicts of interest. The conflicts of interest stem from the fact that the broker has an incentive to recommend strategies and sell products that pay generous commissions and to ignore strategies and products that pay no or low commissions.

Financial advisers who are fee-only sometimes make most of their fees from money-management services. (*Fee-only* or *fee-based* means that the advisers' fees are paid by their clients, not by companies whose products they recommend.) This can mean focusing on clients who have already accumulated significant wealth. Some fee-based advisers may also gravitate toward strategies and recommendations that involve their ongoing management of your money, and they may ignore or dismiss tactics that diminish the pool of investment money that they can manage for you for an ongoing fee.

The following sections describe some of the problems associated with finding a good planner.

Regulatory problems

The financial-planning field has a problem when it comes to oversight. Oversight is minimal *at best.* Except in Quebec, anyone can hang out a shingle and call him- or herself a financial planner. Provincial securities commissions generally police only those financial planners who provide investment advice; these advisers must register with the provincial securities regulator. These bodies provide no oversight of planners who do not provide investment advice. Similarly, those who sell mutual funds must be licensed as Mutual Fund Sales Representatives (MFSR), but there is no requirement to offer competent comprehensive financial planning advice.

Prior to working with a client, financial planners should be required to disclose, in writing, how they're compensated. This disclosure would make it easier for people to know how the planner earns a living. And it would eliminate much of the need for more formal government regulation.

Recognizing financial planners' conflicts of interest

All professions have conflicts of interest. Some fields have more than others, and the financial-planning field is one of those. Knowing where some of the land mines are located can certainly help. Here, then, are the most common reasons why planners may not have 20/20 vision when giving financial directions.

Selling and pushing products that pay commissions

If a financial planner isn't charging you a fee for his time, you can rest assured that he's earning commissions on the products he tries to sell you. In order to sell financial products, this planner must have a broker's licence. People who sell financial products and then earn commissions from those products often operate as salespeople, *not* financial planners. Financial planning involves taking an objective, holistic look at your financial puzzle to determine which pieces fit it well — something that brokers are neither trained nor financially motivated to do.

"Financial planning" in banks

Over recent decades, banks have witnessed an erosion of the money in their coffers and vaults because increasing numbers of investors realized that banks are generally lousy places to build wealth. The highest-yielding bank savings accounts and GICs barely keep an investor ahead of inflation. If you factor in both inflation and taxes, these bank "investments" provide no real growth on your investment dollars.

Increasingly, banks have "financial representatives" and "investment specialists" sitting in their branches, waiting to pounce on bank customers with big balances. In some banks, these "financial planners" are simply brokers who are out to sell investments that pay them (and the bank) hefty sales commissions.

Although you may expect your bank account balances to be confidential and off-limits to the eager eyes of investment salespeople in banks, numerous studies have demonstrated that banks are betraying customer trust.

Customers often have no idea that these bank reps are earning commissions, and that those commissions are being siphoned out of customers' investment dollars. Many customers are mistaken (partly due to the banks' and salespeople's poor disclosure) in believing that these investments, like bank savings accounts, are CDIC-insured and cannot lose value.

To make it even harder for you to discern a planner's agenda, you can't assume that planners who charge fees for their time don't also earn commissions selling products. This compensation is common.

Selling products that provide a commission can skew a planner's recommendations. Because a commission is earned only when a product is sold, such a product or service is inevitably more attractive in the planner's eyes than other options. For example, consider the case of a planner who sells disability insurance that you can obtain at a lower cost through your employer or a group trade association (see Chapter 16). He may overlook or criticize your most attractive option (buying through your employer) and focus on *his* most attractive option — selling you a higher-cost disability policy on which he derives a commission.

Another danger of trusting the recommendation of a commission-based planner is that she may steer you toward the products that have the biggest payback for her. These products are among the *worst* for you because they siphon off even more of your money upfront to pay the commission. They also tend to be among the costliest and riskiest financial products available.

Planners who are commission-greedy may also try to *churn* your investments. They encourage you to buy and sell at the drop of a hat, attributing the need to changes in the economy or the companies you invested in. More trading means more commissions for the broker.

Taking a narrow view

Because of the way they earn their money, many planners are biased in favour of certain strategies and products. As a result, they typically don't keep your overall financial needs in mind. For example, if you have a problem with accumulated consumer debts, some planners may never know (or care) because they're focused on selling you an investment product. Likewise, a planner who sells a lot of life insurance tends to develop recommendations that require you to purchase it.

Not recommending saving through your employer's retirement plan

Taking advantage of saving through your employer's retirement savings plan(s) is one of your best financial options. Although this method of saving may not be as exciting as risking your money in cattle futures, it's not as dull as watching paint dry — and, most importantly, your contributions are generally tax-deductible. Some planners are reluctant to recommend taking full advantage of this option: It doesn't leave much money for the purchase of their commission-laden investment products.

Ignoring debts

Sometimes paying off outstanding loans — such as credit card, auto, or even mortgage debts — is your best investment option. But most financial planners don't recommend this strategy, because paying down debts depletes the capital with which you could otherwise buy investments — the investments that the broker may be trying to sell you to earn a commission, or that the adviser would like to manage for an ongoing fee.

Not recommending real estate and small-business investments

Investing in real estate and small business, like paying off debts, takes away from your interest and ability to invest elsewhere. Most planners won't help with these choices. They may even tell you tales of real-estate and small-business-investing disasters to try to give you cold feet.

The value of real estate can go down just like any other investment. But over the long haul, owning real estate makes good financial sense for most people. With small business, the risks are higher but so are the potential returns. Don't let a financial planner convince you that these options are foolish — in fact, if you do your homework and know what you're doing, you can make higher rates of return investing in real estate and small business than you can in traditional securities such as stocks and bonds. See Part III to read more about your investing options.

Selling ongoing money-management services

The vast majority of financial planners who don't work on commission make their money by managing your money for an ongoing fee percentage (typically 1 to 3 percent of your investment annually).

An ongoing fee percentage can still create a conflict of interest; the financial planner may tend to steer you away from beneficial financial strategies that reduce the asset pool from which he derives his percentage. Financial strategies such as maximizing contributions to your employer's retirement savings plan, paying off debts like your mortgage, investing in real estate or small business, and so on may make the most sense for you. Advisers who work on a percentage-of-assets-under-management basis may be biased against such beneficial strategies.

Selling legal services

Some planners are in the business of drawing up *trusts* and providing other estate-planning services for their clients. Although these and other legal documents may be right for you, legal matters are often complex enough that the competence of someone who isn't a full-time legal specialist should be carefully scrutinized. And lower-cost options may be available if your situation is not complicated.

If you need help determining whether you need these legal documents, do a little investigating: Do some additional reading or consult an adviser who won't actually perform the work. If you do ultimately hire someone to perform estate-planning services for you, make sure that it's someone who specializes and works at it full-time. See Chapter 16 to find out more about estate planning.

Scaring you unnecessarily

Some planners put together nifty computer-generated projections that show you that you're going to need millions of dollars by the time you retire to maintain your standard of living, or that show that tuition will cost tens of thousands of dollars by the time your two-year-old is ready for university.

Waking up a client to the realities of his or her financial situation is an important and difficult job for good financial planners. But some unscrupulous planners take this task to an extreme, deliberately scaring you into buying what they're selling. They paint a bleak picture and imply that you can fix your problems only if you do what they say. Don't let them scare you — read this book and get your financial life in order.

Creating dependency

Many financial planners create dependency by making things seem so complicated that their clients feel as though they could never manage their finances on their own. If your adviser is reluctant to tell you how you can educate yourself about personal money management, or if she tells you that your time would be better spent learning yoga, you probably have a self-perpetuating consultant.

BEWARE

Watching for possible warning signs in planners' cultivation techniques

The channel through which you hear of a planner may provide clues to the planner's integrity and way of doing business. Beware of planners you find (or that find you) through these avenues:

✔ **Cold calling:** You've just come home after a hard day. No sooner has your posterior hit the recliner to settle in for the night when the phone rings. It's Joe the financial planner, and he wants to help you achieve all your financial dreams. Cold calling (the salesperson calls you, without an appointment) is the most inefficient way for a planner to get new clients. Cold calling is intrusive, and it's typically used by aggressive salespeople who work on commission.

✔ **Adult education classes:** Here's what often happens at the adult education classes that are offered at local schools: You pay a reasonable fee for the course. You go to class giddy at the prospect of learning how to manage your finances. And then the instructor ends up being a broker or financial planner hungry for clients. He confuses more than he conveys. He's short on specifics. But he's more than happy to show you the way if you contact (and hire) him outside of class.

The instructors for these courses are paid to teach. They don't need to solicit clients in class, and, in fact, it's unethical for them to do so. We should note, however, that part of the problem is that some universities take advantage of the fact that such "teachers" want to solicit business, setting the pay at a low level. So *never* assume that someone who is teaching a financial-planning course at a local college is ethical, competent, or looking out for your best interests. Although we may sound cynical in saying so, assume that these people are none of the above until they clearly prove otherwise.

Ethical instructors who are there to teach do *not* solicit clients. In fact, they may actively discourage students from hiring them. Smart schools pay their instructors well and weed out the instructors who are more interested in building up their client base than they are in teaching.

✔ **"Free" seminars:** This is a case of "you get what you pay for." Because you don't pay a fee to attend "free seminars," and the "teachers" don't get paid either, these events tend to be clear-cut sales pitches. The "instructor" may share some information, but smart seminar leaders know that the goal of a successful seminar is to establish himself or herself as an expert and to whet the prospects' appetites.

Note: Be especially wary of seminars targeted at select groups, such as special seminars for people who have received retirement-plan distributions or seminars touting "Financial Planning for Women." In most cases, financial planning is not specific to gender, ethnicity, or marital status.

Don't assume, either, that the financial planner giving a presentation at your employer's office is the right planner for you. You may be surprised at how little some corporate benefits departments investigate the people they let in. In most cases, planners are accepted simply because they don't charge. One organization gave preference to planners who, in addition to doing free presentations, also brought in a catered lunch! Guess what — this preference attracted a lot of brokers who sell high-commission products.

Finding a Good Financial Planner

Locating a good financial planner who is willing to work with the not-yet-rich-and-famous and who doesn't have conflicts of interest can be a challenge. Personal referrals and associations are two methods that can serve as good starting points.

Soliciting personal referrals

Getting a personal referral from a satisfied customer you trust is one of the best ways to find a good financial planner. Finding a referral from an accountant or lawyer whose judgment you have tested can help as well.

The best financial planners continue to build their practices through word of mouth. Satisfied customers are a professional's best and least costly marketers.

However, you should *never* take a recommendation from anyone as gospel. We don't care *who* is making the referral — even if it's your mother or the Pope. You must do your homework: Ask the planner the interview questions we list in the "Interviewing Financial Advisers: Asking the Right Questions" section later in this chapter. We've seen people get into real trouble because of blindly accepting someone else's recommendation. Remember that the person making the recommendation is (probably) not a financial expert. He or she may be just as bewildered as you are.

You may get referred to a planner or broker who returns the favour by sending business to the tax, legal, or real estate person who referred you. Good professionals don't do tit for tat. Hire professionals who make referrals to others based on their competence and ethics.

Seeking advisers through associations

Associations of financial planners are more than happy to refer you to planners in your area. But as we discuss earlier in this chapter, the major trade associations are composed of planners who sell products and work on commission.

Here are two of the best places to start searching for good financial planners:

> ✔ **The Institute of Advanced Financial Planners (IAFP)** (1-888-298-3292; www.iafp.ca) was founded in 2002 by Registered Financial Planners, after their existing association — the Canadian Association of Financial Planners — merged with the Canadian Association of Insurance and Financial Advisors to form Advocis. (In French, the designation is Planificateur financier certifié, or PFC.) In addition to letting you find RFPs in your area, the IAFP site lets you search for planners that meet a

number of different criteria. In particular, you can narrow your search by specifying the type of compensation — commission only, fee only, fee and commission, or salary. Put another way, this lets you come up with a shortlist of advisers according to how you want to pay for their services.

✔ **Advocis** (1-800-563-5822; www.advocis.ca) is the organization that resulted from the merger of the Canadian Association of Financial Planners and the Canadian Association of Insurance and Financial Advisors. Like the IAFP site, the Advocis Web site also has a feature that allows you to search for financial planners. Be sure to scroll down on the search page so you can specify the credentials.

Interviewing Financial Advisers: Asking the Right Questions

Don't consider hiring a financial adviser until you read the rest of this book. If you're not educated about personal finance, how can you possibly evaluate the competence of someone you may hire to help you make important financial decisions?

We firmly believe that you are your own best financial adviser. However, we know that some people don't want to make financial decisions without getting assistance. Perhaps you're busy, or you simply can't stand making money decisions.

You need to recognize that you have a lot at stake when you hire a financial adviser. Besides the cost of his services, which generally don't come cheap, you're placing a lot of trust in his recommendations. The more you know, the better the adviser you end up working with, the fewer services you may need to buy and the better the outcome.

The following questions will help you get to the core of an adviser's competence and professional integrity. Get answers to these questions *before* you decide to hire a financial adviser.

What percentage of your income comes from clients' fees vs. commissions from the products that you sell?

Anything less than 100 percent means that the person you're speaking to is at least partly a salesperson with a vested interest in recommending certain strategies and products.

Sadly, more than a few financial advisers don't tell the truth. In an undercover investigation done by *Money* magazine, nearly one-third of advisers who claimed that they were fee-only turned out to be brokers who also sold investment and insurance products on a commission basis.

How can you ferret these people out? The simplest way is to have them put down in writing exactly how they are compensated.

What percentage of fees paid by your clients is for ongoing money management vs. hourly financial planning?

The answer to how the adviser is paid provides clues to whether he has an agenda to convince you to hire him to manage your money. If you want objective and specific financial planning recommendations, in general it's wise to give preference to advisers who derive their income from hourly fees. Many counsellors and advisers call themselves "fee-based," which usually means that they make their living managing money for a percentage.

If you want a money manager, you can hire the best quite inexpensively through a mutual fund. Or, if you have substantial assets, you can hire an established money manager (refer to Chapter 9).

What is your hourly fee?

The rates for financial advisers vary all over the map (as they do with legal and tax advisers). We've seen and heard of fees that range from as low as $50 per hour all the way up to several hundred dollars per hour. If you shop around, you can find terrific planners who charge around $125 to $225 per hour and work faster than a snail's pace.

Because good planners spend a reasonable portion of their time researching and running their business, don't assume that they're getting rich at your expense by charging you around $125 to $125 per hour. Running a business is costly, but you shouldn't pay several hundreds of dollars per hour unless you're wealthy and you want an adviser who works only with people like you. You also need to be aware that a number of planners who manage money or sell products charge very high hourly rates because they don't really want to work with people on an hourly-fee basis.

What work and educational experience qualifies you to be a financial planner?

This question doesn't have one right answer. Ideally, a planner should have experience in the business or financial services field. Some say to look for planners with at least five or ten years of experience. We've always wondered how planners earn a living their first five or ten years if folks won't hire them until they reach these benchmarks! A good planner should also be good with numbers, speak plainly, and have good interpersonal skills.

Education is sort of like food. Too little leaves you hungry. Too much can leave you feeling stuffed and uncomfortable. And a small amount of high quality is better than a lot of low quality.

Because investment decisions are a critical part of financial planning, take note of the fact that the most common designations of educational training among professional money managers are MBA (master of business administration) and CFA (chartered financial analyst).

Have you ever sold limited partnerships? Options? Futures? Commodities?

The correct answers here are *no, no, no,* and *no.* If you don't know what these disasters are, refer to Chapter 8. You also need to be wary of any financial adviser who used to deal in these areas but now claims to have seen the light and reformed his ways.

Professionals with poor judgment may not repeat the same mistakes, but they're more likely to make some new ones at your expense. Our experience is that even advisers who have been "reformed" are unlikely to be working by the hour. Most of them either work on commission or want to manage your money for a hefty fee.

Do you carry liability (errors and omissions) insurance?

Some advisers may be surprised by this question or think that you're a problem customer looking for a lawsuit. On the other hand, accidents happen; that's why insurance exists. So if the planner doesn't have liability (errors and omissions) insurance, she missed one of the fundamental concepts of planning: Insure against risk. Don't make the same mistake by hiring her.

You wouldn't (and shouldn't) let contractors into your home to do work without knowing that they have insurance to cover any mistakes they make. Likewise, you should insist on hiring a planner who carries protection in case she makes a major mistake for which she is liable. Make sure that she carries enough coverage given what she is helping you with. RFPs are required to have this insurance, as are full members of Advocis.

Can you provide references from clients with needs similar to mine?

Take the time to talk to other people who have used the planner. Ask what the planner did for them, and find out what the adviser's greatest strengths and weaknesses are. You can learn a bit about the planner's track record and style. And because you want to have as productive a relationship as possible with your planner, the more you find out about him, the easier it will be for you to hit the ground running if you hire him.

Some financial advisers offer a "free" introductory consultation. If an adviser offers a free consultation to allow you to check him out, and it makes you feel more comfortable about hiring him, fair enough. But be careful: Most free consultations end up being a big sales pitch for certain products or services the adviser offers.

The fact that a planner doesn't offer a free consultation may be a good sign. Counsellors who are busy and who work strictly by the hour can't afford to burn an hour of their time for an in-person free session. They also need to be careful of folks seeking free advice. Such advisers usually are willing to spend some time on the phone answering background questions. They should also be able to send background materials by mail and provide references.

Will you provide specific strategies and product recommendations that I can implement on my own if I choose?

This is an important question. Some advisers may indicate that you can hire them by the hour. But then they provide only generic advice without specifics. Some planners even *double dip* — they charge an hourly fee initially to make you feel like you're not working with a salesperson, and they try selling commission-based products. Also be aware of advisers who say that you can choose to implement their recommendations on your own and then recommend financial products that carry commissions.

How is implementation handled?

Ideally, you should find an adviser who lets you choose whether you want to hire him to help with implementation after the recommendations have been presented to you. If you know that you're going to follow through on the advice, and you can do so without further discussions and questions, don't hire the planner to help you implement his recommendations.

On the other hand, if you hire the counsellor because you lack the time, desire, and/or expertise to manage your financial life in the first place, building implementation into the planning work makes good sense.

Chapter 19

Computer Money Management

• •

In This Chapter

▶ Evaluating the different types of software and Web sites

▶ Performing financial tasks with your computer

• •

*P*retty much everybody these days owns a computer. So should you join the crowd and start running your life — including your finances — in the cyberuniverse?

The short answer is . . . not necessarily. We know plenty of people who either don't own a computer or who use one sparingly and still do an excellent job managing their money.

Although a computer may be able to assist you with your personal finances, it simply represents one of many tools. Computers are best for performing routine tasks faster (such as processing lots of bills or performing many calculations) and to aid you with research.

Surveying Software and Web Sites

You can access two major repositories of personal finance information using your computer. Although the lines are sometimes a bit blurry between these two categories, they're roughly defined as software and the Internet. If you're familiar with computers, you can skip over the next two paragraphs. However, in case you're not comfortable with computer jargon, here's the difference between software and the Internet.

✔ *Software* refers to computer programs that are either packaged in a box or CD-ROM case or available to be downloaded online. (If you've ever used a word-processing program such as Word or WordPerfect, or a spreadsheet program such as Excel, then you've used software.) Most of the mass-marketed financial software packages sell for under $100.

✔ *The Internet* is a vast ocean of information that you can generally access via a modem, cable modem, or DSL (Digital Subscriber Line). These devices allow your computer to talk with other computers. To access the Internet, you need a Web browser, which you can obtain through your Internet service provider (ISP). Most of the financial stuff on the Internet is supplied by companies marketing their wares and, hence, is available for free. Some sites sell their content for a fee.

Adding up financial software benefits

Although the number of personal finance software packages and Web sites is large and growing, quality is having a hard time keeping up. The best software can;

✔ Guide you to better organization and management of your personal finances

✔ Help you complete mundane tasks or complex calculations more quickly and easily, and provide basic advice in unfamiliar territory

✔ Make you feel in control of your life.

Mediocre and bad software, on the other hand, can make you feel stupid or, at the very least, make you want to tear your hair out. Lousy packages usually end up in the software graveyard.

Having reviewed many of the packages available, we can assure you that if you are having a hard time with some of the programs out there (and sometimes even with the more useful programs), you are not at fault. Too many packages assume that you already know things such as your tax rate, your mortgage options, and the difference between stock and bond mutual funds. Much of what's out there is too technically oriented and isn't user-friendly. Some of it is even flawed in its financial accuracy.

A good software package, like a good tax or financial adviser, should help you better manage your finances. It should simply and concisely explain financial terminology, and it should help you make decisions by offering choices and recommendations, allowing you to play with alternatives before following a particular course of action.

With increasing regularity, financial software packages are being designed to perform more than one task or to address more than one area of personal finances. But remember that no software package covers the whole range of issues in your financial life. Later in this chapter, we recommend some of our favourite financial software.

Treading carefully on the Web

Like the information you receive from any medium, you have to sift out the good from the bad when you look for financial information or help online. If you blindly navigate the Internet, and you naively think that everything out there is useful "information," "research," or "objective advice," you're going to be in for a rude awakening.

Most personal-finance sites on the Internet are free, which means that these sites are basically advertisements. At the very least, they are probably dominated and driven by advertising. If you're looking for written material by unbiased experts or writers — well, you can find some on the Web, but you'll find far more biased and uninformed stuff.

Consider the source

A report on the Internet published by a leading investment-banking firm provides a list of the "coolest" finance sites. On the list is the Web site of a major bank. Because it's been a long time since we were in high school, we're not quite sure what "cool" means anymore. If cool can be used to describe a well-organized and graphically pleasing Web site, then we guess we can say that the bank's site is cool.

However, if you're looking for sound information and advice, then the bank's site is decidedly "uncool." It (not surprisingly) steers you in a financial direction that benefits the bank, and not you. For example, in the real-estate section, users are asked to plug in their gross monthly income and down payment. The information is then used to spit out the supposed amount that users can "afford" to spend on a home. No mention is given to the other financial goals and concerns — such as saving for retirement — that affect one's ability to spend a particular amount of money on a home.

Consider this advice in the lending area of the site: "Maybe you *can* have it now. When you don't have the cash on hand for important purchases, we can help you borrow what you need. From a new car, to that vacation you've been longing for, to new kitchen appliances, you can make these dreams real now." Click on a button at the bottom of the screen, and presto — you're on your way to racking up credit card and auto debt. Why bother practising delayed gratification, living within your means, or buying something used if getting a loan is "easy" and comes with "special privileges"?

Watch out for sponsored content

Sponsored content, a euphemism for advertising under the guise of editorial content, is another problem to watch out for on Web sites. You may find a disclaimer or note, which is often buried in small print in an obscure part of the Web site, saying that an article is "sponsored by" (in other words, advertising paid for by) the author.

For example, one mutual fund site states that its "primary purpose is to provide viewers with an independent guide that contains information and articles they can't get anywhere else." The content of the site suggests otherwise. In the "Expert's Corner" section, material is reprinted from a newsletter that advocates frequent trading in and out of mutual funds to time market moves. Turns out that the article is "sponsored by" the featured expert: In other words, it's a paid advertisement. (The track record of the newsletter's past recommendations, which isn't discussed on the site, is poor.)

Steer clear of biased financial planning advice

We also suggest skipping the financial planning advice offered by most financial service companies with financial products to sell. Such companies generally can't take the necessary objective, holistic view required to render useful advice.

For example, on one major mutual fund company's Web site, you'll find a good deal of material on the company's mutual funds. The site's financial planning advice is, unfortunately, off the mark: It urges readers to think of investing as putting money into financial instruments, and quickly moves on to — you guessed it — the benefits of mutual funds. It makes no mention of the fact that paying off high-cost consumer debt usually offers the best return, and that real estate and even small business are also worth considering. If you did that, though, you would put less money into mutual funds, which this area of the site prods you to do.

Shun short-term thinking

Many financial Web sites provide real-time stock quotes as a hook to some site that is cluttered with advertising. Our experience with individual investors is that the more short-term they think, the worse they do. And checking your portfolio during the trading day certainly promotes short-term thinking.

Be especially leery of tips offered around the electronic water cooler — message boards. As in the real world, chatting with strangers and exchanging ideas is sometimes fine. However, if you don't know the identity and competence of message-board posters or chat-room participants, why would you follow their financial advice or stock tips? Getting ideas from various sources is okay, but educate yourself and do your homework before making personal financial decisions.

If you want to best manage your personal finances and find out more, remember that the old expression "You get what you pay for" contains a grain of truth. Free information on the Internet, especially information provided by companies in the financial services industry, is often self-serving. Stick with information providers who have proven themselves offline or who don't have anything to sell except objective information and advice.

Accomplishing Money Tasks Using Your Computer

In the remainder of this chapter, we detail important personal financial tasks that your computer can help you accomplish. We look at using the Internet to do your banking, along with chequebook software programs and online bill payment services. We also provide our recommendations for the best software and Web sites to help you accomplish these chores.

Doing your banking online

You can avoid dealing with paper cheques — written or printed — by paying your bills online. You save on stamps and envelopes, and the cost of the service may be comparable to what you're spending on those supplies. Such services are available to anyone with a chequing account through almost all banks and credit unions.

The most straightforward way to pay your bills is to arrange to have your monthly payments automatically paid for out of your chequing account. In most cases, all you need to do is fill out a form to sign up for a *PAC* — short for *pre-authorized cheque plan* — and provide a sample voided cheque (just write the word "VOID" across the front of the cheque). This service is available with most companies that send you a regular bill. This includes cable, Internet, and phone service providers, your utilities (hydro, water, heating, etc.) as well as other bills you pay on a monthly basis, including your insurance premiums.

You can even skip this step in many cases. Most banks and credit unions have set up automatic accounts with many of the companies that people make payments to on a regular basis. These includes utility companies, cable TV and internet service providers, and sometimes local tax departments. Your financial institution's online banking site should tell you the steps needed to set your account up to have these bills pay as they come due. If the instructions aren't clear — which too often is the case — just call up the bank and have someone walk you through the process.

Using chequebook software

Chequebook software can help you get organized around paying your bills. When you have to make your monthly phone bill payment, for example, your monthly cheque, already made payable to the phone company, pops up on-screen at your command. All you have to do is fill in the new amount that you have to pay and print your cheque on your computer's printer.

Chequebook programs can track your cheque writing and prepare reports that detail your spending by category, so you can get a handle on where the fat is in your budget. One drawback of using these programs to track your spending is that they capture only what is entered. So the amount and spending category of your individual credit card and cash purchases, which for most people are substantial, may be omitted. However, most financial institutions and credit cards companies will provide this information to you in an electronic form so that you can typically enter an entire month's worth of transactions with a few commands. For a complete discussion on how to track your spending, see Chapter 3.

Quicken and Microsoft Money are good programs that we've reviewed in this category. In addition to offering the printed cheque and electronic bill-payment features, both of these packages are financial organizers. The programs allow you to list your investments and other assets, along with your loans and other financial liabilities. In addition, most financial institutions allow you to download an electronic list of your transaction which can then be easily inputted into these programs. Both Quicken and Microsoft's Money are available in Canadian versions.

In addition to the significant investment of time necessary to figure out how to use the software program, another drawback is cost — computer cheques are pricey. If you order cheques directly from the software manufacturers (order forms come with your software), expect to pay around $120 to $150 for 500 cheques. You can beat those prices by ordering from other companies. ChequeDirect Co., (www.chequedirect.com), for example, sells 500 cheques for $50.

Using online bill payment services

You don't need a chequebook program or use your bank's site to pay your bills online. One option is to use an intermediary company that receives your electronic instructions and pays the bill for you. There are a number of Web sites offering this service. One good choice is Canada Post's ePost (www.epost.ca). The service is free for consumers — the institutions that receive money through ePost pay the "freight." Because most online bill-payment services charge a minimum monthly fee, you can find cheaper ways to avoid cheque writing and stamp licking. For example, many businesses that you must pay monthly allow you to establish a pre-authorized monthly electronic payment service directly with them. Depending on your financial institution's schedule of service fees, this may mean paying a small charge for each transaction. In this case, inquire about the cost of a monthly plan that buys you up to a certain number of transactions a month, which is usually cheaper than paying the individual charge on each transaction.

Planning for retirement

Good retirement-planning software and online tools can help you plan for retirement by crunching the numbers for you. But they can also teach you how particular changes — such as your investment returns, rate of inflation, or your savings rate — can affect when, and in what style, you can retire. The biggest time-saving aspect of retirement-planning software and Web sites is that they let you more quickly play with and see the consequences of changing the assumptions.

Some of the major investment companies we profile in Part III of this book are sources for some high-quality, low-cost retirement planning tools. Here are some good ones to consider:

✔ Scotiabank's Web site (www.scotiabank.com) has several tools that can help you determine where you stand in terms of reaching a given retirement goal. You can calculate what you should be saving for retirement, and the site allows you to enter information about non-registered investments and private pension plans, and lets you try out different what-if scenarios.

✔ BMO InvestorLine's Web site (www.bmoinvestorline.com) has a comprehensive tool called the Financial Planner that allows you to do year-by-year projections. It takes into account tax considerations, and lets you include income from different sources.

✔ Credential Direct's Web site (www.credentialdirect.com) has a useful tool called the Life Events Planner that includes retirement planning and asset allocation tools.

Preparing your taxes

Good, properly used tax-preparation software can save you time and money. The best programs "interview" you to gather the necessary information and select the appropriate forms based on your responses. Of course, you're still the one responsible for locating all the information needed to complete your return. More-experienced taxpayers can bypass the interview and jump directly to the forms they know they need to complete. These programs also help flag overlooked deductions and identify other tax-reducing strategies.

QuickTax, UFile, and Taxtron are among the better tax-preparation programs we've reviewed. And if you're using an Apple computer, Taxtron happily comes in a Mac version.

If you're mainly looking for tax forms, you can get them at no charge in tax-preparation books or through the Canada Revenue Agency Web site (www.cra-arc.gc.ca).

Tracking your investment returns often isn't worth the headache

Accurately tracking the return on your investments can be an extremely complicated, tedious, and time-consuming task — exactly the type of chore that computers were designed to relieve us of. You'd think that a number of excellent investment-tracking software packages would be on the market today, but we feel that the available packages are too often complicated, tedious, and time-consuming. Many programs aren't any more efficient than the old-fashioned method of pencil, paper, and a calculator.

Our big gripe with many investment-tracking software programs is that most of them don't allow you to determine your investment's total return, and the programs that do allow you to calculate total return require a lot of time to get to that point. Your *effective* or *internal rate of return* (IRR), which compares your original amounts invested to the current market value, is the best way to measure the success of your investments over time.

Most of the other packages calculate your *cost basis,* which is your original investment plus reinvested dividends and capital gains, for which you would have already paid taxes in a regular investment account (as opposed to investments inside an RRSP or other tax-sheltered plan). When you sell an investment held outside such tax-favoured plans, you need to know the cost basis for tax purposes (see Chapter 6). Cost-basis reports make your returns look less generous because reinvested distributions increase your original investment and seemingly reduce your returns. We know from direct experience that investors often look at the cost-basis reports — which are

sometimes misleadingly named "investment performance" or "investment analysis" — and assume that the reports tell them their total investment returns. Using software for cost-basis calculations is generally not worthwhile, because most investment companies provide cost-basis information to you upon request or when you sell an investment.

If you want to analyze your historical returns, you need to gather all your old account statements (if you can find them) and enter every investment you made, as well as all reinvestments of dividends, interest, and capital-gains distributions.

For buy-and-hold mutual fund investors, investment-tracking software has limited benefit given the time required to enter your data. Mutual funds and many other published resources tell you what the funds' total return was for the past year, so you don't need to enter every dividend and capital gain distribution for yourself.

As for calculating the return of your overall portfolio with the old-fashioned method of paper and pencil, simply weight the return of each investment by the portion of your portfolio invested in it. For example, with a simple portfolio equally divided between two investments that returned 10 percent and 0 percent, respectively, your overall portfolio return would be 5 percent.

Investment-tracking software may be more useful for stock traders. In our experience, stock traders don't usually track their overall returns. If they actually used one of these programs, they could at least see how all their trading depresses their returns.

Researching investments

Rather than schlepping off to the library and fighting over the favourite investing reference manuals, ponying up hundreds of dollars to buy print versions for your own use, or slogging through voice-mail hell when you call government agencies, you can access a variety of materials with your computer. You can also often pay for just what you need:

- **Sedar.com:** This site provides free access to the various documents publicly traded Canadian companies and mutual funds must file with the regulators. You'll find everything from annual reports and financial statements to news releases here. The site is also loaded full of promotion-free material on mutual funds. You can find performance details here for most funds, as well as financial statements and annual reports that offer a breakdown on just which securities each fund holds. Sedar is also a useful place to start if you already have particular stocks in mind and want to find out more about the companies' businesses and financials.

- **FreeEdgar.com:** This Web site supplies information from Securities and Exchange Commission filings and other sources on U.S. public companies. If you want to access more than the one free report per day allowed by this service, you must upgrade to Edgar Online Premium for US$14.95 per month. To sidestep these charges, you can get unlimited free access to SEC documents directly via the SEC's Web site (www.sec.gov), but be aware that navigating this site takes patience. All public corporations, as well as mutual funds, file with the agency.

- **Globeandmail.com:** The home site to the various sites run by *The Globe and Mail,* it gives access to many of the business stories published in the paper. You'll also find articles from the *Globe*'s helpful personal finance section, including Tony's "Me and My Money" column. On the investment-selection front, both the *Globe*'s mutual fund and stock market sites offer excellent filtering features. For example, in a few clicks you can get a detailed list of low-cost, low-fee index funds that mirror the return of the major stock markets.

- **Morningstar.ca:** This site provides access to Morningstar's mutual fund reports, as well as reports on U.S. stocks. The reports are free, but they're watered-down versions of the company's comprehensive software and paper products.

Trading online

If you do your investing homework, trading securities online may save you money and perhaps some time. By eliminating the overhead of branch offices, and by accepting and processing trades by computer, online brokers keep their costs and brokerage charges to a minimum. However, some of these brokers have limited products and services. It's also worth noting that our own experience with reaching live people at some online brokers has been trying — we've waited on hold for more than ten minutes before a customer service representative answered the call.

While online trading may save you on transaction costs, it can also encourage you to trade more than you should, resulting in higher total trading costs, lower investment returns, and higher income tax bills. Following investments on a daily basis encourages you to think short term. Remember that the best investments are bought and held for the long haul (see Part III for more information).

Commissions are a key part of assessing online brokers. Lower costs are your compensation for not getting hands-on help and personal advice. But this doesn't mean you should accept poor service and substandard Web sites. Better online brokers offer their customers quality stock and mutual fund reports. The Web site itself should be user-friendly, straightforward, and flexible enough that you can enter trades easily. The better online brokers also offer a wide range of government and corporate bonds at competitive prices.

Here are some of the best online brokers to choose from:

- **BMO InvestorLine** (www.bmoinvestorline.com; 1-888-776-6886)
- **E*Trade Canada** (www.canada.etrade.com; 1-888-872-3388)
- **TD Waterhouse** (www.tdwaterhouse.ca; 1-800-465-5463)

Reading and searching periodicals

Many business and financial publications are going online to offer investors news and financial-market data. *The Globe and Mail* offers most of its current and recent stories for free at www.globeandmail.com. If you subscribe to its Insider Edition service, you can set up a personalized edition of the paper, get e-mail alerts for stories that are of interest to you, and have access to more of the paper's archives and premium features, as well as stories from the *Wall Street Journal*. The service costs $6.95 a month for six-day subscribers to the print version of *The Globe and Mail*. Otherwise, the cost is $14.95 a month.

For keeping up with U.S. business news, the *Wall Street Journal* lets you customize an online edition of the paper to fit your needs. The cost is $99 U.S. per year ($49 U.S. if you're already a *Journal* subscriber).

Leading business publications such as *Report on Business* magazine (www.theglobeandmail.com/special/robmagazinecover), *Forbes* (www.forbes.com) and *BusinessWeek* (www.businessweek.com) put their magazines' content on the Internet, with some allowing you to conduct searches for articles on specific topics that interest you. Be careful, though, to take what you read and hear in the mass media with many grains of salt (see Chapter 20). Much of the content revolves around tweaking people's anxieties and dwelling on the latest crises and fads.

Buying life insurance

If loved ones are financially dependent on you, you probably know that you need some life insurance. But add together the dread of life-insurance salespeople and a fear of death and you have a recipe for procrastination. While your computer can't stave off the grim reaper, it can help you find a quality, low-cost policy that can be more than 80 percent less costly than the most expensive options, without having to deal with high-pressure sales tactics.

The best way to shop for term life insurance online is through one of the quotation services that we discuss in Chapter 15. At each of these sites, you fill in your date of birth, whether you smoke, how much coverage you'd like, and for how long you'd like to lock in the initial premium. When you're done filling in this information, a new Web page pops up with a list of low-cost quotes (based on assumed good health) from highly rated (for financial stability) insurance companies.

Invariably, the quotes are ranked by how cheap they are. While cost is certainly an important factor, many of these services don't do as good a job explaining the other important factors to consider when doing your comparison shopping. For example, the projected and maximum rates after the initial term has expired are sometimes not covered. Be sure to ask about these other future rates before you agree to a specific policy.

If you decide to buy a policy from one of the online agencies, you can fill out an online application form. The quotation agency will then mail you a detailed description of the policy and insurer, and your completed application. In addition to having to deal with snail mail, you're also likely going to have to deal with a *medical technician* who will drop by your home to check on your health status . . . at least until some computer genius figures out a way for you to give a blood and urine sample online!

Preparing legal documents

Just as you can prepare a tax return with the advice of a software program, you can also prepare common legal documents. This type of software may save you from the often difficult task of finding a competent and affordable attorney.

Using legal software is generally preferable to using fill-in-the-blank documents. Software has the built-in virtues of directing and limiting your choices and preventing you from making common mistakes. Quality software also incorporates the knowledge and insights of the legal eagles who developed the software. And it can save you money.

If your situation isn't unusual, legal software may work well for you. As to the legality of documents that you create with legal software, remember that a will, for example, is made legal and valid by your witnesses; the fact that a lawyer prepares the document is *not* what makes it legal.

Wills are important documents, and you may still want to have a lawyer go over what you've prepared to ensure that it will have the effects that you intended. Another useful role that lawyers can perform is to make sure that you have covered all the possible eventualities.

Even if you plan on having a lawyer draft your will, using a will-drafting program will familiarize you with the process and terminology, as well as help you organize your thoughts. This can not only save you legal fees, but also help to ensure your will truly reflects your wishes.

A good package for preparing your own will is WillExpert, which is published by Intuit. In addition to allowing you to prepare wills, WillExpert can also help you prepare a power of attorney document (see Chapter 17). WillExpert also allows you to create a living will (a *personal care directive*) that lets you appoint someone to make medical decisions on your behalf if the event you are unable to do so on your own.

Chapter 20

On Air and in Print

In This Chapter

▶ Recognizing the mass media's impact on investors

▶ Deciding whether to tune in or tune out radio and television investing coverage

▶ Surfing safely for investing information on the Internet

▶ Evaluating newspapers and magazines

▶ Finding the best investing books

You aren't going to lack for options when it comes to finding radio and television news, Web sites, newspapers, magazines, and books that talk about money and purport to help you get rich. Tuning out poor resources and focusing on the best ones is the real challenge.

Because you probably don't consider yourself a financial expert, more often than not you aren't going to know what to believe and whom to listen to. We help you solve that problem in this chapter.

Observing the Mass Media

For better and for worse, the mass media have a profound influence on our culture. On the positive side, news is widely disseminated these days. So if a product is recalled or a dangerous virus breaks out in your area, you'll probably hear about it — perhaps more than you want to — through the media. (Or perhaps from tuned-in family members!)

The downsides of the mass media are plenty, though.

Alarming or informing us?

Imagine sitting down to watch the evening news and hearing the following stock market report:

> *"On Bay Street today, stock prices dropped a bit less than one percent, extending the market's decline of the past week. The reason: There were more people wanting to sell than there were people wanting to buy. For the year, the Canadian market is still up 15 percent, which is well above the historical average annual return of 10 percent."*

Now contrast that report with the following report for the same day:

> *"Stocks plunged sharply today as the S&P/TSX index plummeted more than 100 points to close at its lowest level in the past 168 hours. Banking stocks got hammered again, and the sector is now off more than 20 percent from its peak this past spring. Mining stocks also fell for the third day in a row."*

While the second news report goes into more detail, it is meant to be more provocative and anxiety producing. Most of the daily stock market reports we hear in the media sound more like the second report than they do the mundane — dare we say calming — first report. News producers, in their quest for ratings and advertising dollars, try to be alarming. The more you watch, the more unnerved you get over short-term negative events. Don't let yourself be manipulated.

Teaching what kind of values?

Daily doses of mass media, including all the advertising that comes with it, essentially communicate the following messages to us:

- ✔ Your worth as a person is directly related to your physical appearance (including the quality of clothing and jewellery you wear) and your material possessions — cars, homes, electronics, and other gadgets.

- ✔ The more money you make, the more "successful" you clearly are.

- ✔ The more famous you are (especially movie, music, and sports stars), the more you're worth listening to and admiring.

- ✔ Don't bother concerning yourself with possible consequences before engaging in negative behaviour.

- ✔ Delaying gratification and making sacrifices is for boring losers.

Continually inundating yourself with poor messages can cause you to behave in a way that undermines your long-term happiness and financial success. Don't support (by watching, listening, or reading) forms of media that don't reflect your values and morals.

Perpetuating prognosticating pundits?

Quoting and interviewing experts is perhaps the only thing that the media loves more than hyping short-term news events. What's the economy going to do next quarter? What's stock XYZ going to do next month? What's the stock market going to do in the next hour? No, we're not kidding about that last one — stock market channels regularly have interviews with floor traders from stock exchanges late in the trading day to get their opinions about what the market will do in the last hour before closing!

Prognosticating pundits keep many people tuned in because their advice is constantly changing (and therefore entertaining and anxiety producing), and they lead investors to believe that investments can be manoeuvred in advance to outfox future financial market moves. Common sense suggests, though, that no one has a working crystal ball — and if they did, they certainly wouldn't share such insights with the mass media for free. (For more on experts who purport to predict the future, see Chapter 18.)

Rating Radio and Television Financial Programs

Over the years, money issues have received increased coverage through the major media of radio and television. Is managing your money much more complicated than it was a generation ago? Not really — while we do have more financial products and services to choose from these days, the best of these resources simplify rather than complicate your financial life. For example, while there are far more mutual funds to choose from today than in decades past, many of the better fund companies offer funds of funds (see Chapter 9) to simplify the process of building a portfolio of mutual funds.

Some topics gain more coverage in radio and television because they help draw more advertising dollars (which follow what people are watching). When you click on the radio or television, you don't pay a fee to tune in to a particular channel (pay cable channels are an exception). Advertising doesn't necessarily prevent a medium from delivering coverage that is objective and in your best interest, but it sure doesn't help foster this type of coverage, either.

For example, can you imagine a financial radio or television correspondent saying:

> *"We've decided to stop providing financial market updates every five minutes because we've found it causes some investors to become addicted to tracking the short-term movements in the markets and to lose sight of the bigger picture. We don't want to encourage people to make knee-jerk reactions to short-term events."*

Soundbite-itis is another problem with both of these media. Producers and network executives believe that if you go into too much detail, viewers and listeners will change the channel.

Now, radio and television are hardly the only types of media that offer poor advice and cause investor myopia. The Internet, for example, can be even worse. And we've read plenty of lousy money books over the years.

Surveying the Internet

Yes, the Internet is changing the world, but certainly not always for the better and not always in such a big way. Consider the way we shop. Sure, you can buy things online that you couldn't in the past. Big deal — what's the difference between buying something by calling a toll-free number or doing mail order (which many of us did for years before the Internet got commercialized), and buying something by clicking your computer mouse? Purchasing things online simply broadens the avenues through which you can spend money. We see a big downside here: Overspending is easier to do when you surf the Internet a lot.

Some of the best Web sites allow you to more efficiently access information that may help you make important investing decisions. However, this doesn't mean that your computer allows you to compete at the same level as a professional money manager. No, the playing field isn't level. The best pros work at their craft full time and have far more expertise and experience than the rest of us. Some non-professionals have been fooled into believing that investing online makes them better investors. Our experience has been that most people who spend time online every day dealing with investments tend to trade and react more to short-term events and have a harder time keeping the bigger picture and their long-term goals and needs in focus.

If you know where to look, you can more easily access some types of information. However, you often find a lot of garbage online — just as you do on other advertiser-dominated media like television and radio. In Chapter 19, we explain how to safely navigate online to find the best of what's out there.

Navigating Newspapers and Magazines

Compared with radio and television, print publications generally offer lengthier discussions of topics. And, in the more financially focused publications, the editors who work on articles generally have more background in the topics they write about.

Even within the better publications, we find a wide variety of quality, so don't instantly believe what you read, even if you read a piece in a publication you like. Most publications have had their budgets continually squeezed over the last couple of decades. In many cases, writers are getting the same rate that they were 20 years ago. What does that say about the publications' commitment to quality — not to mention their ability to hire seasoned, knowledgeable writers who can put things in the proper perspective?

Here's how to get the most from financial periodicals:

- ✔ **Read some back issues.** Go to your local library (or perhaps visit the publication's Web site) and read some issues that are at least one to two years old. While reading old issues may seem silly and pointless, it can actually be enlightening. By reviewing a number of past issues in one sitting, you can begin to get a flavour for a publication's style, priorities, and philosophies. You can often get old content for free.

- ✔ **Look for solid information and perspective.** Headlines reveal a lot about how a publication perceives its role. Publications with cover stories such as "10 hot stocks to buy now!" and "Funds that will double your money in the next three years!" are probably best avoided. Look for articles that seek to educate with accuracy, not predict.

- ✔ **Note bylines.** As you read a given publication over time, you should begin to make note of the different writers. After you get to know who the better writers are, you can skip over the ones you don't care for and spend your limited free time reading the best.

- ✔ **Don't react.** Here's a common example of how *not* to use information and advice you glean from publications. You've got some cash you want to invest. You read an article about investing in real estate investment trusts and then go out the next week and buy several of them. Then you see a mention of some technology stocks that are supposedly coming back from the dead, and you put some money into the shares of those companies. Next, you come across a few headlines that say China is the place to be, so you buy several mutual funds that focus on China.

  Follow this approach and eventually your portfolio will be a mess of investments that end up reflecting the history of what you've read, rather than an orchestrated, well-thought-out investment portfolio.

Betting on Books

Reading a good book is one of our favourite ways to get a crash course on a given financial topic. As with the other types of resources we discuss in this chapter, you definitely have to choose carefully — there's plenty of mediocrity and garbage out there (see the sidebar "Don't book publishers exercise due diligence?").

Don't book publishers exercise due diligence?

Book publishers are businesses first. And, like most businesses, their business practices vary. Some have a reputation for care and quality; some just want to push a product out the door with maximum hype and minimum effort.

For instance, you may think that book publishers check out an author before they sign him or her to write an entire book. Well, you may be surprised to find out that some publishers don't do their homework.

What most publishers care about first is how marketable an author is. Some authors are marketable because of their well-earned reputation for sound advice. Others are marketable because of stellar promotional campaigns built on smoke and mirrors. Still others may have the potential for marketability if a publisher is willing to take a chance on them, but most publishers like a sure thing.

Even more troubling is that few publishers require advice guides to be technically reviewed for accuracy by an expert in the field other than the author, who sometimes is not an expert. You, the reader, are expected to be your own technical reviewer. But do you have the expertise to do that? (Don't worry; this book has been checked for accuracy.)

As authors, we know that financial ideas and strategies can differ considerably. Different is not necessarily wrong. When a technical reviewer looks at our text and tells us that a better way is out there, we take a second look. We may even see things in a new way. If we're the only experts who see our book before publication, we're not going to get this second expert opinion. How do you know whether a book's been technically reviewed? Check the credits page or the author's acknowledgments.

Authors write books for many reasons other than to teach and educate. The most common reason financial book authors write books is to further their own business interests. Taking care of business interests may not always be a bad thing, but it's not the best thing for you when you're trying to educate yourself and better manage your own finances. For example, some investment books are written by investment newsletter sellers. Rather than teach you how to make good investments, the authors make the investment world sound complicated so that you feel the need to subscribe to their ongoing newsletters.

Good books can go into depth on a topic in a way that simply isn't possible with other resources. Books also aren't cluttered with advertising and the conflicts inherent therein.

Here's a list of some of our favourite financial titles:

- *Dematerializing: Taming the Power of Possessions* by Jane Hammerslough (Perseus)
- *The Ultimate Credit Handbook: How to Cut Your Debt and Have a Lifetime of Great Credit* by Gerri Detweiler (Plume)

- *Tax Planning for You and Your Family*, produced by KPMG (Thomson Carswell)

- *Money Logic: Financial Strategies for The Smart Investor* by Moshe A. Milevsky with Michael Posner (Stoddart)

- *A Random Walk Down Wall Street* by Burton Malkiel (Norton)

- *Built to Last: Successful Habits of Visionary Companies* by James Collins and Jerry Porras (HarperCollins)

- *Good to Great: Why Some Companies Make the Leap and Others Don't* by James Collins (HarperCollins)

- *Canadian Small Business Survival Guide* by Benj Gallander (Dundurn Press)

- *Starting a Successful Business in Canada* by Jack D. James (Self Counsel Press)

- Self-Counsel Press's legal titles

- And, not surprisingly, our *Investing For Canadians For Dummies*, published by Wiley Publishing, Inc.

Part VI
The Part of Tens

The 5th Wave · By Rich Tennant

"...and don't tell me I'm not being frugal enough. I hired a man last week to do nothing but clip coupons!"

In this part . . .

You find some fun and useful chapters that will help you with financial strategies for ten life changes and provide a reality check with ten things more important than money. Why "Tens"? Why not?

Chapter 21

Survival Guide for Ten Life Changes

. . . .

In This Chapter

▶ Handling the financial challenges that arise during life changes

▶ Minimizing financial worries so you can focus on your life

. . . .

Some of life's changes come unexpectedly, like earthquakes. Others you can see coming when they're still far off on the horizon, like a big storm moving in off the ocean. Whether a life change is predictable or not, your ability to navigate successfully through its challenges and adjust quickly to its new circumstances depends largely on your degree of preparedness.

Perhaps you find our comparison of life changes to earthquakes and storms to be a bit negative. After all, some of the changes we discuss in this chapter should be occasions for joy, and here we are comparing them to natural disasters. But understand that what one defines as a "disaster" has everything to do with his or her preparedness. To the person who has no emergency rations stored in his basement, the big snowstorm that traps him in his home can lead to problems. But to the prepared person with plenty of food and water, that same storm may mean a vacation from work and some relaxing days in the midst of a winter wonderland.

Before we discuss critical financial issues for you to deal with before and during major life changes, here are some general tips that apply to all types of life changes:

- ✔ **Stay in financial shape.** An athlete is best able to withstand physical adversities during competition by training and eating well in advance. Likewise, the more sound your finances are to begin with, the better you'll be able to deal with life changes.

- ✔ **Changes require change.** Even if your financial house is in order, a major life change — starting a family, buying a home, starting a business, divorcing, retiring — should prompt you to review your personal financial strategies. Why? Because life changes often affect your income, spending, insurance needs, and ability to take financial risk.

✔ **Don't procrastinate.** With a major life change on the horizon, procrastination can be costly. You (and your family) may overspend and accumulate high-cost debts, lack proper insurance coverage, or take other unnecessary risks. Early preparation can save you from these pitfalls.

✔ **Manage stress and your emotions.** Life changes often are accompanied by stress and other emotional upheavals. Don't make knee-jerk decisions during these changes. Take the time to become fully informed and recognize and acknowledge your feelings. Educating yourself is key. You may want to hire experts to help (see Chapter 18), but don't abdicate decisions and responsibilities to advisers — the advisers may not have your best interests at heart or fully appreciate your needs.

Here, then, are the major life changes that you may have to deal with at some point in your life. We wish you more of the good changes than the bad.

Starting Out: Your First Job

If you just graduated from university or some other program, or you're otherwise entering the workforce, your increased income and reduction in educational expenses are probably a welcome relief. You'd think, then, that more young adults would be able to avoid financial trouble and challenges. But they face these challenges largely because of poor financial habits picked up at home or from the world at large. Here's how to get on the path to financial success:

✔ **Don't use consumer credit.** The use and abuse of consumer credit can cause long-term financial pain and hardship. You want furniture, a new television, and lots of fun vacations, but all these things cost money. To get off on the right financial foot, young workers need to shun the habit of making purchases on credit cards that they can't pay for in full when the bill arrives in the mail. Here's the simple solution for overspending and running up outstanding credit card balances: Don't carry a credit card. Cash and cheques worked fine for decades before credit cards arrived on the scene. If you need the convenience of making purchases with a piece of plastic instead of with cash or cheques, use a debit card (see Chapter 4).

✔ **Get in the habit of saving and investing.** If you hope to someday own a home and cease working full-time, you'll need to save over many years. Ideally, your savings should be directed into retirement accounts that offer tax benefits, unless you want to accumulate down-payment money for a home or small business purchase (see Chapter 2). Thinking about a home purchase or retirement is usually not part of the active thought patterns of first-time job seekers. We're often asked, "At what age should a person start saving?" To us, that's similar to asking at what age you should start brushing your teeth. Well, when you have teeth to brush! So we say you should start saving and investing money from your first pay-cheque. Try saving 5 percent of every paycheque and then eventually increase the amount to 10 percent. If you're having trouble saving money, track your spending and make cutbacks as needed (refer to Chapters 3 and 5).

✔ **Get insured.** Many people who are starting out are able to rationalize not buying insurance. When you're young and healthy, imagining yourself feeling otherwise is hard. Many twentysomethings give little thought to the potential for health care expenses. But because accidents and unex-pected illnesses can strike at any age, forgoing coverage can be finan-cially devastating. Buying disability coverage, which replaces income lost to a long-term disability, in your first full-time job with more limited bene-fits is wise. And as you begin to build your assets, consider making out a will so that your assets go where you want in the event of your death.

✔ **Continue your education.** After you get out in the work force, you (like many other people) may realize how little you learned in formal school-ing that can actually be used in the real world — and, conversely, how much you need to learn (like personal financial management) that school never taught you. Read, learn, and continue to grow. Continuing education will help you advance in your career and learn to enjoy the world around you.

Changing Jobs or Careers

During your adult life, you'll almost surely change jobs — perhaps as often as several times a decade. We hope that most of the time you'll be changing by your own choice. But let's face it: Job security is not what it used to be. Corporate downsizing has made victims of even the most talented workers.

Always be prepared for a job change. No matter how happy you are in your current job, knowing that your world won't fall apart if you're not working tomorrow will give you an added sense of security and encourage an open-ness to new opportunities and possibilities. Whether you're changing your job by choice or necessity, the following financial manoeuvres will help ease the transition:

✔ **Structure your finances to weather an income dip.** Spending less than you earn always makes good financial sense, but if you're coming up to a possible job change, spending less is even more important. This is par-ticularly true if you're entering a new field or starting your own company and you expect a short-term drop in your income. Many people view a lifestyle of thriftiness as restrictive, but ultimately those thrifty habits can give you more freedom to do what you want to do. Be sure to keep an emergency reserve fund (refer to Chapter 8).

If you lose your job, batten down the hatches. You normally get little advance warning when you lose your job — this does not mean, however, that you can't do anything financially. Evaluating and slashing your current level of spending may be necessary. Everything should be fair game, from how much you spend on housing to how often you eat out to where you do your grocery shopping. Avoid at all costs the temptation to maintain your level of spending by accumulating consumer debt.

✔ **Evaluate the total financial picture when relocating.** At some point in your career, you may have the option of relocating. But don't call the moving company until you understand the financial consequences of such a move. You can't simply compare salaries and benefits between two jobs. You also need to compare the cost of living between the two areas: That includes housing, commuting, income and property taxes, food, utilities, and all the other major expenditure categories that we discuss in Chapter 3.

Getting Married

Ready to tie the knot with the one you love? Congratulations — we hope that you'll have a long, healthy, and happy life together. In addition to the emotional and moral commitments that you and your spouse are going to be making to one another, you're probably going to be merging many of your financial decisions and resources. There's a good chance your money personalities may be quite different; after all, opposites often attract. Even if you're largely in agreement about your financial goals and strategies, managing as two is different from managing as one.

✔ **Take a compatibility test.** Many couples never discuss their financial goals and plans before marriage; failing to do so breaks up way too many marriages. Finances are just one of the many issues you need to discuss. Others include expectations for having and raising children, dealing with in-laws, career goals, and so on. Ensuring that you know what you're getting yourself into is a good way to minimize your chances for heartache. Ministers, priests, and rabbis sometimes offer premarital counselling to help bring issues and differences to the surface. Don't let romance blind you to important issues that are vital to the long-term health of your marriage.

✔ **Consider taxes.** More than a few couples actually allow their joint tax burdens to influence when and even if they marry. The only way to know what will happen to your tax bill is to get out a tax return and plug in the relevant numbers and see what the Canada Revenue Agency will do to you after you're married. Put strategies to work to cut your household's total tax bill. Have the higher-earning spouse pay all the household expenses. This leaves the lower-earning spouse with more money for investments, which are then taxed at a lower rate. Consider setting up a spousal RRSP. (See Chapter 7 for more details.) Be sure to prepare your tax returns together to make the best use of your household's credits and deductions. (Refer to Chapter 6 for more details.)

✔ **Discuss and set joint goals.** After you're married, you and your spouse should set aside time once a year, or every few years, to discuss personal and financial goals for the years ahead. When you talk about where you want to go, you help ensure that you're both rowing your financial boat in the same direction.

✔ **Decide whether to keep finances separate or jointly managed.** Some couples choose to keep separate financial accounts, and others decide to pool their resources. Philosophically, we like the idea of pooling better. After all, marriage is a partnership, and it shouldn't be a his-versus-hers affair. In some marriages, however, spouses may choose to keep some money separate, particularly for personal spending, so that they don't feel the scrutiny of a spouse with different spending preferences. Spouses who have been through divorce may choose to keep the assets they bring into the new marriage separate in order to earmark and protect their money in the event of another divorce. As long as you're jointly accomplishing what you need to financially, some separation of money is okay. But for the health of your marriage, don't hide money from one another — and, if you're the higher-income spouse, don't assume power and control over your joint income.

✔ **Coordinate and maximize employer benefits.** If one or both of you have access to a package of employee benefits through an employer, understand how best to make use of those benefits. Coordinating and using the best that each package has to offer is like giving yourselves a pay raise. For example, if you both have access to health insurance, compare which of you has better benefits. Likewise, one of you may have a better company retirement savings plan — one that matches your contributions and offers superior investment options. Unless you can afford to save the maximum through both your plans, saving more in the better plan will increase your combined assets. (*Note:* If you're concerned about what will happen if you save more in one of your retirement plans and then you divorce, rest assured that in most provinces the money is considered part of your joint assets to be divided equally.)

✔ **Discuss life and disability insurance needs.** If you and your spouse can make do without each other's income, you may not need any income-protecting insurance. However, if, like many husbands and wives, you both depend on each other's incomes, or if one of you depends fully or partly on the other's income, you may each need long-term disability and term life insurance policies (refer to Chapter 16).

✔ **Update your wills.** When you marry, you should update your wills. If you haven't gotten around to making a will, having a will is potentially more valuable when you're married, especially if you want to leave money to others in addition to your spouse, or if you have children for whom you need to name a guardian. See Chapter 16 for more on wills.

✔ **Reconsider beneficiaries on investment and life insurance.** With retirement plans and life insurance policies, you name beneficiaries to whom the money or value in those accounts will go in the event of your passing. When you marry, you'll probably want to rethink your beneficiaries.

Buying a Home

Most Canadians eventually buy a home. You don't need to own a home to be a financial success, but home ownership certainly offers financial rewards. Over the course of your adult life, the real estate that you own is likely going to appreciate in value. Additionally, you're going to pay off your mortgage someday, which will greatly reduce your housing costs. As a renter, on the other hand, your full housing costs are going to increase over time with inflation.

If you're thinking about buying a home:

✔ **Get your overall finances in order.** Before buying, you need to analyze your current budget, your ability to afford debt, and your future financial goals. Make sure that your expected housing expenses still allow you to save properly for retirement and other long- or short-term objectives. Don't buy a home based on what lenders are willing to lend. Read and digest the relevant portions of this book so that you can get your financial house in order before you buy.

✔ **Determine if now's the time.** Buying a house when you don't see yourself staying put for three to five years rarely makes financial sense, especially if you're a first-time home buyer. Buying and selling a home gobbles up a good deal of money in transaction costs — you'll be lucky to recoup those costs even within a five-year period. Also, if your income is likely to drop or you have other pressing goals, such as starting a business, you may want to wait to buy.

To find out more about buying a home, be sure to read Chapter 14.

Having Children

If you think that being a responsible adult, holding down a job, paying your bills on time, and preparing for your financial future are tough, wait 'til you add kids to the equation. Most parents find that, with kids in the family, the already precious commodities of free time and money become even more precious — sometimes even extinct. The more efficiently you're able to manage your time and money, the better able you'll be to have a sane, happy, and financially successful life as a parent.

Budgeting for life changes

One thing is certain about life: It changes. Marriage, buying a home, family expansion, starting a business, divorce, retirement, or the death of a spouse — although some life events bring joy and others sorrow, all bring financial change. If you don't manage this change, it may end up managing and ruling you.

We've seen the best of savers turn into deficit financiers due to the financial upheaval and shock waves from a major life event — even events that were anticipated. You should budget ahead for life changes.

For example, if you want to take the entrepreneurial plunge and leave your full-time job, you need to determine whether you can afford to do that, and what impact the change in your expenses and income is going to have on your ability to save money. Those considering becoming parents likewise need to consider how increased expenses and a likely reduction in income are going to affect their monthly budget.

Going through this budgeting exercise is a great way to estimate what impact a child or other significant life change will have on your financial situation. Consider the nervous expectant parents who went through this exercise because they were wondering what financial impact having a baby would have on their household finances. Their findings: Given their expected spending, they would go from saving 12 percent of their annual incomes to spending 5 percent more than they earned. But the lower-income spouse was also surprised to see that, by working half-time rather than full-time, their net savings would actually increase thanks largely to lower taxes and work-related expenses, as well as reduced child care costs.

In Chapter 3, we provide suggested categories for tallying your expenses — such as housing, clothing, auto, cable TV, furniture, insurance, telephone, utilities, education, and so on. You can adjust and create new spending and income categories to match your personal financial situation.

As you plan for your next life change, remember the limitations of quantitative analysis. It can't factor in the non-financial considerations such as how you feel about working more or less because of a life change. Crunching numbers may also mistakenly give you the illusion of control. Those expectant parents that we just told you about found out that they were getting not one but *three* new additions to their family!

Here are some key things to recognize and do both before and after you begin your family:

> ✔ **Set your priorities.** You can't do it all and have it all. As with many other financial decisions, starting or expanding a family requires you to plan ahead. Set your priorities and structure your finances and living situation accordingly. Is having a bigger home in a particular community important, or would you rather feel less pressure to work hard, giving you more time to spend with your family? Keep in mind that a less hectic work life not only gives you more free time but it also often reduces your cost of living by decreasing meals out, dry-cleaning costs, daycare expenses, and so on.

- ✔ **Take a hard look at your budget.** If you had a hard time living within your means before having children, then you definitely should take an honest look at how your income and spending will change after your family grows. In addition to diaper changes and less sleep at night, having children requires you to increase your spending. At a minimum, expenditures for food and clothing will increase. But you're also likely to spend more on housing, insurance, daycare, and education. On top of that, if you want to play an active role in raising your children, working at a full-time job will not be possible for both parents. So while you consider the added expenses, you may also need to factor in a decrease in income.

    No simple rules exist for estimating how children will affect your household's income and expenses. On the income side, figure out how much you want to cut back on work. On the expense side, statistics show that the average household with school-age children spends about 20 percent more than those without children. Going through your budget category by category and estimating how kids will change your spending is a more scientific approach. (You can use the worksheets in Chapter 3).

- ✔ **Boost insurance coverage** *before* **getting pregnant.** Before you try to have a baby, women should make sure they have adequate disability insurance, as pregnancy is usually considered a pre-existing condition. This means that if you don't already have coverage in place and get pregnant, a disability that is the result of your pregnancy will generally not enable you to receive benefits. (Ask about waiting periods that may exclude coverage for a pregnancy within the first year or so of the insurance.) And most families-to-be should buy life insurance. Waiting to buy life insurance *after* the bundle of joy comes home from the hospital is a risky proposition — if one of the parents develops a health problem, he or she may be denied coverage. You should also consider buying life insurance for a stay-at-home parent. Even though the stay-at-home parent is not bringing in income, if he or she were to pass away, hiring assistance could cripple the family budget.

- ✔ **Check maternity leave with your employers.** Many of the larger employers offer some maternity leave for women and, in rare but thankfully increasing cases, for men. Some employers offer paid leaves, while others may offer unpaid leaves. Understand the options and the financial ramifications before you consider the leave and, ideally, before you get pregnant.

- ✔ **Update your will.** If you have a will, you'll need to update it. If you don't have a will, make one now. With children in the picture, you need to name a guardian who will be responsible for raising your children should you and your spouse both pass away. Although choosing a guardian is a daunting decision, the thought of letting the courts decide who should raise your children can be even more frightful.

- ✔ **Understand child care tax benefits.** If you have children under the age of 18, you may be eligible for the Canada Child Tax Benefit (CCTB), a non-taxable benefit. In 2005, the annual basic benefit was set at $1,228 per child, plus an extra $86 for the third and subsequent children. There is an additional benefit set at $243 in 2005 for each child under age 7. This amount is reduced by 25 percent of any child care expenses you claim in the previous year. These benefits are decreased on a sliding scale if your household income exceeds a certain amount, which in 2005 was $35,595. If you have one child, the basic benefit is reduced by 2 percent of the amount your net family income exceeds that level. If you have two or more children, it's reduced by 4 percent. (Note that Alberta has different payment schedules than the rest of the country.)

In addition, the CCTB also includes the National Child Benefit Supplement for low-income families. The amounts in 2005 were $1,722 for the first child, $1,502 for the second, and $1,420 for any additional children. This benefit also gets gradually phased out if your family's net income exceeds a certain level, which in 2005 was $21,480.

Child care expenses can also be deducted if they were incurred in order for you or your spouse to earn an income. In a two-parent family, the deduction must usually be claimed by the lower-earning spouse. Single parents who are students, as well as households where both spouses are studying at a postsecondary institution, can also claim this deduction. In 2005, you could claim up to $7,000 in expenses for each child under the age of 7, and $4,000 for children age 7 to 16. The total you can claim is limited to two-thirds of your earned income. Some provinces also have an additional child care tax credit for lower-income families.

✔ **Don't indulge the children.** Toys, art classes, sports, field trips, and the like can rack up big bills, especially if you don't control your spending. Some parents fail to set guidelines or limits when spending on children's programs. Others mindlessly follow the examples set by the families of their children's peers. Parents sometimes feel some insecurity about providing the best for their children. The parents (and kids) that seem the happiest and most financially successful are the ones who clearly distinguish between material luxuries and family necessities.

As children get older and become indoctrinated into the world of shopping, all sorts of other purchases come into play. Consider giving your kids a weekly allowance and letting them discover how to spend and manage it. And when they're old enough, having your kids get a part-time job can help teach financial responsibility, as well.

Starting a Small Business

Many people aspire to be their own bosses, but far fewer people actually leave their jobs in order to achieve that dream. Giving up the apparent security of a job with benefits and a built-in network of co-workers is difficult for most people, both psychologically and financially. Starting a small business is not for everyone, but don't let inertia stand in your way. Here are some tips to help get you started and increase your chances for long-term success:

✔ **Prepare to ditch your job.** Do you spend all or nearly all that you earn, and have you failed to accumulate a nest egg? Many people in such a situation never leave their jobs behind to pursue their entrepreneurial dreams, because they feel dependent upon their paycheques. To maximize your ability to save money, live as Spartan a lifestyle as you can while you're employed; you'll simultaneously be developing thrifty habits that will help you weather the reduced income and increased expenditure period that comes with most small-business start-ups. You may also want to consider easing into your small business by working at it part-time in the beginning, with or without cutting back on your normal job.

✔ **Develop a business plan.** If you research and think through your business idea, you'll not only reduce the likelihood of your business failing and increase its success if it thrives, but you'll also feel more comfortable taking the entrepreneurial plunge. A good business plan should be a blueprint for how you expect to build the business. It should describe in detail the business idea, the marketplace you'll be competing in, your marketing plans, and expected revenue and expenses.

✔ **Replace your insurance coverage.** Before you finally leave your job, get proper insurance coverage. With disability insurance, you want to secure coverage before you leave your job so that you have income to qualify for coverage. If you have life insurance through your employer, secure new individual coverage as soon as you know you're going to leave your job. (See Chapter 16 for more details.)

✔ **Establish a retirement savings plan.** After your business starts making a profit, consider establishing a Registered Retirement Savings Plan. We explain the ins and outs of RRSPs in Chapter 10.

Caring for Aging Parents

There comes a time for many of us when we reverse roles with our parents. As your parents age, they may need help with a variety of issues and living tasks — instead of being the one who is cared for, you become the caregiver. Although it's unlikely that you'll have the time or ability to perform all these functions yourself, you may well end up being the coordinator of service providers who will perform these functions.

Here are some things to consider when caring for aging parents:

✔ **Get help where possible.** In most communities, a variety of non-profit organizations offer information and sometimes even counselling to families who are caring for elderly parents. You may be able to find your way to such resources through your province's ministry of health, as well as through recommendations from local hospitals and doctors. You'll especially want to get assistance and information if your parents need some sort of home care, nursing home care, or assisted living arrangement.

✔ **Get involved in their health care.** Your aging parents may already have a lot on their minds, or they simply may not be able to coordinate and manage all the health care providers that are giving them medications and advice. Try, as best as you can, to be their advocate. Speak with their doctors so that you can understand their current medical condition and need for various medications, and how to help coordinate caregivers. Visit home care providers and nursing homes, and speak with prospective care providers.

✔ **Understand tax breaks.** If you're financially supporting your parents, you may be eligible for a number of tax credits and deductions for elder care. You can generally claim most related medical expenses as a tax credit. If you are single, widowed, divorced, or separated and supporting a parent, you can also claim the eligible dependant credit (formerly the equivalent-to-married credit). If an elderly or infirm relative lives with you and you provide in-home care, you may also be eligible for the caregivers credit. In 2005, this credit was worth up to $605. However, if you claim the eligible dependant or other dependant tax credits, you cannot claim the caregivers credit.

✔ **Discuss getting the estate in order.** Parents don't like talking and thinking about their demise, and they may feel awkward discussing this issue with their children. But opening a dialogue between you and your folks about such issues can be healthy in many ways. Discussing wills, living wills, living trusts, and estate planning strategies (see Chapter 17) not only makes you aware of your folks' situation but it can also improve their plans to both their benefit and yours.

✔ **Take some time off.** Caring for an aging parent, particularly one who is having health problems, can be time-consuming and emotionally draining. If you were already juggling the responsibilities of a job, marriage, and parenthood before your parents needed help, you may now feel completely overwhelmed. Do your parents and yourself a favour by using some vacation time to help get things in order. Although this time off may not be the kind of vacation you were envisioning, it should help you reduce your stress and get more on top of things.

Divorcing

In most marriages that are destined to split up, there are usually early warning signs that both parties recognize. Sometimes, however, one spouse may surprise the other with an unexpected request for divorce. Whether the divorce is planned or unexpected, here are some key things to consider:

✔ **Question the divorce.** Some say that divorcing is too easy, and we tend to agree. Although some couples are indeed better off parting ways, others give up too easily, thinking that the grass is greener elsewhere, only to later discover that all lawns have weeds and crabgrass. Just as with lawns that aren't watered and fertilized, relationships can wither without nurturing.

Money and disagreements over money are often major contributing factors to marital unhappiness. Unfortunately, in many relationships, money is wielded as power by the spouse who earns more of it. Try talking things over, perhaps with a marital counsellor. If you invest in making your relationship stronger, you'll reap the dividends for years to come.

✔ **Separate your emotions from the financial issues.** Separating your feelings from your finances is easier said than done. Feelings of revenge may be common in some divorces, but they'll probably only help ensure that the lawyers get rich at your expense as you and your spouse butt heads. If you really want a divorce, work at doing it efficiently and harmoniously so that you can get on with your lives.

✔ **Detail resources and priorities.** Draw up a list of all the assets and liabilities that you and your spouse have. Make sure that you list all the financial facts, including investment account records and statements. After you know the whole picture, begin to think about what is and is not important to you financially and otherwise.

✔ **Educate yourself about personal finance and legal issues.** Divorce sometimes forces non–financially oriented spouses to get a crash course in personal finance at a difficult emotional time. This book can help educate you financially. In terms of the legal issues of divorce, visit a bookstore and pick up a good legal guide or two about divorce.

✔ **Choose advisers carefully.** Odds are that you will retain the services of one or more specialists to assist you with the myriad issues, negotiations, and concerns of your divorce. Legal, tax, and financial advisers can help, but make sure that you recognize their limitations and conflicts of interest. The more complicated things become and the more you haggle with your spouse, the more lawyers, unfortunately, benefit financially. Don't use your divorce lawyer for financial or tax advice — your lawyer probably knows no more than you do in these areas. Also, realize that you don't need a lawyer to get divorced in most provinces. As for choosing tax and financial advisers, if you think you need that type of help, refer to Chapters 6 and 18 for advice on how to find good advisers.

✔ **Analyze your spending.** Although your "household" expenses will surely be less when you go back to being single, you'll probably have to make do with less income. Some divorcees find themselves financially squeezed in the early years following a divorce. Analyzing your spending needs pre-divorce will help you adjust to a new budget, as well as negotiate a fairer settlement with your spouse.

✔ **Review needed changes to your insurance.** If you're covered under your spouse's employer's insurance plan, make sure that you get this coverage replaced (see Chapter 16). If you or your children will still be financially dependent upon your spouse post-divorce, make sure that the divorce agreement mandates life insurance coverage. You should also revise your will (see Chapter 17).

✔ **Revamp your retirement plan.** With changes to your income, expenses, assets, liabilities, and future needs, your retirement plan will surely need a post-divorce overhaul. Refer to Chapter 2 for a reorientation.

Receiving a Windfall

Whether through inheritance, stock options, small-business success, or lottery winnings, you may receive a financial windfall at some point in your life. Like many people who are totally unprepared psychologically and organizationally for their sudden good fortune, you may well find that a flood of money can create more problems than it solves. You may be saying, "We should have such problems." Fair enough. Few people would rather be poor than rich.

Here are a few tips to help you make the most of your financial windfall:

✔ **Take the time to educate yourself.** If you've never had to deal with significant wealth, we don't expect you to know how to handle it. Don't rush and pressure yourself to invest it as soon as possible. Leaving the money where it is or stashing it in one of the higher-yielding money market funds we recommend in Chapter 12 is a far better short-term solution than jumping into investments that you don't understand and haven't taken the time to research.

✔ **Beware of the sharks.** You may begin to wonder if someone has posted your net worth, address, and home telephone number in the local newspaper and on the Internet. Brokers and financial advisers may flood you with marketing materials, telephone solicitations, and lunch date requests. These folks pursue you for a reason: They want to convert your money into their income, either by selling you investments and other financial products or by managing your money. Stay away from the sharks, educate yourself, and take charge of your own financial moves. Decide on your own terms whom to hire, and then seek them out. Most of the best advisers we know don't have the time or philosophical orientation to chase after prospective clients.

✔ **Recognize the emotional side of coming into a lot of money.** One of the side effects of accumulating wealth quickly is that you may have feelings of guilt or otherwise be unhappy, especially if you expected money to solve your problems. If you didn't invest in your relationship with your parents, and, after their passing, you regret how you interacted with them, getting a big inheritance from your folks may make you feel guilty. As another example, if you poured endless hours into a business venture that finally paid off, all that money sitting in your investment accounts may leave you with a hollow feeling if you're divorced and you lost friends by neglecting your relationships.

✔ **Pay down debts.** Paying off your debts is one of the simplest and best investments you can make when you come into wealth. Consider the multi-millionaire who was looking for advice because he was frustrated that he didn't know how to invest several million dollars. He was worried about losing money on investments partly because he had worked so hard to build his wealth. He had a decent-sized home mortgage, which made complete sense for him to pay off. We generally borrow money to buy things that we otherwise can't buy in one fell swoop. Getting rid of debts is an especially good move when you have plenty of money.

✔ **Diversify.** If you want to protect your wealth, don't keep it all in one pot. Mutual funds (see Chapter 9) and exchange-traded funds are ideally diversified, professionally managed investment vehicles to consider. And if you want your money to continue growing, consider the wealth-building investments — stocks, real estate, and small-business options — that we discuss in Part III of this book.

✔ **Make use of the opportunity.** Most people work for a paycheque their whole lives so that they can pay a neverending stream of monthly bills. Although we're not advocating a hedonistic lifestyle, why not take some extra time to travel, spend time with your family, and enjoy the hobbies you've long been putting off? And how about trying a new career that you may find more fulfilling and that may make the world a better place? Many people have little flexibility. Don't waste flexibility if you have it.

Retiring

If you spent the bulk of your adult life working, retiring can be a challenging life transition. Most Canadians have an idealized vision of how wonderful retirement will be. No more irritating bosses and pressure of work deadlines. Unlimited time to travel, play, and lead the good life. Sounds great, huh? Well, the reality for most Canadians is far different, especially for those who don't plan ahead (financially and otherwise).

Here are some tips to help you through retirement:

✔ **Plan both financially and personally.** Leaving behind a full-time career creates big challenges, such as what to do with all your free time — the opposite problem that new parents have. You can get too much of a good thing, which is why planning for your time and activities in retirement is even more important than planning financially. If the focus during your working years is solely on your career and saving money, you may lack interests, friends, and the ability to know how to spend money when you retire.

✔ **Take stock of your resources.** Many people worry and wonder if they have sufficient assets for cutting back on work or retiring completely, yet they don't crunch any numbers to see where they stand. Sometimes ignorance can be blissful, but this is a case where ignorance may cause you to misunderstand how little or how much you really have for retirement when compared to what you need. See Chapter 2 for help with retirement planning.

✔ **Re-evaluate your insurance needs.** During your working years, you carry disability and perhaps some life insurance to protect you and your dependants should you not be able to earn an income. When you have sufficient assets to retire, you don't need to retain insurance to protect your employment income any longer. On the other hand, as your assets grow over the years, you may be underinsured with regards to liability insurance (refer to Chapter 16).

✔ **Decide on health care/living options.** Medical expenses in your retirement years (particularly the cost of nursing home care) can be daunting. Which course of action you take — supplemental insurance, buying into a retirement community, or not doing anything — depends upon your financial and personal situation. Early preparation increases your options. If you wait until you have major health problems, it may be too late to choose specific paths. (See Chapter 16 for more details.)

✔ **Decide what to do with your RRSP.** When you're set to retire, you may have to elect what to do with your RRSP funds. Making the right choice is similar to choosing a good investment — different features carry different risks, benefits, and tax consequences. Read Chapter 7 for information on how to assess your different options for taking money out of your RRSP. Read Part III of this book to learn about investing.

✔ **Pick a pension option.** Pensions are structured by actuaries, who based them on reasonable life expectancies. The younger you are when you start collecting your company pension and Canada Pension Plan (or Quebec Pension Plan) benefits, the less you get per month. Check to see if the amount of your monthly company pension stops increasing past a certain starting age. You obviously don't want to delay access to your pension benefits past that age, because you won't receive a reward for waiting any longer, and you'll collect the benefit for fewer months.

If you know that you have a health problem that shortens your life expectancy, you may benefit from drawing your company pension and CPP/QPP benefits sooner. If you plan to continue working in some capacity and earning a decent income after you leave your employer, waiting for higher pension benefits when you're in a lower tax bracket is probably wise.

As for your other choices that affect what amount your surviving spouse receives from your employer's pension plan should you die first, at one end of the spectrum you have the risky single life option, which pays benefits until you pass away, and then provides no benefits for your spouse thereafter. This option maximizes your monthly take while you are alive. Consider this option only if your spouse can do without this income. The least risky option, and thus least financially rewarding while the pensioner is still living, is the 100-percent joint and survivor option, which pays your survivor the same amount that you received while still alive. The other joint and survivor options fall somewhere in between these two extremes and generally make sense for most couples who desire decent pensions early in retirement but want a reasonable amount to continue should the pensioner die first.

✔ **Get your estate in order.** Confronting your mortality is never a joy, but when you're considering retirement or you're already retired, getting your estate in order makes all the more sense. Find out about wills and trusts that may benefit you and your heirs. You may also want to consider giving monetary gifts now if you have more than you need. You can't take it with you, and if you're worried about taxes that will be triggered by your death, gifting money to your heirs will generally reduce those taxes.

Chapter 22

Ten Things More Important Than Money

. . . .

In This Chapter

▶ Understanding what's really important

▶ Taking time to appreciate the good things in life

. . . .

*T*hroughout this book, we provide information and advice that enable you to make the most of your money. Whether you've been sticking with us since Chapter 1, or you've simply been skimming a few chapters, you probably know that we take a holistic approach to money decisions.

Although we hope that our financial advice serves you well, we also want to be sure that you remember the many things in life (we chose our ten favourites) that are far more important than the girth of your investment portfolio or the size of your latest paycheque. Too often in our capitalistic society, we place too much emphasis on financial success and status, and too little importance on living with a higher purpose. We hope this chapter makes a small contribution to keeping you on the best path.

Putting Your Family First

In North American culture, men (and increasingly, women) see their primary role as being the financial provider for their families. Such a focus seems to permit people to feel comfortable making sacrifices for the sake of their work and careers. We also seem to psychologically justify placing work before family, because we're taught the virtues of a strong work ethic.

Some employees rightfully fear that their bosses may not be sympathetic to the needs of their families, especially when those needs get in the way of getting the job done as efficiently as an impatient boss would like. Others put their companies first because that's what their peers do, and because they don't want to rock the boat.

Your spouse, your parents, and your kids, of course, should come first. They're much more important than your next promotion, and you should treat them that way. Balance is key. If your boss doesn't respect or value the importance of family, perhaps it's time to find a new boss.

Making and Keeping Friends

The older some people get, the less time they seem to have for friends. People who are too busy climbing the career ladder may not even make time for friends.

So many items in our consumer-oriented society are disposable, and unfortunately, friends too often fall into that category. Many friends aren't really friends as much as they are acquaintances who can further our careers, and when that function has been fulfilled, they're tossed aside.

What friends do you really care for? Do you have friends you can turn to in a time of need who can really listen and be there for you? Take the time to invest in your friendships, both old and new.

Investing in Your Health

Stress, poor diet, lack of exercise, problematic relationships within your family — all of these bad habits can have adverse personal health consequences. People neglect their health for different reasons. In some cases, as with money management, people lack the knowledge of the keys to good personal health. Getting too caught up in your career and working endless hours also often lead to the neglect of your health.

Some people don't fully realize what the downside may be of neglecting their bodies. The worst case, of course, is your untimely demise. But plenty of people suffer from ongoing conditions that damage the body and can make them feel far less well than they could feel. Unless you believe in reincarnation, you only get one body — take care of it and treat it with the respect it deserves!

Caring for Kids

Investing in your children is absolutely one of the best investments you can make. Understanding how to relate to and care for kids can help make you a better and more fulfilled person. (And we think that understanding kids can help you better understand what makes grown-ups tick, too!)

Our children are our future. You should care about children even if you don't have any. Why? Do you care about the quality of our society? Do you have any concerns about crime? Do you care about the economy? How about entertainment and the arts?

All of these issues depend to a large extent on our nation's children and what kind of teenagers and adults they will someday become. We know that many parents struggle to balance the demands of work and raising kids. We think that everyone benefits when parents find ways to work at their careers less and spend more time with their children. Find ways to make do with what money (and things) you have. When your children are grown, they won't remember — or appreciate — whether you were able to buy them more computer software or Yu-Gi-Oh! cards by working harder at your career. They will remember — and won't appreciate — a lack of attention.

Knowing Your Neighbours

Your neighbours can be sources of friendship, happiness, and comfort. Too often, we see people getting caught up in their daily routines and neglecting their neighbours.

Of course, you may not want to get to know all your neighbours better. But give them a chance. Don't write them off because they aren't the same age or race, or because they don't have the same occupation as you. Part of our coherence with our greater society comes from where we live, and our neighbours are an important piece of that connection. Don't miss out on it.

Appreciating What You Do Have

In our work in the personal finance world, we have the opportunity to interact with many people from all walks of life. Despite the overall level of affluence in our society, we continue to be struck by how many people focus on and lament the material things they lack (a bigger house, more costly cars, and so on) rather than appreciate the material and non-material things they do have.

Right now, make a list of at least ten things you appreciate. Periodically (daily, weekly, or monthly), make a similar list. Our culture sometimes causes us to dwell on what we don't have, which is usually not nearly as important as what we do have.

Minding Your Reputation

What do you think of when we say Jean Chrétien, Brian Mulroney, Alan Eagleson, or Conrad Black? All of these people can be deemed successful in a career and monetary sense, but is that what first came to your mind?

As one sage summed it up, "It can take a lifetime to build a reputation but only moments to lose it." As people chase after more fame, power, money, and possessions, they often devalue and underinvest in relationships, and breach the other commandments along the way.

Think of the people you most admire in your life. Although we're sure that none of them are perfect, we bet each has a superior reputation with you.

Continuing Your Education

Education is a lifelong process — it's not just about attending a fancy university and perhaps getting an advanced degree. Whether the education is related to your career or a new-found hobby, you can always find something to learn. As long as you have your mental capacities, you can keep learning and building on what you already know.

And, who knows, maybe someday you'll gain an understanding of the meaning of life. The older we get, the more we have to reflect on and learn from.

Having Fun

In the quest to earn more, save more, and invest smarter, some people get so caught up in society's money game that money becomes the purpose of their existence. Whether you call it an addiction or obsession, having such a financial focus will surely steer you from the good things in life. We've known plenty of people who realize too late in life that sacrificing personal relationships and one's health isn't worth any amount of financial success.

Therapists' offices are filled with unhappy people who spend too much time and energy chasing promotions and money. We come across these people as well. Often, they seem to worry about having enough money. When we tell them that they have "enough," the conversation usually turns to the personal things lacking in their lives.

Solving Social Problems

Although Canada may well have a strong economy and a high per capita income, by other more important measures Canadians have a good deal of room for improvement. Illiteracy, child poverty, gun violence, degradation of the environment, violence against women, and global warming are all major problems.

Why not be part of the solution rather than part of the problem? You can find plenty of causes worthy of your volunteer time or donations, such as Big Brothers Big Sisters, which partners adults with children for informal mentoring, Mothers Against Drunk Driving (MADD), which works to reduce drunk driving accidents, and Habitat for Humanity, which helps build affordable housing.

Find a cause that gets your juices flowing, and get involved. Join a group dedicated to protecting the environment such as the World Wildlife Fund (www.wwfcanada.org) or Greenpeace (www.greenpeace.ca). Consider service clubs that raises money for everything from medical aid in the developing world to deserving local area students, such as Rotary (www.rotary.org) or the Lion's Club (www.lionnct.com/canada.html). And don't overlook local or neighbourhood clubs and volunteers groups, from helping out with the local school's parents' association, to Scouts Canada (Beavers, Cubs, Scouts, and other programs for boys), Girl Guides (Sparks, Brownies, Guides, and other programs for girls), library or hospital volunteer groups, or youth and sports organizations.

Glossary

· ·

adjusted cost basis: For capital gains tax purposes, the adjusted cost basis is how Canada Revenue Agency determines your profit or loss when you sell an asset such as a home or a security. For an investment such as a mutual fund or stock, your cost basis is what you originally invested plus any reinvested money. For real estate, you arrive at the adjusted cost basis by adding the original purchase price to the cost of any capital improvements (expenditures that increase your property's value and life expectancy).

alternative minimum tax (AMT): The name given to a sort of shadow tax system that may cause you to pay a higher amount in income taxes than you otherwise would. The AMT was designed to prevent higher-income earners from lowering their tax bills too much through large deductions.

American Stock Exchange (AMEX): The second largest stock exchange in the United States; it typically lists mid-sized firms and many of the new exchange-traded stock funds.

annuity: An investment that is a contract backed by an insurance company. An annuity is frequently purchased for retirement purposes. Its main benefit is that it allows your money to compound and grow without taxation until withdrawal. Selling annuities is a lucrative source of income for insurance agents and financial planners who work on commission, so don't buy an annuity until you're sure that it makes sense for your situation.

asset allocation: When you invest your money, you need to decide how to proportion it (allocate) between risky, growth-oriented investments (such as stocks), with values that fluctuate, and more stable, income-producing investments (like bonds). How soon you will need the money and how tolerant you are of risk are two important determinants when deciding how to allocate your money.

audit: A Canada Revenue Agency examination of your financial records to substantiate your tax return. Audits are among life's worst experiences.

bank prime rate: *See* **prime rate.**

bankruptcy: Legal action that puts a halt to creditors' attempts to collect unpaid debts from you. If you have a high proportion of consumer debt to annual income, filing for bankruptcy may be your best option.

bear market: A period (such as the early 2000s) when the stock market experiences a strong downward swing. It is often accompanied by (and sometimes precedes) an economic recession. Imagine a bear in hibernation, because this is what happens in a bear market: investors hibernate, the market falters, and the value of stocks can decrease significantly. The market usually has to drop at least 20 percent before it is considered a bear market.

beneficiaries: The people to whom you want to leave your assets — or, in the case of life insurance or a pension plan, benefits — in the event of your death. You denote beneficiaries for each of your retirement plans.

blue-chip stock: The stock of the largest and most consistently profitable corporations. This term comes from poker, where the most valuable chips are blue. The list of these stocks is unofficial and changes.

bond: A loan investors make to a corporation or government. Bonds generally pay a set amount of interest on a regular basis. They're an appropriate investment vehicle for conservative investors who don't feel comfortable with the risk involved in investing in stocks and who want to receive a steady income. All bonds have a maturity date when the bond issuer must pay back the bond at par (full) value to the bondholders (lenders). Bonds should not be your primary long-term investment vehicle, because they produce little real growth on your original investment after inflation is factored in.

bond rating: *See* **Standard & Poor's ratings** and **Moody's ratings.**

bond yield: A yield is quoted as an annual percentage rate of return that a bond will produce based on its current value if it makes its promised interest payments. How much a bond will yield to an investor depends on three important factors: the stated interest rate paid by the bond, changes in the creditworthiness of the bond's issuer, and the maturity date of the bond. The better the rating a bond receives, the less risk involved and, thus, the lower the yield. As far as the maturity date is concerned, the longer you loan your money, the higher the risk (because it is more likely that rates will fluctuate) and the higher your yield generally will be.

broker: A person who acts as an intermediary for the purchase or sale of investments. When you buy a house, insurance, or stock, you most likely do so through a broker. Most brokers are paid on commission, which creates a conflict of interest with their clients. The more the broker sells, the more he or she makes. But more is not necessarily better for you. Some insurance companies let you buy their policies directly, and many mutual fund families bypass stockbrokers. If you're going to work with a broker, a discount broker can help you save on commissions.

bull market: A period (such as most of the 1990s in Canada and the United States) when the stock market experiences a strong upward swing, usually accompanied and driven by a growing economy and increasing corporate profits.

callable bond: A bond for which the lender can decide to pay the holder earlier than the previously agreed-upon maturity date. If interest rates are relatively high when a bond is issued, lenders may prefer issuing callable bonds because they have the flexibility to call back these bonds and issue new, lower-interest-rate bonds if interest rates decline. Callable bonds are risky for investors, because if interest rates decrease, the bond holder will get his investment money returned early and may have to reinvest his money at a lower interest rate.

capital gain: The profit from selling your stock at a higher price than the price for which it was purchased. For example, if you buy 50 shares of Rocky and Bullwinkle stock at $20 per share, and two years later you sell your shares when the price rises to $25 per share, your profit or capital gain is $5 per share, or $250. If you hold this Rocky and Bullwinkle stock outside of a tax-sheltered retirement plan, you'll owe tax on this profit when you sell the stock.

capital gains distribution: Taxable distribution by a mutual fund or real estate investment trust (REIT) created by securities that are sold within the fund or REIT at a profit.

cash value insurance: A type of life insurance that is extremely popular with insurance salespeople because it commands a high commission. In a cash value policy, you buy life insurance coverage but also get a savings-type account. Avoid cash value insurance unless you're looking for ways to limit your taxable estate (if you're extremely wealthy, for example). The investment returns tend to be mediocre, and your contributions are not tax-deductible.

closed-end mutual fund: A mutual fund that decides upfront exactly how many shares it is going to issue to investors. After all the shares are sold, an investor seeking to invest in the closed-end fund can do so only by purchasing shares from an existing investor. Shares of closed-end funds trade on the major stock exchanges and therefore sell at either a discount if the sellers exceed the buyers, or at a premium if demand exceeds supply.

commercial paper: A short-term debt or IOU issued by larger, stable companies to help make their businesses grow and prosper. Creditworthy companies can sell this debt security directly to large investors and thus bypass borrowing money from bankers. Money market funds invest in soon-to-mature commercial paper.

commission: The percentage of the selling price of a house, stock, bond, or other investment that is paid to agents and brokers. Because most agents and brokers are paid by commission, understanding how the commission can influence their behaviour and recommendations is important for investors and homebuyers. Agents and brokers make money only when you make a purchase, and they make more money when you make a bigger purchase. Choose an agent carefully, and take your agent's advice with a grain of salt, because this inherent conflict of interest can often set an agent's visions and goals at odds with your own.

commodity: A financial instrument whose value is derived from the performance of an underlying security such as a stock or bond. Commodities are a form of derivatives. Raw materials (gold, wheat, sugar, and gasoline, for example) are commodities traded on the futures market.

common stock: Shares in a company that don't offer a guaranteed amount of dividend to investors; the amount of dividend distributions, if any, is at the discretion of company management. While common stock investors may or may not make money through dividends, they hope that the stock price is going to appreciate as the company expands its operations and increases its profits. Common stock tends to offer you a better return (profit) than other investments, such as bonds or preferred shares. However, if the company falters, you may lose some or all of your original investment.

comparable market analysis (CMA): A written analysis of similar houses currently being offered for sale and that have recently sold. CMAs are usually completed by real estate agents.

consumer debt: Debt on consumer items that depreciate in value over time. Credit card balances and auto loans are examples of consumer debt. This type of debt is bad for your financial health because it is high-interest and it encourages you to live beyond your means.

Consumer Price Index (CPI): The Consumer Price Index reports price changes, on a monthly basis, in the cost of living for such items as food, housing, transportation, health care, entertainment, clothing, and other miscellaneous expenses. The CPI is used to adjust government benefits and is used by many employers to determine cost-of-living increases in wages and pensions. An increase in prices is also known as inflation.

credit report: A report that details your credit history. It is the main report that a lender uses to determine whether or not to give you a loan. You must generally pay the lender to obtain this report.

debit card: When you use a debit card, the cost of the purchase is deducted from your bank account. Thus, a debit card gives you the convenience of a credit card without the danger of building up a mountain of consumer debt.

deductible: With insurance, the deductible is the amount you pay when you file a claim. For example, say that your car sustains $800 of damage. If your deductible is $500, the insurance covers $300 and you pay $500 out of your own pocket for the repairs. The higher the deductible, the lower your insurance premiums, and the less paperwork you expose yourself to when filing claims (because small losses that are less than the deductible don't require filing a claim). Take the highest deductibles that you can afford when selecting insurance.

deduction: An expense you may subtract from your income to lower your taxable income. Examples include childcare expenses, business losses, and most retirement plan contributions.

derivative: An investment instrument whose value is derived from other securities. For example, an option to buy IBM stock does not have value in itself; the value is derived from the price of IBM's stock.

disability insurance: During your working years, you have a lot riding on your ability to earn an income. Without it, you'd be in big trouble (unless a wealthy relative, wife, husband, or friend can support you). Disability insurance replaces a portion of your employment income in the unlikely event that you suffer a disability that keeps you from working.

discount broker: Unlike a full-service broker, a discount broker generally offers no investment advice and has employees who work on salary rather than on commission. Using a discount broker helps you avoid the conflict of interest that will inevitably come up with a so-called full-service broker. In addition to trading individual securities, most discount brokerage firms also offer no-load (commission-free) mutual funds.

diversification: If you put all of your money into one type of investment, you're potentially setting yourself up for a big shock. If that investment collapses, so does your investment world. By spreading (diversifying) your money among different investments — bonds, Canadian stocks, international stocks, and so on — you ensure yourself a better chance of investing success and fewer sleepless nights.

dividend: Quotient, divisor, dividend? Forget elementary school math. The dividend is the income paid to investors holding an investment. With stock, the dividend is the portion of a company's profits paid to its shareholders. For example, if a company has an annual dividend of $2 per share and you own 100 shares, your total dividend is $200. Usually, established and slower-growing companies pay dividends, while smaller and faster growing companies reinvest their profits for growth.

Dow Jones Industrial Average (DJIA): A widely followed stock market index comprised of 30 large, actively traded U.S. company stocks. Senior editors at the *Wall Street Journal* select the stocks in the DJIA.

down payment: The part of the purchase price for a house that the buyer pays in cash upfront and does not finance with a mortgage. Generally, the larger the down payment, the better the deal you can get on a mortgage. You can usually get access to the best mortgage programs with a down payment of at least 25 percent of the home's purchase price.

earthquake insurance: Although the West Coast is often associated with earthquakes, other areas are also quake-prone. An earthquake insurance rider (which usually comes with a deductible of 5 to 10 percent of the cost to rebuild the home) on a homeowner's policy pays to repair or rebuild your home if it is damaged in an earthquake. If you live in an area with earthquake risk, get earthquake insurance coverage!

Emerging Markets Index: The Emerging Markets Index, which is published by Morgan Stanley, tracks stock markets in developing countries. The main reason for investing in emerging markets is that these economies typically experience a higher rate of economic growth than developed markets. However, the potential for higher returns is coupled with greater risk.

equity: In the real estate world, this term refers to the difference between the market value of your home and what you owe on it. For example, if your home is worth $200,000, and you have an outstanding mortgage of $140,000, your equity is $60,000. Equity is also a synonym for stock.

estate: The value, at the time of your death, of your assets minus your loans and liabilities.

estate planning: The process of deciding where your assets will go when you die, and structuring your assets during your lifetime so as to minimize taxes due upon your death.

financial assets: A property or investment (such as real estate or a stock, mutual fund, bond, and so on) that has value that can be realized if sold.

financial liabilities: Your outstanding loans and debts. To determine your net worth, you must subtract your financial liabilities from your financial assets.

financial planners: A sometimes motley crew that professes an ability to manage your money. Financial planners come with varying backgrounds and degrees: MBAs and Certified Financial Planners, to name a few. A useful way to distinguish among this mixed bag of nuts is to determine whether the planners are commission-, fee-, or hourly-based.

fixed-rate mortgage: The granddaddy of all mortgages. You lock into an interest rate (for example, 7 percent), and it never changes during the life (term) of your mortgage. Your mortgage payment will be the same amount each and every month. If you become a cursing, frothing maniac when you miss your morning coffee or someone is five minutes late, then this mortgage may be for you!

flood insurance: If there's even a remote chance that your area may flood, having flood insurance, which reimburses rebuilding your home and replacing its contents in the event of a flood, is prudent.

full-service broker: A broker who gives advice and charges a high commission relative to discount brokers. Because the brokers work on commission, they have a significant conflict of interest: namely, to advocate strategies that will be of financial benefit to them.

futures: An obligation to buy or sell a commodity or security on a specific day for a preset price. When used by most individual investors, futures represent a short-term gamble on the short-term direction of the price of a commodity. Companies and farmers use futures contracts to hedge their risks of changing prices.

guaranteed investment certificates (GICs): Investments offered by most financial institutions that appeal to skittish investors. GICs generally tell you in advance what your interest rate will be for the term of the loan you are making, generally one to ten years. Thus, you don't have to worry about fluctuations and losses in your investment value. On the other hand, GICs offer you little upside, because the interest rate is comparable to what you may get on a high-interest savings account.

home equity: *See* **equity.**

home-equity loan: Technical jargon for what used to be called a second mortgage. With this type of loan, you borrow against the equity in your house. If used wisely, a home-equity loan can help pay off high-interest consumer debt or be tapped for other short-term needs (such as a remodelling project). In contrast with consumer debt, mortgage debt is usually at a lower interest rate.

homeowner's insurance: Dwelling coverage that covers the cost of rebuilding your house in the event of fire or other calamity. The liability insurance portion of this policy protects you against lawsuits associated with your property. Another essential element of homeowner's insurance is the personal property coverage, which pays to replace your damaged or stolen worldly possessions.

index: A security market index, such as the S&P/TSX Index, is a statistical composite that measures the performance of a particular type of security. Indexes exist for various stock and bond markets and are typically set at a round number such as 100 at a particular point in time. *See also* **S&P/TSX composite index** and **Dow Jones Industrial Average.**

inflation: The technical term for a rise in prices. Inflation usually occurs when too much money is in circulation and not enough goods and services are available to spend it on. As a result of this excess demand, prices rise. A link is present between inflation and interest rates: If interest rates do not keep up with inflation, no one will invest in bonds issued by the government or corporations. When the interest rates on bonds are high, it usually reflects a high rate of inflation that will eat away at your return.

initial public offering (IPO): The first time a company offers shares to the investing public. An IPO typically occurs when a company wants to expand more rapidly and seeks additional money to support its growth. A number of studies have demonstrated that buying into IPOs in which the general public can participate produces subpar investment returns. A high level of IPO activity may indicate a cresting stock market, as companies and their investment bankers rush to cash in on a "pricey" marketplace. (IPO could stand for It's Probably Overpriced.)

interest rate: The rate lenders charge you to use their money. The higher the interest rate, the higher the risk entailed in the loan. With bonds of a given maturity, a higher rate of interest means a lower quality of bond — one that is less likely to return your money.

international stock markets: Stock markets outside of Canada account for a significant portion of the world stock market capitalization (value). Some specific stock indices track international markets (*see* **Morgan Stanley EAFE index** and **Emerging Markets Index**). International investing offers one way for you to diversify your portfolio and reduce your risk. In addition to the U.S., some of the foreign countries with major stock exchanges include Japan, Britain, France, and Germany.

junk bond: A bond rated Ba (Moody's) or BB (Standard & Poor's) and lower. Historically, these bonds have had a 1- to 2-percent chance of default, which is not exactly "junky." Of course, the higher risk is accompanied by a higher interest rate.

leverage: Financial leverage affords its users a disproportionate amount of financial power relative to the amount of their own cash invested. In some circumstances, you can borrow up to 50 percent of a stock price and use all funds (both yours and those that you borrow) to make a purchase. You repay this so-called margin loan when you sell the stock. If the stock price rises, you make money on what you invested plus what you borrowed. While this money sounds attractive, remember that leverage cuts both ways — when prices decline, you lose money not only on your investment but also on the money you borrowed.

limited partnership (LP): These partnerships, which are often promoted in a way that promises high returns, generally limit one thing: your investment return. Why? Because they're burdened with high commissions and management fees. Another problem is that they're typically not liquid for many years.

load mutual fund: A mutual fund that includes a sales load, which is the commission paid to brokers who sell commission-based mutual funds. The commission typically ranges up to 6 percent. This commission is deducted from your investment money, so it reduces your returns.

marginal tax rate: The rate of income tax you pay on the last dollars you earn over the course of a year. Why the complicated distinction? Because all income is not treated equally: You pay less tax on your first dollars of your annual earnings and more tax on the last dollars of your annual income. Knowing your marginal tax rate is helpful because it can help you analyze the tax implications of important personal financial decisions.

market capitalization: The value of all the outstanding stock of a company. Market capitalization is the quoted price per share of a stock multiplied by the number of shares outstanding. Thus, if Rocky and Bullwinkle Corporation has 100 million shares of outstanding stock, and the quoted price per share is $20, the company has a market capitalization of $2 billion (100 million = $20).

Moody's ratings: Moody's rating service measures and rates the credit (default) risks of various bonds. Moody's investigates the financial condition of a bond issuer. Its ratings use the following grading system, which is expressed from highest to lowest: Aaa, Aa, A, Baa, Ba, B, Caa, Ca, C. Higher ratings imply a lower risk but also mean that the interest rate will be lower.

Morgan Stanley EAFE (Europe, Australia, Far East) index: The Morgan Stanley EAFE index tracks the performance of the more established countries' stock markets in Europe and Asia. This index is important for international-minded investors who want to follow the performance of overseas stock investments.

mortgage broker: Mortgage brokers buy mortgages wholesale from lenders and then mark the mortgages up (typically from 0.5 to 1 percent) and sell them to borrowers. A good mortgage broker is most helpful for people who don't want to shop around on their own for a mortgage, or people who have blemishes on their credit reports.

mortgage life insurance: Mortgage life insurance guarantees that the lender will receive its money in the event that you meet an untimely demise. Many people may try to convince you that you need this insurance to protect your dependants and loved ones. Mortgage life insurance is relatively expensive given the cost of the coverage provided. If you need life insurance, buy low-cost, high-quality term life insurance instead.

mutual fund: A portfolio of stocks, bonds, or other securities that is owned by numerous investors and managed by an investment company. *See also* **no-load mutual fund.**

NASDAQ (National Association of Securities Dealers Automated Quotation) system: An electronic network that allows brokers to trade from their offices all over the U.S. With NASDAQ, brokers buy and sell shares using constantly updated prices that appear on their computer screens.

negative amortization: Although it may sound like a description of the cause of dinosaur extinction, negative amortization occurs when your outstanding mortgage balance increases despite the fact that you're making the required monthly payments. Negative amortization occurs with adjustable-rate mortgages that cap the increase in your monthly payment but do not cap the interest rate. Therefore, your monthly payments do not cover all the interest that you actually owe. Avoid loans with this "feature."

net asset value (NAV): The dollar value of one share of a mutual fund. For a no-load fund, the market price is its NAV. For a load fund, the NAV is the "buy" price minus the commission.

New York Stock Exchange (NYSE): The largest stock exchange in the world in terms of total volume and value of shares traded. It lists companies that tend to be among the world's oldest, largest, and best-known.

no-load mutual fund: A mutual fund that doesn't come with a commission payment attached to it. Because of the lack of a load and the generally lower management fees of these funds, they tend to have better returns than load funds. Some funds claim to be no-load, but they simply hide their sales commissions as an ongoing sales charge. You can avoid these funds by educating yourself and reading the prospectuses carefully.

open-end mutual fund: A mutual fund that issues as many shares as investors demand. These open-end funds do not generally limit the number of investors or amount of money in the fund. Some open-end funds have been known to close to new investors, but investors with existing shares can often still buy more shares from the company.

option: The right to buy or sell a specific security (such as a stock) for a preset price during a specified period of time. Options differ from futures in that with an option you pay a premium fee upfront, and you can either exercise the option or let it expire. If the option expires worthless, you lose 100 percent of your original investment. The use of options is best left to companies as hedging tools. Investment managers may use options as a hedging tool to reduce the risk in their investment portfolio. Like with futures, when most individual investors buy an option they're doing so as a short-term gamble, not as an investment. For example: You have an option to buy 100 shares of Rocky and Bullwinkle Co. stock at $20 per share in the next six months. You pay $3 per share upfront as the premium. During this time period, R&B's share price rises to $30, and you exercise your right to buy at $20. You then sell your shares at the market price of $30; you make a $10 profit per share, which is a return more than three times larger than your original investment.

pension: Pensions are a benefit offered by some employers. These plans generally pay you a monthly retirement income based on your years of service with the employer, or based on the value of your pension plan contributions when you retire.

performance: You traditionally judge an investment's performance by looking at the historical rate of return. The longer the period over which these numbers are tallied, the more useful they are. Considered alone, these numbers are practically meaningless. You must also note how well a fund has performed in comparison to competitors with the same investment objectives. Beware of advertisements that tout the high returns of a mutual fund, because they may not be looking at risk-adjusted performance, or they may be promoting performance over a short time period. Keep in mind that high return statistics are usually coupled with high risk, and that this year's star may turn out to be next year's crashing meteor.

preferred stock: Stock that offers a guaranteed number of dividend payments to investors. Preferred stock dividends must be paid before any dividends are paid to the common stock shareholders. Although preferred stock reduces your risk as an investor (because of the more secure dividend and greater likelihood of getting your money back if the company fails), it also often limits your reward if the company expands and increases its profits.

price/earnings (P/E) ratio: The current price of a stock divided by the current (or sometimes the projected) earnings per share of the issuing company. This ratio is a widely used stock analysis statistic that helps an investor get an idea of how cheap or expensive a stock price is. In general, a relatively high P/E ratio indicates that investors believe the company's earnings are likely to grow quickly.

prime rate: The rate of interest that major banks charge their most creditworthy corporate customers. Why should you care? Well, because the interest rates on various loans you might be interested in are often based on the prime rate. And, guess what — you pay a higher interest rate than those big corporations!

principal: No, we're not talking about the big boss from elementary school who struck fear into the hearts of most eight-year-olds. The principal is the amount you borrow for a loan. If you borrow $100,000, your principal is $100,000. Principal can also refer to the amount you originally placed in an investment.

prospectus: Individual companies and mutual funds are required by securities regulators to issue a prospectus. For a company, the prospectus is a legal document presenting a detailed analysis of that company's financial history, its products and services, its management's background and experience, and the risks of investing in the company. A mutual fund prospectus tells you about the fund's investment objectives, costs, risk, and performance history.

real estate investment trust (REIT): Real estate investment trusts are like a mutual fund of real estate investments. Such trusts invest in a collection of properties (from shopping centres to apartment buildings). REITs trade on the major stock exchanges. If you want to invest in real estate while avoiding the hassles inherent in owning property, real estate investment trusts may be the right choice for you.

refinance: Refinance is a fancy word for taking out a new mortgage loan (usually at a lower interest rate) to pay off an existing mortgage (generally at a higher interest rate). Refinancing is not automatic, nor is it guaranteed. Refinancing can also be a hassle and expensive. Weigh the costs and benefits of refinancing carefully before proceeding.

Registered Education Savings Plan (RESP): A special account in which you can save money to pay for a post-secondary education. The money you put in does not earn you a tax deduction. The money inside the plan, however, can grow tax free. The profits are taxed when the money is withdrawn to pay for education costs, but it is taxed as income to the student. Since their overall income is likely to be very low, they will generally have to pay little if any tax on the proceeds.

Registered Retirement Income Fund (RRIF): A type of retirement savings account that allows your investments to grow tax free. Unlike an RRSP, you cannot make annual contributions to an RRIF. Instead, you are required to withdraw at least a certain minimum amount each year, which is taxed as regular income.

Registered Retirement Savings Plan (RRSP): A type of retirement savings plan available to almost everybody who has earned some money either through a job or by being self-employed. Your contributions are usually exempt (yes!) from federal and provincial income taxes and compound without taxation over time. The money, however, is taxed as income when you withdraw it from the plan.

return on investment: The percentage of profit you make on an investment. If you put $1,000 into an investment, and then one year later it's worth $1,100, you make a profit of $100. Your return on investment is the profit ($100) divided by the initial investment ($1,000) — in this case, 10 percent.

reverse mortgage: A reverse mortgage enables elderly homeowners, typically those who are low on cash, to tap into their home's equity without selling their home or moving from it. Specifically, a lending institution makes a cheque out to you each month, and you can use the cheque as you want. This money is really a loan against the value of your home, so it is tax-free when you receive it. The downside of these loans is that they deplete your equity in your estate, the fees and interest rates tend to be on the high side, and some require repayment within a certain number of years.

S&P/TSX composite index: This index measures the broad performance of the Toronto Stock Exchange. If you invest in larger-company Canadian stock or stock funds, this is a good benchmark to compare the performance of your investments to.

S&P/TSX Venture composite index: This index measures the broad performance of the TSX Venture Exchange, where the shares of many smaller and emerging Canadian companies trade.

Securities and Exchange Commission (SEC): The U.S. federal agency that administers U.S. securities laws and regulates and monitors investment companies, brokers, and financial advisers.

Standard & Poor's 500 index: An index that measures the performance of 500 large-company U.S. stocks that account for about 80 percent of the total market value of all stocks traded in the United States. If you invest in larger-company U.S. stock or stock funds, the S&P 500 index is an appropriate benchmark for the performance of your investments.

Standard & Poor's (S&P) ratings: Standard & Poor's rating service is one of two services that measure and rate the risks in buying a bond. The S&P ratings use the following grading system, listed from highest to lowest: AAA, AA, A, BBB, BB, B, CCC, CC, C. *See also* **Moody's ratings.**

stock: Shares of ownership in a company. When a company goes public, it issues shares of stock to the public (*see also* **initial public offering**). Many, but not all, stocks pay dividends — a distribution of a portion of company profits. In addition to dividends, the other way you make money investing in stock is via appreciation in the price of the stock, which normally results from growth in revenues and corporate profits. You can invest in stock by purchasing individual shares or by investing in a stock mutual fund that offers a diversified package of stocks.

stripped (strip) bond: A bond that doesn't pay explicit interest during the term of the loan. Such bonds are purchased at a discounted price relative to the principal value paid at maturity. The interest-bearing coupons have been removed or stripped off. Thus, the interest is implicit in the discount.

term life insurance: If people are dependent on your income for their living expenses, you may need this insurance. Term life insurance functions simply: You determine how much protection you would like and then pay an annual premium based on that amount. Although it is much less touted by insurance salespeople than cash value insurance, it is the best life insurance out there for the vast majority of people.

Treasury bill (T-bills): IOUs from the federal government that mature within a year.

underwriting: The process an insurance company uses to evaluate a person's likelihood of filing a claim on a particular type of insurance policy. If significant problems are discovered, an insurer will often propose much higher rates or refuse to sell the insurance coverage.

will: A legal document that ensures that your wishes regarding your assets and the care of your minor children are heeded when you die.

Wilshire 5000: Despite the name, this index actually tracks closer to 6,000 companies of all sizes on major U.S. stock exchanges. If you invest in U.S. stock or stock funds of companies of all sizes, this index is an appropriate benchmark.

zero-coupon bond: A bond that doesn't pay explicit interest during the term of the loan. Zero-coupon bonds are purchased at a discounted price relative to the principal value paid at maturity. Thus, the interest is implicit in the discount. These bonds do not offer a tax break, because the investor must pay taxes on the interest he would have received.

Index

• A •

accessories, cost of, 110
accident benefits coverage, 357
addiction
  credit as, 62–63, 86–87
  reducing cost of, 118–119
adjustable mortgages. *See* variable-rate
    mortgages
adjusted cost basis, defined, 433
adult education classes, 381
Advocis, 367, 383
age credit, 136
agents. *See* insurance agents; real estate
    agents
aging parents, 420–421
alcohol, cost of, 118–119
alimony deduction, 129
allocation. *See* asset allocation
alternative medicine, cost of, 116
alternative minimum tax (AMT), 124, 433
American Stock Exchange (AMEX), 433
AMEX. *See* American Stock Exchange
    (AMEX)
amortization, 283–284
AMT. *See* alternative minimum tax (AMT)
annual reports, and mutual funds, 207–208
annuities, 194, 232–234, 244–245, 260,
    325, 433
appraisals, and mortgage application, 289
asset allocation
  defined, 159–162, 433
  and investments, 257–260
  and retirement plans, 235–239
  and RRSPs, 239–244
asset allocation funds. *See* hybrid funds
assets, 25–27, 438
attribution rules, 362
audits, 141–143, 433
auto insurance, 354–358

• B •

back-end loads, defined, 209
backup loans, and mortgages, 297
bad debt. *See* debt
balanced funds. *See* hybrid funds
balancing chequebook, 70
banking online, 393
bankruptcy, 79–83, 433
basic personal tax credit, 132
BBB. *See* Better Business Bureau (BBB)
bear market, defined, 434
beneficiaries, defined, 434
Better Business Bureau (BBB), 96
bill-payment online, 394
blue-chip stock, defined, 434
bodily injury liability coverage, 354–355
bond funds, 202, 237, 257
bond yield, defined, 434
bonds, 154–155, 177–179, 434
books, financial, 405–407
brand names, 94
broker–dealer networks, 166
brokerage-house RRSPs, 228
brokerages. *See* investment firms
brokers. *See also* insurance brokers
    defined, 434
budgeting, 99, 417
bull market, defined, 434
business losses deduction, 129
business purchase, saving for, 41
buyer's brokers, 302

• C •

callable bonds, 179, 435
Canada Access Grants, 271
Canada Education Savings Grants (CESGs),
    265–267
Canada Pension Plan (CPP), 46–47, 333–334

Canada Revenue Agency (CRA), and tax help, 138
Canada Student Loan Program (CSLP), 269–271
capital gains, 126, 215, 361–362, 435
capital gains distribution, defined, 435
car loans, 61–62
caregiver's credit, 135
carpooling, 109
cars, purchasing, 107–109
CAs. *See* chartered accountants (CAs)
cash-value life insurance, 40, 75, 195, 273, 334–338, 340–341, 362, 435
catastrophes, and insurance, 316–317
CCS. *See* Credit Counselling Service (CCS)
cell phones, reducing cost, 105
certified financial planners (CFPs), 367
certified general accountants (CGAs), 140
CESG. *See* Canada Education Savings Grants (CESGs)
CFAs. *See* chartered financial analysts (CFAs)
CFPs. *See* certified financial planners (CFPs)
CGAs. *See* certified general accountants (CGAs)
charge card, defined, 85
charitable donations credit, 132–133
chartered accountants (CAs), 140–141
chartered financial analysts (CFAs), 385
chequebook software, 393–394
chequing accounts, 176, 252–254
child support deduction, 129
childcare expenses deduction, 128
children, and financial challenges, 416–419
children's benefit, and CPP/QPP, 47, 334
claims, insurance, 326–329
clone funds, 240
closed mortgages, 286
closed-end mutual funds, defined, 435
clothing costs, reducing, 109–110
CMA. *See* comparable market analysis (CMA)
COLAs. *See* cost-of-living adjustments (COLAs)

cold calling, 381
collectibles, 194–195
college. *See* education expenses
collision deductibles, 356
commercial paper, defined, 435
commissions
    defined, 167, 435
    and financial planners, 371–372, 377–378
    and insurance, 322–325, 337–338
    and mutual funds, 208–210
commodities, 151, 436
common stock, defined, 436
common-law couples, and taxes, 130
commuter passes, 109
company shares, 238–239
comparable market analysis (CMA), 436
comprehensive deductibles, 356
computers
    and financial tasks, 393–400
    types of software and Web sites, 389–392
condominiums, defined, 298
conflicts of interest
    and financial planners, 167–169, 377–380
    and real estate agents, 300–301
consumer credit, defined, 42
consumer debt, defined, 436
Consumer Price Index (CPI), 436
consumer proposals, 84–85
contact lens insurance, 320
contribution deadline, and RRSPs, 225
contribution limits, and RRSPs, 222–225
contribution rate, to CPP/QPP, 46
contribution room, and RRSPs, 223
convertible mortgages, 288
cooperatives, defined, 298
corporate bonds, 179
cost-basis reports, 396
cost-of-living adjustments (COLAs), 344
coupon, defined, 177
coverage, and insurance, 320–321, 325–326
CPI. *See* Consumer Price Index (CPI)
CPP. *See* Canada Pension Plan (CPP)
CRA. *See* Canada Revenue Agency (CRA)

credit
    addiction to, 62–63, 86–87
    and overspending, 60–61
    reducing limit, 85
    reducing temptation, 85–86
    and renting to own, 98
credit cards
    benefits of, 24
    best choices, 110–112
    living without, 77–78
    low-interest-rate, 75–77
    and overspending, 60–61
Credit Counselling Service (CCS), 82
credit disability insurance, 319
credit life insurance, 319
credit reports, 87–89, 289, 296, 436
credits. *See* tax credits
CSLP. *See* Canada Student Loan Program
    (CSLP)
custodian, and mutual funds, 199

• *D* •

DA. *See* Debtors Anonymous (DA)
daytrading, 152–153
DCA. *See* dollar-cost averaging (DCA)
deal making, and real estate, 303–305
death benefit, and CPP/QPP, 47
debit cards, 78–79, 436
debt
    and bankruptcy, 79–83
    and consumer proposals, 84–85
    cost of, 110–112
    ending cycle, 85–87
    evaluating, 22–24, 73
    paying off as investment, 250
    reducing, 74–79
Debtors Anonymous (DA), 63, 86–87
deductibles, 117, 317–318, 353, 356, 436
deductions. *See* tax deductions
deferred profit-sharing plans (DPSPs), 225
deferred sales charges (DSCs), 209
defined-benefit plans, 49, 225
defined-contribution plans, 50
defined-term annuities, 233
dental insurance, 319
derivatives, 151, 437

detached homes, defined, 298
direct trustee to trustee transfer, 246–248
disability credit, 134–135
disability insurance, 341–344, 437
disability pension, and CPP/QPP, 47, 342
discharging debt, and bankruptcy, 80
discount brokers, 166, 242–243, 244, 437
diversification, 157–163, 198, 437
dividend funds, 259–260
dividends, 214–215, 437
divorce, 421–423
DJIA. *See* Dow Jones Industrial Average
    (DJIA)
dollar-cost averaging (DCA), 162–163
Dow Jones Industrial Average (DJIA), 437
down payments, 289–291, 437
DPSPs. *See* deferred profit-sharing plans
    (DPSPs)
drug abuse, cost of, 118–119
dry cleaning, 110
DSCs. *See* deferred sales charges (DSCs)
dwelling coverage, 350

• *E* •

early-withdrawal penalties, and RRSPs, 39
earned income, defined, 222, 223
earthquake insurance, 352–353, 438
eating out, 102
education expenses
    investment options, 264–268, 272–274
    loans, grants, and scholarships, 269–272
    and overspending, 63–64
    planning for, 41, 261–264
emergency reserves, 40–41, 251–256
Emerging Markets Index, defined, 438
employer insurance plans, 322–324
employment income taxes, reducing,
    125–126
entertainment costs, reducing, 112
equity, 25, 49, 75, 438
equity funds. *See* stock funds
equivalent-to-married credit. *See* wholly
    dependent person credit
estate, defined, 438
estate planning, 359–362, 438

ETFs. *See* exchange-traded funds (ETFs)
excess liability insurance. *See* umbrella insurance
exchange-traded funds (ETFs), 243–244, 273
expense shifting, and taxes, 153
extended warranties, 318–319

• *F* •

fee-based advisers, 372
financial assets, 25–27, 438
financial catastrophes, and insurance, 316–317
financial liabilities, 26–28, 438
financial net worth, 25–28
financial planners
  defined, 438
  finding, 382–383
  interviewing, 383–387
  options, 369–374
  problems with, 365–369, 376–381
  whether to hire, 374–376
Financial Planning Standards Council (FPSC), 367
financing. *See* mortgages
first job, 412–413
fixed-rate mortgages, 287–288, 438
flood insurance, 352–353, 438
food costs, reducing, 100–102
FPSC. *See* Financial Planning Standards Council (FPSC)
full-service broker, defined, 439
fund managers, 197–198, 212
funds of funds, 203
future insurability, defined, 344
futures, 151, 439

• *G* •

gambling, 119, 150–153
GICs. *See* guaranteed investment certificates (GICs)
gift costs, reducing, 113
GIS. *See* Guaranteed Income Supplement (GIS)

global funds, 204–205
goals. *See also* retirement preparation
  business purchase, 41
  defining, 33–36
  education expenses, 41, 263–264
  emergency reserves, 40–41
  home purchase, 41
  importance of, 63
  for investment, 147–148
  prioritizing, 37–39
  purchases, 42
going long, defined, 200
good debt. *See* debt
grace period, and credit cards, 24
grants, for education, 272
gross debt-service ratio, 278
group insurance plans, 322–324
growth stocks, defined, 203
guaranteed annuity, 233
Guaranteed Income Supplement (GIS), 48–49, 333
guaranteed investment certificates (GICs), 178, 237–238, 258, 439
guaranteed renewability, and insurance policies, 339, 343
guaranteed renewal rates, and insurance policies, 339
guaranteed replacement cost, 350, 351
guaranteed RRSPs, 227–228
guides, for tax-preparation, 139
gurus, investment, 172–173

• *H* •

hair care, cost of, 114
health club expenses, 114
hedge funds, 200–201
high-interest savings accounts, 252–254
high-ratio mortgages, 290–291
high-risk pool coverage, 326
Home Buyers' Plan, 291–293
home inspections, 304–305
home purchase, 41, 416. *See also* real estate
home warranty plans, 319
home-equity loan, defined, 439
homeowner expenses, reducing, 103–104

homeowner's insurance, 349–354, 439
hourly-based advisers, 372–373
housing costs, reducing, 102–104
hybrid funds, 204, 238

• *I* •

IAFP. *See* Institute of Advanced Financial
    Planners (IAFP)
implementation, of financial advice,
    386–387
in trust for (ITF) accounts. *See* in-trust
    accounts
in-trust accounts, 267–268
income shifting, defined, 126
income trusts, 185–186
incorporating, and taxes, 137
independent agent, defined, 326
index, defined, 439
index funds, 205–206, 243–244
indexed annuity, 233
indexed bonds, 259
inflation, defined, 439
initial public offering (IPO), defined, 440
inspections. *See* home inspections
Institute of Advanced Financial Planners
    (IAFP), 382–383
insurance
  buying, 315–325
  claims, 325–329
  disability policies, 341–344
  life policies, 332–341
  premium reduction, 116–117
  travel medical policies, 345–346
insurance agents, 322–325
insurance brokers, 322–325
interest on investment loans deduction,
    129–130
interest rate, defined, 440
interest-rate differential (IRD) penalty, 307
intermediate-term investments, defined,
    257
internal rate of return (IRR), 396
international funds, 204–205
international stock market, defined, 440
international stocks, 180

Internet
  banking, 393
  bill payment, 394
  financial Web sites, 391–392, 404
  finding periodicals, 398–399
  investment research, 397
  life insurance purchase, 399
  retirement planning, 395
  tax preparation, 139
  trading online, 397–398
investment banking, defined, 170
investment concepts
  advice, 173–174
  diversifying, 157–163
  goals, 147–148
  predictions, 171–173
  returns, 153–154
  risks, 154–156
  types of, 148–153
investment firms, 165–170, 243
investment gurus, 172–173
investment income taxes, reducing,
    126–127
investment insurance, 358
investment vehicles
  annuities, 194
  bonds, 177–179
  collectibles, 194–195
  income trusts, 185–186
  life insurance, 195
  precious metals, 193–194
  real estate, 186–191
  savings and money market accounts,
    176–177
  small businesses, 191–193
  stocks, 179–185
  transaction/chequing accounts, 176
IPO. *See* initial public offering (IPO)
IRD penalty. *See* interest-rate differential
    (IRD) penalty
IRR. *See* internal rate of return (IRR)
ITF accounts. *See* in-trust accounts

• *J* •

job changes, 413–414
joint-life annuity, 232
junk bonds, 179, 440

• L •

large cap, defined, 181
legal software, 399–400
lender, defined, 148
lending investments, 148–149, 175–179
leverage, defined, 187–188, 440
liabilities, 26–28, 438
liability insurance, 351
life annuity, 232
life changes
    aging parents, 420–421
    divorce, 421–423
    first job, 412–413
    having children, 416–419
    home purchase, 416
    job change, 413–414
    marriage, 414–416
    preparing for, 411–412, 417
    retiring, 424–426
    small business start-up, 419–420
    windfalls, 423–424
life income funds (LIFs), 234
life insurance
    buying online, 399
    cash-value policies, 340–341
    choosing, 332–338
    term policies, 338–340
Lifelong Learning Plan, 268
LIFs. *See* life income funds (LIFs)
limited partnerships (LPs), 189, 245, 440
LIRAs. *See* locked-in retirement accounts (LIRAs)
list billing, defined, 344
living trusts, 360–361
living wills, 359–360
load mutual funds, defined, 440
loads. *See* commissions
locked-in retirement accounts (LIRAs), 234, 248
locked-in retirement income funds (LRIFs), 234
locked-in RRSPs, 234, 248
long-term care (LTC) insurance, 346–347
long-term investments, defined, 257
long-term mortgages, 284–286
LPs. *See* limited partnerships (LPs)

LRIFs. *See* locked-in retirement income funds (LRIFs)
LTC insurance. *See* long-term care (LTC) insurance

• M •

magazines, financial, 404–405
maintenance payments deduction, 129
managed accounts, 170
marginal tax rate, 122–123, 441
market capitalization, defined, 181, 441
market neutral, defined, 200
marriage, 130, 414–416
masters of business administration (MBA), 385
maturing, of RRSPs, 228–234
MBA. *See* masters of business administration (MBA)
media, financial information in, 401–407
medical expenses, reducing, 115–116
medical expenses credit, 133–134
medical information report, 325–326
medical powers of attorney, 359–360
money market funds, 176–177, 201–202, 237, 254–255
money-purchase pension plans, 225
Moody's ratings, defined, 441
Morgan Stanley EAFE index, defined, 441
mortgage brokers, 295–296, 441
mortgage life insurance, 307–308, 441
mortgages
    as cost of owning, 280
    eligibility, 277–278
    and lenders, 294–297
    refinancing, 306–307
    types of, 282–288
moving expenses deduction, 130–131
mutual fund RRSPs, 228
mutual funds
    benefits of, 181–182, 197–199
    choosing, 207–213
    defined, 441
    and diversification, 157
    performance of, 213–216
    selling, 216
    types of, 199–207

• N •

NASDAQ system, defined, 441
NAV. *See* net asset value (NAV)
negative amortization, defined, 442
negotiating
  and insurance claims, 328–329
  and real estate, 303–304
net asset value (NAV), defined, 442
net worth, calculating, 25–28
New York Stock Exchange (NYSE), 442
newsletters, investment, 171, 183
newspapers
  cost of, 115
  financial information in, 404–405
no-load insurance, 325
no-load mutual funds, 165, 198, 208–210,
  273, 442
non-cancellable insurance policies, 343
non-refundable credits, defined, 131
NYSE. *See* New York Stock Exchange
  (NYSE)

• O •

OAS. *See* Old Age Security (OAS)
Old Age Security (OAS), 48
open mortgages, 286
open-end mutual funds, defined, 442
operating expenses, and mutual funds,
  210–211
opportunity cost of owning, defined, 279
options, 151, 442
overspending, causes of, 59–64
own-occupation disability policies, 343
owner, defined, 149
owner-occupied property, defined, 275
ownership investments
  defined, 149–150
  income trusts, 185–186
  real estate, 186–191
  small businesses, 191–193
  stocks, 179–185

• P •

P/E ratio. *See* price/earnings (P/E) ratio
PA. *See* pension adjustment (PA)

PAC. *See* pre-authorized cheque plan (PAC)
past service pension adjustment (PSPA),
  226
pension adjustment (PA), 137, 223, 224–225
pension adjustment reversal (PAR), 226
pension income credit, 135–136
pensions, 49–50, 442
percentage-of-assets-under-management
  advisers, 372
performance, defined, 211–212, 443
periodicals, financial, 398–399, 404–405
personal care costs, reducing, 114
personal property coverage, 350–351
phone bills, reducing, 105–106
playing the credit card float, defined, 24
postal insurance, 319
pre-authorized cheque plan (PAC), 393
preapproval for mortgage, 297
precious metals, 193–194
predictions, and investments, 171–173
preferred stock, defined, 443
premium adjustment, 338–339
prepaid tuition plans, 273–274
preparers, and taxes, 140
prequalification for mortgage, 297
prescription drugs, costs of, 116
price/earnings (P/E) ratio, 179, 443
prime rate, defined, 443
principal, defined, 148, 176, 443
priorities, non-monetary, 427–431
private asset management, 273–274
private investment management, 373–374
privately held companies, 180, 192–193
probate, 360–361
professional expenses, reducing, 115
professional fees deduction, 129
professional liability insurance, 137
profits, and taxes, 128
property coverage. *See* personal property
  coverage
property damage liability coverage,
  354–355
property taxes, as cost of owning, 280
property-tax assessment, appealing, 104
prospectus, and mutual funds, 207–208,
  443
public transit, 109
publicly held companies, defined, 180
put options, defined, 200

• Q •

Quebec Pension Plan (QPP). *See* Canada Pension Plan (CPP)

• R •

radio, and financial information, 403–404
real estate
  deal making, 303–305
  deciding to buy, 275–282
  financing, 282–297
  finding property, 297–299
  as investment vehicle, 186–191, 260
  post-buying, 305–311
real estate agents, 300–303, 309–310
real estate investment trusts (REITs), 189, 190, 443
record keeping
  and insurance claims, 327
  and taxes, 124–125
recreation costs, reducing, 112–114
refinancing mortgage, 306–307, 444
refunds for items, 94–95, 97
Registered Education Savings Plans (RESPs), 265–267, 444
Registered Retirement Income Funds (RRIFs), 230–232, 444
Registered Retirement Savings Plans (RRSPs). *See also* retirement plans
  allocating money in, 239–241
  benefits of, 217–220
  contribution rules, 222–227
  defined, 444
  Home Buyers' Plan, 291–293
  Lifelong Learning Plan, 268
  maturing, 228–234
  maximizing, 220–222
  and taxes, 125–126
  types of, 227–228
regulation, of financial planners, 377
reinvestment plans, stock dividend, 184
REITs. *See* real estate investment trusts (REITs)
renewability guarantee, 339, 343
renewal rates guarantee, 339

rental costs, reducing, 103
renter's insurance, 349–354
renting, versus buying, 279–282
renting to own, 98
replacement cost guarantees, 350, 351
residual benefits, defined, 343
RESPs. *See* Registered Education Savings Plans (RESPs)
retirement plans. *See also* Registered Retirement Savings Plans (RRSPs)
  allocating money in, 235–245
  and self-employment, 137
  and taxes, 125–126, 127
  transferring, 246–248
  valuing, 38
retirement preparation. *See also* retirement plans
  calculating needs, 44–45
  catching up, 52–54
  and computers, 395
  facing challenges, 424–426
  government benefits, 46–49
  importance of, 42–43, 54–56
  pensions, 49–50
  worksheet for, 50–52
returns on investment
  defined, 153–154, 444
  and RRSPs, 221–222
reverse mortgages, 53, 308–309, 444
risk
  and insurance, 321
  and investments, 154–156, 198
RRIFs. *See* Registered Retirement Income Funds (RRIFs)
RRSPs. *See* Registered Retirement Savings Plans (RRSPs)

• S •

S&P ratings. *See* Standard & Poor's (S&P) ratings
S&P/TSX composite index, defined, 444
S&P/TSX Venture composite index, defined, 444
same-sex couples. *See* common-law couples

savings accounts, 176–177, 237, 252–254
scholarships, 272
SEC. *See* Securities and Exchange Commission (SEC)
second homes, as investments, 190–191
sector funds. *See* specialty funds
secured credit cards, defined, 82–83
secured debt, defined, 84
Securities and Exchange Commission (SEC), 445
self-directed RRSPs, 228, 242–243
self-employment, and taxes, 136–137
self-employment expenses credit, 136–137
selling short, defined, 200
seminars, on financial planning, 381
share price changes, and mutual funds, 215
shifting expenses, and taxes, 153
short-term investments, defined, 256–257
short-term mortgages, 284–286
small businesses
  as investments, 191–193, 260
  starting, 419–420
small cap, defined, 181
smoking, cost of, 118
socially responsible funds, 205
software
  benefits of, 390
  chequebook, 393–394
  investment-tracking, 39
  legal document preparation, 399–400
  retirement-planning, 395
  tax preparation, 139, 395–396
specialty funds, 206–207
spending. *See also* overspending
  addictions and, 118–119
  analyzing, 64–71
  clothing costs, 109–110
  debt costs, 110–112
  food costs, 100–102
  insurance premiums, 116–117
  medical expenses, 115–116
  personal care, 114–115
  phone bills, 105–106
  professional expenses, 115
  recreation, 112–114
  shelter, 102–104
  strategies for, 92–99
  taxes, 117–118
  transportation costs, 106–109

sponsored content, 391–392
spousal credit, 132
spousal RRSPs, 226–227
Standard & Poor's 500 index, defined, 445
Standard & Poor's (S&P) ratings, defined, 445
stock funds, 202–203, 238, 258
stockbrokers, 184
stocks, 154–155, 179–185, 187, 445
stripped bonds, defined, 445
student loans, 269–271
survivor's pension, and CPP/QPP, 47, 333–334

• *T* •

T-bills, 255, 445
tax credits, 131–137
tax deductions, 128–131, 437
tax lawyers, 141
tax professionals, 139–141
tax-on-income (TONI) method, defined, 131
tax-on-tax method, defined, 131
taxable income, defined, 123
taxes
  audits, 141–143
  credits, 131–137
  deductions, 128–131
  and employment income, 125–126
  and estate planning, 361–362
  and investment income, 126–128, 250–251
  and mutual funds, 212–213
  preparation software, 395–396
  and record keeping, 124–125
  reducing, 117–118
  resources, 138–141
  and RRSPs, 218–220
  understanding, 121–124
television, and financial information, 403–404
term, of mortgage, 284–286
term life insurance, 334–340, 445
testamentary trusts, 362
therapy, costs of, 116
three months' interest penalty, 306–307
timeshares, 189–190
TONI method. *See* tax-on-income (TONI) method
total debt-service ratio, 278

town homes, defined, 298
trading, 161–162, 397–398
trailer fees, defined, 209
transaction accounts, 176
transportation costs, reducing, 106–109
travel medical insurance, 345–346
Treasury bills, 255, 445
TSX composite index, defined, 444
TSX Venture composite index, defined, 444
tuition fees credit, 133

• U •

umbrella insurance, 358–539
underwriting, defined, 445
uninsured or underinsured motorist liability coverage, 355–356
union fees deduction, 129
university. *See* education expenses
unused contribution room, defined, 222–223
utility costs, reducing, 104

• V •

vacation costs, reducing, 112–114
value stocks, defined, 203
variable-rate mortgages, 287–288
vegetarian diets, 101
vested, defined, 50

• W •

waiting periods, defined, 343
warranties, 318–319
wealth, defining, 33–36
Web sites. *See* Internet
wholesale superstores, 101–102
wholly dependent person credit, 132
wills, 359–360, 445
Wilshire 5000, defined, 446
windfalls, 423–424
withdrawals
   from RRIFs, 231–232
   from RRSPs, 226
workers' compensation, 342
wrap accounts, 170

• Y •

yields, defined, 176

• Z •

zero-coupon bonds, defined, 446